METAMORPHOSES V-VIII

In memory of

MY MOTHER

who died just as this book was finished

OVID

Metamorphoses V- VIII

Edited with Translation and Notes by

D.E. HILL

ARIS & PHILLIPS

PUBLISHERS

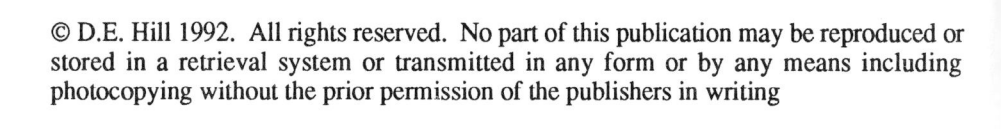

© D.E. Hill 1992. All rights reserved. No part of this publication may be reproduced or stored in a retrieval system or transmitted in any form or by any means including photocopying without the prior permission of the publishers in writing

British Library Cataloguing-in-Publication Data
A catalogue record for this book is available from the British Library.

ISBN cloth 0 85668 394 9
         limp 0 85668 395 7

The illustration on the front cover is reproduced by courtesy of Dr A.J.S. Spawforth, Curator of the Greek Museum, University of Newcastle upon Tyne. It depicts a terracotta antefix in the form of a Gorgon's face from Sicily, dating to about 500 B.C.

Reprinted with corrections 1997

Printed and published in England by Aris & Phillips Ltd., Teddington House, Warminster, Wiltshire BA12 8PQ

Contents

Preface	vii
Introduction	1
Metamorphoses	
Book V	10
Book VI	38
Book VII	68
Book VIII	104
Commentary	141
Bibliography	239
Index	245

PREFACE

Since the appearance of my edition of the first four books of Ovid's *Metamorphoses* in 1985, I have not lost my sense of the importance of treating students of classical literature in translation with proper respect. Too often, the student's need for a translation has been taken to mean that he or she is incapable of doing any significant independent study. My recent work at Newcastle has reinforced my belief that there is every reason to expect genuinely original and penetrating analyses from our students in translation; it is my hope that this sort of edition will help to encourage more such students to explore what they can do in this direction.

Scholars and students owe much to the vision of John Aris and there are very many who, like me, treasure personal memories of his warmth, kindness and encouragement. Perhaps the best testimony to the strength of his vision is the vigour with which, in spite of his sad loss, his family have been able to continue what they all started together.

Once again, it is a great privilege to record my indebtedness to Professor R.J. Tarrant who has not only provided me with a draft of his forthcoming Oxford text but has also made countless fruitful suggestions towards improving the translation. His patience in enduring my importunate demands for the next section is, I hope, rewarded by seeing this project now a little beyond the half-way stage. Once again, I must stress that the text I print does not necessarily enjoy Professor Tarrant's endorsement; it is, however, much better than it would have been without his help.

Seven years ago, in the preface to the first four books, I included a deeply felt tribute to the department I then served in Cardiff. Subsequent events have given me a superstitious disinclination to express in this preface the warm feelings I have towards my new department in Newcastle. However, I cannot pass over the enormous contribution made towards the translation by Professor David West. His natural translation style is very different from mine, as a glance at his *Aeneid* (Penguin, 1990) will make clear; and yet he was able so to enter into the spirit of what I was trying to do that he was able to help me to see how to execute my style better without ever trying to persuade me to do it his way. This most unusual generosity of spirit was matched only by the generosity with which he gave me his time.

It has taken me much longer than I had hoped to complete this book; it would have taken longer still but for the support of the Research Committee at the University of Newcastle who provided replacement teaching for one term so that I could have an uninterrupted period to bring the work to a conclusion. Their enlightened policy has been of great value to many of my colleagues too, and I hope they will be able to continue to support useful projects in this way.

Once again, I owe a great deal to the skill of Miss Judith Grey. I have received many compliments on the appearance of the previous book, compliments owed not to me but to her and to the staff at Warminster. This time, with the help of more advanced technology (most sympathetically assisted by the computing experts of Newcastle, by Mrs Barbara Ingman of the Newcastle Centre for Health Services Research and by the computing staff of the University of Wales College of Cardiff who were also most generous with their facilities), I dare to hope that it has been possible to produce something with an even better appearance. I should also mention many hours of tedious proof-reading uncomplainingly provided by Miss Judith Grey and by one of our post-graduate students, Miss Rhiannon Evans.

viii] PREFACE

Proof-reading is, however, an inadequate term for the contribution once again made by the general editor of this series, Professor Malcolm Willcock. He has saved me from more errors and worse blunders than I care to remember. My gratitude to him and to all the others who have helped me is overwhelming, and they are to be assured that the usual indemnity offered in this context will be fully honoured.

I have, as before, gained great pleasure from working on this book. The act of translation compels the reader into a deeper understanding of the text and Ovid rewards deeper understanding most generously, especially in this, the work of his best years. I hope that I have been able successfully to share something of my own enthusiasm for this most witty and urbane poet, yet one whose humanity is never far from the surface.

Newcastle upon Tyne
October, 1992

INTRODUCTION

This Introduction is only slightly adapted and updated from my Introduction to Books 1-4. This volume is intended to stand alone, if so desired, so that, where it is important for understanding, I have not scrupled to repeat information from the notes of 1-4. On the other hand, in less important matters, I have referred to my notes to 1-4 as I might to any other work.

1. *Ovid's life and works*

Ovid was born in the small Italian town of Sulmo (now Sulmona) on the 20th March 43 B.C., five days after the first anniversary of Caesar's assassination. When Octavian (soon to be known as Augustus) made himself undisputed master of the Roman world by defeating Antony and Cleopatra at Actium, Ovid was only twelve. The difference between the social and political outlook of his generation and that of Virgil, who was born only twenty-seven years before him, must have been as profound as the difference today between those who remember Europe in the tumult of the Fascist era, and those who do not.

For a century before Ovid's birth, Rome had been racked by political upheavals, frequently breaking out into violence and, eventually, full civil war. Catullus (c.84-c.54 B.C.), Virgil (70-19 B.C.), Horace (65-8 B.C.), Tibullus (55/48-19 B.C.) and Propertius (54/47-16/2 B.C.) had all been touched by these upheavals and all reflect the political issues of their day to a greater or lesser extent in their poetry. The last four lived to see the end of the civil war and the establishment of the Augustan regime. Indeed, in their more optimistic moments, Virgil and Horace can dare to hope that they are witnessing the birth of a new Golden Age, though all four clearly suffer from doubts too. With Ovid, however, politics are ignored. Just as the fall of the Greek city states and the rise of the Hellenistic world some four centuries earlier had driven poetry from the centre stage of politics into the study, the countryside and the boudoir, so again, the collapse of the Roman Republic rendered politics neither interesting nor safe for any but the most robust of poets. Even so, Ovid fell disastrously foul of Augustus' authority and spent the last years of his life, from A.D. 8 until his death about a decade later, in exile.

As a boy and young man, he received the conventional education of a reasonably prosperous and ambitious Italian family. First at home, then at Rome and finally on the Grand Tour (including Athens, Sicily and Asia Minor) he was given also the training and polish necessary for a legal or political career. At the core of this training was a grounding in rhetoric achieved largely through exercises known as *controuersiae* and *suasoriae*; in the former, the student would prepare an argument based on an unusual or even exotic situation arising out of a point of law; in the latter, he would prepare a speech to sway a figure of history or mythology confronted by some dramatic or momentous decision. No reader of Ovid will be surprised to learn that Ovid preferred the latter and, for good or ill, the influence of these exercises is to be found throughout his work.

Ovid did embark briefly on the political career his father had wanted for him but his own inclinations and genius and the influence of his friends soon drove him to abandon politics and the law in favour of poetry.

All his early work, except for his lost play *Medea*, was written in elegiac couplets (the metres are discussed in the next section), a medium well suited to his witty and epigrammatic style. His subject matter ranged from the plight of various mythological women in a whole range of disastrous love affairs to a number of mock

2] INTRODUCTION

didactic works purporting to give practical advice to both sexes on every aspect of the conduct of a love affair including even a poem on cosmetics. Such poetry did, however, have a more serious side. Ovid, like Catullus as well as the Augustan poets, was amazingly well read and his work is packed with witty and learned allusions to his predecessors in both Greek and Latin. Roman poets, such as Catullus, Tibullus and Propertius, as well as the almost entirely lost Gallus, had established elegiac as a prime form for amatory poetry, and Ovid's work was firmly established in that tradition.

He was exiled in A.D. 8, though we do not know precisely why. There is, however, no need to doubt his own account that it arose from *carmen et error,* 'a poem and a mistake'. For a brief discussion, see the note on 3.142 in the earlier volume. Ovid's rather cavalier attitude to authority and sexual propriety throughout his amatory elegiacs must have earned him disapprobation at a time when Augustus was constantly legislating in an attempt to enforce high moral standards. A single famous example must suffice here to make the point. In 23 B.C., M. Marcellus fell sick and died. He had recently married Augustus' daughter, Julia (they were cousins, for Marcellus' mother was Augustus' sister). The young man had clearly been marked out as Augustus' successor though he was only nineteen (he was the same age as Ovid) and the grief that followed his death was quite unrestrained. Virgil made him the final tragic figure in his famous parade of Roman heroes at the end of the sixth book of the *Aeneid* and, it is said, the boy's mother swooned when she heard Virgil recite the lines. Austin's note on *Aen.* 6.868 gives a full account of the elaborate memorials constructed for him by his grieving family. Among them was a marble portico and library dedicated by his mother. There must, accordingly, be real mischief in Ovid when, in a list of places which are particularly good for picking up a girl, he included this very monument (*Ars Amat.* 1.69-70).

However, Ovid was a man of great literary ambition. The clever trifles discussed above were so packed with wit, charm and learning that they would alone have secured him a place among the famous poets of antiquity. Nevertheless, true greatness seemed to require a major work in weighty dactylic hexameters, the metre of Homer and of Virgil whose *Aeneid* (published in 19 B.C. shortly after its author's death and when Ovid was still a young man) had come to dominate Latin letters in a wholly unprecedented way. No direct challenge to the master of epic, Virgil, was possible, but Ovid had conceived a rival plan and by the time of his exile it was essentially complete. In his *Metamorphoses*, Ovid turned to the dactylic hexameter to produce a mythological *tour de force* of epic scale that wholly transcended anything he had produced before. This, his greatest work, was essentially complete when he was sent into exile, and he had even completed the first half of another serious work, this time in elegiac couplets again, the *Fasti*, a calendar of the Roman year, which afforded ample scope for a display of religious, historical, mythological and astronomical learning.

The *Metamorphoses* is a very long poem (15 books in all) in the form of a highly idiosyncratic 'history' of the world from Creation to the death and deification of Julius Caesar. Its special peculiarity is that each of the stories it tells involves a metamorphosis (transformation) and each is so attached to the next that the whole gives the illusion of a seamless garment. There was, of course, a long tradition of more or less large poems using a single theme to unite a collection of stories. Hesiod (or, perhaps more probably, a sixth century imitator) had produced a *Catalogue of Women*, now largely lost, which consisted simply of a string of tales about women each starting with the simple formula, 'Or like...', the origin of its alternative title, *Eoiae*. This work had had a considerable influence on the Hellenistic writers. Callimachus' *Aetia*, for instance, an elegiac poem of over 4,000 lines (though only fragments survive now) was a string of legends united by the fact that all related the 'causes' (*aitia*) of some Greek custom, religious rite etc. In the 2nd century B.C., Nicander had composed a *Heteroeumena* (an alternative Greek word for *Metamorphoses*; it is lost but Antoninus Liberalis, frequently cited in the notes, has left us a prose paraphrase of many of its stories) and Ovid's older contemporaries, Parthenius and Theodorus, were also each said to have composed a *Metamorphoses*. This is a very complex issue and those who wish to follow it up should consult Wilkinson (144-46), the authorities cited by him and my own notes on 1.1 and 1.4.

One of the most obvious features of Ovid's *Metamorphoses* is the attention paid to achieving the effect of a continuous narrative, or *perpetuum...carmen* as he himself put it at 1.4. He achieved this sometimes by clever links (at 6.146, we have just listened to the fate of Arachne who had scorned Minerva when we are introduced to her former neighbour, Niobe, who had not learnt from her example but...), sometimes by arranging for one character to narrate a story to another (at 8.577, Theseus' journey has been blocked by the flooded Achelous who, entertains him and, in the course of conversation, begins the story of the Echinades) and sometimes by bringing together a series of stories with a common theme (from 7.402 to 9.97, the stories are linked by the common thread of Theseus). The situation is further complicated, however, by the fact that it is possible to detect other structures, such as the simple chronological one, or more subtle groupings, such as Otis's (83) four-fold division, 'The Divine Comedy' (Books 1-2), 'The Avenging Gods' (3.1-6.400), 'The Pathos of Love' (6.401-11.795) and 'Rome and the Deified Ruler' (12-15), each section itself subdivided, according to Otis, into smaller sections as discussed in his following pages. Some readers may well find the specific analyses of Otis and others, at least in part, unconvincing, but few if any will deny that the unity of the *Metamorphoses* is achieved by Ovid's genius in relating one story to another in a bewildering variety of ways. The original decision to start this edition with the first four books was quite arbitrary; indeed, it necessitated breaking off before the Perseus story was complete. Similarly, this edition of books 5-8 leaves us wondering why Achelous is groaning. It will, however, become obvious that there are no clean breaks in the *Metamorphoses* and the whole, in this format, would make a cumbrous volume indeed. However, now that we are more than half way through, I do hope to be able to complete the whole project.

In spite of Augustus' decision to banish Ovid as an offender against public morality, many readers detect a strong moral and humane theme throughout the *Metamorphoses*. Cruelty and treachery are almost invariably punished, but all the more venial of the foibles and weaknesses of human nature are depicted with a constant, gentle humour. One of the recurrent motifs is that the metamorphosis is only the revelation of some ultimate truth about the victim (see the note on 6.97) and the mediaeval writers who treated the *Metamorphoses* as a storehouse of paradigms for moral instruction (see Rand 131-37, Wilkinson 366-98) were exaggerating rather than falsifying. There are so many verbal pyrotechnics, so much showing off of learning, so much wit and humour (some subtle, some not, but none cruel) that the fundamental humanity of Ovid can be lost sight of. Many may even agree with the elder Seneca (*Contr. 2.10.12*) who complained that Ovid did not lack the judgement to restrain his excesses but the will. For my own part, I find his charm and sensitivity too overwhelming to be much exercised by his occasional blemishes. For a particularly trenchant view of Ovid's moral purpose, see W.R. Johnson in *Ancient Writers, Greece and Rome*, ed. T.J. Ince (New York, 1982) II 783-806.

Exile was a bitter pill for Ovid, the ultimate sophisticate, to swallow. The last six months of the *Fasti* were abandoned and there flowed from his pen instead a great

4] INTRODUCTION

outpouring of elegiac verse devoted largely to complaints about his punishment, nostalgia for happier days and pleadings to a variety of friends for help to secure a return home. Eventually, some four years after the death of Augustus, he died himself, still in exile at Tomis (a small town on the Black Sea, now Constanta in modern Romania). In his ten years there, he never tired of bemoaning the climate of the place and its remoteness, but he did learn the local language and he did acknowledge the kindness that his hosts had afforded him.

A much fuller account of the issues raised in this section will be found in Wilkinson and in Kenney, *Cambridge History of Classical Literature II* (Cambridge, 1982) 420-57. See also J.C. Thibault, *The Mystery of Ovid's Exile* (Beverley and Los Angeles, 1964).

2.   Metre

English verse is based on stress; it is, essentially, a recognizable pattern of stressed and unstressed syllables.

> Mad dogs and Englishmen go out in the mid-day sun.

It would be possible to substitute for 'Englishmen' words such as 'antelopes' or 'terriers' without disturbing the metre because all three words have the same stress pattern; substitute 'alsatians', however, and the metre is lost, not because the number of syllables is wrong, but because the stress pattern is.

Classical Greek, on the other hand, had no stress so that its verse was not stress based. It was founded instead on a pattern of 'long' (marked   ) and 'short' (marked   ) syllables, sometimes called 'heavy' and 'light', though both sets of terms are misleading because not all 'long' syllables take longer to say than 'short' syllables and 'heavy' and 'light' suggest stress which is quite wrong. It will suffice to say that the distinction for the Greek speaker between 'long' and 'short' syllables was different from, but no less important than, the distinction between stressed and unstressed syllables for the English speaker.

The Homeric poems, and all Classical epic and didactic poetry thereafter (and much more besides), were written in the dactylic hexameter. This rhythm consists of six dactyls ($- \cup \cup$) which may (in the case of the last foot, must) become spondees ($- -$), like this:

$$\cup\cup - \cup\cup - \cup\cup - \cup\cup - \cup\cup - -$$

(As in all metres, Greek and Latin, a short syllable may count long at the end of a line). By translating length into stress, it is possible to gain some sense of the rhythm from the schoolboy mnemonic:

> Down in a deep dark ditch sat an old cow munching a turnip.

But, as the pattern above indicates and as any reading of the text will illustrate, the dactylic hexameter enjoys great inherent variety. Add to that the fact that sentences could, and more and more frequently did, run over from line to line, coming to rest at a considerable variety of points within the line, and it will be seen that this is a metre well suited for narrative poetry.

The elegiac couplet, on the other hand, is, as its name indicates, a two line metre and is a rhythm which clearly lends itself to end-stopping. Indeed, the second line of the couplet is often no more than a restatement of the first. It is, accordingly, a superb metre for cleverness and wit, but it lacks the epic weight of the dactylic hexameters, though it never lost its rôle in brief epitaphs where its very simplicity could lend real dignity.

Latin, like English, is a stressed language and its very earliest verse, like much of its mediaeval or modern (*gaudeamus igitur*, for instance, or *adeste fideles*), was based wholly on stress patterns, just like English verse. However, during the classical period and beyond, for at least a millenium from the second century B.C., Latin verse was based on the principles of Greek quantitative verse, as it is called, though, gradually, with some extra refinements that almost certainly arose because Latin was a stressed language.

The reader who wishes to know more should consult L.P. Wilkinson, *Golden Latin Artistry* (Cambridge, 1970) 89-134. Further exploration of the purely technical aspects of this section could usefully begin with W. Sidney Allen, *Accent and Rhythm* (Cambridge, 1973) and D.E. Hill, 'Quaestio Prosodiae', *Glotta 52* (1974) 218-31.

3. *The text*

The *Metamorphoses* was one of the most popular of classical works during the Middle Ages and, as a consequence, we possess a bewildering number of mediaeval manuscripts, though none earlier than the ninth century and no complete manuscript earlier than the twelfth. In addition, we possess a translation into Greek by the 13th century monk, Maximus Planudes. All the ordinary difficulties of such a tradition are further complicated by the apparent existence from time to time of ancient alternatives which may or may not have arisen from two editions from Ovid's own hand. For the details, see R.J. Tarrant in *Texts and Transmission*, edited L.D. Reynolds, (Oxford, 1983) *276-82*.

Professor Tarrant is preparing a text for the O.C.T. series and he has very kindly sent me copies of his draft typescript of the text for the first eight books. In choosing between well known variants or emendations I have, far more often than not, been guided by him. His text will obviously become the standard one; in view of its imminence, I have contented myself with producing a readable text without apparatus or serious pretensions to originality. The punctuation style is my own.

4. *The translation*

Before any attempt to outline the principles on which this translation is based, it may help to consider other possible approaches and discuss why they have been discarded.

It might be argued that verse for a lengthy work is as alien to a modern audience as Latin itself and any attempt, therefore, to use verse cloaks the translation with a quaintness that is quite wrong. There are, of course, translations available for anyone of that persuasian and the theoretical position is advanced in perhaps its most trenchant form in E.V. Rieu's introduction to his Penguin translation of the *Odyssey*. This translation of the *Metamorphoses*, however, is based on the proposition that the 'otherness' of Ovid is part of his importance and appeal and that to make him seem like a contemporary is not the task of his translator.

It might be argued that Ovid's verse was composed according to the strictest rules and that the appropriate English equivalent would involve strict metre at least and, probably, rhyme as well. Arthur Golding, whose translation was known to Shakespeare, A.E. Watts (University of California Press, 1954), whose translation was lavishly praised by Otis, and now A.D. Melville (Oxford, 1986) are among the best known to have adopted this approach. On rhyme I cannot do better than cite Milton's preamble to *Paradise Lost*:

> The measure is English *Heroic Verse without Rime, as that of* Homer in Greek and of Virgil *in Latin; Rime being no necessary Adjunct or true Ornament of Poem or good Verse, in longer Works especially, but the Invention of a barbarous Age, to set off wretched matter and lame Metre; grac't indeed since by the use of some famous modern Poets, carried away by Custom, but much to thir own vexation, hindrance, and constraint to express many things otherwise, and for the most part worse than else they would have exprest them. This neglect then of Rime so little is to be taken for a defect, though it may seem so perhaps to vulgar Readers, that it rather is to be esteem'd an example set, the first in* English, *of ancient liberty recover'd to Heroic Poem from the troublesome and modern bondage of Riming.*

Furthermore, rhyme must restrict vocabulary and, therefore, fidelity and, even more important, it produces either end-stopped lines or constant comic effect. For all these reasons, rhyme is possibly appropriate for Ovid's elegiacs but certainly not for his hexameter poem. Most of these arguments apply also, to a greater or lesser extent, to strict verse but, in any case, the argument for strict verse is based on something of a fallacy. While it is perfectly true that Ovidian hexameters are written to very precise rules they are, nevertheless, rules which permit an astonishing range of tempos which would be wholly lost in the strait-jacket of English strict verse. For all these reasons, I have settled on a six-beat blank verse effect though I have not scrupled, from time to time, to stretch my metre even to the point where the reader may think that it has become prose, if fidelity to Ovid's meaning was not, apparently, otherwise attainable. In broad terms, I took the view that once a rhythm had been established, it would be easier for the reader to imagine that it had been sustained than to identify and correct an infidelity. The principle advantage of the line for line translation is that it minimises the distortions inevitable in any translation. It must be wrong to use six words where Ovid uses only one, or seriously to distort the order of his ideas. I have tried to preserve either the order of Ovid's words or his sentence structure, whichever seemed more significant in each case. Where Ovid uses a common Latin word, I have sought a common English word, but where his vocabulary is highly poetic, deliberately archaic or, as so often, where he has deliberately coined a new word, I have attempted the same effect in English. In the notes, I have tried to draw attention to particular instances where the translation has failed or might mislead. I hope that I have done this often enough so that the reader never wholly forgets that this is a translation, and not so frequently that the reader loses all trust. Ideally, the reader will so enjoy the translation and the insights that it, together with the notes, provides, that he will be driven to a desire to master the Latin. For a full account of the history of Renaissance English translations of Ovid, see Wilkinson 406-38. For more on the principles behind this particular translation, see D.E. Hill, 'What sort of Translation of Virgil do we need?', *G & R* 25 (1978) 59-68 (now reprinted in *Virgil* (Greece and Rome Studies) edited Ian McAuslan and Peter Walcot, Oxford, 1990, pp. 180-8).

5.   *The notes*

As has already been indicated, Ovid's *Metamorphoses* is an amazingly rich poem full of learning, allusion and wit. Apart from the very important observations on the limits of the translation, as discussed above, the main purposes of the notes are to elucidate passages likely to be unclear, to indicate something of Ovid's possible sources and to discuss how he treated them, to give some indication of how Ovid's work has influenced his successors and to add anything else which seems valuable or interesting. The notes make no pretence whatsoever of completeness and, inevitably, reflect one man's tastes and prejudices. The hope is, however, that the notes will alert readers to the sort of questions that can be asked, challenge readers to notice, from their own reading, important points that have been omitted and bring to readers' attention classical authors and modern scholarly works they might otherwise have ignored. Students of classics in translation (and some readers will surely fall into that category) are often far too diffident to approach the notes of the standard editions of classical authors. In an attempt to overcome this, I have quoted from such works extensively and directed to them very freely in the hope that any reader with access to a standard university library will feel drawn to use its resources and thus, in a relatively painless way, acquire a wider and deeper knowledge of classical literature with Ovid as the spur. However, the genius of Ovid is such that, although a full appreciation does indeed depend on a close familiarity with classical literature, much profit and pleasure can still be gained from a relatively superficial reading. Accordingly, a reader coming to the work for the first time should consult the notes only when puzzled by the translation or text. Second or subsequent readings can then be enriched by following up the leads given in the notes.

The notes include almost no linguistic discussion; it would be burdensome for those without Latin and, with a facing translation present, largely superfluous for those with Latin, especially since they can turn to Anderson and Hollis for more linguistically based notes on books 6-8.

Two points about Ovid's 'sources' should be made plain. Much classical and Hellenistic literature known to Ovid is lost to us. Accordingly, it should not be assumed that a note's reference to an earlier treatment of a myth or idea necessarily involves a suggestion that it is Ovid's source. Each case must be judged on its merits; an understanding of Ovid cannot, however, be complete without as much knowledge as possible about the ancient tradition behind him and a full appreciation of his sense of detail.

Some readers may be disappointed that the notes are not much fuller on Ovid's influence on later times, though those already well versed in mediaeval literature and art will find much in the text and notes that they will recognize. The best general treatments of this subject are to be found in Rand, Wilkinson, the essays by Robathan and Jameson in *Ovid*, edited J.W. Binns (London, 1973) 191-242, Hanne Carlsen, *A Bibliography to the Classical Tradition in English Literature* (Copenhagen, 1985), and *Ovidian influences on literature and art from the Middle Ages to the twentieth century*, edited by Charles Martindale, Cambridge, 1988.

METAMORPHOSES V-VIII

LIBER V

     Dumque ea Cephenum medio Danaeius heros
     agmine commemorat, fremida regalia turba
     atria complentur, nec coniugialia festa
     qui canat est clamor, sed qui fera nuntiet arma;
5   inque repentinos conuiuia uersa tumultus
     adsimilare freto possis, quod saeua quietum
     uentorum rabies motis exasperat undis.
     primus in his Phineus, belli temerarius auctor;
     fraxineam quatiens aeratae cuspidis hastam
10   'en,' ait 'en adsum praereptae coniugis ultor!
     nec mihi te pennae nec falsum uersus in aurum
     Iuppiter eripiet.' conanti mittere Cepheus
     'quid facis?' exclamat 'quae te, germane, furentem
     mens agit in facinus? meritisne haec gratia tantis
15   redditur? hac uitam seruatae dote rependis?
     quam tibi non Perseus, uerum si quaeris, ademit,
     sed graue Nereidum numen, sed corniger Ammon,
     sed quae uisceribus ueniebat belua ponti
     exsaturanda meis. illo tibi tempore rapta est
20   quo peritura fuit—nisi si crudelis id ipsum
     exigis, ut pereat, luctuque leuabere nostro.
     scilicet haud satis est, quod te spectante reuincta est
     et nullam quod opem patruus sponsusue tulisti;
     insuper a quoquam quod sit seruata dolebis
25   praemiaque eripies? quae si tibi magna uidentur,
     ex illis scopulis, ubi erant adfixa, petisses!
     nunc sine qui petiit, per quem haec non orba senectus,
     ferre quod et meritis et uoce est pactus, eumque
     non tibi, sed certae praelatum intellege morti.'
30   ille nihil contra, sed et hunc et Persea uultu
     alterno spectans petat hunc ignorat an illum;
     cunctatusque breui contortam uiribus hastam,
     quantas ira dabat, nequiquam in Persea misit.
     ut stetit illa toro, stratis tum denique Perseus
35   exsiluit teloque ferox inimica remisso
     pectora rupisset, nisi post altaria Phineus
     isset; et (indignum!) scelerato profuit ara.
     fronte tamen Rhoeti non inrita cuspis adhaesit;
     qui postquam cecidit ferrumque ex osse reuulsum est,
40   calcitrat et positas aspergit sanguine mensas.
     tum uero indomitas ardescit uulgus in iras
     telaque coniciunt, et sunt qui Cephea dicunt
     cum genero debere mori; sed limine tecti
     exierat Cepheus, testatus Iusque Fidemque
45   hospitiique deos ea se prohibente moueri.
          bellica Pallas adest et protegit aegide fratrem

BOOK 5

And while the Danaeian hero was recalling this in the midst
of the host of the Cephenes, a roaring mob filled
the royal halls, and theirs was not a shout that sings
for the wedding feast, but one that calls to cruel arms;
and the banquet turned to sudden rioting   5
you could compare to the sea whose quiet the fierce
raging of the winds has roughened by its rousing of the waves.
First of these men was Phineus, the reckless instigator of the war;
shaking his ash-wood spear with its bronze tip,
'Look,' he said, 'look, I am here to avenge the snatching of my wife!   10
neither your wings nor Jupiter turned into false gold
will snatch you away from me.' As he tried to throw it, Cepheus
cried out to him, 'What are you doing? What thought is driving you,
brother, raging into crime? Are these the thanks returned for such
deserts? Is it with this dowry you repay the saving of her life?   15
It is not Perseus, if you seek the truth, that has taken her from you,
but the grim deity of the Nereids, but horned Ammon,
but the sea monster that came to sate itself
upon the bowels of my own one. It was at that time she was snatched from you
when she was about to perish—unless, perhaps, you cruelly demand   20
that very thing, that she perish, and you will be relieved by our grief.
It is not enough, I suppose, that you looked on while she was chained
and that you brought no help as her uncle or as her betrothed;
and will you also grieve that she was saved by anyone
and snatch his reward away? If it seems so great to you,   25
would that you had sought it from the cliffs where it was fixed!
Now let him who did seek, him through whom this old man is not bereft,
carry off what he has secured by his merits and my word, and understand
that it is not to you he is preferred but to her certain death.'
He said nothing in reply but faced both him and Perseus   30
gazing to and fro and did not know whether to aim at one or at the other;
he paused briefly, then sent his spear whirling with all the strength
that anger gave him, and threw it in vain at Perseus.
As it stuck into the couch then, finally, Perseus leapt up
from the coverlets and, throwing back the weapon, would have in his ferocity   35
burst his enemy's breast if Phineus had not gone behind
the altar; and (for shame!) the altar helped the criminal.
Yet the tip, not without effect, lodged in Rhoetus' forehead;
after he had fallen and the weapon had been wrenched from the bone,
he kicked, and spattered the set tables with his blood.   40
Then truly did the crowd catch fire with an anger beyond control,
hurling their weapons, and there were those who said that Cepheus
ought to die together with his son-in-law; but Cepheus had gone outside
the doorway of his house and called upon Right and Faith
and the gods of hospitality to witness that he had forbidden what was now being set in motion.
    Warrior Pallas was there to protect her brother with her aegis   46

datque animos. erat Indus Athis, quem flumine Gange
edita Limnaee uitreis peperisse sub undis
creditur, egregius forma, quam diuite cultu
augebat, bis adhuc octonis integer annis,
indutus chlamydem Tyriam, quam limbus obibat
aureus; ornabant aurata monilia collum
et madidos murra curuum crinale capillos.
ille quidem iaculo quamuis distantia misso
figere doctus erat, sed tendere doctior arcus;
tum quoque lenta manu flectentem cornua Perseus
stipite, qui media positus fumabat in ara,
perculit et fractis confudit in ossibus ora.
hunc ubi laudatos iactantem in sanguine uultus
Assyrius uidit Lycabas—iunctissimus illi
et comes et ueri non dissimulator amoris—
postquam exhalantem sub acerbo uulnere uitam
deplorauit Athin, quos ille tetenderat arcus
arripit et 'mecum tibi sint certamina,' dixit
'nec longum pueri fato laetabere, quo plus
inuidiae quam laudis habes.' haec omnia nondum
dixerat; emicuit neruo penetrabile telum
uitatumque tamen sinuosa ueste pependit.
uertit in hunc harpen spectatam caede Medusae
Acrisioniades adigitque in pectus; at ille
iam moriens oculis sub nocte natantibus atra
circumspexit Athin seque acclinauit ad illum
et tulit ad manes iunctae solacia mortis.
    ecce Suenites, genitus Metione, Phorbas
et Libys Amphimedon, auidi committere pugnam,
sanguine, quo late tellus madefacta tepebat,
conciderant lapsi; surgentibus obstitit ensis,
alterius costis, iugulo Phorbantis adactus.
at non Actoriden Erytum, cui lata bipennis
telum erat, hamato Perseus petit ense, sed altis
exstantem signis multaeque in pondere massae
ingentem manibus tollit cratera duabus
infligitque uiro; rutilum uomit ille cruorem
et resupinus humum moribundo uertice pulsat.
inde Semiramio Polydegmona sanguine cretum
Caucasiumque Abarin Sperchionidenque Lycetum
intonsumque comas Helicen Phlegyanque Clytumque
sternit et exstructos morientum calcat aceruos.
    nec Phineus ausus concurrere comminus hosti
intorquet iaculum, quod detulit error in Idan
expertem frustra belli et neutra arma secutum.
ille tuens oculis immitem Phinea toruis
'quandoquidem in partes' ait 'abstrahor, accipe, Phineu,
quem fecisti, hostem pensaque hoc uulnere uulnus.'
iamque remissurus tractum de uulnere telum
sanguine defectos cecidit conlapsus in artus.

BOOK V   [13

and give him courage. There was Indian Athis whom Limnaee, sprung
from the river Ganges, had brought forth beneath her glassy waters,
it is believed; his beauty was outstanding and enhanced by his rich
apparel; twice eight years old, still fresh,   50
he was clad in a Tyrian cloak round which there ran a fringe
of gold; a golden collar adorned his neck
and a curved hairband his myrrh-drenched locks.
He was skilled at throwing a javelin and piercing things
however far away they stood, but he was more skilled at drawing the bow;   55
then too he was bending the pliant bow with his hand, when Perseus
used a stick which lay smoking in the middle of the altar
to strike him, mangling his face upon its broken bones.
When Assyrian Lycabas saw that face he admired
writhing in blood—he was his closest   60
companion and no concealer of his true love—
he first wept for Athis as he breathed his life out
beneath that bitter wound, then seized the bow
which he had drawn and said, 'Let your battle be with me
and you will not for long rejoice in that boy's fate from which   65
you will have more hatred than praise.' He had not yet said
all of this; the penetrating shaft flashed from the string
and, though he avoided it, it still hung from the folds of his clothing.
Acrisius' son turned on him with the harpe, well known from the slaughter
of Medusa, and drove it in his breast; but he,   70
now dying, his eyes swimming beneath dark night,
looked round for Athis, leant himself upon him
and took to the shades the solace that they were joined in death.
       Look, Phorbas of Syene, born to Metion,
and Amphimedon of Libya, in their eagerness to join the fight,   75
slipped and fell down in the blood which drenched and warmed
the earth on every side; as they were getting up they were stopped by a sword
driven into the latter's ribs and into Phorbas' throat.
But Erytus, son of Actor, whose weapon was a broad   79
two-edged axe, Perseus did not look for with his hook-shaped sword, but with his two
hands he lifted up a huge mixing bowl, outstanding
for the height of its reliefs and of a very massive weight,
and smashed it down upon the man; he spewed forth crimson blood
and face up in his death throes beat the earth with the crown of his head.
Then Polydegmon, sprung from the blood-line of Semiramis,   85
and Abaris of the Caucasus, and Lycetus, a descendant of Spercheus,
and Helices of the unshorn hair, and Phlegyas and Clytus
he laid low and piled up heaps of dying men and trampled on them.
       Nor did Phineus dare to charge his foe up close
but hurled a javelin which his poor aim carried off into Idas   90
who had vainly kept out of the war and followed neither side.
He gazed at pitiless Phineus with a grim look in his eyes
saying, 'Since I am dragged into taking part, accept, Phineus,
the enemy you have made and pay me wound for wound.'
He drew the weapon from his body and was about to send it back   95
when, with his limbs deprived of blood, he collapsed and fell.

14] LIBER V

```
         tum quoque Cephenum post regem primus Hodites
         ense iacet Clymeni; Prothoenora percutit Hypseus,
         Hypsea Lyncides. fuit et grandaeuus in illis
100      Emathion, aequi cultor timidusque deorum,
         qui, quoniam prohibent anni bellare, loquendo
         pugnat et incessit scelerataque deuouet arma;
         huic Chromis amplexo tremulis altaria palmis
         decutit ense caput, quod protinus incidit arae
105      atque ibi semianimi uerba exsecrantia lingua
         edidit et medios animam exspirauit in ignes.
              hinc gemini fratres Broteasque et caestibus Ammon
         inuicti, uinci si possent caestibus enses,
         Phinea cecidere manu Cererisque sacerdos
110      Ampycus albenti uelatus tempora uitta.
         tu quoque, Lampetide, non hos adhibendus ad usus,
         sed qui, pacis opus, citharam cum uoce moueres,
         iussus eras celebrare dapes festumque canendo.
         quem procul astantem plectrumque imbelle tenentem
115      Paetalus inridens 'Stygiis cane cetera' dixit
         'manibus' et laeuo mucronem tempore fixit;
         concidit et digitis morientibus ille retemptat
         fila lyrae, casuque ferit miserabile carmen.
         nec sinit hunc impune ferox cecidisse Lycormas
120      raptaque de dextro robusta repagula posti
         ossibus inlisit mediae ceruicis; at ille
         procubuit terrae mactati more iuuenci.
         demere temptabat laeui quoque robora postis
         Cinyphius Pelates; temptanti dextera fixa est
125      cuspide Marmaridae Corythi lignoque cohaesit;
         haerenti latus hausit Abas, nec corruit ille,
         sed retinente manum moriens e poste pependit.
              sternitur et Melaneus, Perseia castra secutus,
         et Nasamoniaci Dorylas ditissimus agri,
130      diues agri Dorylas, quo non possederat alter
         latius aut totidem tollebat farris aceruos.
         huius in obliquo missum stetit inguine ferrum
         (letifer ille locus); quem postquam uulneris auctor
         singultantem animam et uersantem lumina uidit
135      Bactrius Halcyoneus, 'hoc, quod premis,' inquit 'habeto
         de tot agris terrae' corpusque exsangue reliquit.
         torquet in hunc hastam calido de uulnere raptam
         ultor Abantiades, media quae nare recepta
         ceruice exacta est in partesque eminet ambas.
140      dumque manum Fortuna iuuat, Clytiumque Claninque,
         matre satos una, diuerso uulnere fudit;
         nam Clytii per utrumque graui librata lacerto
         fraxinus acta femur, iaculum Clanis ore momordit.
         occidit et Celadon Mendesius, occidit Astreus,
145      matre Palaestina, dubio genitore creatus,
         Aethionque sagax quondam uentura uidere,
```

BOOK V [15

Then Hodites too, first of the Cephenes after the king,
lay dead from Clymenus' sword; Prothoenor was struck down by Hypseus,
Hypseus by Lynceus' son. Among them too there was the aged
Emathion, who cultivated what is right and feared the gods;   100
he, since his years forbade him to make war, used speech
to fight and advancing cursed their wicked arms;
as he embraced the altar with his trembling hands, Chromis
struck his head off with a sword; at once it fell onto the altar
and let forth words of execration from its half-alive   105
tongue and breathed out its soul into the middle of the fires.
   Next twin brothers, Broteas and Ammon, unconquerable
with boxing gloves, if boxing gloves could conquer swords,
fell at the hand of Phineus, as did the priest of Ceres,
Ampycus, his temples veiled by a white headband.   110
You too, Lampetides, who should not have been employed in such a task,
but one to fit the lyre to your voice, a work of peace,
you had been asked to honour the festal banquet with your singing.
And, as he stood apart, holding his unwarlike plectrum,
Paetalus mocked him saying, 'Sing the rest to the Stygian   115
shades,' and lodged his sword point in his left temple;
he fell and with his dying fingers tried the strings
of his lyre again, and with his fall he struck a pitiable song.
But fierce Lycormas did not let his fall go unpunished;
he snatched the oaken bar from the door-post on the right   120
and smashed it on the bones in the middle of his neck; and he
fell down upon the ground like a bullock sacrificed.
Cinyphian Pelates tried to take the oak away from the door-post
on the left as well; as he tried, his right hand was pierced
by the spear-tip of Corythus from Marmarica and pinned to the wood;   125
pinned there as it was, Abas gouged out his flank, but he did not
fall but hung, dying, from the door-post that still held his hand.
   Melaneus too, who had followed the standards of Perseus, was laid low
and so was Dorylas, the richest man in the Nasamonian land;
Dorylas was rich in land, no other estate had been broader   130
than his or raised up so many heaps of corn.
A weapon was thrown and stood at an angle in his groin
(that is a fatal place); after the author of that wound,
Halcyoneus of Bactria, had seen him gasping out his soul
and rolling his eyes, 'From so much of the earth's land,' he said,   135
'may you have just this much that you press upon,' and he left the bloodless body.
The spear was snatched from the warm wound and hurled against him
by Abas' avenging son; it entered by the middle of the nose
and was driven out at the neck, protruding in both directions.
And, while Fortune helped his hand, he slew Clytius   140
and Clanis, both born to one mother but each wounded differently;
for he aimed his ash-wood spear with his stout arm and drove it
through both of Clytius' thighs, while Clanis' mouth bit upon his javelin.
Celadon of Mendes also fell, Astreus fell,
born of a Palestinian mother and an uncertain father,   145
and so did Aethion, once shrewd to see what was to come,

tunc aue deceptus falsa, regisque Thoactes
armiger et caeso genitore infamis Agyrtes.
    plus tamen exhausto superest; namque omnibus unum
150 opprimere est animus, coniurata undique pugnant
agmina pro causa meritum impugnante fidemque.
hac pro parte socer frustra pius et noua coniunx
cum genetrice fauent ululatuque atria complent;
sed sonus armorum superat gemitusque cadentum,
155 pollutosque simul multo Bellona penates
sanguine perfundit renouataque proelia miscet.
circueunt unum Phineus et mille secuti
Phinea; tela uolant hiberna grandine plura
praeter utrumque latus praeterque et lumen et aures.
160 applicat hic umeros ad magnae saxa columnae
tutaque terga gerens aduersaque in agmina uersus
sustinet instantes; instabat parte sinistra
Chaonius Molpeus, dextra Nabataeus Echemmon.
tigris ut auditis diuersa ualle duorum
165 exstimulata fame mugitibus armentorum
nescit utro potius ruat et ruere ardet utroque,
sic dubius Perseus dextra laeuane feratur
Molpea traiecti summouit uulnere cruris
contentusque fuga est; neque enim dat tempus Echemmon,
170 sed furit et, cupiens alto dare uulnera collo,
non circumspectis exactum uiribus ensem
fregit in extrema percussae parte columnae;
lammina dissiluit dominique in gutture fixa est.
non tamen ad letum causas satis illa ualentes
175 plaga dedit; trepidum Perseus et inertia frustra
bracchia tendentem Cyllenide confodit harpe.
    uerum ubi uirtutem turbae succumbere uidit,
'auxilium,' Perseus 'quoniam sic cogitis ipsi,'
dixit 'ab hoste petam. uultus auertite uestros,
180 si quis amicus adest' et Gorgonis extulit ora.
'quaere alium, tua quem moueant miracula' dixit
Thescelus, utque manu iaculum fatale parabat
mittere, in hoc haesit signum de marmore gestu.
proximus huic Ampyx animi plenissima magni
185 pectora Lyncidae gladio petit, inque petendo
dextera deriguit nec citra mota nec ultra est.
at Nileus, qui se genitum septemplice Nilo
ementitus erat, clipeo quoque flumina septem
argento partim, partim caelauerat auro,
190 'aspice,' ait 'Perseu, nostrae primordia gentis;
magna feres tacitas solacia mortis ad umbras,
a tanto cecidisse uiro --' pars ultima uocis
in medio suppressa sono est, adapertaque uelle
ora loqui credas, nec sunt ea peruia uerbis.
195 increpat hos 'uitio' que 'animi, non uiribus' inquit
'Gorgoneis torpetis;' Eryx 'incurrite mecum

then misled by a deceiving bird, and Thoactes, the king's
armour-bearer and Agyrtes, infamous for the slaying of his father.
　　But more remained than had been accomplished; for they all had a mind
to crush him alone, throngs conspired together from every side　　　　　　　150
to fight for a cause that fought against merit and faithfulness.
On his side were his father-in-law, vainly loyal, and his new wife
together with her mother, to favour him and fill the halls with screaming;
but the sound of arms and the groans of those who fell outdid them,
while Bellona polluted the penates by drenching them　　　　　　　　　　　155
in much blood and stirring up the strife she had renewed.
Alone he was surrounded by Phineus and by a thousand who had followed
Phineus; more weapons flew than hailstones in the winter
past both his sides and past his eyes and ears.
He leant his shoulders up against the stones of a great column　　　　　　　160
and, with his back safe, turned on the throngs turned against him
and held them back as they pressed on; pressing on the left flank was
Molpeus of Chaonia, and on the right Echemmon of Nabataea.
Just as a tigress hears the mooing of two herds
in separate valleys and goaded on by hunger　　　　　　　　　　　　　　　　165
does not know which to rush upon and burns to rush on both,
so Perseus, in doubt whether he should move right or left,
disposed of Molpeus with a wound that went right through his leg
and was content for him to flee, since Echemmon was giving him no time,
but was raging and, wanting to give him deep wounds in the neck,　　　　　170
drove the sword with unconsidered force
and broke it by striking it against the column's outer edge;
the blade split off and lodged in its master's throat.
The blow, however, was not strong enough to be
a cause of death; terrified, he vainly stretched out　　　　　　　　　　　　　175
his helpless arms, but Perseus ran him through with his Cyllenian harpe.
　　But when he saw his strength was succumbing to the mob,
Perseus said, 'Since you yourselves compel me to it,
I shall seek help from my enemy. Turn away your faces,
if any of my friends is here,' and he lifted up the Gorgon's head.　　　　　　180
'Look for another to be moved by your miracles,' said
Thescelus and, as he prepared to throw the fatal javelin
from his hand, he was fixed in that posture, a marble statue.
Next to him, Ampyx' sword was seeking the breast
of Lynceus' most high spirited descendant, and, as it sought,　　　　　　　　185
his right hand stiffened moving neither to nor fro.
But Nileus, whose lying claim had been that he was born
to the seven-branched Nile, and had also engraved upon his shield the seven
streams, partly in silver, partly in gold,
said, 'Look, Perseus, at the origins of my race;　　　　　　　　　　　　　　190
great is the consolation for your death that you will take to the silent shades
that you have fallen to so great a man --' The last part of his words
was stifled in mid sound, and you would believe his mouth
had opened up wanting to speak, but words could not pass through it.
Eryx reproached them and said, 'It is a defect in your courage, not the power　　195
of the Gorgon, that has numbed you; charge with me

LIBER V

et prosternite humi iuuenem magica arma mouentem.'
incursurus erat: tenuit uestigia tellus,
immotusque silex armataque mansit imago.
200 hi tamen ex merito poenas subiere, sed unus
miles erat Persei, pro quo dum pugnat, Aconteus,
Gorgone conspecta saxo concreuit oborto.
quem ratus Astyages etiamnum uiuere, longo
ense ferit; sonuit tinnitibus ensis acutis.
205 dum stupet Astyages, naturam traxit eandem
marmoreoque manet uultus mirantis in ore.
nomina longa mora est media de plebe uirorum
dicere; bis centum restabant corpora pugnae,
Gorgone bis centum riguerunt corpora uisa.
210   paenitet iniusti tum denique Phinea belli.
sed quid agat? simulacra uidet diuersa figuris
agnoscitque suos et nomine quemque uocatum
poscit opem credensque parum sibi proxima tangit
corpora; marmor erant. auertitur atque ita supplex
215 confessasque manus obliquaque bracchia tendens
'uincis,' ait 'Perseu; remoue tua monstra tuaeque
saxificos uultus, quaecumque ea, tolle Medusae,
tolle, precor. non nos odium regnique cupido
compulit ad bellum; pro coniuge mouimus arma.
220 causa fuit meritis melior tua, tempore nostra.
non cessisse piget. nihil, o fortissime, praeter
hanc animam concede mihi, tua cetera sunto.'
talia dicenti neque eum, quem uoce rogabat,
respicere audenti 'quod,' ait 'timidissime,' Perseus
225 'et possum tribuisse et magnum est munus inerti
(pone metum) tribuam: nullo uiolabere ferro.
quin etiam mansura dabo monimenta per aeuum,
inque domo soceri semper spectabere nostri,
ut mea se sponsi soletur imagine coniunx.'
230 dixit et in partem Phorcynida transtulit illam,
ad quam se trepido Phineus obuerterat ore.
tum quoque conanti sua uertere lumina ceruix
deriguit, saxoque oculorum induruit umor;
sed tamen os timidum uultusque in marmore supplex
235 summissaeque manus faciesque obnoxia mansit.
    uictor Abantiades patrios cum coniuge muros
intrat et immeriti uindex ultorque parentis
adgreditur Proetum; nam fratre per arma fugato
Acrisioneas Proetus possederat arces.
240 sed nec ope armorum nec quam male ceperat arce
torua colubriferi superauit lumina monstri.
    te tamen, o paruae rector, Polydecta, Seriphi,
nec iuuenis uirtus per tot spectata labores
nec mala mollierant, sed inexorabile durus
245 exerces odium, nec iniqua finis in ira est;
detrectas etiam laudem fictamque Medusae

and stretch out on the ground this youth who plies the magic arms.'
He was about to charge: the earth held him in his tracks,
and he stayed an unmoving stone, an image of an armed man.
These men endured their punishment deservedly, but Perseus   200
had one soldier, Aconteus, who, while fighting for him,
caught sight of the Gorgon and was hardened into rock that grew over him.
Astyages thought that he was still alive and struck him
with a long sword; the sword rang with a sharp sound.
While Astyages was still stunned, he took on the same nature,   205
and the look of wonder stayed in his marble face.
It would take much time to tell the names of all the common
soldiers; twice a hundred bodies were left from the fight,
twice a hundred bodies had seen the Gorgon and solidified.
     Then at last Phineus regretted his unjust war.   210
But what was he to do? He saw the statues with their different features
and recognized his own men and called them each by name
demanding help and, in disbelief, he touched the bodies closest
to himself; they were marble. He turned away, and in supplication
stretched out to the side hands and arms that confessed defeat,   215
saying, 'You win, Perseus; remove your monster and put away,
I beg you, put away the petrifying face of your Medusa,
whoever she may be. It was not hate or lust to rule
that drove me to war; it was for my bride I took up arms.
In point of merit yours was the better case, in point of time, mine.   220
I am sorry not to have given way. Grant, oh bravest man, nothing
except this life of mine and let the rest be yours.'
As he spoke thus, not daring to look round at the one
his voice was beseeching, Perseus said to him, 'Most timid man, what
I can grant and what is a great boon to the unmanly   225
(put away your fear) I shall grant: no sword will do you harm.
But rather I shall give you a monument to last for ever,
and you will be gazed at always in the house of my father-in-law
so that my wife may console herself with the image of her betrothed.'
He spoke, and carried Phorcus' daughter across in the direction   230
where Phineus had turned his terrified face.
As he tried even then to turn his eyes away, his neck
grew stiff and the moisture of his eyes hardened into stone;
but still in the marble his face remained timid and his look supplicating,
his hands submissive and subservient his expression.   235
     Abas' victorious descendant entered his father's walls together with
his wife and, as champion and avenger of his undeserving
grandfather, attacked Proetus; for, with his brother put to flight by force of arms,
Proetus had seized Acrisius' citadel.   239
But, neither with the help of his arms nor with the citadel that he had basely taken,
could he overcome the grim eyes of the snake-bearing monster.
     But you, oh Polydectes, ruler of small Seriphos,
neither the young man's courage, well known throughout so many toils,
nor his misfortunes had softened, but you stubbornly maintained
a relentless hate, and there was no end to your unjust anger;   245
you even belittled his renown and asserted that Medusa's

arguis esse necem. 'dabimus tibi pignora ueri;
parcite luminibus' Perseus ait oraque regis
ore Medusaeo silicem sine sanguine fecit.
          hactenus aurigenae comitem Tritonia fratri
se dedit; inde caua circumdata nube Seriphon
deserit, a dextra Cythno Gyaroque relictis,
quaque super pontum uia uisa breuissima, Thebas
uirgineumque Helicona petit. quo monte potita
constitit et doctas sic est adfata sorores:
'fama noui fontis nostras peruenit ad aures,
dura Medusaei quem praepetis ungula rupit.
is mihi causa uiae. uolui mirabile factum
cernere; uidi ipsum materno sanguine nasci.'
excipit Vranie: 'quaecumque est causa uidendi
has tibi, diua, domos, animo gratissima nostro es.
uera tamen fama est: est Pegasus huius origo
fontis' et ad latices deduxit Pallada sacros.
quae mirata diu factas pedis ictibus undas
siluarum lucos circumspicit antiquarum
antraque et innumeris distinctas floribus herbas,
felicesque uocat pariter studioque locoque
Mnemonidas. quam sic adfata est una sororum:
'o, nisi te uirtus opera ad maiora tulisset,
in partem uentura chori Tritonia nostri,
uera refers meritoque probas artesque locumque,
et gratam sortem, tutae modo simus, habemus.
sed (uetitum est adeo sceleri nihil) omnia terrent
uirgineas mentes, dirusque ante ora Pyreneus
uertitur, et nondum tota me mente recepi.
Daulida Threicio Phoceaque milite rura
ceperat ille ferox iniustaque regna tenebat.
templa petebamus Parnasia; uidit euntes
nostraque fallaci ueneratus numina uultu
"Mnemonides," (cognorat enim) "consistite" dixit
"nec dubitate, precor, tecto graue sidus et imbrem"
(imber erat) "uitare meo; subiere minores
saepe casas superi." dictis et tempore motae
adnuimusque uiro primasque intrauimus aedes.
desierant imbres, uictoque Aquilonibus Austro
fusca repurgato fugiebant nubila caelo.
impetus ire fuit; claudit sua tecta Pyreneus
uimque parat, quam nos sumptis effugimus alis.
ipse secuturo similis stetit arduus arce
"qua" que "uia est uobis, erit et mihi" dixit "eadem,"
seque iacit uecors e summae culmine turris
et cadit in uultus discussisque ossibus oris
tundit humum moriens scelerato sanguine tinctam.'
          Musa loquebatur; pennae sonuere per auras,
uoxque salutantum ramis ueniebat ab altis.
suspicit et linguae quaerit tam certa loquentes

BOOK V [21]

death had been a lie. 'I shall give you proofs of what is true;
watch out for your eyes,' said Perseus and with Medusa's face
he made the king's face bloodless stone.
  Till then Tritonia had given herself as a companion to her golden-born   250
brother; but now, wrapped in a hollow cloud, she abandoned
Seriphos, leaving Cynthos and Gyaros to the right,
and, by what seemed the shortest way across the sea, sought
Thebes and Helicon of the Virgins. And when she had reached that mountain,
she stopped and spoke thus to the learned sisters: 255
'To my ears has come the story of a new spring
which the hard hoof of Medusa's flyer made burst forth.
That is the reason for my journey. I wanted to behold this
miracle; I saw him even being born from his mother's blood.'
Urania replied, 'Whatever your reason is, goddess,   260
for coming to see our homes, you are most welcome to our hearts.
But the story is true: Pegasus is the source of this
spring,' and she led Pallas down to the sacred waters.
She marvelled for a long time at the waters made by hoof blows,
then looked around at the groves of ancient woods,   265
at the caves and at the grass bedecked with countless flowers,
and called the daughters of Memory lucky alike in their craft and in their
home. Then one of the sisters spoke to her so:
'Oh you who, if your merits had not borne you off for greater works,
would have come, Tritonia, to be a part of our chorus,   270
you speak the truth and you are right to admire our arts and home,
and we have a favoured lot, if only we were safe.
But (for there is nothing indeed forbidden to crime) all things terrify
virgins' minds, and dreadful Pyreneus goes to and fro before
our faces and as yet I have not fully recovered in my mind.   275
He had, in his ferocity, taken Daulis and the Phocean
countryside with his Thracian soldiery and was holding those realms unjustly.
We were seeking the temple of Parnassus; he saw us coming and,
paying homage to our divinity with his deceitful face,
"Daughters of Memory" (for he knew us), "stop," he said,   280
"and do not hesitate, I beg you, to escape the heavy sky and rainstorm"
(there was a rainstorm) "in my house; gods have often
entered smaller huts." Moved by his words and by the weather,
we nodded our assent to the man and entered the first part of his house.
The rainstorms had stopped, Aquilo had defeated Auster   285
and the dark clouds were fleeing from the sky now swept clean again.
Our impulse was to go; Pyreneus closed his house
and was preparing to use violence, which we escaped by taking to our wings.
He stood high up on his citadel like one about to follow us
and, "Wherever there is a way for you," he said, "there too will be one for me,"   290
and in his frenzy threw himself from the roof at the top of his tower
and fell onto his face smashing its bones
and, as he died, pounded the earth stained with his wicked blood.'
  The Muse was still speaking; wings sounded through the air
and a voice of greeting came from the branches on high.   295
Jove's daughter looked up and asked where tongues that spoke

unde sonent hominemque putat Ioue nata locutum;
ales erat, numeroque nouem sua fata querentes
institerant ramis imitantes omnia picae.
300 miranti sic orsa deae dea: 'nuper et istae
auxerunt uolucrum uictae certamine turbam.
Pieros has genuit Pellaeis diues in aruis,
Paeonis Euippe mater fuit; illa potentem
Lucinam nouiens, nouiens paritura, uocauit.
305 intumuit numero stolidarum turba sororum
perque tot Haemonias et per tot Achaidas urbes
huc uenit et tali committit proelia uoce:
"desinite indoctum uana dulcedine uulgus
fallere; nobiscum, si qua est fiducia uobis,
310 Thespiades, certate, deae. nec uoce nec arte
uincemur, totidemque sumus. uel cedite uictae
fonte Medusaeo et Hyantea Aganippe,
uel nos Emathiis ad Paeonas usque niuosos
cedemus campis. dirimant certamina nymphae."
315 turpe quidem contendere erat, sed cedere uisum
turpius; electae iurant per flumina nymphae
factaque de uiuo pressere sedilia saxo.
tum sine sorte prior quae se certare professa est
bella canit superum falsoque in honore Gigantas
320 ponit et extenuat magnorum facta deorum;
emissumque ima de sede Typhoea terrae
caelitibus fecisse metum cunctosque dedisse
terga fugae, donec fessos Aegyptia tellus
ceperit et septem discretus in ostia Nilus.
325 huc quoque terrigenam uenisse Typhoea narrat
et se mentitis superos celasse figuris:
"dux" que "gregis" dixit "fit Iuppiter, unde recuruis
nunc quoque formatus Libys est cum cornibus Ammon;
Delius in coruo, proles Semeleia capro,
330 fele soror Phoebi, niuea Saturnia uacca,
pisce Venus latuit, Cyllenius ibidis alis."
      'hactenus ad citharam uocalia mouerat ora:
poscimur Aonides -- sed forsitan otia non sint,
nec nostris praebere uacet tibi cantibus aures?'
335 'ne dubita uestrumque mihi refer ordine carmen'
Pallas ait nemorisque leui consedit in umbra.
Musa refert: 'dedimus summam certaminis uni.
surgit et immissos hedera collecta capillos
Calliope querulas praetemptat pollice chordas
340 atque haec percussis subiungit carmina neruis:
      "prima Ceres unco glaebam dimouit aratro,
prima dedit fruges alimentaque mitia terris,
prima dedit leges; Cereris sunt omnia munus.
illa canenda mihi est; utinam modo dicere possim
345 carmina digna dea! certe dea carmine digna est.
      "uasta Giganteis ingesta est insula membris

BOOK V [23

so clearly sounded from, thinking a human had spoken.
It was a bird; indeed there were nine in number complaining about their fate
and perched upon the branches mimicking everything, they were magpies.
Goddess began to speak to marvelling goddess so: 'Recently they too,   300
after defeat in a contest, increased the throng of birds.
They had been born to Pieros, rich in fields at Pella,
Paeonian Euippe was their mother; she had called out
to powerful Lucina nine times, nine times about to give birth.
Their number made this throng of stupid sisters puff themselves up   305
and, passing through so many Haemonian and so many Achaean cities,
they came here and joined battle with such words as these:
"Stop deceiving the unlearned mob with your empty
sweetness; if you have any confidence in yourselves, contest,
goddesses of Thespiae, with us. Neither in voice nor skill   310
shall we be defeated, and we are just as many as you. Either withdraw, if defeated,
from Medusa's spring and Hyantean Aganippe
or we shall withdraw from the Emathian plains all the way
to the snowbound Paeones. Let the nymphs settle the contest."
It was shameful, indeed, to compete, but to give way seemed   315
more shameful; nymphs were chosen and swore by the rivers
and pressed down on seats made from the living rock.
Then, without drawing lots, the one who first had offered herself for the contest
sang of the wars of the gods, giving false honour
to the Giants and belittling the deeds of the great gods;   320
how Typhoeus, sent out from earth's lowest abode
had brought fear to the heavenly ones who had all turned
their backs in flight until, tired out, they were received by the land
of Egypt and by the Nile which is divided into seven mouths.
She told how Typhoeus, the earth-born one, had come here too   325
and that the gods had concealed themselves in lying shapes:
and, "Jupiter," she said, "became the leader of the flock, hence Libyan
Ammon is depicted even now with horns curving back;
the Delian hid as a raven, Semele's offspring as a goat,
as a cat Phoebus' sister, Saturnia as a snowy cow,   330
as a fish Venus, Cyllenius as a winged ibis."
    Thus far she had fitted the words of her mouth to the lyre:
we Aonides were called forth -- but perhaps you have not the leisure,
and you are not free to lend your ear to our verses?'
'Don't hesitate, but tell me your song in order,'   335
said Pallas, and she sat down in the soft shade of the copse.
The Muse replied: 'We gave sole charge in the contest to one of us.
There rose, her flowing locks bound up with ivy,
Calliope who tried the plaintive strings with her thumb
and then continued with this song striking the notes out: 340
    "Ceres was the first to part the clods with the curved plough,
the first to give corn and gentle nourishment to the lands,
the first to give laws; all things are a gift from Ceres.
I must sing of her; if only I could perform
songs worthy of the goddess! Truly the goddess is worthy of a song.   345
    Heaped upon the limbs of the Giants was the vast island

Trinacris et magnis subiectum molibus urget
aetherias ausum sperare Typhoea sedes.
nititur ille quidem pugnatque resurgere saepe,
350 dextra sed Ausonio manus est subiecta Peloro,
laeua, Pachyne, tibi, Lilybaeo crura premuntur;
degrauat Aetna caput, sub qua resupinus harenas
eiectat flammamque ferox uomit ore Typhoeus.
saepe remoliri luctatur pondere terrae
355 oppidaque et magnos deuoluere corpore montes;
inde tremit tellus, et rex pauet ipse silentum
ne pateat latoque solum retegatur hiatu
immissusque dies trepidantes terreat umbras.
hanc metuens cladem tenebrosa sede tyrannus
360 exierat curruque atrorum uectus equorum
ambibat Siculae cautus fundamina terrae.
postquam exploratum satis est loca nulla labare
depositique metus, uidet hunc Erycina uagantem
monte suo residens natumque amplexa uolucrem
365 'arma manusque meae, mea, nate, potentia,' dixit
'illa, quibus superas omnes, cape tela, Cupido,
inque dei pectus celeres molire sagittas,
cui triplicis cessit fortuna nouissima regni.
tu superos ipsumque Iouem, tu numina ponti
370 uicta domas ipsumque regit qui numina ponti.
Tartara quid cessant? cur non matrisque tuumque
imperium profers? agitur pars tertia mundi.
et tamen in caelo (quae iam patientia nostra est!)
spernimur, ac mecum uires minuuntur Amoris.
375 Pallada nonne uides iaculatricemque Dianam
abscessisse mihi? Cereris quoque filia uirgo,
si patiemur, erit; nam spes adfectat easdem.
at tu pro socio, si qua est ea gratia, regno
iunge deam patruo.' dixit Venus; ille pharetram
380 soluit et arbitrio matris de mille sagittis
unam seposuit, sed qua nec acutior ulla
nec minus incerta est nec quae magis audiat arcum,
oppositoque genu curuauit flexile cornum
inque cor hamata percussit harundine Ditem.
385   "haud procul Hennaeis lacus est a moenibus altae,
nomine Pergus, aquae; non illo plura Caystros
carmina cycnorum labentibus audit in undis.
silua coronat aquas cingens latus omne suisque
frondibus ut uelo Phoebeos summouet ictus.
390 frigora dant rami, uarios humus umida flores;
perpetuum uer est. quo dum Proserpina luco
ludit et aut uiolas aut candida lilia carpit,
dumque puellari studio calathosque sinumque
implet et aequales certat superare legendo,
395 paene simul uisa est dilectaque raptaque Diti
(usque adeo est properatus amor). dea territa maesto

of Trinacria which pressed down with its great mass on Typhoeus
lying underneath, for he had dared to hope for an ethereal abode.
He struggled indeed and often fought to rise again,
but his right hand was lying under Ausonian Pelorus,   350
his left under you, Pachynos, his legs were pressed beneath Lilybaeon;
Etna weighed down his head, and, flat on his back beneath, belching
sand and fiercely spewing flame from his mouth, lay Typhoeus.
Often he strained to heave the weight of land away
and to roll the towns and great mountains off his body;   355
then the earth shuddered and the king of the silent ones himself was afraid
that the ground would open and be revealed in a wide crack
and that daylight would be let in and terrify the trembling shades.
Afraid of this disaster, the king had come out from his shadowy
abode and, in a chariot drawn by two black horses,   360
he cautiously went round the Sicilian land's foundations.
After his inspection had satisfied him that there was no slippage anywhere
and he had laid his fears aside, Erycina saw him roaming
as she sat upon her mountain and, embracing her winged son,
'My arms and hands, oh son, my power,' she said,   365
'take up the weapons, Cupid, with which you overcome all
and shoot swift arrows into the breast of the god
to whom befell the last lot of the triple kingdom.
By you the gods and Jupiter himself, by you the sea's divinities
are conquered and subdued, as is the one who rules the sea's divinities.   370
Why is Tartarus left out? Why do you not extend your mother's
jurisdiction and your own? A third part of the world is at stake.
And yet in heaven (what patience we have now!)
we are spurned and, together with myself, the strength of Love is diminished.
Do you not see that Pallas and the spearwoman Diana   375
have forsaken me? And Ceres' daughter too will be,
if we allow it, a virgin; for she aspires to the same hopes.
But, on behalf of our shared rule, if that finds any favour with you,
join the goddess to her uncle.' Venus had spoken; he undid
his quiver and, as his mother wanted, from his thousand arrows   380
picked out one; but there was no other that was sharper
or less untrue or that would respond better to the bow;
putting the supple horn to his knee he bent it
and struck Dis to the heart with a barbed shaft.

    Not far from the walls of Henna there is a lake of deep   385
water, Pergus by name; Cayster hears no more
songs from the swans upon its gliding waves than does that lake.
A wood crowns the waters, ringing them on every side, and with its
leaves like an awning keeps out Phoebus' blows.
The branches give coolness and the damp earth a variety of flowers;   390
there is perpetual spring. While Proserpina played in this
grove gathering either violets or white lilies
and was filling up her baskets and her lap with girlish
enthusiasm striving to outdo her companions in collecting them,
almost in one moment she was seen, adored and ravished by Dis   395
(so hurried was his love). The terrified goddess cried out

et matrem et comites, sed matrem saepius, ore
clamat et, ut summa uestem laniarat ab ora,
collecti flores tunicis cecidere remissis.
400 (tantaque simplicitas puerilibus adfuit annis,
haec quoque uirgineum mouit iactura dolorem.)
raptor agit currus et nomine quemque uocando
exhortatur equos, quorum per colla iubasque
excutit obscura tinctas ferrugine habenas;
405 perque lacus altos et olentia sulphure fertur
stagna Palicorum rupta feruentia terra
et qua Bacchiadae, bimari gens orta Corintho,
inter inaequales posuerunt moenia portus.
    "est medium Cyanes et Pisaeae Arethusae
410 quod coit angustis inclusum cornibus aequor;
hic fuit, a cuius stagnum quoque nomine dictum est
inter Sicelidas Cyane celeberrima Nymphas.
gurgite quae medio summa tenus exstitit aluo
agnouitque deam 'nec longius ibitis!' inquit
415 'non potes inuitae Cereris gener esse; roganda,
non rapienda fuit. quod si componere magnis
parua mihi fas est, et me dilexit Anapis;
exorata tamen, nec, ut haec, exterrita nupsi.'
dixit et in partes diuersas bracchia tendens
420 obstitit. haud ultra tenuit Saturnius iram
terribilesque hortatus equos in gurgitis ima
contortum ualido sceptrum regale lacerto
condidit; icta uiam tellus in Tartara fecit
et pronos currus medio cratere recepit.
425 at Cyane, raptamque deam contemptaque fontis
iura sui maerens, inconsolabile uulnus
mente gerit tacita lacrimisque absumitur omnis
et, quarum fuerat magnum modo numen, in illas
extenuatur aquas. molliri membra uideres,
430 ossa pati flexus, ungues posuisse rigorem;
primaque de tota tenuissima quaeque liquescunt,
caerulei crines digitique et crura pedesque
(nam breuis in gelidas membris exilibus undas
transitus est); post haec umeri tergusque latusque
435 pectoraque in tenues abeunt euanida riuos;
denique pro uiuo uitiatas sanguine uenas
lympha subit, restatque nihil quod prendere possis.
    "interea pauidae nequiquam filia matri
omnibus est terris, omni quaesita profundo.
440 illam non udis ueniens Aurora capillis
cessantem uidit, non Hesperus: illa duabus
flammiferas pinus manibus succendit ab Aetna
perque pruinosas tulit inrequieta tenebras;
rursus ubi alma dies hebetarat sidera, natam
445 solis ab occasu solis quaerebat ad ortus.
fessa labore sitim conceperat oraque nulli

BOOK V [27

in mournful tone both to her mother and to her companions, but more often
to her mother, and, when she had torn her clothing down from its upper hem,
the flowers she had gathered fell from her loosened tunic.
(And so great was the innocence of her girlish years   400
that this loss too moved the virgin's grief.)
The ravisher drove his chariot off and urged his horses on by calling to them
each by name, and along their neck and mane
he shook out their dark-rust dyed reins.
And he was carried through deep lakes and the sulphur smelling   405
ponds of the Palici seething through a fissure in the earth,
and where the Bacchiadae, a race that began in Corinth of two seas,
had set their walls between unequal harbours.
    There is between Cyane and Pisaean Arethusa
a point where the sea is compressed, enclosed by narrow horns;   410
here was she from whom the pond too was called,
Cyane, the most famous among the nymphs of Sicily.
And she stood out from the middle of the flood as far as her belly's top
and she recognized the goddess and, 'You shall go no further,' said,
you cannot be the son-in-law of Ceres against her will; she should have been courted,
not ravished. But, if it is right for me   416
to compare great things with small, I too was loved, by Anapis;
but I was wooed, not terrified like her, before I married him.
She spoke and, stretching her arms in opposite directions,
blocked his way. No longer did the Saturnian hold his anger back,   420
but, urging his fearsome horses into the depths of the flood,
he sent his royal sceptre whirling with his mighty arm
and plunged it in; where it was struck, the earth made a way to Tartarus
and received the headlong chariot in the middle of the crater.
But Cyane, grieving for the ravished goddess and the mocking   425
of her own spring's rights, sustained an inconsolable wound
silently in her mind and was all consumed in tears
and was reduced into the waters of which she had been just now
the great divinity. You could have seen her limbs soften,
her bones suffer bending, her nails lose their hardness;   430
it was the smallest of all her parts that were the first to liquefy,
her aquamarine hair, her fingers, her legs and her feet
(for it is a short passage from slender limbs
to cool waters); after that her shoulders, back, side
and breast vanished away into narrow streams;   435
at last, instead of living blood, into her ruined veins
there entered water, and there was nothing left you could have grasped.
    Meanwhile, the fearful mother vainly sought
her daughter in all the lands and in all the deep.
Dawn, coming with dampened locks, did not see her   440
lingering, nor did Hesperus: she lit
from Etna flame-bearing pines for her two hands
and bore them unresting through the frosty dark;
and again, when bounteous day had dulled the stars, she sought
her daughter from the setting of the sun to its rising.   445
Tired out from her effort, she had developed thirst, and no springs

                    conluerant fontes, cum tectam stramine uidit
                    forte casam paruasque fores pulsauit; at inde
                    prodit anus diuamque uidet lymphamque roganti
450   dulce dedit, tosta quod texerat ante polentam.
                    dum bibit illa datum, duri puer oris et audax
                    constitit ante deam risitque auidamque uocauit.
                    offensa est neque adhuc epota parte loquentem
                    cum liquido mixtae perfudit diua polentae.
455   combibit os maculas et, quae modo bracchia gessit,
                    crura gerit; cauda est mutatis addita membris,
                    inque breuem formam, ne sit uis magna nocendi,
                    contrahitur, paruaque minor mensura lacerta est.
                    mirantem flentemque et tangere monstra pauentem
460   fugit anum latebramque petit aptumque pudori
                    nomen habet, uariis stellatus corpora guttis.
                         "quas dea per terras et quas errauerit undas,
                    dicere longa mora est; quaerenti defuit orbis.
                    Sicaniam repetit, dumque omnia lustrat eundo,
465   uenit et ad Cyanen. ea ni mutata fuisset,
                    omnia narrasset; sed et os et lingua uolenti
                    dicere non aderant, nec qua loqueretur habebat.
                    signa tamen manifesta dedit notamque parenti
                    illo forte loco delapsam in gurgite sacro
470   Persephones zonam summis ostendit in undis.
                    quam simul agnouit, tamquam tum denique raptam
                    scisset, inornatos laniauit diua capillos
                    et repetita suis percussit pectora palmis.
                    nescit adhuc ubi sit; terras tamen increpat omnes
475   ingratasque uocat nec frugum munere dignas,
                    Trinacriam ante alias, in qua uestigia damni
                    repperit. ergo illic saeua uertentia glaebas
                    fregit aratra manu parilique irata colonos
                    ruricolasque boues leto dedit aruaque iussit
480   fallere depositum uitiataque semina fecit.
                    fertilitas terrae latum uulgata per orbem
                    laesa iacet; primis segetes moriuntur in herbis,
                    et modo sol nimius, nimius modo corripit imber,
                    sideraque uentique nocent, auidaeque uolucres
485   semina iacta legunt; lolium tribolique fatigant
                    triticeas messes et inexpugnabile gramen.
                         "tum caput Eleis Alpheias extulit undis
                    rorantesque comas a fronte remouit ad aures
                    atque ait: 'o toto quaesitae uirginis orbe
490   et frugum genetrix, immensos siste labores,
                    neue tibi fidae uiolenta irascere terrae;
                    terra nihil meruit patuitque inuita rapinae.
                    nec sum pro patria supplex; huc hospita ueni.
                    Pisa mihi patria est et ab Elide ducimus ortus.
495   Sicaniam peregrina colo, sed gratior omni
                    haec mihi terra solo est; hos nunc Arethusa penates,

BOOK V [29

had rinsed her mouth, when she chanced to see a hut
roofed with straw, and she knocked on its low doors; and from within
emerged an old woman who saw the goddess and, when she asked for water,
gave her something sweet which she had first covered with roasted barley.   450
While she drank what she had been given, a boy hard of face and bold
stood before the goddess and laughed and called her greedy.
She was annoyed and, while there was a part she had not yet drunk down, the goddess
drenched him as he spoke with the liquid barley mixture.
His face was stained with spots and, where just now he had had arms,   455
he had legs; a tail was added to these altered limbs
and, so that he would not have a great power to do harm, he was reduced
to a little size, he was a lizard of less than small scale.
As the old woman marvelled and wept and was frightened to touch the monster,
he fled from her and looked for a lair and took a name   460
to fit the disgrace of a body starred with varied spots.

    To tell what lands and what waters the goddess
wandered through would take much time; the world was not enough for the searcher.
She returned to Sicania and, as she went scouring through it all,
she came at last to Cyane. If she had not been changed,   465
she would have told everything; but, though she wished to talk,
her mouth and her tongue were not there, she did not have the means to speak.
And yet she gave clear signs; so well known to her mother,
there had chanced to slip off at that place in her sacred flood
Persephone's girdle, and she displayed it on the surface of her waters.   470
As soon as she had recognized it, as if then at last she knew she had been
ravished, the goddess tore at her dishevelled hair
and beat her breast again and again with her palms.
She still did not know where she was; but she reproached all lands
calling them ungrateful and not worthy of the gift of corn,   475
Trinacria above the others where she had found the traces
of her loss. So then, with savage hand, she broke
the ploughs that turn the clods and in her anger sent the farmers
and the oxen that tilled the soil to a like fate and told the fields
to default on their deposits and blighted the seeds.   480
The land's fertility, well known throughout the wide world,
lay ruined; the crops died in the first blade,
and now too much sun, now too much rain destroyed them,
both stars and winds caused harm, and greedy birds
picked up the scattered seeds; darnel and caltrop wore down   485
the wheat harvest as did the unconquerable grass.

    Then Alpheias lifted her head from the Elean waters
and pushed back her dripping hair from her brow to her ears
and said, 'Oh mother of a maiden sought in all the world
and of the grain crops, stop your immeasurable labours,   490
do not be violent and angry with your faithful land;
the land has not deserved it at all, it opened for the rape unwillingly.
And I am not supplicating for my country; I came here as a stranger,
Pisa is my country and I trace my origins to Elis.
In Sicania I dwell as a foreigner, but this land   495
is dearer to me than all the earth; these now do I, Arethusa, have as my penates,

LIBER V

       hanc habeo sedem—quam tu, mitissima, serua!
       mota loco cur sim tantique per aequoris undas
       aduehar Ortygiam, ueniet narratibus hora
500   tempestiua meis, cum tu curaque leuata
       et uultus melioris eris. mihi peruia tellus
       praebet iter subterque imas ablata cauernas
       hic caput attollo desuetaque sidera cerno.
       ergo dum Stygio sub terris gurgite labor,
505   uisa tua est oculis illic Proserpina nostris;
       illa quidem tristis neque adhuc interrita uultu,
       sed regina tamen, sed opaci maxima mundi,
       sed tamen inferni pollens matrona tyranni.'
         'mater ad auditas stupuit ceu saxea uoces
510   attonitaeque diu similis fuit; utque dolore
       pulsa graui grauis est amentia, curribus auras
       exit in aetherias. ibi toto nubila uultu
       ante Iouem passis stetit inuidiosa capillis
       'pro' que 'meo ueni supplex tibi, Iuppiter,' inquit
515   'sanguine proque tuo; si nulla est gratia matris,
       nata patrem moueat, neu sit tibi cura, precamur,
       uilior illius, quod nostro est edita partu.
       en quaesita diu tandem mihi nata reperta est,
       si reperire uocas amittere certius, aut si
520   scire ubi sit reperire uocas. quod rapta, feremus,
       dummodo reddat eam; neque enim praedone marito
       filia digna tua est, si iam mea filia non est.'
       Iuppiter excepit: 'commune est pignus onusque
       nata mihi tecum. sed si modo nomina rebus
525   addere uera placet, non hoc iniuria factum,
       uerum amor est; neque erit nobis gener ille pudori,
       tu modo, diua, uelis. ut desint cetera, quantum est
       esse Iouis fratrem! quid quod non cetera desunt
       nec cedit nisi sorte mihi? sed tanta cupido
530   si tibi discidii est, repetet Proserpina caelum,
       lege tamen certa, si nullos contigit illic
       ore cibos; nam sic Parcarum foedere cautum est.'
         'dixerat; at Cereri certum est educere natam.
       non ita fata sinunt, quoniam ieiunia uirgo
535   soluerat et, cultis dum simplex errat in hortis,
       puniceum curua decerpserat arbore pomum
       sumptaque pallenti septem de cortice grana
       presserat ore suo. solusque ex omnibus illud
       Ascalaphus uidit, quem quondam dicitur Orphne,
540   inter Auernales haud ignotissima Nymphas,
       ex Acheronte suo siluis peperisse sub atris;
       uidit et indicio reditum crudelis ademit.
       ingemuit regina Erebi testemque profanam
       fecit auem sparsumque caput Phlegethontide lympha
545   in rostrum et plumas et grandia lumina uertit.
       ille sibi ablatus fuluis amicitur in alis

this is my home -- which you, most gentle one, must save!
Why it was I moved from my place and travelled through the waters of so great
a sea to Ortygia, there will come a fitting hour
for me to tell when you are relieved of care   500
and are looking better. The porous earth showed
me a path, and when I had been carried off within its lowest caverns,
here I lifted up my head and saw the stars that I was now unused to.
And so, while I was gliding under the earth in the Stygian flood,
there I saw with my own eyes your Proserpina;   505
she was sad indeed and had still not lost her look of fear,
but still she was a queen, still the greatest lady in the world of darkness,
still indeed the powerful consort of the king below.'
   The mother was stunned as if turned to stone at the words she had heard,
and for a long time she was like one thunderstruck; but, as her great   510
frenzy was driven out by great grief, she went off in her chariot
into the ethereal air. There, with face all clouded,
and hair flowing loose, she stood resentfully in front of Jove
and, 'I have come as a suppliant to you, Jupiter,' she said,
'for my blood and for yours; if a mother finds no favour,   515
let a daughter move her father, and do not, I pray, let your care
for her be meaner because I gave her birth.
Look, the daughter I have sought so long has at last been found
if you call it finding to lose her more surely, or if   519
you call it finding merely to know where she is. That she was ravished, I shall bear,
provided only that he gives her back; for your daughter does not
deserve a robber husband, if now she's not my daughter.'
Jupiter replied: 'She is my daughter and yours,
our common pledge and concern. But if you wish to give things
their true names, this deed is not an injustice   525
but love; nor will he be a disgrace to us as a son-in-law,
provided only, goddess, you are willing. If it weren't for the rest, how great a thing
it is to be Jove's brother! And what of the fact that he does not lack all the rest
and, except in his portion, he does not yield to me? But if your desire
to separate them is so great, Proserpina will return to heaven,   530
but on this clear condition, that she has not touched any food
there with her mouth; for so it was decided by the compact of the Fates.'
   He had spoken; but Ceres was determined to bring her daughter out.
The fates did not allow it, since the maiden had broken
her fast and, while wandering innocently in the well-kept gardens,   535
had plucked a crimson fruit from a bending tree
and taken seven seeds from its pale rind
and pressed them to her mouth. The only one at all to see it
was Ascaphalus; Orphne, not the least known among
the Nymphs of Avernus, once bore him,   540
it is said, to her Acheron within the dark woods;
he saw and, by informing, cruelly deprived her of her return.
The queen of Erebus groaned and made the sacrilegious witness
into a bird, and sprinkled his head with Phlegethontic water
and turned it into a beak, feathers and large eyes.   545
He was taken from himself and covered by tawny wings

inque caput crescit longosque reflectitur ungues
uixque mouet natas per inertia bracchia pennas;
foedaque fit uolucris, uenturi nuntia luctus,
ignauus bubo, dirum mortalibus omen.
    "hic tamen indicio poenam linguaque uideri
commeruisse potest; uobis, Acheloides, unde
pluma pedesque auium, cum uirginis ora geratis?
an quia, cum legeret uernos Prosperpina flores,
in comitum numero, doctae Sirenes, eratis?
quam postquam toto frustra quaesistis in orbe,
protinus, ut uestram sentirent aequora curam,
posse super fluctus alarum insistere remis
optastis facilesque deos habuistis at artus
uidistis uestros subitis flauescere pennis.
ne tamen ille canor mulcendas natus ad aures
tantaque dos oris linguae deperderet usum,
uirginei uultus et uox humana remansit.
    "at medius fratrisque sui maestaeque sororis
Iuppiter ex aequo uoluentem diuidit annum:
nunc dea, regnorum numen commune duorum,
cum matre est totidem, totidem cum coniuge menses.
uertitur extemplo facies et mentis et oris;
nam modo quae poterat Diti quoque maesta uideri
laeta deae frons est, ut sol, qui tectus aquosis
nubibus ante fuit, uictis e nubibus exit.
    "exigit alma Ceres, nata secura recepta,
quae tibi causa fugae, cur sis, Arethusa, sacer fons.
conticuere undae, quarum dea sustulit alto
fonte caput uiridesque manu siccata capillos
fluminis Elei ueteres narrauit amores.
    "pars ego nympharum quae sunt in Achaide' dixit
'una fui, nec me studiosius altera saltus
legit nec posuit studiosius altera casses.
sed quamuis formae numquam mihi fama petita est,
quamuis fortis eram, formosae nomen habebam.
nec mea me facies nimium laudata iuuabat,
quaque aliae gaudere solent, ego rustica dote
corporis erubui crimenque placere putaui.
lassa reuertebar (memini) Stymphalide silua;
aestus erat, magnumque labor geminauerat aestum.
inuenio sine uertice aquas, sine murmure euntes,
perspicuas ad humum, per quas numerabilis alte
calculus omnis erat, quas tu uix ire putares.
cana salicta dabant nutritaque populus unda
sponte sua natas ripis decliuibus umbras.
accessi primumque pedis uestigia tinxi,
poplite deinde tenus; neque eo contenta recingor
molliaque impono salici uelamina curuae
nudaque mergor aquis. quas dum ferioque trahoque
mille modis labens excussaque bracchia iacto,

and grew into the head and was bent over onto his long claws,
and hardly moved the feathers that had formed over his sluggish arms;
and he had become a loathsome bird, a messenger of grief to come,
the slothful owl, omen of dread for mortals. 550
  Now he might seem to have deserved punishment
for his informer's tongue; but you, Acheloides, whence
your feathers and birds' feet, though you still have maidens' faces?
Was it because, when Proserpina was picking spring flowers,
you, learned Sirens, were in the number of her companions? 555
And after you had vainly sought her in all the world,
immediately, so that the seas might feel your concern,
you prayed to be able to tread upon the billows with the oarage
of wings, and you found the gods agreeable and saw
your limbs grow golden with sudden feathers. 560
But, so that your song, made for soothing ears,
and that great endowment of your mouth might not lose the use of speech,
your maiden faces and your human voice remained.
  But, mediating between his brother and his grieving sister,
Jupiter divided the revolving year equally: 565
now the goddess, a deity common to the two realms,
is with her mother for as many months as the months she is with her husband.
At once the demeanour of her mind and of her face was changed;
for the goddess' brow, which just now could have seemed sad
even to Dis, was happy, just as the sun, which before was 570
covered by watery clouds, comes out from the clouds it has conquered.
  But kindly Ceres, free of care with the return of her daughter, asked
what was the reason for your flight, Arethusa, and why you are a sacred spring.
The waters fell silent, and their goddess raised her head
from the deep spring, dried her green locks with her hand 575
and told of the old loves of the Elean river.
  I was part', she said, 'of the nymphs who are
in Achais, and no other more keenly than I traversed
the glades, and no other more keenly set the snares.
But though a fame for beauty was never what I sought, 580
though I was strong, it was the reputation of a beauty that I had.
But my looks, though greatly praised, did not please me,
and what other girls will delight in, the endowments of their body,
I, a country girl, blushed at and thought it was a crime to please.
I was returning (I remember) tired from the Stymphalian wood; 585
it was hot and my exertions had doubled that great heat.
I found some waters flowing without an eddy, without a murmur,
clear to the bottom; you could count deep through them
every pebble and you would hardly think that they were flowing.
White willows and a poplar tree fed by the waters gave 590
natural shade to the sloping banks.
I approached, and first dipped the sole of my foot in,
then up to my knee; and, not content with that, I undid
my soft clothing and put it on a bending willow
and plunged naked into the waters. And while I struck them, drawing them along 595
and gliding in a thousand ways, shaking and tossing my arms,

nescioquod medio sensi sub gurgite murmur
territaque insisto propiori margine fontis.
'quo properas, Arethusa?' suis Alpheus ab undis,
'quo properas?' iterum rauco mihi dixerat ore. 600
sicut eram, fugio sine uestibus (altera uestes
ripa meas habuit); tanto magis instat et ardet,
et quia nuda fui, sum uisa paratior illi.
sic ego currebam, sic me ferus ille premebat,
ut fugere accipitrem penna trepidante columbae, 605
ut solet accipiter trepidas urgere columbas.
usque sub Orchomenon Psophidaque Cyllenenque
Maenaliosque sinus gelidumque Erymanthon et Elin
currere sustinui, nec me uelocior ille;
sed tolerare diu cursus ego uiribus impar 610
non poteram, longi patiens erat ille laboris.
[per tamen et campos, per opertos arbore montes,
saxa quoque et rupes et, qua uia nulla, cucurri.]
sol erat a tergo; uidi praecedere longam
ante pedes umbram, nisi si timor illa uidebat. 615
sed certe sonitusque pedum terrebat et ingens
crinales uittas adflabat anhelitus oris.
fessa labore fugae 'fer opem, deprendimur,' inquam
'armigerae, Diana, tuae, cui saepe dedisti
ferre tuos arcus inclusaque tela pharetra.' 620
mota dea est spissisque ferens e nubibus unam
me super iniecit; lustrat caligine tectam
amnis et ignarus circum caua nubila quaerit
bisque locum, quo me dea texerat, inscius ambit
et bis 'io Arethusa, io Arethusa!' uocauit. 625
quid mihi tunc animi miserae fuit? anne quod agnae est,
si qua lupos audit circum stabula alta frementes,
aut lepori, qui uepre latens hostilia cernit
ora canum nullosque audet dare corpore motus?
non tamen abscedit (neque enim uestigia cernit 630
longius ulla pedum); seruat nubemque locumque.
occupat obsessos sudor mihi frigidus artus
caeruleaeque cadunt toto de corpore guttae;
quaque pedem moui, manat locus eque capillis
ros cadit, et citius, quam nunc tibi facta renarro, 635
in latices mutor. sed enim cognoscit amatas
amnis aquas positoque uiri, quod sumpserat, ore
uertitur in proprias, ut se mihi misceat, undas.
Delia rupit humum caecisque ego mersa cauernis
aduehor Ortygiam, quae me cognomine diuae 640
grata meae superas eduxit prima sub auras.'
        "hac Arethusa tenus. geminos dea fertilis angues
curribus admouit frenisque coercuit ora
et medium caeli terraeque per aera uecta est,
atque leuem currum Tritonida misit in urbem 645
Triptolemo partimque rudi data semina iussit

I sensed some murmur or other in the middle of the flood
and stood terrified upon the nearer bank of the spring.
'Where, Arethusa, are you rushing to?' it was Alpheus from his waters,
'Where are you rushing to?' he had said to me again in his hoarse voice. 600
Just as I was, without my clothes, I fled (the other bank
held my clothes); he was all the more insistent and burned for me
and, naked as I was, I seemed to him more ready.
So I ran and so that wild one pursued me
as doves on trembling wing will flee a hawk, 605
as a hawk will chase trembling doves.
All the way to Orchomenos, Psophis and Cyllene,
the hollows of Maenalos, cold Erymanthos and Elis
I kept on running nor was he swifter than me;
but I, unequal in strength, could not for long endure 610
the chase, but he could tolerate long effort.
[But even through plains, through mountains covered with trees,
rocks too and crags and where there was no way I ran,]
The sun was at my back; I saw a long shadow
going ahead of my feet, unless it was my fear that saw it. 615
But certainly the sound of his feet began to terrify me and a huge
gasping from his mouth breathed on the bands upon my hair.
Tired out from the effort of my flight, 'I am being caught, bring help,' I said,
'Diana, to your armour-bearer whom you have often let
carry your bows and the arrows encased in your quiver.' 620
The goddess was moved and taking one of the dense clouds,
she threw it over me; covered in darkness I was circled
by the river who, in his ignorance, searched around the hollow clouds
and twice unwittingly went round the place where the goddess had concealed me,
and twice he called, 'Oh Arethusa! Oh Arethusa!' 625
What then were my thoughts in my unhappiness? Were they not a lamb's
if ever she hears wolves howling around the high pens,
or a hare's when he is hiding in a thornbush, sees the hostile
mouths of the dogs and dares not make a move with his body?
But he did not go away (for he did not see any 630
footprints further on); he watched both the cloud and the place.
A cold sweat assailed and seized my limbs,
the blue-green drops fell from the whole of my body;
and where I put my foot the place grew wet and from my hair
dew fell and, more swiftly than I now retell the fact, 635
I was changed into water. And yet the river recognized
the waters that he loved; he laid aside the man's face he had taken on
and turned into his own waters so as to mix with me.
Delia cleft the ground and I plunged into the dark caverns
and arrived at Ortygia which, cherished by me because it bore the surname 640
of my goddess, was the first to bring me out to the air above.'
    Thus Arethusa. The fruitful goddess attached her twin
dragons to her chariot, restrained their mouths with bits,
rode through the air between the sky and earth,
took her light chariot to the city of Tritonis 645
to Triptolemus, and told him to scatter some of the seeds she had given him

```
           spargere humo, partim post tempora longa recultae.
           iam super Europam sublimis et Asida terram
           uectus erat iuuenis; Scythicas aduertitur oras.
650        rex ibi Lyncus erat; regis subit ille penates.
           qua ueniat causamque uiae nomenque rogatus
           et patriam, 'patria est clarae mihi' dixit 'Athenae,
           Triptolemus nomen. ueni nec puppe per undas,
           nec pede per terras; patuit mihi peruius aether.
655        dona fero Cereris, latos quae sparsa per agros
           frugiferas messes alimentaque mitia reddant.'
           barbarus inuidit, tantique ut muneris auctor
           ipse sit, hospitio recipit somnoque grauatum
           adgreditur ferro; conantem figere pectus
660        lynca Ceres fecit rursusque per aera iussit
           Mopsopium iuuenem sacros agitare iugales."
              'finierat doctos e nobis maxima cantus;
           at Nymphae uicisse deas Helicona colentes
           concordi dixere sono. conuicia uictae
665        cum iacerent, "quoniam" dixi "certamine uobis
           supplicium meruisse parum est maledictaque culpae
           additis et non est patientia libera nobis,
           ibimus in poenas et, qua uocat ira, sequemur."
           rident Emathides spernuntque minacia uerba;
670        conantesque oculis magno clamore proteruas
           intentare manus, pennas exire per ungues
           aspexere suos, operiri bracchia plumis,
           alteraque alterius rigido concrescere rostro
           ora uidet uolucresque nouas accedere siluis;
675        dumque uolunt plangi, per bracchia mota leuatae
           aere pendebant, nemorum conuicia, picae.
           nunc quoque in alitibus facundia prisca remansit
           raucaque garrulitas studiumque immane loquendi.'
```

BOOK V [37

upon the virgin soil and some where he had ploughed again after a long time.
Now the young man rode up high over Europe
and the land of Asia; he reached the Scythian regions.
The king there was Lyncus; he entered the penates of the king; 650
asked from where he came, the reasons for his journey, his name
and his country. 'My country is,' he said, 'famous Athens,
Triptolemus my name. I came neither by ship over the waves,
nor on foot over land; a way through the ether opened for me.
I bring the gift of Ceres which, if scattered over the broad fields, 655
would return fruitful harvests and gentle nourishment.'
The barbarian was jealous and, so that he might be the bringer of so great a gift
himself, he took him in hospitably and, when sleep was heavy on him,
attacked him with a sword; as he tried to pierce his breast,
Ceres made him into a lynx and told the Mopsopian young man once again 660
to drive the sacred team through the air."

    The eldest of us had finished her learned song;
and the Nymphs in harmony declared that the goddesses
who tend Helicon had won. When those who had been defeated
hurled insults, "Since," I said, "it is not enough 665
that you have deserved punishment for the contest but you are adding
to your guilt with these taunts and our patience is not unlimited,
we shall go on to punishments and follow where anger calls."
The Emathides laughed and scorned my threatening words;
and as they tried with a great shout to shake their insolent 670
fists into our faces, they noticed feathers coming out
through their fingernails, their arms being covered with plumage,
each saw the other's mouths hardening
into stiff beaks and new birds being added to the woods;
and when they wished to beat their breasts, lifted by the motion of their arms, 675
they hung in the air, those scolds of the copses, magpies.
Even now, in the birds, their ancient garrulity has remained,
their raucous chatter and their vast passion for talking.'

LIBER VI

    Praebuerat dictis Tritonia talibus aures,
carminaque Aonidum iustamque probauerat iram.
tum secum: 'laudare parum est; laudemur et ipsae,
numina nec sperni sine poena nostra sinamus.'
Maeoniaeque animum fatis intendit Arachnes,
quam sibi lanificae non cedere laudibus artis
audierat. non illa loco nec origine gentis
clara, sed arte fuit. pater huic Colophonius Idmon
Phocaico bibulas tingebat murice lanas;
occiderat mater, sed et haec de plebe suoque
aequa uiro fuerat. Lydas tamen illa per urbes
quaesierat studio nomen memorabile, quamuis
orta domo parua paruis habitabat Hypaepis.
huius ut aspicerent opus admirabile, saepe
deseruere sui nymphae uineta Timoli,
deseruere suas nymphae Pactolides undas.
nec factas solum uestes, spectare iuuabat
tum quoque cum fierent: tantus decor adfuit arti!
siue rudem primos lanam glomerabat in orbes,
seu digitis subigebat opus repetitaque longo
uellera mollibat nebulas aequantia tractu,
siue leui teretem uersabat pollice fusum,
seu pingebat acu, scires a Pallade doctam.
quod tamen ipsa negat tantaque offensa magistra
'certet' ait 'mecum; nihil est quod uicta recusem.'
Pallas anum simulat falsosque in tempora canos
addit et infirmos baculo quos sustinet artus.
tum sic orsa loqui: 'non omnia grandior aetas
quae fugiamus habet; seris uenit usus ab annis.
consilium ne sperne meum. tibi fama petatur
inter mortales faciendae maxima lanae;
cede deae ueniamque tuis, temeraria, dictis
supplice uoce roga: ueniam dabit illa roganti.'
aspicit hanc toruis inceptaque fila relinquit
uixque manum retinens confessaque uultibus iram
talibus obscuram resecuta est Pallada dictis:
'mentis inops longaque uenis confecta senecta,
et nimium uixisse diu nocet. audiat istas,
si qua tibi nurus est, si qua est tibi filia, uoces.
consilii satis est in me mihi, neue monendo
profecisse putes, eadem est sententia nobis.
cur non ipsa uenit? cur haec certamina uitat?'
tum dea 'uenit' ait formamque remouit anilem
Palladaque exhibuit. uenerantur numina nymphae
Mygdonidesque nurus, sola est non territa uirgo;

BOOK 6

Tritonia had lent her ears to such words
and had approved the songs of the Aonides and their just anger.
Then to herself: 'To praise is not enough; let me be praised myself,
and not allow my godhead to be scorned without punishment.'
And she turned her mind to the fate of Maeonian Arachne 5
who, she had heard, did not yield to her in renown for skill
at working wool. She was famous not for her birthplace nor for the origin
of her family, but for her skill. Her father, Colophonian Idmon,
used to dye absorbent wool with Phocaean murex;
her mother had died but she too was from the plebs, 10
an equal to her husband. Still she had passionately sought for herself
a memorable name throughout the Lydian cities, though
sprung from a small house and living in small Hypaepa.
To look at her admirable work, often
the nymphs left the vineyards of their Timolus, 15
and the Pactolid nymphs left their waters.
And it delighted them to look at the clothes not only when they had been made
but also then when they were being made: so great was the splendour of her skill!
Whether she was forming the raw wool into its first balls,
or working the stuff with her fingers and softening the fleeces 20
that resembled clouds with a repeated long drawing out,
whether she was turning the smooth spindle with a light thumb,
or embroidering with a needle, you would know she had been taught by Pallas.
But she herself denied it and, annoyed that there was so great a
mistress, 'Let her compete,' she said, 'with me; there is nothing I would refuse if
    defeated.'
Pallas made herself like an old woman adding false white hair 26
to her temples and frail limbs which she supported with a staff.
Then she began to speak thus: 'Not everything that getting older
brings is to be shunned; experience comes with advancing years.
Do not scorn my advice. You may seek 30
the greatest fame amongst mortals for making wool;
but give way to the goddess and with humble voice, rash girl,
ask her pardon for your words: she will give you pardon if you ask.'
She looked grimly at her, let go the threads she had begun,
and, scarcely holding back her hand and revealing her anger in her face, 35
she went after the disguised Pallas with such words as these:
'You come here out of your wits and enfeebled with long old age,
and having lived too long is your undoing. If you have a daughter-in-law,
if you have a daughter, let her hear those words of yours.
I have counsel enough for me within myself, and in case you think 40
that you've achieved something by your warning, my opinion is still the same.
Why does she not come herself? Why does she avoid this contest?'
Then the goddess said, 'She has come,' and she discarded her old woman's appear-
    ance,
and revealed Pallas. The nymphs adored her divinity,
so did the young Mygdonian wives; the maiden alone was not terrified. 45

sed tamen erubuit, subitusque inuita notauit
ora rubor rursusque euanuit, ut solet aer
purpureus fieri, cum primum Aurora mouetur,
et breue post tempus candescere solis ab ortu.
perstat in incepto stolidaque cupidine palmae
in sua fata ruit; neque enim Ioue nata recusat
nec monet ulterius nec iam certamina differt.
     haud mora, constituunt diuersis partibus ambae
et gracili geminas intendunt stamine telas;
tela iugo uincta est, stamen secernit harundo,
inseritur medium radiis subtemen acutis,
quod digiti expediunt, atque inter stamina ductum
percusso pauiunt insecti pectine dentes.
utraque festinant cinctaeque ad pectora uestes
bracchia docta mouent, studio fallente laborem,
illic et Tyrium quae purpura sensit aenum
texitur et tenues parui discriminis umbrae,
qualis ab imbre solet percusso solibus arcus
inficere ingenti longum curuamine caelum,
in quo diuersi niteant cum mille colores,
transitus ipse tamen spectantia lumina fallit.
usque adeo quod tangit idem est; tamen ultima distant.
illic et lentum filis immittitur aurum
et uetus in tela deducitur argumentum.
     Cecropia Pallas scopulum Mauortis in arce
pingit et antiquam de terrae nomine litem.
bis sex caelestes medio Ioue sedibus altis
augusta grauitate sedent. sua quemque deorum
inscribit facies: Iouis est regalis imago;
stare deum pelagi longoque ferire tridente
aspera saxa facit medioque e uulnere saxi
exsiluisse fretum, quo pignore uindicet urbem;
at sibi dat clipeum, dat acutae cuspidis hastam,
dat galeam capiti, defenditur aegide pectus,
percussamque sua simulat de cuspide terram
edere cum bacis fetum canentis oliuae
mirarique deos; operis Victoria finis.
ut tamen exemplis intellegat aemula laudis
quod pretium speret pro tam furialibus ausis,
quattuor in partes certamina quattuor addit,
clara colore suo, breuibus distincta sigillis.
Threiciam Rhodopen habet angulus unus et Haemum,
nunc gelidos montes, mortalia corpora quondam,
nomina summorum sibi qui tribuere deorum.
altera Pygmaeae fatum miserabile matris
pars habet; hanc Iuno uictam certamine iussit
esse gruem populisque suis indicere bellum.
pinxit et Antigonen ausam contendere quondam
cum magni consorte Iouis, quam regia Iuno
in uolucrem uertit; nec profuit Ilion illi

But still she blushed; a sudden blush appeared
on her unwilling cheeks and vanished again, as the sky will
become crimson when Dawn first rises
and, after a short time, grows white from the rising of the sun.
She persisted in what she had begun and in her stupid lust for victory   50
rushed into her fate; for Jove's daughter neither refused her
nor warned her further nor any longer put the contest off.
    Without delay they both set up their twin looms
in separate places and strung them with the slender warp;
the loom was joined to the beam, a reed parted the warp,   55
the woof was inserted between them by sharp shuttles,
and their fingers pulled it through, and, after it was drawn between the warp threads,
teeth cut in a comb struck against it and tamped it down.
Each sped along, their robes girt to their breasts,
and plied skilled hands, their zeal belying their toil.   60
There purple which had felt the Tyrian vat
was woven in, also a close range of fine shades
just as, after the sun has been struck by a shower, the rainbow
will paint the length of the sky with its huge arc,
and though a thousand various colours gleam within it,   65
yet the transitions themselves deceive the watching eye.
So much are they the same where they touch; yet those at the edges are so different.
There too pliant gold was worked in with the threads
and an old story was spun out with the cloth.
    Pallas depicted Mars' rock on the Cecropian   70
citadel and the ancient dispute about the name of the land.
Twice six heavenly ones, with Jupiter in the middle, were sitting on their high
seats in august solemnity. In each case, the face
identified the god; Jove's was a regal image;
she made the sea god stand and strike the rough   75
rocks with his long trident and from the middle of the rock's wound
there leapt up a salt spring and with this token he laid claim to the city;
but to herself she gave a shield, she gave a spear with sharp tip,
she gave a helmet to her head, her breast was defended by the aegis,
and she portrayed the earth, struck by her spear tip,   80
producing a hoary olive tree together with its berry,
and the gods wondering; Victory ended the work.
But, so that her rival for renown might understand from examples
what reward to hope for from such frenzied daring,
in the four corners she added four contests,   85
bright in colour and embellished with small miniatures.
One corner had Thracian Rhodope and Haemus,
now cold mountains, mortal bodies once;
who had ascribed to themselves the names of the highest gods.
The second corner had the pitiable fate   90
of the Pygmaean mother; she was defeated in a contest and Juno ordered
that she be a crane and declare war on her own people.
She depicted Antigone too who once had dared to compete
with the wife of great Jupiter, and queenly Juno
turned her into a bird; Ilion did not save her   95

Laomedonue pater, sumptis quin candida pennis
ipsa sibi plaudat crepitante ciconia rostro.
qui superest solus, Cinyran habet angulus orbum,
isque gradus templi, natarum membra suarum,
amplectens saxoque iacens lacrimare uidetur.
circuit extremas oleis pacalibus oras
(is modus est) operisque sua facit arbore finem.
  Maeonis elusam designat imagine tauri
Europam; uerum taurum, freta uera putares.
ipsa uidebatur terras spectare relictas
et comites clamare suas tactumque uereri
adsilientis aquae timidasque reducere plantas.
fecit et Asterien aquila luctante teneri,
fecit olorinis Ledam recubare sub alis;
addidit ut satyri celatus imagine pulchram
Iuppiter implerit gemino Nycteida fetu,
Amphitryon fuerit cum te, Tirynthia, cepit,
aureus ut Danaen, Asopida luserit ignis,
Mnemosynen pastor, uarius Deoida serpens.
te quoque mutatum toruo, Neptune, iuuenco
uirgine in Aeolia posuit; tu uisus Enipeus
gignis Aloidas, aries Bisaltida fallis,
et te flaua comas frugum mitissima mater
sensit equum, sensit uolucrem crinita colubris
mater equi uolucris, sensit delphina Melantho.
omnibus his faciemque suam faciemque locorum
reddidit. est illic agrestis imagine Phoebus,
utque modo accipitris pennas, modo terga leonis
gesserit, ut pastor Macareida luserit Issen,
Liber ut Erigonen falsa deceperit uua,
ut Saturnus equo geminum Chirona crearit.
ultima pars telae, tenui circumdata limbo,
nexilibus flores hederis habet intertextos.
  non illud Pallas, non illud carpere Liuor
possit opus. doluit successu flaua uirago
et rupit pictas, caelestia crimina, uestes;
utque Cytoriaco radium de monte tenebat,
ter quater Idmoniae frontem percussit Arachnes.
non tulit infelix laqueoque animosa ligauit
guttura; pendentem Pallas miserata leuauit
atque ita 'uiue quidem, pende tamen, improba,' dixit
'lexque eadem poenae, ne sis secura futuri,
dicta tuo generi serisque nepotibus esto.'
post ea discedens sucis Hecateidos herbae
sparsit, et extemplo tristi medicamine tactae
defluxere comae, cum quis et naris et aures,
fitque caput minimum, toto quoque corpore parua est;
in latere exiles digiti pro cruribus haerent,
cetera uenter habet, de quo tamen illa remittit
stamen et antiquas exercet aranea telas.

BOOK VI [43

nor Laomedon her father from taking on white feathers
and applauding herself with clattering beak, a stork.
The only corner left had the bereaved Cinyras,
and he was embracing the temple steps, the limbs
of his daughters, and as he lay on the rock he seemed to weep. 100
She surrounded the outermost edges with the olive leaves of peace
(that was the end) and she finished the work with her own tree.
    The Maeonian woman depicted the tricking by a bull's guise
of Europa; you would think it was a real bull and real sea.
She herself seemed to be looking at the lands she had left behind, 105
to be crying out to her companions and, afraid of being touched
by the water leaping up at her, to be drawing her timid feet away.
She made Asterie too to be held by a struggling eagle,
she made Leda lie back under the swan's wings;
she added how Jupiter, concealed in the guise of a satyr, 110
had filled the beautiful Nycteis with twin offspring,
how he had been Amphitryon when he took you, Tirynthian one,
how, as golden, he had tricked Danaë, as fire, Asopis,
as a shepherd, Mnemosyne and, as a spotted snake, Deois.
You too, Neptune, she placed there, changed into a grim 115
bullock, for the Aeolian maiden; to you, when you seemed to be Enipeus,
the Aloidae were born, as a ram you deceived Bisaltis,
and the fair-haired, gentlest mother of the grain crops
saw you as a horse, as a bird were you seen by the snake-haired
mother of the bird-horse, and as a dolphin were you seen by Melantho. 120
To all of these she gave their own likeness and a likeness
of their settings. Phoebus was there in the guise of a countryman,
and here how he was wearing a hawk's feathers, here a lion's
skin, how as a shepherd he tricked Macareus' daughter, Isse,
how Liber deceived Erigone with false grapes, 125
and how Saturn used a horse to beget the two-formed Chiron.
The last part of the cloth, surrounded by a narrow border,
had flowers interwoven with twining ivy leaves.
    Not Pallas, not Spite could cavil at
that work. The fair-haired manly-maid, galled by her success, 130
tore at the cloth and its pictures of heavenly crimes;
and as she was holding the shuttle from mount Cytorus
three times or four she struck it on the forehead of Idmonian Arachne.
The unhappy girl could not bear it and she tied her spirited throat
in a noose; as she hung there Pallas in pity raised her up 135
saying this, 'Live then, but hang, presumptuous girl,
and, so that you are not free of care for the future, let the same terms of punishment
be declared for your family and all your descendants.'
And then, as she departed, she sprinkled her with the juices of Hecatean
herbs, and immediately on being touched by the grim drug 140
her hair dropped off, and with it both nose and ears;
her head became very small, and indeed her whole body was small,
to her flank slender fingers were stuck instead of legs,
the rest of her was belly, yet from it she gave out
a strand and, as a spider, practised her weaving as before. 145

Lydia tota fremit Phrygiaeque per oppida facti
rumor it et magnum sermonibus occupat orbem.
ante suos Niobe thalamos cognouerat illam
tum cum Maeoniam uirgo Sipylumque colebat;
nec tamen admonita est poena popularis Arachnes
cedere caelitibus uerbisque minoribus uti.
multa dabant animos, sed enim nec coniugis arte˘
nec genus amborum magnique potentia regni
sic placuere illi (quamuis ea cuncta placerent)
ut sua progenies; et felicissima matrum
dicta foret Niobe, si non sibi uisa fuisset.
 nam sata Tiresia uenturi praescia Manto
per medias fuerat diuino concita motu
uaticinata uias: 'Ismenides, ite frequentes
et date Latonae Latonigenisque duobus
cum prece tura pia lauroque innectite crinem;
ore meo Latona iubet.' paretur, et omnes
Thebaides iussis sua tempora frondibus ornant
turaque dant sanctis et uerba precantia flammis.
 ecce uenit comitum Niobe celeberrima turba,
uestibus intexto Phrygiis spectabilis auro
et, quantum ira sinit, formosa; mouensque decoro
cum capite immissos umerum per utrumque capillos
constitit, utque oculos circumtulit alta superbos,
'quis furor auditos' inquit 'praeponere uisis
caelestes? aut cur colitur Latona per aras,
numen adhuc sine ture meum est? mihi Tantalus auctor,
cui licuit soli superorum tangere mensas;
Pleiadum soror est genetrix mea; maximus Atlas
est auus, aetherium qui fert ceruicibus axem;
Iuppiter alter auus; socero quoque glorior illo.
me gentes metuunt Phrygiae, me regia Cadmi
sub domina est, fidibusque mei commissa mariti
moenia cum populis a meque uiroque reguntur.
in quamcumque domus aduerti lumina partem,
immensae spectantur opes; accedit eodem
digna dea facies; huc natas adice septem
et totidem iuuenes et mox generosque nurusque.
quaerite nunc, habeat quam nostra superbia laudem
nescioquoque audete satam Titanida Coeo
Latonam praeferre mihi, cui maxima quondam
exiguam sedem pariturae terra negauit.
nec caelo nec humo nec aquis dea uestra recepta est;
exsul erat mundi, donec miserata uagantem
"hospita tu terris erras, ego" dixit "in undis"
instabilemque locum Delos dedit. illa duorum
facta parens; uteri pars haec est septima nostri.
sum felix; quis enim neget hoc? felixque manebo;
hoc quoque quis dubitet? tutam me copia fecit.
maior sum quam cui possit Fortuna nocere,

BOOK VI [45

    All Lydia murmured and the story of what had happened went
throughout the towns of Phrygia and filled the wide world with talk.
Before her marriage Niobe had known her
when as a maiden she was living in Maeonia and Sipylus;
yet she was not warned by the punishment of Arachne her compatriot   150
to give way to the heavenly ones and to use more humble words.
Many things made her proud, but still neither her husband's skills
nor the families of both of them and the power of their great kingdom
pleased her as much (though all those things did please her)
as did her children; and Niobe would have been called   155
the luckiest of mothers if she had not seemed so to herself.
    For Tiresias' daughter, Manto, with her foreknowledge of what was to come,
aroused by a divine urge, had prophesied
through the middle of the streets: 'Ismenides, come in throngs,
and give to Latona and to the two Latona-born   160
incense with pious prayer and bind up your hair with laurel;
Latona orders you through my mouth.' She was obeyed and all
Thebaides adorned their temples with the foliage as ordered,
and offered incense and words of prayer to the sacred flames.
Look there comes Niobe all encompassed by a crowd of her companions   165
a fine sight in her Phrygian clothes with inwoven gold
and, as far as her anger allowed, beautiful; shaking her resplendent
head and the hair that flowed across each shoulder
she stood there and, as she haughtily cast her proud eyes around,
'What is this madness,' she said, 'preferring gods that you have heard of   170
to those that you have seen? And why is Latona worshipped on the altars
but my divinity is still without incense? Tantalus was my father,
the only one allowed to touch the banquets of the gods;
my mother was a sister of the Pleiades; Atlas most great
was my grandfather, he who bears the ethereal world on his neck;   175
Jupiter was my other grandfather; I boast in him as my father-in-law too.
The Phrygian races are in awe of me, Cadmus' palace has me
for its mistress, and the walls assembled by my husband's
lyre, together with their peoples, are ruled by me and my husband.
To whatever part of the house I turn my eyes   180
immeasurable wealth is seen; and, in addition,
my looks are worthy of a goddess; add to this seven daughters
and as many sons and soon sons and daughters-in-law.
Now ask what renown my pride receives
and dare to prefer Latona, the Titan daughter   185
of some Coeus or other, to me, when all the great earth
once refused a tiny lodging for her to give birth.
Your goddess was accepted neither by sky nor earth nor waters;
she was an exile from the world till, pitying her as she roamed,
"You are wandering, a stranger, on the lands, but I," said Delos, "on the waves,"   190
and she gave her an unstable place. She became
a mother of two; that is a seventh part of my child-bearing.
I am lucky; for who would deny it? And lucky I shall remain;
who would doubt that too? My plenty has made me safe.
I am too great for fortune to be able to hurt me,   195

multaque ut eripiat, multo mihi plura relinquet.
excessere metum mea iam bona. fingite demi
huic aliquid populo natorum posse meorum:
non tamen ad numerum redigar spoliata duorum,
200 Latonae turbam, qua quantum distat ab orba?
infectis propere ite sacris laurumque capillis
ponite.' deponunt et sacra infecta relinquunt,
quodque licet, tacito uenerantur murmure numen.
  indignata dea est summoque in uertice Cynthi
205 talibus est dictis gemina cum prole locuta:
'en ego uestra parens, uobis animosa creatis,
et nisi Iunoni nulli cessura dearum,
an dea sim dubitor perque omnia saecula cultis
arceor, o nati, nisi uos succurritis, aris.
210 nec dolor hic solus; diro conuicia facto
Tantalis adiecit uosque est postponere natis
ausa suis et me, quod in ipsam reccidat, orbam
dixit et exhibuit linguam scelerata paternam.'
adiectura preces erat his Latona relatis:
215 'desine;' Phoebus ait 'poenae mora longa querella est.'
dixit idem Phoebe, celerique per aera lapsu
contigerant tecti Cadmeida nubibus arcem.
  planus erat lateque patens prope moenia campus,
adsiduis pulsatus equis, ubi turba rotarum
220 duraque mollierat subiectas ungula glaebas.
pars ibi de septem genitis Amphione fortes
conscendunt in equos Tyrioque rubentia suco
terga premunt auroque graues moderantur habenas.
e quibus Ismenus, qui matri sarcina quondam
225 prima suae fuerat, dum certum flectit in orbem
quadripedis cursus spumantiaque ora coercet,
'ei mihi!' conclamat medioque in pectore fixa
tela gerit, frenisque manu moriente remissis
in latus a dextro paulatim defluit armo.
230 proximus audito sonitu per inane pharetrae
frena dabat Sipylus, ueluti cum praescius imbres
nube fugit uisa pendentiaque undique rector
carbasa deducit, ne qua leuis effluat aura;
frena tamen dantem non euitabile telum
235 consequitur, summaque tremens ceruice sagitta
haesit et exstabat nudum de gutture ferrum.
ille ut erat pronus per crura admissa iubasque
uoluitur et calido tellurem sanguine foedat.
Phaedimus infelix et auiti nominis heres
240 Tantalus, ut solito finem imposuere labori,
transierant ad opus nitidae iuuenale palaestrae;
et iam contulerant arto luctantia nexu
pectora pectoribus, cum tento concita neruo,
sicut erant iuncti, traiecit utrumque sagitta.
245 ingemuere simul, simul incuruata dolore

let her snatch much away, she will leave me much more.
My blessings now have passed beyond fear. Suppose that some part
could be taken from this tribe of my children:
though despoiled, I still would not be brought down to a count of two,
Latona's crowd, with which how far is she from childlessness? 200
Hurry away from your unfinished sacrifice and take the laurel
from your hair.' They took it off and left the sacrifice unfinished,
but, in a quiet murmur, which they could do, they adored the divinity.
 The goddess was indignant and on the very top of Cynthus
spoke to her twin offspring in such words as these: 205
'Look, here I am, your mother, proud of your birth,
ready to give way to none of the goddesses save Juno,
and my divinity is doubted, I am being kept for all time
from being worshipped at the altars, oh my children, unless you hurry to my help.
And this is not the only hurt; to her dreadful deed the Tantalid 210
has added insults and has dared to prefer
her children to you and, may it rebound on herself, she has called me
childless and in her wickedness displayed her father's tongue.'
Latona was about to add entreaties to her telling of these things:
'Stop,' Phoebus said, 'a long complaint will delay the punishment.' 215
Phoebe said the same; and with a swift glide through the air
and covered in clouds they had reached the Cadmeian citadel.
 There was a level plain, wide and open, near the city walls,
constantly pounded down by horses where a host of wheels
and the hardness of the hoof had softened the ground beneath. 220
There some of the seven sons of Amphion were mounting
their strong horses, pressing down upon their backs that were red
from Tyrian juice and controlling them with bridles heavy with gold.
One of them, Ismenus, who had once been his
mother's first burden, while he was turning the course of his 225
steed into a sure circuit and restraining its foaming mouth,
'Ah me!' he screamed as he took a shaft that pierced
the middle of his breast and, as the reins dropped from his dying hand,
he gradually sank from the right forequarter down onto his flank.
Next, hearing the sound of the quiver through the void, 230
Sipylus began to give full rein, just as when a helmsman with foreknowledge
sees a cloud and flees the rainstorms and stretches down the hanging
sails on every side in case any light breeze eludes him.
But as he was giving full rein, the inescapable shaft
caught up with him and the trembling arrow stuck in the top 235
of his neck and the bare iron tip protruded from his throat.
He, leaning forward as he was, rolled over the free-running legs
and mane and defiled the earth with his warm blood.
Unhappy Phaedimus and the inheritor of his grandfather's name,
Tantalus, having brought their usual toil to an end, 240
had passed on to the youthful exercise of the gleaming wrestling-floor;
and now they had joined together in a tight hold striving
breast to breast when, driven from the taut bowstring,
an arrow transfixed them joined as they were.
They groaned together, together they dropped their limbs 245

membra solo posuere, simul suprema iacentes
lumina uersarunt, animam simul exhalarunt.
aspicit Alphenor laniataque pectora plangens
aduolat ut gelidos complexibus adleuet artus,
250   inque pio cadit officio; nam Delius illi
intima fatifero rupit praecordia ferro.
quod simul eductum est, pars est pulmonis in hamis
eruta cumque anima cruor est effusus in auras.
at non intonsum simplex Damasicthona uulnus
255   adficit. ictus erat, qua crus esse incipit et qua
mollia neruosus facit internodia poples,
dumque manu temptat trahere exitiabile telum
altera per iugulum pennis tenus acta sagitta est;
expulit hanc sanguis seque eiaculatus in altum
260   emicat et longe terebrata prosilit aura.
ultimus Ilioneus non profectura precando
bracchia sustulerat 'di' que 'o communiter omnes,'
dixerat (ignarus non omnes esse rogandos)
'parcite!' motus erat, cum iam reuocabile telum
265   non fuit, Arquitenens; minimo tamen occidit ille
uulnere, non alte percusso corde sagitta.
    fama mali populique dolor lacrimaeque suorum
tam subitae matrem certam fecere ruinae,
mirantem potuisse irascentemque quod ausi
270   hoc essent superi, quod tantum iuris haberent;
nam pater Amphion ferro per pectus adacto
finierat moriens pariter cum luce dolorem.
heu, quantum haec Niobe Niobe distabat ab illa,
quae modo Latois populum summouerat aris
275   et mediam tulerat gressus resupina per urbem,
inuidiosa suis, at nunc miseranda uel hosti!
corporibus gelidis incumbit et ordine nullo
oscula dispensat natos suprema per omnes;
a quibus ad caelum liuentia bracchia tollens
280   'pascere, crudelis, nostro, Latona, dolore,
pascere' ait 'satiaque meo tua pectora luctu!
[corque ferum satia' dixit 'per funera septem]
efferor; exsulta uictrixque inimica triumpha.
cur autem uictrix? miserae mihi plura supersunt
285   quam tibi felici; post tot quoque funera uinco.'
dixerat, et sonuit contento neruus ab arcu,
qui praeter Nioben unam conterruit omnes;
illa malo est audax. stabant cum uestibus atris
ante toros fratrum demisso crine sorores.
290   e quibus una trahens haerentia uiscere tela
imposito fratri moribunda relanguit ore;
altera solari miseram conata parentem
conticuit subito duplicataque uulnere caeco est.
[oraque compressit, nisi postquam spiritus ibat.]
295   haec frustra fugiens conlabitur, illa sorori

BOOK VI [49

bent with pain upon the ground, together they lay rolling
their eyes around for the last time and together they breathed out their lives.
Alphenor saw it and, tearing and beating his breast,
flew to lift their cold limbs in his arms
and, in that pious duty, fell; for the Delian burst   250
his inmost vitals with his fateful iron tip.
And, as it was taken out, part of the lung was wrenched out with it
on the barbs, and his blood together with his spirit poured out into the air.
But it was not a single wound that disposed of unshorn
Damasichthon. He had been struck where the lower leg begins, where   255
the sinews behind the knee leave soft flesh between,
and while he tried to drag the deadly shaft out with his hand,
a second arrow was driven through his throat up to its feathers;
his blood drove it out and jetted up on high
and spurted gushing far as it drilled through the air.   260
Last Ilioneus in the act of prayer had raised
arms that would achieve nothing and, 'Oh, company of all the gods,
had said (unaware that it was not all of them he had to ask)
'spare me!' He was moved, was the Archer-god, when the shaft
could no longer be called back; but he fell to the smallest   265
wound, his heart was not struck deeply by the arrow.
    Rumour of this woe, the grief of the people and the tears of her friends
informed the mother of so sudden a disaster;
she marvelled that the gods could have done it and was angry that
they had dared to, that they had such powers;   270
for the father, Amphion, had driven a sword through his breast
and by dying had brought an end to grief and life together.
Alas, how far was this Niobe from that Niobe
who just before had moved the people away from Latona's altars
and with head tossed high had made her way through the middle of the city,   275
envied by her friends, but now pitiable even to an enemy!
She fell upon the cold bodies and distributed
her last kisses haphazardly to all her sons;
then, raising her livid arms from them towards heaven,
'Feed yourself, cruel Latona, on our pain,   280
feed yourself' she said, 'and glut your breast with my grief!
[Glut your wild heart', she said, 'through seven funerals]
I am being carried out; exult and triumph as my victorious enemy.
But why victorious? In my misery more are left to me
than are to you in your good fortune; after so many deaths I am still the victor.' 285
She had spoken and the string sounded from the stretched bow,
which terrified all save Niobe alone;
woe had made her bold. The sisters stood before their brothers' biers,
all dressed in black and with their hair unbound.
One of them, while dragging out a shaft stuck in his bowels,   290
collapsed in her death throes face down upon her brother.
A second, after trying to console her unhappy mother,
suddenly fell silent doubled over by an unseen wound.
[She pressed her mouth shut, except after her spirit was gone.]
One vainly fleeing collapsed, another died   295

immoritur; latet haec, illam trepidare uideres.
sexque datis leto diuersaque uulnera passis
ultima restabat; quam toto corpore mater,
tota ueste tegens 'unam minimamque relinque;
300 de multis minimam posco' clamauit 'et unam.'
dumque rogat, pro qua rogat, occidit. orba resedit
exanimes inter natos natasque uirumque
deriguitque malis. nullos mouet aura capillos,
in uultu color est sine sanguine, lumina maestis
305 stant immota genis; nihil est in imagine uiuum.
ipsa quoque interius cum duro lingua palato
congelat, et uenae desistunt posse moueri;
nec flecti ceruix nec bracchia reddere motus
nec pes ire potest; intra quoque uiscera saxum est.
310 flet tamen et ualidi circumdata turbine uenti
in patriam rapta est; ibi fixa cacumine montis
liquitur, et lacrimas etiam nunc marmora manant.
    tum uero cuncti manifestam numinis iram
femina uirque timent cultuque impensius omnes
315 magna gemelliparae uenerantur numina diuae.
utque fit, a facto propiore priora renarrant;
e quibus unus ait: 'Lyciae quoque fertilis agris
non impune deam ueteres spreuere coloni.
res obscura quidem est ignobilitate uirorum,
320 mira tamen. uidi praesens stagnumque locumque
prodigio notum. nam me iam grandior aeuo
impatiensque uiae genitor deducere lectos
iusserat inde boues gentisque illius eunti
ipse ducem dederat; cum quo dum pascua lustro,
325 ecce lacu medio sacrorum nigra fauilla
ara uetus stabat tremulis circumdata cannis.
restitit et pauido "faueas mihi" murmure dixit
dux meus, et simili "faueas" ego murmure dixi.
Naiadum Faunine foret tamen ara rogabam
330 indigenaene dei, cum talia rettulit hospes:
"non hac, o iuuenis, montanum numen in ara est.
illa suam uocat hanc, cui quondam regia coniunx
orantem accepit, tum cum leuis insula nabat;
335 illic incumbens cum Palladis arbore palmae
edidit inuita geminos Latona nouerca.
hinc quoque Iunonem fugisse puerpera fertur
inque suo portasse sinu, duo numina, natos.
iamque Chimaeriferae, cum sol grauis ureret arua,
340 finibus in Lyciae longo dea fessa labore
sidereo siccata sitim collegit ab aestu,
uberaque ebiberant auidi lactantia nati.
forte lacum mediocris aquae prospexit in imis
uallibus; agrestes illic fruticosa legebant
345 uimina cum iuncis gratamque paludibus uluam.

on her sister; one hid, another you could see trembling.
When six had been dealt their death after suffering a variety of wounds,
the last one was left; her mother covered her with all
her body and with all her robe; 'Leave me one, the youngest;
from my many children I beg for the youngest,' she cried, 'and her alone.' 300
And while she asked, the one she asked for died. Childless she sank back
among her lifeless sons, daughters and husband
and grew rigid from her woes. The breeze moved not a hair,
the colour in her face was bloodless, her eyes stood
unmoving in their sad sockets; there was nothing living in her appearance. 305
Even her tongue itself froze inside her together with her hardened
palate, and her veins lost the ability to be moved;
her neck could not be bent nor her arms make movements
nor her foot go; inside her bowels too it was stone.
And yet she wept and, wrapped in a mighty whirlwind, 310
was snatched off to her native land; there fixed to a mountain peak
she melts away and even now as marble flows with tears.
    Then indeed was the anger of the divinity made plain, and every
man and woman feared it and all in their worship more unstintingly
adored the great divinity of the twin-bearing goddess. 315
And, as happens, because of the nearer event they retold earlier ones;
and one of them said, 'In the fields of fertile Lycia too
the farmers of old did not go unpunished when they scorned the goddess.
The affair, though little known from the obscurity of those men,
is, even so, amazing. I have been there and seen both the pond and the place 320
made famous by the miracle. For my father, already too advanced in age
and unable to endure the journey, had ordered me to choose
some cattle from there and lead them back, and as I went he had himself
given me a guide from that tribe; and while I roamed the pastures with him,
look, in the middle of the lake there stood an old altar 325
black with smoke of sacrifice and surrounded by trembling
reeds. My guide stopped and in a timid murmur said, "Be gracious
to me," and in a similar murmur I said, "Be gracious."
I began to ask whether the altar was to the Naiads or to Faunus
or to a native god when my host replied so: 330
"In this altar, oh young man, there is no mountain divinity.
She calls it hers whom once the king's wife
debarred from the world, whom, though she begged, wandering Delos
scarcely accepted even when she was a light, swimming island.
There, leaning on a palm and on Pallas' tree, 335
Latona gave birth to twins against the will of their stepmother.
From here too, they say, the new mother fled
carrying her children in her bosom, the two divinities.
And now, within the borders of Chimera-bearing Lycia, while the oppressive
sun was burning the fields, the goddess, tired out by her long toil, 340
and dried up by the starry heat, built up a thirst
when her children had greedily drained her milky breasts.
By chance she saw before her a lake of moderate size at the bottom
of the valley; the country people were gathering bushy osiers
there and rushes and the sedge that favours marshes. 345

accessit positoque genu Titania terram
pressit, ut hauriret gelidos potura liquores.
rustica turba uetat; dea sic adfata uetantes:
'quid prohibetis aquis? usus communis aquarum est.
nec solem proprium natura nec aera fecit
nec tenues undas; ad publica munera ueni.
quae tamen ut detis, supplex peto. non ego nostros
abluere hic artus lassataque membra parabam,
sed releuare sitim; caret os umore loquentis
et fauces arent uixque est uia uocis in illis.
haustus aquae mihi nectar erit, uitamque fatebor
accepisse simul; uitam dederitis in unda.
hi quoque uos moueant, qui nostro bracchia tendunt
parua sinu' (et casu tendebant bracchia nati).
quem non blanda deae potuissent uerba mouere?
hi tamen orantem perstant prohibere minasque,
ni procul abscedat, conuiciaque insuper addunt.
nec satis est; ipsos etiam pedibusque manuque
turbauere lacus imoque e gurgite mollem
huc illuc limum saltu mouere maligno.
distulit ira sitim; neque enim iam filia Coei
supplicat indignis nec dicere sustinet ultra
uerba minora dea tollensque ad sidera palmas
'aeternum stagno' dixit 'uiuatis in isto.'
eueniunt optata deae; iuuat esse sub undis
et modo tota caua submergere membra palude,
nunc proferre caput, summo modo gurgite nare,
saepe super ripam stagni consistere, saepe
in gelidos resilire lacus; sed nunc quoque turpes
litibus exercent linguas pulsoque pudore,
quamuis sint sub aqua, sub aqua maledicere temptant.
uox quoque iam rauca est inflataque colla tumescunt
ipsaque dilatant patulos conuicia rictus.
terga caput tangunt, colla intercepta uidentur,
spina uiret, uenter, pars maxima corporis, albet,
limosoque nouae saliunt in gurgite ranae.'"
    sic ubi nescioquis Lycia de gente uirorum
rettulit exitium, Satyri reminiscitur alter,
quem Tritoniaca Latous harundine uictum
adfecit poena. 'quid me mihi detrahis?' inquit;
'a! piget, a! non est' clamabat 'tibia tanti.'
clamanti cutis est summos derepta per artus,
nec quidquam nisi uulnus erat; cruor undique manat
detectique patent nerui trepidaeque sine ulla
pelle micant uenae; salientia uiscera possis
et perlucentes numerare in pectore fibras.
illum ruricolae, siluarum numina, Fauni
et satyri fratres et tum quoque carus Olympus
et nymphae flerunt, et quisquis montibus illis

Titania approached and knelt down
upon the ground to scoop up the cool water to drink it.
The rustic mob forbade her; as they forbade the goddess spoke to them so:
'Why do you keep me from the water? There is a common right to water.
Nature has made neither the sun private nor the air   350
nor the clear waters; I have come to a public facility.
Still, I ask you as a suppliant to give it to me. I was not preparing
to wash my limbs here or my wearied body
but to relieve my thirst; as I speak, my mouth lacks moisture,
my throat is dry and there is scarcely a way for my voice through it. 355
A drink of water will be nectar to me, and I shall admit I have received
life with it; you will have given life to me in the water.
Let these too move you as they stretch out their little
arms from my bosom' (and it happened that the children were stretching out their arms).
Who could have been unmoved by the goddess' pleading words?   360
But though she begged they persisted in keeping her away, and added
threats besides and insults unless she went far away.
And that was not enough; they even disturbed the lake itself
with their hands and feet and by spiteful jumping moved
the soft silt up from the bottom of the flood.   365
Anger deferred thirst; for Coeus' daughter no longer
entreated the unworthy men nor endured any more to speak
words too humble for a goddess and, raising her hands up to the stars,
'May you live for eternity,' she said, 'in that pond.'   369
It turned out as the goddess had prayed; it delighted them to be beneath the waves
and sometimes to submerge their whole bodies under the deep marsh
and now to hold their head out, and sometimes to swim on the top of the flood,
often to stay on the pond's bank, often
to leap back into the cool lake; but even now they exercised
their foul tongues in disputation and, with shame dismissed,   375
although they were under water, under water they tried to speak ill.
Their voice too was hoarse and their inflated necks swelled up
and their very insults expanded their gaping jaws.
Their backs touched their head, their necks seemed to be cut short,
their spine was green, their belly, the biggest part of their body, white, 380
and they leapt in the muddy flood as new frogs.'"
  When whoever it was had thus told of the destruction of the men
from the Lycian tribe, a second recalled the Satyr
whom Latous had defeated on the Tritoniac reed,
and given punishment to. 'Why do you tear me from myself?' he said;   385
'Ah! I am sorry, ah! the flute,' he cried, 'it is not worth so much.'
As he cried the skin was stripped from the surface of his limbs,
and he was nothing but wound; blood flowed from everywhere,
the sinews were uncovered and lay open and the veins without any
skin trembled and throbbed; you could count the pulsating   390
organs and the glistening tissues in the breast.
The country-dwelling Fauns, divinities of the woods,
his brother satyrs and Olympus even then dear to him
and the nymphs wept for him and so did anyone who on those mountains

lanigerosque greges armentaque bucera pauit.
fertilis immaduit madefactaque terra caducas
concepit lacrimas ac uenis perbibit imis;
quas ubi fecit aquam, uacuas emisit in auras.
inde petens rapidum ripis decliuibus aequor
Marsya nomen habet, Phrygiae liquidissimus amnis.
　　　　　talibus extemplo redit ad praesentia dictis
uulgus et extinctum cum stirpe Amphiona luget.
mater in inuidia est; tamen hanc quoque dicitur unus
flesse Pelops umeroque, suas a pectore postquam
deduxit uestes, ebur ostendisse sinistro.
concolor hic umerus nascendi tempore dextro
corporeusque fuit; manibus mox caesa paternis
membra ferunt iunxisse deos, aliisque repertis,
cui locus est iuguli medius summique lacerti
defuit; impositum est non comparentis in usum
partis ebur, factoque Pelops fuit integer illo.
　　　　　finitimi proceres coeunt, urbesque propinquae
orauere suos ire ad solacia reges,
Argosque et Sparte Pelopeiadesque Mycenae
et nondum toruae Calydon inuisa Dianae
Orchomenosque ferax et nobilis aere Corinthus
Messeneque ferox Patraeque humilesque Cleonae
et Nelea Pylos neque adhuc Pittheia Troezen,
quaeque urbes aliae bimari clauduntur ab Isthmo,
exteriusque sitae bimari spectantur ab Isthmo.
credere quis posset? solae cessastis Athenae.
obstitit officio bellum, subuectaque ponto
barbara Mopsopios terrebant agmina muros.
　　　　　Threicius Tereus haec auxiliaribus armis
fuderat et clarum uincendo nomen habebat;
quem sibi Pandion opibusque uirisque potentem
et genus a magno ducentem forte Gradiuo
conubio Procnes iunxit. non pronuba Iuno,
non Hymenaeus adest, non illi Gratia lecto;
Eumenides tenuere faces de funere raptas,
Eumenides strauere torum, tectoque profanus
incubuit bubo thalamique in culmine sedit.
hac aue coniuncti Procne Tereusque, parentes
hac aue sunt facti. gratata est scilicet illis
Thracia, disque ipsi grates egere diemque,
quaque data est claro Pandione nata tyranno
quaque erat ortus Itys, festam iussere uocari;
usque adeo latet utilitas! iam tempora Titan
quinque per autumnos repetiti duxerat anni,
cum blandita uiro Procne 'si gratia' dixit
'ulla mea est, uel me uisendae mitte sorori,
uel soror huc ueniat. redituram tempore paruo
promittes socero; magni mihi muneris instar
germanam uidisse dabis.' iubet ille carinas

grazed wool-bearing flocks and horned herds. 395
The fertile earth was drenched and, being drenched, took in
the falling tears and drank them down into her deepest veins;
and when she had made them into water, she sent them out into the empty air.
Thence, as from its sloping banks it seeks the rushing sea,
the river, the clearest in Phrygia, has the name Marsyas. 400
    With such words the people returned immediately
to the present and mourned the destruction of Amphion and his offspring.
The blame fell on the mother; but there was one Pelops, said to have wept
even for her and, when he pulled his cloak
from his breast, to have shown the ivory on his left shoulder. 405
This shoulder was at the time of his birth the same colour
as his right one and made of flesh; they say that later his limbs had been cut up
by his father's hands and joined by the gods; they found the rest,
but the place between the throat and the top of the arm
was missing; ivory was placed there to serve for the part 410
that had not appeared and by this action Pelops was made whole.
    The neighbouring princes came together and the nearby cities
begged their kings to go to console them,
Argos and Sparta and Pelopian Mycenae
and Calydon not yet hated by grim Diana 415
and fertile Orchomenos and Corinth famous for its bronze
and fierce Messene and Patrae and low-lying Cleonae
and Nelean Pylos and Troezen not yet Pitthean
and the other cities confined by the Isthmus of two seas,
and those sited outside and seen from the Isthmus of two seas. 420
Who could believe it? You alone, Athens held back.
War impeded duty, for barbarian hosts
had sailed across the sea and were terrifying the Mopsopian walls.
    Thracian Tereus had routed these with his relieving
forces and had a name made famous by his victory; 425
he was endowed with wealth and men and traced his family,
as it chanced, to great Gradivus, so Pandion joined him
to himself through marriage with Procne. No *pronuba* Juno,
no Hymenaeus was there, no Grace attended at the bed;
Eumenides held the torches, they had snatched them from a funeral, 430
Eumenides spread the couch and, on the house, an accursed
owl settled perching on the roof of the bridal chamber.
Under this bird of omen were Procne and Tereus joined, parents
under this bird of omen did they become. Thrace of course
congratulated them, and they themselves gave thanks to the gods; and the day 435
on which Pandion's daughter had been given to the famous king
and on which Itys was born they ordered should be called a festal day;
So hidden is what will benefit us! Already had Titan brought on
the times of the repeating year through five autumns,
when Procne coaxing her husband said, 'If I have 440
any favour with you, either send me to visit my sister,
or let my sister come here. You will promise your father-in-law
she will return in a little while; to have seen my sister will be like
your giving me a great gift.' He ordered the ship

```
445   in freta deduci ueloque et remige portus
      Cecropios intrat Piraeaque litora tangit.
              ut primum soceri data copia, dextera dextrae
      iungitur et fausto committitur omine sermo.
      coeperat aduentus causam, mandata referre
450   coniugis et celeris missae spondere recursus:
      ecce uenit magno diues Philomela paratu,
      diuitior forma; quales audire solemus
      Naidas et Dryadas mediis incedere siluis,
      si modo des illis cultus similisque paratus.
455   non secus exarsit conspecta uirgine Tereus,
      quam si quis canis ignem supponat aristis
      aut frondem positasque cremet faenilibus herbas.
      digna quidem facies, sed et hunc innata libido
      exstimulat, pronumque genus regionibus illis
460   in Venerem est; flagrat uitio gentisque suoque.
      impetus est illi comitum corrumpere curam
      nutricisque fidem, nec non ingentibus ipsam
      sollicitare datis totumque impendere regnum,
      aut rapere et saeuo raptam defendere bello;
465   et nihil est quod non effreno captus amore
      ausit, nec capiunt inclusas pectora flammas.
      iamque moras male fert cupidoque reuertitur ore
      ad mandata Procnes et agit sua uota sub illa.
      facundum faciebat amor, quotiensque rogabat
470   ulterius iusto, Procnen ita uelle ferebat;
      addidit et lacrimas, tamquam mandasset et illas.
      pro superi, quantum mortalia pectora caecae
      noctis habent! ipso sceleris molimine Tereus
      creditur esse pius laudemque a crimine sumit.
475   quid quod idem Philomela cupit patriosque lacertis
      blanda tenens umeros, ut eat uisura sororem,
      perque suam contraque suam petit ipsa salutem?
      spectat eam Tereus praecontrectatque uidendo,
      osculaque et collo circumdata bracchia cernens
480   omnia pro stimulis facibusque ciboque furoris
      accipit; et quotiens amplectitur illa parentem,
      esse parens uellet. (neque enim minus impius esset!)
      uincitur ambarum genitor prece; gaudet agitque
      illa patri grates et successisse duabus
485   id putat infelix, quod erit lugubre duabus.
              iam labor exiguus Phoebo restabat, equique
      pulsabant pedibus spatium decliuis Olympi.
      regales epulae mensis et Bacchus in auro
      ponitur; hinc placido dantur sua tempora somno.
490   at rex Odrysius, quamuis secessit, in illa
      aestuat et, repetens faciem motusque manusque,
      qualia uult fingit quae nondum uidit et ignes
      ipse suos nutrit cura remouente soporem.
      lux erat, et generi dextram complexus euntis
```

BOOK VI [57

to be launched upon the sea and with the help of sail and oar he entered 445
the Cecropian port and the shores of the Piraeus.
　　As soon as he was admitted to his father-in-law, right hand was joined
with right hand and with that happy omen they joined in conversation.
He had begun to relate the reason for his coming and his wife's
requests, and to pledge the swift return of the girl if she were sent; 450
look, there came Philomela rich in her great adornment,
richer in her beauty; she was like the Naiads and the Dryads
that we are used to hear of advancing through the woods,
if only you gave them the same costume and adornments.
When he beheld the maiden, Tereus caught fire no differently 455
than if someone were to apply fire to white corn
or burn leaves and hay laid up in barns.
Her looks indeed were worth it, but his inborn lust too
goaded him on, and the race in those regions is
inclined to Venus; he was ablaze with a vice that was his race's and his own. 460
His impulse was to corrupt her companions' care
and her nurse's fidelity, and also to entice the girl herself
with sumptuous gifts and spend his whole kingdom on her,
or to ravish her and to defend the ravishing with cruel war;
he was held by unbridled love, there was nothing that 465
he would not dare, and his breast could not hold the flames it enclosed.
And now he bore delays ill and returned with eager words
to Procne's requests and worked for his own wishes under cover of hers.
Love made him eloquent, and whenever what he asked for
was beyond what was fair, he told them Procne wanted it so; 470
he added tears too as if she had commanded them as well.
Ye gods, how much dark night there is
in mortal breasts! From his very efforts for his crime Tereus
was believed to be pious and gained praise for his guilt.
What of the fact that Philomela wanted the same thing and, clasping 475
her father's shoulders in her arms to coax him, asked by her life,
and against it, that she might go to see her sister?
Tereus gazed at her and in looking prefondled her,
and as he saw her kisses and her arms encircling his neck
he took it all as spurs and torches and food 480
for his passion; and whenever she embraced her father,
he would wish to be her father. (And he would be no less impious!)
The father was won over by the prayer of both girls; she rejoiced and gave
thanks to her father and, unhappy one, thought the two girls
had won success through what was to be grievous for the two girls. 485
　　By now very little toil was left for Phoebus, and his horses
were pounding the slope down from Olympus with their feet.
Royal feasts were placed upon the tables and Bacchus
in gold cups; then due time was given to peaceful sleep.
But the Odrysian king, although he had retired, raged 490
for her and, remembering her face, her movements and her hands,
and imagining what he had not yet seen just as he wanted it, he fed
his own fires himself with a care that banished sleep.
It was light and Pandion clasped his son-in-law's right hand

58] LIBER VI

495   Pandion comitem lacrimis commendat obortis:
             'hanc ego care gener, quoniam pia causa coegit
             et uoluere ambae (uoluisti tu quoque, Tereu),
             do tibi perque fidem cognataque pectora supplex,
             per superos oro, patrio ut tuearis amore
500   et mihi sollicitae lenimen dulce senectae
             quam primum (omnis erit nobis mora longa) remittas.
             tu quoque quam primum (satis est procul esse sororem),
             si pietas ulla est, ad me, Philomela, redito.'
             mandabat pariterque suae dabat oscula natae,
505   et lacrimae mites inter mandata cadebant.
             utque fide pignus dextras utriusque poposcit
             inter seque datas iunxit natamque nepotemque
             absentes pro se memori rogat ore salutent,
             supremumque 'uale' pleno singultibus ore
510   uix dixit timuitque suae praesagia mentis.
                  ut semel imposita est pictae Philomela carinae
             admotumque fretum remis tellusque repulsa est,
             'uicimus!' exclamat 'mecum mea uota feruntur'
             [exultatque et uix animo sua gaudia differt]
515   barbarus et nusquam lumen detorquet ab illa,
             non aliter quam cum pedibus praedator obuncis
             deposuit nido leporem Iouis ales in alto;
             nulla fuga est capto, spectat sua praemia raptor.
             iamque iter effectum iamque in sua litora fessis
520   puppibus exierant, cum rex Pandione natam
             in stabula alta trahit, siluis obscura uetustis,
             atque ibi pallentem trepidamque et cuncta timentem
             et iam cum lacrimis ubi sit germana rogantem
             includit fassusque nefas et uirginem et unam
525   ui superat, frustra clamato saepe parente,
             saepe sorore sua, magnis super omnia diuis.
             illa tremit uelut agna pauens, quae saucia cani
             ore excussa lupi nondum sibi tuta uidetur,
             utque columba suo madefactis sanguine plumis
530   horret adhuc auidosque timet, quibus haeserat, ungues.
             mox ubi mens rediit, passos laniata capillos,
             [lugenti similis, caesis plangore lacertis,]
             intendens palmas 'o diris barbare factis,
             o crudelis,' ait 'nec te mandata parentis
535   cum lacrimis mouere piis nec cura sororis
             nec mea uirginitas nec coniugialia iura?
             [omnia turbasti; paelex ego facta sororis,
             tu geminus coniunx, hostis mihi debita poena.]
             quin animam hanc, ne quod facinus tibi, perfide, restet,
540   eripis? atque utinam fecisses ante nefandos
             concubitus; uacuas habuissem criminis umbras.
             si tamen haec superi cernunt, si numina diuum
             sunt aliquid, si non perierunt omnia mecum,
             quandocumque mihi poenas dabis. ipsa pudore

BOOK VI [59

as she went and with tears welling up entrusted her to be accompanied by him. 495
'I give her to you, dear son-in-law, since a pious reason
has compelled me, and both my girls wanted it (and you wanted it too,
Tereus), and as a suppliant I beg you, by your good faith and our kindred
breasts and by the gods, that you protect her with a father's love
and that you send me back the sweet consolation of my anxious 500
old age as soon as possible (any delay will be long to me).
You too, Philomela, if you have any piety, return to me
as soon as possible (it is enough that your sister is far away).'
He was instructing him and at the same time giving kisses to his daughter,
and his gentle tears fell in the midst of his instructions. 505
And as he begged both for their right hands as a pledge of good faith,
and, when given them, joined them together, he asked them to greet
his absent daughter and grandson for him with words of remembrance,
and he hardly spoke his last 'farewell' for his words
were full of sobs and he feared the forewarnings of his mind. 510
    Once Philomela was embarked on the painted ship,
and the oars had brought the sea near and pushed back the land,
'I have conquered!' he cried out, 'My prayers are being borne along with me,'
[and he exulted and scarcely put off his pleasure]
barbarian that he was, and he turned his eye nowhere away from her, 515
just as when the predatory bird of Jove
has with his hooked claws set a hare down in his high nest;
there is no escape for the captive, the plunderer gazes at his prize.
At last the journey was done and at last they had left the tired boats
for their own shores when the king dragged Pandion's 520
daughter into a high pen hidden in ancient woods,
and there the pale, trembling girl, afraid of everything,
and already asking with tears where her sister was,
he shut away, and declared his wickedness and violently overcame her,
a maiden and alone, as she vainly cried out often for her father, 525
often for her sister, but above all for the great gods.
She trembled like a frightened lamb tossed out wounded
from the mouth of a hoary wolf and not yet seeming safe to herself,
or like a dove that shudders at her plumage soaked with her own
blood and still fears the greedy claws in which she has been caught. 530
Soon when her senses had returned she tore at her streaming hair,
[like a mourner as she cut and beat her arms,]
and, stretching out her hands, 'Oh barbarian, what dreadful deeds,
oh cruel one,' she said, 'have neither my father's instructions and pious
tears moved you, nor your care for my sister, 535
nor my virginity, nor the obligations of your marriage?
[You have overturned everything; I am made my sister's supplanter,
you a double husband, I deserve a foe's punishment.]
Why do you not, so that no crime be left for you, you traitor, snatch
my life away? And would that you had before the abomination 540
of lying with me; I would have had a shade free of guilt.
If, even so, the gods see this, if the divine powers
are something, if everything has not perished with me,
at some time I shall see you pay the penalty. I myself shall cast aside

```
545     proiecto tua facta loquar: si copia detur,
        in populos ueniam; si siluis clausa tenebor,
        implebo siluas et conscia saxa mouebo.
        audiet haec aether et si deus ullus in illo est.'
        talibus ira feri postquam commota tyranni
550     nec minor hac metus est, causa stimulatus utraque,
        quo fuit accinctus, uagina liberat ensem
        arreptamque coma flexis post terga lacertis
        uincla pati cogit. iugulum Philomela parabat
        spemque suae mortis uiso conceperat ense;
555     ille indignantem et nomen patris usque uocantem
        luctantemque loqui comprensam forcipe linguam
        abstulit ense fero. radix micat ultima linguae,
        ipsa iacet terraeque tremens immurmurat atrae,
        utque salire solet mutilatae cauda colubrae,
560     palpitat et moriens dominae uestigia quaerit.
        hoc quoque post facinus (uix ausim credere) fertur
        saepe sua lacerum repetisse libidine corpus.
        sustinet ad Procnen post talia facta reuerti.
        coniuge quae uiso germanam quaerit; at ille
565     dat gemitus fictos commentaque funera narrat,
        et lacrimae fecere fidem. uelamina Procne
        deripit ex umeris auro fulgentia lato
        induiturque atras uestes et inane sepulcrum
        constituit falsisque piacula manibus infert
570     et luget non sic lugendae fata sororis.
              signa deus bis sex acto lustrauerat anno.
        quid faciat Philomela? fugam custodia claudit,
        structa rigent solido stabulorum moenia saxo,
        os mutum facti caret indice. grande doloris
575     ingenium est, miserisque uenit sollertia rebus.
        stamina barbarica suspendit callida tela
        purpureasque notas filis intexuit albis,
        indicium sceleris, perfectaque tradidit uni,
        utque ferat dominae, gestu rogat. illa rogata
580     pertulit ad Procnen; nescit quid tradat in illis.
        euoluit uestes saeui matrona tyranni
        germanaeque suae stamen miserabile legit
        et (mirum potuisse) silet. dolor ora repressit,
        uerbaque quaerenti satis indignantia linguae
585     defuerunt; nec flere uacat, sed fasque nefasque
        confusura ruit poenaeque in imagine tota est.
              tempus erat, quo sacra solent trieterica Bacchi
        Sithoniae celebrare nurus. nox conscia sacris,
        nocte sonat Rhodope tinnitibus aeris acuti,
590     nocte sua est egressa domo regina deique
        ritibus instruitur furialiaque accipit arma.
        uite caput tegitur, lateri ceruina sinistro
        uellera dependent, umero leuis incubat hasta.
        concita per siluas turba comitante suarum
```

my shame and tell of your deeds: if given the chance 545
I shall go to the people; if I am held shut up in the woods,
I shall fill the woods and move the stones that know your guilt.
The ether will hear this and whatever god is in it.'
After the anger of the wild king had been stirred up by such words,
and his fear no less than that, goaded on both accounts, 550
he freed from its sheath the sword he had girded on,
seized her by the hair, twisted her arms behind her back
and forced her to endure being bound. Philomela was offering him her throat
and, when she saw his sword, had conceived a hope of death;
as her tongue protested, calling all the time on the name 555
of her father, and struggling to speak, he caught it in pincers
and took it out with his cruel sword. The end of its root flickered
while the tongue itself lay trembling and muttering on the black earth,
and as the tail of a mutilated snake will jump,
it quivered and, as it died, was looking for its mistress's tracks. 560
Even after this crime (I would scarcely dare to believe it), they say
he often sought her torn body again in his lust.
After such deeds he could still bear to return to Procne.
She, seeing her husband, asked about her sister; but he
gave false groans and told a lying tale about her death, 565
and his tears made her believe. Procne tore
from her shoulders her clothes gleaming with broad gold,
put on a black dress, and set up an empty
tomb, bringing offerings to propitiate the false shade,
and mourning for the fate of a sister not to be mourned like that. 570
    The god had gone around the twice six signs and a year had passed.
What was Philomela to do? A guard shut off her escape,
the walls of the pen were firmly built in solid stone,
and her mute mouth had no power to testify to the crime. Great is the ingenuity
of grief, and resourcefulness comes to the unhappy. 575
Skilfully she hung her warp from the barbarian loom
and wove purple signs into the white thread
to bear witness to the crime, and when it was completed she passed it to her only maid
and by gesturing asked her to take it to her mistress. Once asked
she took it to Procne; she did not know what she was passing on in it. 580
The wife of the savage king unfolded the cloth
and read her sister's pitiable warp
and (a wonder that she could be) was silent. Grief stopped up her mouth,
and she searched for words to match her anger, but they failed to come
to her tongue; and she could not weep but rushed on to confound 585
right and wrong and was all engrossed in the idea of punishment.
    It was the time when the Sithonian brides are wont to celebrate
the trieteric rites of Bacchus. Night witnessed their rites,
by night Rhodope resounded with the ringing of sharp bronze,
by night the queen emerged from her house, equipped herself 590
for the rituals of the god and took up the arms of frenzy.
Her head was covered by a vine-wreath, deerskins hung
from her left side and a light spear rested on her shoulder.
As she rushed through the woods with a crowd of her companions,

```
595        terribilis Procne furiisque agitata doloris,
           Bacche, tuas simulat. uenit ad stabula auia tandem
           exululatque euhoeque sonat portasque refringit
           germanamque rapit raptaeque insignia Bacchi
           induit et uultus hederarum frondibus abdit
600        attonitamque trahens intra sua moenia ducit.
                ut sensit tetigisse domum Philomela nefandam,
           horruit infelix totoque expalluit ore.
           nacta locum Procne sacrorum pignora demit
           oraque deuelat miserae pudibunda sororis
605        amplexumque petit; sed non attollere contra
           sustinet haec oculos, paelex sibi uisa sororis,
           deiectoque in humum uultu iurare uolenti
           testarique deos, per uim sibi dedecus illud
           inlatum, pro uoce manus fuit. ardet et iram
610        non capit ipsa suam Procne fletumque sororis
           corripiens 'non est lacrimis hoc' inquit 'agendum,
           sed ferro, sed si quid habes, quod uincere ferrum
           possit. in omne nefas ego me, germana, paraui:
           aut ego cum facibus regalia tecta cremabo,
615        artificem mediis immittam Terea flammis,
           aut linguam atque oculos et quae tibi membra pudorem
           abstulerunt ferro rapiam, aut per uulnera mille
           sontem animam expellam. magnum quodcumque paraui;
           quid sit, adhuc dubito.' peragit dum talia Procne,
620        ad matrem ueniebat Itys; quid possit, ab illo
           admonita est oculisque tuens immitibus 'a! quam
           es similis patri' dixit; nec plura locuta
           triste parat facinus tacitaque exaestuat ira.
                ut tamen accessit natus matrique salutem
625        attulit et paruis adduxit colla lacertis
           mixtaque blanditiis puerilibus oscula iunxit,
           mota quidem est genetrix infractaque constitit ira
           inuitique oculi lacrimis maduere coactis.
           sed simul ex nimia mentem pietate labare
630        sensit, ab hoc iterum est ad uultus uersa sororis
           inque uicem spectans ambos 'cur admouet' inquit
           'alter blanditias, rapta silet altera lingua?
           quam uocat hic matrem, cur non uocat illa sororem?
           cui sis nupta uide, Pandione nata, marito:
635        degeneras; scelus est pietas in coniuge Terei.'
                nec mora, traxit Ityn, ueluti Gangetica ceruae
           lactentem fetum per siluas tigris opacas;
           utque domus altae partem tenuere remotam,
           tendentemque manus et iam sua fata uidentem
640        et 'mater, mater' clamantem et colla petentem
           ense ferit Procne, lateri qua pectus adhaeret,
           nec uultum uertit. satis illi ad fata uel unum
           uulnus erat; iugulum ferro Philomela resoluit,
           uiuaque adhuc animaeque aliquid retinentia membra
```

BOOK VI [63

terrible Procne, driven on by her frenzy of grief,   595
imitated, Bacchus, yours. She came at last to that out of the way pen
and howled out and cried 'euhoe', broke down the gates
and seized her sister and when she was seized put the Bacchic trappings
on her, hiding her face with ivy leaves
and, dragging the astonished girl, led her inside the walls.   600
   When Philomela realized she had reached the accursed house,
the unhappy girl shuddered and grew pale in all her face.
Procne found a place to take off the symbols of the ritual
and uncovered the shamed face of her wretched sister
and sought her embrace; but she could not bear to raise   605
her eyes in response, seeming to herself to be her sister's supplanter,
and when, with her face cast down upon the ground, she wanted to swear
and call the gods to witness that that dishonour had been violently
brought on her, it was her hand that acted for her voice. Procne was on fire
and could not contain her own anger and, rebuking her sister's   610
tears, 'It is not with tears,' she said, 'that this is to be settled,
but with a sword, but with anything you have that can defeat
a sword. I have prepared myself, my sister, for any wickedness:
either I shall with my torches burn the royal palace down
and throw the perpetrator Tereus in the middle of the flames,   615
or with my sword I shall tear out his tongue and eyes and the parts
which took away your modesty, or I shall drive his guilty spirit out
through a thousand wounds. Whatever I have prepared is a great deed;
but I am still in doubt on what it is. While Procne was going over such things,
Itys came to his mother; this suggested to her   620
what she could do; she gazed at him with pitiless eyes, 'Ah!
how like you are to your father,' she said; and, saying no more,
she prepared a bitter crime and seethed in silent anger.
But as her son approached her and brought a greeting
to his mother and drew her neck to him with his little arms   625
and joined kisses mixed with boyish endearments,
the mother was moved and her anger was broken and held still,
and her eyes unwillingly grew wet with tears forced from her.
But as soon as she felt that her mind was wavering from too much
piety, she turned again from him to her sister's face   630
and, looking at them both in turn, 'Why does one,' she said,
employ endearments, while the other is silent, her tongue taken out?
When he calls me mother why doesn't she call me sister?
See what a husband you have married, oh daughter of Pandion:
you are unworthy of your family; piety in a wife of Tereus is a sin.'   635
   Without delay she dragged Itys off as a Ganges tigress would
the suckling offspring of a deer through the dark woods;
and when they had reached a remote part of the high house,
as he stretched out his hands and now saw his fate
and cried out, 'Mother, mother,' and sought her neck,   640
Procne struck him with her sword where his breast met his flank,
and she did not turn her face away. Just one wound was enough
for his fate; Philomela opened up his throat with a blade
and while his limbs, still alive, retained something of his spirit,

```
645       dilaniant. pars inde cauis exsultat aenis,
          pars ueribus stridet; manant penetralia tabo.
          his adhibet coniunx ignarum Terea mensis
          et patrii moris sacrum mentita, quod uni
          fas sit adire uiro, comites famulosque remouit.
650       ipse sedens solio Tereus sublimis auito
          uescitur inque suam sua uiscera congerit aluum;
          tantaque nox animi est, 'Ityn huc accersite' dixit.
          dissimulare nequit crudelia gaudia Procne;
          iamque suae cupiens exsistere nuntia cladis
655       'intus habes, quem poscis' ait. circumspicit ille
          atque ubi sit quaerit; quaerenti iterumque uocanti,
          sicut erat sparsis furiali caede capillis,
          prosiluit Ityosque caput Philomela cruentum
          misit in ora patris nec tempore maluit ullo
660       posse loqui et mentis testari gaudia dictis.
          Thracius ingenti mensas clamore repellit
          uipereasque ciet Stygia de ualle sorores;
          et modo, si posset, reserato pectore diras
          egerere inde dapes immersaque uiscera gestit;
665       flet modo seque uocat bustum miserabile nati,
          nunc sequitur nudo genitas Pandione ferro.
          corpora Cecropidum pennis pendere putares;
          pendebant pennis. quarum petit altera siluas,
          altera tecta subit; neque adhuc de pectore caedis
670       excessere notae, signataque sanguine pluma est.
          ille dolore suo poenaeque cupidine uelox
          uertitur in uolucrem, cui stant in uertice cristae,
          prominet immodicum pro longa cuspide rostrum.
          [nomen epops uolucri, facies armata uidetur.]
675            hic dolor ante diem longaeque extrema senectae
          tempora Tartareas Pandiona misit ad umbras.
          sceptra loci rerumque capit moderamen Erectheus,
          iustitia dubium ualidisne potentior armis.
          quattuor ille quidem iuuenes totidemque crearat
680       femineae sortis, sed erat par forma duarum.
          e quibus Aeolides Cephalus te coniuge felix,
          Procri, fuit; Boreae Tereus Thracesque nocebant,
          dilectaque diu caruit deus Orithyia,
          dum rogat et precibus mauult quam uiribus uti.
685       ast ubi blanditiis agitur nihil, horridus ira,
          quae solita est illi nimiumque domestica uento,
          'et merito!' dixit 'quid enim mea tela reliqui,
          saeuitiam et uires iramque animosque minaces,
          admouique preces, quarum me dedecet usus?
690       apta mihi uis est; ui tristia nubila pello,
          ui freta concutio nodosaque robora uerto
          induroque niues et terras grandine pulso.
          idem ego cum fratres caelo sum nactus aperto
          (nam mihi campus is est), tanto molimine luctor,
```

BOOK VI [65

they tore them apart. Some of them tossed up and down in bronze cauldrons,   645
some hissed on spits; the room flowed with gore.
This was the banquet to which his wife summoned unknowing Tereus,
and she lied, saying it was a ritual custom of her fatherland which only
a husband had the right to attend, and she sent his companions and attendants away.
King Tereus, seated on high on his ancestral throne,   650
took food and stuffed his own flesh into his own belly;
and so great was the night in his mind, 'Fetch Itys here,' he said.
Procne could not disguise her cruel joy;
and wanting now to be seen as the messenger of her disaster,
'You have within the one you want,' she said. He looked around   655
and asked where he was; and as he asked and called him again,
just as she was, her hair spattered from the frenzied slaughter,
Philomela leaped out and threw Itys' bloody
head into his father's face, nor did she wish more at any other time
to be able to speak and testify to the joy of her mind with words.   660
The Thracian pushed back the banquet table with an enormous shout
and summoned the snaky sisters from the valley of the Styx;
and now he longed, if he could, to open up his breast
and spew out from there the dreadful feast and the flesh immersed within him;
now he wept and called himself the pitiable tomb of his son,   665
and now he pursued Pandion's daughters with a naked sword.
You would have thought that the bodies of the Cecropides were hovering on wings;
they were hovering on wings. One of them sought the woods,
the other went up under the roof; and still the signs of the slaughter
have not disappeared from their breasts and their plumage is marked with blood.   670
He, swift in grief and desire to punish,
was turned into a bird, on the crown of whose head stood a crest,
and instead of his long spear there stuck out an immense beak.
[The bird was called the hoopoe, it had an armed look.]
      This grief sent Pandion to the shades of Tartarus   675
too soon and before the last moments of long old age.
Erechtheus took the sceptre of the place and the control of its affairs;
it is doubtful whether he was stronger in justice or in might of arms.
He had begotten four young men and as many
of the female sort, but the beauty of two of the girls was equal.   680
Of these, Cephalus, grandson of Aeolus, was lucky to have you,
Procris, as his wife; Tereus and the Thracians had spoilt things for Boreas,
and for a long time the god was deprived of his beloved Orithyia,
while he wooed her preferring to use entreaties rather than strength.   684
But when nothing had been achieved with his blandishments, bristling with the anger
which was usual and only too familiar with that wind,
'And rightly so!' he said, 'For why have I abandoned my weapons,
savagery and strength, anger and a threatening spirit,
and employed entreaties whose use demeans me?
Violence suits me; with violence I drive the gloomy clouds along,   690
with violence I stir up the seas and overturn the gnarled oaks,
harden the snows and pelt the lands with hail.
I too when I encounter my brothers in the open sky
(for that is my training ground), wrestle with such great energy

```
695   ut medius nostris concursibus insonet aether
      exsiliantque cauis elisi nubibus ignes;
      idem ego cum subii conuexa foramine terrae
      supposuique ferox imis mea terga cauernis,
      sollicito manes totumque tremoribus orbem.
700   hac ope debueram thalamos petiisse, socerque
      non orandus erat, sed ui faciendus Erectheus.'
      haec Boreas aut his non inferiora locutus
      excussit pennas, quarum iactatibus omnis
      adflata est tellus latumque perhorruit aequor;
705   puluereamque trahens per summa cacumina pallam
      uerrit humum pauidamque metu caligine tectus
      Orithyian amans fuluis amplectitur alis.
      dum uolat, arserunt agitati fortius ignes,
      nec prius aerii cursus suppressit habenas,
710   quam Ciconum tenuit populos et moenia raptor.
      illic et gelidi coniunx Actaea tyranni
      et genetrix facta est, partus enixa gemellos,
      cetera qui matris, pennas genitoris haberent.
      non tamen has una memorant cum corpore natas,
715   barbaque dum rutilis aberat submissa capillis,
      implumes Calaisque puer Zetesque fuerunt;
      mox pariter pennae ritu coepere uolucrum
      cingere utrumque latus, pariter flauescere malae.
      ergo ubi concessit tempus puerile iuuentae,
720   uellera cum Minyis nitido radiantia uillo
      per mare non notum prima petiere carina.
```

BOOK VI [67

that the ether between us resounds as we clash 695
and fires struck from the hollow clouds leap up;
I too, when I have gone down into the vaulted cavities of the earth
and fiercely pushed my back down into its lowest caverns,
rouse up the Shades and the whole world with tremors.
It was by these means I should have sought my marriage, and Erechtheus 700
ought not to have been begged to be my father-in-law, but with violence made to be.'
When Boreas had said these words, or words not weaker than these,
he shook out his wings at whose beatings all
the earth was blown upon and the wide seas shuddered;
dragging his cloak of dust across the highest peaks, 705
he swept the earth and, covered in darkness, embraced, as his lover,
fearful panicking Orithyia in his tawny wings.
While he flew, his fires were fanned and burnt more strongly,
and he did not hold back the reins of his airy course
until he had gained the Ciconian walls and peoples with his prey. 710
There the Actaean girl became both the wife of the cold
king and a mother, for she gave birth to twin sons
who had all the rest from their mother, but their father's wings.
But they say that these were not on their bodies at birth;
and while they had no beard coming down from their russet hair, 715
the boy Calais and Zetes too were unfledged;
soon, in the manner of birds, wings began
to gird their flanks, just when their cheeks began to golden.
And so, when boyhood's time had given way to manhood,
they went with the Minyans to seek the radiant fleece of gleaming 720
wool across the unknown sea in the first ship.

LIBER VII

Iamque fretum Minyae Pagasaea puppe secabant,
perpetuaque trahens inopem sub nocte senectam
Phineus uisus erat, iuuenesque Aquilone creati
uirgineas uolucres miseri senis ore fugarant,
5   multaque perpessi claro sub Iasone tandem
contigerant rapidas limosi Phasidos undas.
dumque adeunt regem Phrixeaque uellera poscunt
lexque datur Minyis magnorum horrenda laborum,
concipit interea ualidos Aeetias ignes
10 et luctata diu, postquam ratione furorem
uincere non poterat, 'frustra, Medea, repugnas;
nescioquis deus obstat' ait 'mirumque nisi hoc est,
aut aliquid certe simile huic, quod amare uocatur.
nam cur iussa patris nimium mihi dura uidentur?
15 (sunt quoque dura nimis!) cur, quem modo denique uidi,
ne pereat, timeo? quae tanti causa timoris?
excute uirgineo conceptas pectore flammas,
si potes, infelix. si possem, sanior essem.
sed trahit inuitam noua uis, aliudque cupido,
20 mens aliud suadet; uideo meliora proboque,
deteriora sequor. quid in hospite regia uirgo
ureris et thalamos alieni concipis orbis?
haec quoque terra potest quod ames dare. uiuat an ille
occidat, in dis est; uiuat tamen idque precari
25 uel sine amore licet; quid enim commisit Iason?
quem nisi crudelem non tangat Iasonis aetas
et genus et uirtus? quem non, ut cetera desint,
ore mouere potest? certe mea pectora mouit.
at nisi opem tulero, taurorum adflabitur igne
30 concurretque suae segeti, tellure creatis
hostibus, aut auido dabitur fera praeda draconi.
hoc ego si patiar, tum me de tigride natam,
tum ferrum et scopulos gestare in corde fatebor.
cur non et specto pereuntem oculosque uidendo
35 conscelero? cur non tauros exhortor in illum
terrigenasque feros insopitumque draconem?
di meliora uelint! quamquam non ista precanda,
sed facienda mihi. prodamne ego regna parentis
atque ope nescioquis seruabitur aduena nostra
40 ut per me sospes sine me det lintea uentis
uirque sit alterius, poenae Medea relinquar?
si facere hoc aliamue potest praeponere nobis,
occidat ingratus. sed non is uultus in illo,
non ea nobilitas animo est, ea gratia formae,
45 ut timeam fraudem meritique obliuia nostri;
et dabit ante fidem cogamque in foedera testes
esse deos. quid tuta times? accingere et omnem

BOOK 7

[handwritten: Phineus - A Thracian King / Blind prophet]

And now the Minyans in their Pagasaean ship, were cutting through the sea,
and they had seen Phineus dragging out his helpless old age
in eternal night and the young men born to Aquilo
had chased the virgin birds from the unhappy old man's face,
and, after enduring many things under famous Jason, at last   5
they had reached the swift waters of the muddy Phasis;
and when they approached the king and demanded Phrixus' fleece, *[handwritten: Phrixus gave]*
a dreadful condition of great toils was given to the Minyans. *[handwritten: fleece to Aeetes]*
Meanwhile Aeetes' daughter conceived a mighty fire
and, after a long struggle, when she had not been able to conquer   10
passion with reason, 'In vain, Medea, do you fight against it:
it is some god opposing you,' she said, 'and it's a wonder if this,
or at least something like this, is not what is called to love.
For why do my father's commands seem too hard to me?   14
(And they are indeed too hard!) Why am I afraid that someone I have only just now
seen will die? What is the reason for so great a fear?
Strike from your virgin breast the flames you have conceived there,
if you can, unhappy one. If I could, I would be more in my right mind;
but a strange force draws me against my will, and desire urges
one thing, thought another; I see the better things and admire them,   20
it is the worse I pursue! Why are you on fire, royal virgin,
for a stranger and conceiving of marriage with another part of the world?
This land too can give you something to love. Whether he lives
or dies is up to the gods; yet let him live! I may pray for that
even without loving him; for what has Jason done?   25
Who but a cruel beast would not be touched by Jason's age
and birth and carriage? Who, if it weren't for all the rest of him,
can he not move with that face? My breast for sure has he moved.
But unless I bring him help, he will be breathed on by the bulls' fire
and charge into his own crop of enemies sprung   30
from the earth or be given as wild prey to the greedy snake.
If I allow this, I shall be admitting both that I am born
from a tigress and that I wear iron and stone in my heart.
Why don't I just watch him die and pollute my eyes
with the sight? Why don't I urge the bulls against him   35
and the wild earth-born ones and the unsleeping snake?
May the gods want better things. Though I should not be praying for them
but doing them. Shall I betray my father's kingdom
and will some stranger be rescued by my help
so that, saved by me, he may without me give his canvas to the winds   40
and be another's husband, while I, Medea, am left for punishment?
If he can do this or prefer another girl to me
let him die, ungrateful one. But not with that look upon his face,
not with that nobility of spirit, that handsome charm
am I to fear deceit or forgetfulness of my services.   45
And first he will give his pledge and I shall make the gods witnesses
of our bond. You're safe, what do you fear? Gird yourself up and banish

pelle moram! tibi se semper debebit Iason,
te face sollemni iunget sibi, perque Pelasgas
seruatrix urbes matrum celebrabere turba.
ergo ego germanam fratremque patremque deosque
et natale solum uentis ablata relinquam?
nempe pater saeuus, nempe est mea barbara tellus,
frater adhuc infans; stant mecum uota sororis,
maximus intra me deus est. non magna relinquam,
magna sequar: titulum seruatae pubis Achiuae
notitiamque loci melioris et oppida quorum
hic quoque fama uiget cultusque artesque uirorum
quemque ego non rebus, quas totus possidet orbis,
Aesoniden mutasse uelim, quo coniuge felix
et dis cara ferar et uertice sidera tangam.
quid quod nescioqui mediis concurrere in undis
dicuntur montes ratibusque inimica Charybdis
nunc sorbere fretum, nunc reddere cinctaque saeuis
Scylla rapax canibus Siculo latrare profundo?
nempe tenens quod amo gremioque in Iasonis haerens
per freta longa ferar; nihil illum amplexa uerebor
aut, si quid metuam, metuam de coniuge solo.
coniugiumne putas speciosaque nomina culpae
imponis, Medea, tuae? quin aspice quantum
adgrediare nefas et, dum licet, effuge crimen!'
dixit, et ante oculos Rectum Pietasque Pudorque
constiterant et uicta dabat iam terga Cupido.
　　ibat ad antiquas Hecates Perseidos aras
quas nemus umbrosum secretaque silua tegebat,
et iam fortis erat pulsusque resederat ardor,
cum uidet Aesoniden extinctaque flamma reluxit;
erubuere genae totoque recanduit ore,
utque solet uentis alimenta adsumere quaeque
parua sub inducta latuit scintilla fauilla
crescere et in ueteres agitata resurgere uires,
sic iam lenis amor, iam quem languere putares,
ut uidit iuuenem, specie praesentis inarsit.
et casu solito formosior Aesone natus
illa luce fuit; posses ignoscere amanti.
spectat et in uultu ueluti tum denique uiso
lumina fixa tenet nec se mortalia demens
ora uidere putat nec se declinat ab illo.
ut uero coepitque loqui dextramque prehendit
hospes et auxilium submissa uoce rogauit
promisitque torum, lacrimis ait illa profusis:
'quid faciam uideo, nec me ignorantia ueri
decipiet, sed amor. seruabere munere nostro;
seruatus promissa dato!' per sacra triformis
illa deae lucoque foret quod numen in illo
perque patrem soceri cernentem cuncta futuri
euentusque suos et tanta pericula iurat;

BOOK VII [71

all delay! Jason will always owe himself to you,
he will join you to himself with the ceremonial torch, and throughout the Pelasgian
cities you will be celebrated as a saviour by a throng of mothers.   50
Shall I then, carried off by the winds, leave my sister,
brother, father, gods and native soil?
Yes, for my father is cruel, yes, for my land is barbarous,
my brother still a baby. My sister's prayers are with me
and the greatest god is within me. I shall not be leaving greatness   55
but pursuing it: the credit for saving Achaea's youth,
acquaintance with a better place, and towns whose
fame thrives even here, and the culture and arts of the people,
and the man for whom I would exchange what the whole
world possesses, Aeson's son; and with him as my husband I shall be called   60
blessed and dear to the gods, and with my head I shall touch the stars.
What of that fact that there are some mountains said to rush together
in the middle of the waves, and the enemy of boats, Charybdis
now sucking the sea down, now returning it, and, girt by her savage
dogs, the grasping Scylla, barking in the Sicilian deep?   65
But of course, holding what I love, and clinging close in Jason's arms,
I shall be carried through the long seas: in his embrace, there's nothing I shall fear,
or, if I am to be afraid of anything, I shall be afraid for my husband alone.
Do you think this is a marriage, and do you put fine-sounding names,
Medea, upon your guilt? But look how great   70
a sin you are approaching and, while you may, escape from this crime.'
She spoke and before her eyes Right, Piety and Shame
had taken up their stand, and Cupid was already turning his defeated back.
    She was going to the ancient altars of Hecate, Perse's daughter,
which were hidden by a shady copse and a secluded wood,   75
and she was strong now, and her ardour had been driven away and had subsided,
when she saw Aeson's son, and the extinguished flame grew bright again;
her cheeks grew red and again she glowed over all her face,
and as a spark will draw in nourishment from the winds
and a small one, hidden beneath a spread of ash,   80
will grow, and when stirred up will spring up again with its former strength,
so her love now calm, now one you would have thought was wilting,
when she saw the young man, caught fire at the sight of his presence.
And it happened that Aeson's son was more handsome
than usual that day: you could forgive her for loving him.   85
She gazed at him and kept her eyes fixed on his face as if
she had seen it only then at last, nor in her madness did she think
it was a mortal face she was seeing, nor turn herself away from him.
But when the stranger began to speak and grasped
her right hand and asked in a submissive voice for help   90
and promised her a marriage-bed, she said to him with streaming tears,
'I see what I am doing, and it is not ignorance of the truth
that will mislead me, but love. You will be saved by my favour:
when you are saved, give me what you have promised!' He, by the rites
of the three-formed goddess and by whatever spirit was in that grove   95
and by the all-seeing father of his future father-in-law
and his own successes and dangers so great, swore his oath;

```
             creditus accepit cantatas protinus herbas
             edidicitque usum laetusque in tecta recessit.
100                 postera depulerat stellas aurora micantes:
             conueniunt populi sacrum Mauortis in aruum
             consistuntque iugis; medio rex ipse resedit
             agmine purpureus sceptroque insignis eburno.
             ecce adamanteis Vulcanum naribus efflant
105          aeripedes tauri tactaeque uaporibus herbae
             ardent, utque solent pleni resonare camini
             aut ubi terrena silices fornace soluti
             concipiunt ignem liquidarum aspergine aquarum,
             pectora sic intus clausas uoluentia flammas
110          gutturaque usta sonant. tamen illis Aesone natus
             obuius it; uertere truces uenientis ad ora
             terribiles uultus praefixaque cornua ferro,
             puluereumque solum pede pulsauere bisulco
             fumificisque locum mugitibus impleuerunt.
115          deriguere metu Minyae; subit ille nec ignes
             sentit anhelatos (tantum medicamina possunt),
             pendulaque audaci mulcet palearia dextra
             suppositosque iugo pondus graue cogit aratri
             ducere et insuetum ferro proscindere campum.
120          mirantur Colchi, Minyae clamoribus augent
             adiciuntque animos. galea tum sumit aena
             uipereos dentes et aratos spargit in agros.
             semina mollit humus ualido praetincta ueneno
             et crescunt fiuntque sati noua corpora dentes;
125          utque hominis speciem materna sumit in aluo
             perque suos intus numeros componitur infans
             nec nisi maturus communes exit in auras,
             sic ubi uisceribus grauidae telluris imago
             effecta est hominis, feto consurgit in aruo,
130          quodque magis mirum est, simul edita concutit arma.
             quos ubi uiderunt praeacutae cuspidis hastas
             in caput Aesonii iuuenis torquere parantes,
             demisere metu uultumque animumque Pelasgi.
             ipsa quoque extimuit quae tutum fecerat illum,
135          utque peti uidit iuuenem tot ab hostibus unum,
             palluit et subito sine sanguine frigida sedit;
             neue parum ualeant a se data gramina, carmen
             auxiliare canit secretasque aduocat artes.
             ille grauem medios silicem iaculatus in hostes
140          a se depulsum Martem conuertit in ipsos:
             terrigenae pereunt per mutua uulnera fratres
             ciuilique cadunt acie. gratantur Achiui
             uictoremque tenent auidisque amplexibus haerent.
144          tu quoque uictorem complecti, barbara, uelles;
146          [obstitit incepto pudor. at complexa fuisses,
145          sed te ne faceres tenuit reuerentia famae.]
             quod licet, adfectu tacito laetaris agisque
```

BOOK VII [73

he was believed and took at once her enchanted herbs
and learnt their use and withdrew joyfully to his shelter.
    The next dawn had driven off the twinkling stars: 100
the peoples assembled at Mars' sacred field
and took their places on the slopes; the king himself sat down in the middle
of his host, clad in purple and conspicuous with his ivory sceptre.
Look, the bronze-footed bulls are breathing Vulcan
from their adamantine nostrils, and the grass touched by the heat 105
caught light; and as full forges will resound,
or stones when freed from the earth kiln
catch fire from a sprinkling of clear water,
so did their breasts revolving flames shut up within,
and their burnt throats sound: yet Aeson's son went 110
to meet them: savagely they turned towards his face, as he came on,
their terrible features and their horns tipped with iron,
and they pounded on the dusty ground with cloven hoof
and filled the place with smoke-bearing lowings.
The Minyans went stiff with fear; he went up to them and did not feel 115
them breathing fire on him (so potent were the drugs)
and with bold right hand he soothed their hanging dewlaps
and putting them beneath the yoke he forced them to draw the heavy weight
of the plough and to cut into a plain unused to iron.
The Colchians were amazed, the Minyans' shouts raised 120
and boosted his spirits. Then from the bronze helmet he took
the viper's teeth and scattered them over the fields he had ploughed.
The earth softened the seeds pre-steeped with powerful poison,
and the teeth he had sown grew and became new bodies;
and as a baby takes on human appearance in its mother's 125
womb and is built up within it part by part
and, unless it's due, does not come out into the common air,
so, when human forms had been made in the bowels
of the pregnant earth, they rose up in the fruitful field
and, what was more amazing, they clashed arms produced at the same time. 130
And when they saw them preparing to hurl sharp-tipped
spears against the head of the Aesonian young man,
the Pelasgians dropped their faces and their spirits in fear.
She too was terrified, and she had made him safe,
and when she saw one young man being attacked by so many enemies, 135
she blanched and at once sat down cold and bloodless;
and in case the herbs she had given him were not strong enough, she sang
a relieving chant and summoned up her secret skills.
Hurling a heavy stone into the middle of his enemies
he drove war from himself and turned it against them: 140
the earth-born brothers perished from mutual injuries
and fell in their civil war. The Achaeans congratulated him
and clasped the victor and clung to him in eager embrace.
You too, barbarian, would have wanted to embrace the victor; 144
[shame stopped what had been begun, but you would have embraced him, 146
but, in case you did, respect for your reputation held you back.] 145
but you did enjoy, which you could do, your emotion silently and gave

carminibus grates et dis auctoribus horum.
  peruigilem superest herbis sopire draconem,
150 qui crista linguisque tribus praesignis et uncis
dentibus horrendus custos erat arboris aureae.
hunc postquam sparsit Lethaei gramine suci
uerbaque ter dixit placidos facientia somnos,
quae mare turbatum, quae concita flumina sistunt,
155 somnus in ignotos oculos * ubi uenit et auro
heros Aesonius potitur spolioque superbus
muneris auctorem secum, spolia altera, portans
uictor Iolciacos tetigit cum coniuge portus.
  Haemoniae matres pro natis dona receptis
160 grandaeuique ferunt patres, congestaque flamma
tura liquefaciunt inductaque cornibus aurum
uictima uota cadit; sed abest gratantibus Aeson
iam propior leto fessusque senilibus annis.
tum sic Aesonides: 'o cui debere salutem
165 confiteor, coniunx, quamquam mihi cuncta dedisti
excessitque fidem meritorum summa tuorum,
si tamen hoc possunt (quid enim non carmina possunt?),
deme meis annis et demptos adde parenti.'
nec tenuit lacrimas. mota est pietate rogantis[,
170 dissimilemque animum subiit Aeeta relictus];
nec tamen adfectus tales confessa 'quod' inquit
'excidit ore tuo, coniunx, scelus? ergo ego cuiquam
posse tuae uideor spatium transcribere uitae?
nec sinat hoc Hecate, nec tu petis aequa. sed isto,
175 quod petis, experiar maius dare munus, Iason;
arte mea soceri longum temptabimus aeuum,
non annis renouare tuis, modo diua triformis
adiuuet et praesens ingentibus adnuat ausis.'
  tres aberant noctes, ut cornua tota coirent
180 efficerentque orbem. postquam plenissima fulsit
et solida terras spectauit imagine luna,
egreditur tectis uestes induta recinctas,
nuda pedem, nudos umeris infusa capillos,
fertque uagos mediae per muta silentia noctis
185 incomitata gradus. homines uolucresque ferasque
soluerat alta quies; nullo cum murmure saepes,
186a [sopitae similis, nullo cum murmure serpens;]
immotaeque silent frondes, silet umidus aer.
sidera sola micant, ad quae sua bracchia tendens
ter se conuertit, ter sumptis flumine crinem
190 inrorauit aquis ternisque ululatibus ora
soluit et in dura summisso poplite terra
'Nox,' ait 'arcanis fidissima, quaeque diurnis
aurea cum luna succeditis ignibus astra,
tuque, triceps Hecate, quae coeptis conscia nostris
195 adiutrixque uenis cantusque artisque magorum,
quaeque magos, Tellus, pollentibus instruis herbis,

BOOK VII [75

thanks to your chants and to the gods, their authors.
    It remained to soothe the unsleeping snake with your herbs
which, distinguished by its crest, its three tongues and its curved   150
teeth, was the dread guardian of the golden tree.
After he had sprinkled it with the juice of a Lethaean herb
and said three times the words for making peaceful sleep,
which stay both the troubled sea and swollen rivers,
sleep came to eyes unknown to it, and the Aesonian   155
hero gained the gold and, proud of his spoils,
and carrying with him his provider of service, his other spoils,
touched in victorious at the Iolcan port with a wife.
    For the return of their sons the Haemonian mothers and aged
fathers brought their gifts, heaped up the incense   160
on the flame and melted it, and the vowed victim, its horns
trimmed with gold, fell; but Aeson was absent from the congratulations,
being so near to death and tired out by his old man's years,
when Aeson's son spoke thus: 'Oh wife, to whom I admit
I owe my safety, though you have given everything to me   165
and the sum of your services has gone beyond belief,
if even so they can do this (for what can your chants not do?)
strip from my years, and add what you have stripped to my father!'
And he did not hold back his tears: she was moved by his piety in asking[,
and into her different heart there came the thought of Aeetes left behind];   170
but even so she did not admit to such emotions; 'What crime,'
she said, 'oh husband, has fallen from your lips? Do I, then, seem
able to transfer your span of life to anyone?
Neither would Hecate allow it, nor are you asking for what is right, but I
shall attempt to grant you a greater favour than you ask for, Jason.   175
With my skill we shall try to renew my father-in-law's
great age, not with your years, if only the three-formed goddess
helps and nods her assent in person to our huge daring.'
    It was three days from when the horns would come wholly together
and make an orb. After the moon at its most full   180
had shone and with its full shape had looked upon the lands,
she left the house clad in robes ungirt,
her feet uncovered, her hair uncovered and streaming over her shoulders,
and she took her wandering steps unattended through the hushed silence
of the middle of the night. Men, birds and beasts   185
were relaxed in deep sleep: the hedgerow was without a murmur,
[like one asleep, the snake was without a murmur;]   186a
unmoving and silent was the foliage, silent was the moist air.
The stars twinkled alone, and stretching her arms towards them,
three times she turned round, three times she bedewed her hair with water
taken from the river, and she freed her mouth for triple   190
screams and, lowering her knee onto the hard earth,
said, 'Oh Night, most faithful to my mysteries, and golden stars
who with the moon succeed the fires of day,
and you, three-fold Hecate, who comes as witness to what I
have begun and helper to the incantations and skill of sorcerers,   195
and you, Earth, who provide sorcerers with their potent herbs,

76] LIBER VII

                auraeque et uenti montesque amnesque lacusque,
                dique omnes nemorum dique omnes noctis, adeste.
                quorum ope, cum uolui, ripis mirantibus amnes
200   in fontes rediere suos, concussaque sisto,
                stantia concutio cantu freta, nubila pello
                nubilaque induco, uentos abigoque uocoque,
                uipereas rumpo uerbis et carmine fauces,
                uiuaque saxa sua conuulsaque robora terra
205   et siluas moueo iubeoque tremescere montes
                et mugire solum manesque exire sepulcris.
                te quoque, Luna, traho, quamuis Temesaea labores
                aera tuos minuant; currus quoque carmine nostro
                pallet aui, pallet nostris Aurora uenenis.
210   uos mihi taurorum flammas hebetastis et unco
                impatiens oneris collum pressistis aratro,
                uos serpentigenis in se fera bella dedistis
                custodemque rudem somno sopistis et aurum
                uindice decepto Graias misistis in urbes.
215   nunc opus est sucis per quos renouata senectus
                in florem redeat primosque recolligat annos.
                et dabitis; neque enim micuerunt sidera frustra,
                nec frustra uolucrum tractus ceruice draconum
                currus adest.' (aderat demissus ab aethere currus.)
220   quo simul ascendit frenataque colla draconum
                permulsit manibusque leues agitauit habenas,
                sublimis rapitur subiectaque Thessala Tempe
                despicit et certis regionibus applicat angues;
                et quas Ossa tulit, quas altum Pelion herbas,
225   Othrysque Pindusque et Pindo maior Olympus
                perspicit et placitas partim radice reuellit,
                partim succidit curuamine falcis aenae.
                multa quoque Apidani placuerunt gramina ripis,
                multa quoque Amphrysi, neque eras immunis, Enipeu;
230   nec non Peneos, nec non Spercheides undae
                contribuere aliquid iuncosaque litora Boebes;
                carpsit et Euboica uiuax Anthedone gramen,
                nondum mutato uulgatum corpore Glauci.
                et iam nona dies curru pennisque draconum
235   nonaque nox omnes lustrantem uiderat agros
                cum rediit; neque erant tacti nisi odore dracones,
                et tamen annosae pellem posuere senectae.
                      constitit adueniens citra limenque foresque
                et tantum caelo tegitur refugitque uiriles
240   contactus statuitque aras e caespite binas,
                dexteriore Hecates, ast laeua parte Iuuentae.
                has ubi uerbenis siluaque incinxit agresti,
                haud procul egesta scrobibus tellure duabus
                sacra facit cultrosque in guttura uelleris atri
245   conicit et patulas perfundit sanguine fossas.
                tum super inuergens liquidi carchesia mellis

BOOK VII [77

and breezes and winds, mountains, streams and lakes,
and all the gods of the copses and all the gods of night, be present.
With your help, when I have wished it, streams, to the wonder of their banks,
have returned to their sources, with my incantation I stay   200
the seas when they are shaken and shake them when they are still, I dispel clouds
and bring clouds back, winds I both drive away and summon,
with words and chant I break the viper's throat,
living rocks and oaks and woods I wrench from
their earth and move, and I order mountains to quake,   205
the ground to roar and shades to come out from their tombs.
You too, oh Moon, I draw down, though the Temesaean bronzes
diminish your toils; even my grandfather's chariot at my chant
grows dim and Dawn grows dim from my poisons.
You dulled the bulls' flames for me and pressed   210
the neck that had never felt a burden under the curved plough,
you gave the serpent-born cruel wars against themselves,
you stupefied the rough guardian with sleep and sent
the gold to the cities of Greece by tricking its defender.
Now I need the juices by which old age may be renewed,   215
return to its bloom and regain its first years.
And you will give them! For neither have the stars twinkled in vain,
nor is it in vain that the chariot drawn by the necks of flying
snakes is present.' (And it was present, the chariot sent down from the ether.)
As soon as she climbed up onto it, soothed the bridled necks   220
of the snakes and shook the light reins with her hands,
she was snatched up on high, looked down on Thessalian
Tempe lying below, brought the snakes to certain regions,
and searched out the herbs which Ossa and which high Pelion
bore and Othrys, Pindus and, greater than Pindus,   225
Olympus, and some of those that pleased her she tore up by the root,
others she cut away with her curved brazen sickle.
Many herbs too from the banks of the Apidanus pleased her,
many too from Amphrysus, and you were not exempt, Enipeus;
and also the streams of Peneus and also those of Spercheius   230
contributed something as did the rushy shores of Boebe.
And she plucked a long-lived herb from Euboean Anthedon
not yet widely known for Glaucus' change of body.
And now the ninth day in her chariot with its winged snakes
and the ninth night had seen her scouring all the fields,   235
when she returned; and her snakes had not been touched except by the smell,
and even so they shed their skin of old age and its years.
    She stopped as she came this side of the threshold and doors
and, covered only by the sky, and shunning male
contact, she built a pair of altars out of turf,   240
on the right to Hecate but on the left side to Youth.
When she had girt these with branches and foliage from the fields,
not far off she dug out two trenches in the earth
and made a sacrifice thrusting the knife into the throat of a black
fleece and drenching the gaping ditches with blood.   245
Then tipping over them chalices of clear honey

alteraque inuergens tepidi carchesia lactis
uerba simul fudit terrenaque numina ciuit,
umbrarumque rogat rapta cum coniuge regem
ne properent artus anima fraudare senili.
quos ubi placauit precibusque et murmure longo,
Aesonis effetum proferri corpus ad auras
iussit et in plenos resolutum carmine somnos
exanimi similem stratis porrexit in herbis.
hinc procul Aesoniden, procul hinc iubet ire ministros
et monet arcanis oculos remouere profanos.
diffugiunt iussi, passis Medea capillis
bacchantum ritu flagrantes circuit aras
multifidasque faces in fossa sanguinis atra
tingit et infectas geminis accendit in aris
terque senem flamma, ter aqua, ter sulphure lustrat.
interea ualidum posito medicamen aeno
feruet et exsultat spumisque tumentibus albet.
illic Haemonia radices ualle resectas
seminaque floresque et sucos incoquit atros;
adicit extremo lapides Oriente petitos
et quas Oceani refluum mare lauit harenas;
addit et exceptas luna pernocte pruinas
et strigis infames ipsis cum carnibus alas
inque uirum soliti uultus mutare ferinos
ambigui prosecta lupi; nec defuit illis
squamea Cinyphii tenuis membrana chelydri
uiuacisque iecur cerui, quibus insuper addit
ora caputque nouem cornicis saecula passae.
his et mille aliis postquam sine nomine rebus
propositum instruxit mortali barbara maius,
arenti ramo iampridem mitis oliuae
omnia confudit summisque immiscuit ima.
ecce uetus calido uersatus stipes aeno
fit uiridis primo nec longo tempore frondes
induit et subito grauidis oneratur oliuis;
at quacumque cauo spumas eiecit aeno
ignis et in terram guttae cecidere calentes,
uernat humus floresque et mollia pabula surgunt.
quae simul ac uidit, stricto Medea recludit
ense senis iugulum ueteremque exire cruorem
passa replet sucis; quos postquam combibit Aeson
aut ore acceptos aut uulnere, barba comaeque
canitie posita nigrum rapuere colorem,
pulsa fugit macies, abeunt pallorque situsque,
adiectoque cauae supplentur corpore rugae,
membraque luxuriant. Aeson miratur et olim
ante quater denos hunc se reminiscitur annos.
uiderat ex alto tanti miracula monstri
Liber et admonitus iuuenes nutricibus annos

BOOK VII [79

and tipping out other chalices of warm milk,
at the same time she poured out words and summoned the gods of earth
and asked the king of the shades together with his ravished wife
not to rush to deprive his body of its old man's soul. 250
And when she had placated them with prayers and lengthy murmurings,
she ordered Aeson's worn out body to be brought forth
into the air and relaxing him with her chant into full sleep
she stretched him out onto strewn herbs like a dead man.
She ordered Aeson's son to go far from her and his attendants 255
and warned them to turn their profane eyes away from the mysteries.
They fled away as ordered; Medea, her hair flowing loose,
circled the blazing altars like one of the bacchants,
and dipped the much-split torches into a black ditch 259
of blood, and when they had been immersed she ignited them from the twin altars
and purified the old man three times with fire, three times with water and three times
with sulphur.

Meanwhile, the powerful drug in the cauldron she had put on
boiled and seethed and whitened with swelling froth.
She cooked in with it roots cut from a Haemonian
valley and seeds, flowers and black juices. 265
She threw in stones sought from the farthest East
and sands which had been washed by the ebbing sea of Ocean;
she added frost too collected under an all-night moon,
and the ill-famed wings of an owl together even with its carrion,
and the entrails of a changeling wolf used to changing 270
from a bestial appearance to a man; and they were not without
the thin scaly skin of the Cinyphian water-snake
or the liver of a long-lived stag, to which she added besides
the beak and head of a crow that had experienced nine generations.
After the barbarian woman had with these things and a thousand other 275
nameless ones arranged her more than mortal plan,
with a long since dried branch of sweet olive
she stirred it all up and mixed the bottom with the top.
Look, the old stick which had been worked round in the hot cauldron
first became green and in no long time put on 280
leaves and suddenly was loaded with swelling olives;
and wherever the froth was spewed out from the hollow cauldron
by the fire, and scalding drops fell upon the earth,
the ground was as in spring, flowers and soft pasture grew up.
And, as soon as she had seen it, Medea drew her sword 285
and opened up the old man's throat and, having let the old blood
flow out, she refilled it with her juices; and after Aeson had drunk them down,
taking them either in his mouth or in his wound, his beard and hair
shed their greyness and instantly took on a black colour,
his thinness was put to flight, his pallor and his decay went from him, 290
his hollow wrinkles were filled out with added flesh,
and his limbs swelled out: Aeson was amazed and remembered
that this was himself of old four times ten years ago.
    Liber had seen from high how marvellous was
this miracle and realizing that his nurses could 295

posse suis reddi capit hoc a Colchide munus.
     neue doli cessent, odium cum coniuge falsum
Phasias adsimulat Peliaeque ad limina supplex
confugit; atque illam, quoniam grauis ipse senecta est,
300 excipiunt natae. quas tempore callida paruo
Colchis amicitiae mendacis imagine cepit,
dumque refert inter meritorum maxima demptos
Aesonis esse situs atque hac in parte moratur,
spes est uirginibus Pelia subiecta creatis
305 arte suum parili reuirescere posse parentem,
idque petunt pretiumque iubent sine fine pacisci.
illa breui spatio silet et dubitare uidetur
suspenditque animos ficta grauitate rogantum;
mox ubi pollicita est, 'quo sit fiducia maior
310 muneris huius,' ait 'qui uestri maximus aeuo est
dux gregis inter oues, agnus medicamine fiet.'
protinus innumeris effetus laniger annis
attrahitur flexo circum caua tempora cornu.
cuius ut Haemonio marcentia guttura cultro
315 fodit et exiguo maculauit sanguine ferrum,
membra simul pecudis ualidosque uenefica sucos
mergit in aere cauo; minuunt medicamina corpus
cornuaque exurunt nec non cum cornibus annos,
et tener auditur medio balatus aeno;
320 nec mora, balatum mirantibus exsilit agnus
lasciuitque fuga lactantiaque ubera quaerit.
obstipuere satae Pelia, promissaque postquam
exhibuere fidem, tum uero impensius instant.
     ter iuga Phoebus equis in Hiberno flumine mersis
325 dempserat et quarta radiantia nocte micabant
sidera, cum rapido fallax Aeetias igni
imponit purum laticem et sine uiribus herbas.
iamque neci similis resoluto corpore regem
et cum rege suo custodes somnus habebat,
330 quem dederant cantus magicaeque potentia linguae.
intrarant iussae cum Colchide limina natae
ambierantque torum; 'quid nunc dubitatis inertes?
stringite' ait 'gladios ueteremque haurite cruorem,
ut repleam uacuas iuuenali sanguine uenas.
335 in manibus uestris uita est aetasque parentis;
si pietas ulla est nec spes agitatis inanes,
officium praestate patri telisque senectam
exigite et saniem coniecto emittite ferro.'
his ut quaeque pia est hortatibus impia prima est
340 et, ne sit scelerata, facit scelus; haud tamen ictus
ulla suos spectare potest, oculosque reflectunt
caecaque dant saeuis auersae uulnera dextris.
ille cruore fluens cubito tamen adleuat artus
semilacerque toro temptat consurgere et inter

be given back their youthful years, he received it as a gift from the Colchian.
   And so that there should be no rest for her trickery, the Phasian falsely pretended
hatred in her husband and fled to Pelias' threshold
as a suppliant and, since he was himself weighed down by old age,
his daughters took her in; and in a short time the wily Colchian   300
had taken them in with her deceitful picture of friendship,
and, while she was relating among the greatest of her merits the stripping off
of Aeson's decay and lingered on that part,
the hope was implanted in the virgins sprung from Pelias
that with a like skill their father could grow young again,   305
and this is what they wanted and they told her to set a price without limit.
For a brief time she was silent and seemed to hesitate
and kept their demanding minds in suspense with a pretended earnestness:
soon, when she had promised, 'So that you may have greater confidence
in this gift,' she said, 'the leader of the flock, and greatest in age   310
among your sheep, will with my drug become a lamb.'
At once, a wool-bearer worn out by countless years
was dragged before her, its horn bent around its hollow temples;
and as she pierced its withered throat with her Haemonian
knife and stained the iron blade with its meagre blood,   315
the sorceress plunged the limbs of the sheep together with the powerful
juices into the hollow bronze pot; the drugs shrank its body,
burnt up its horns and also, with its horns, its years,
and a gentle bleating was heard from the cauldron;
without delay, while they were wondering at the bleating, a lamb leapt out   320
and ran frolicking off and looked for milky udders.
Pelias' daughters were dumbfounded, and now that her promises
had shown their reliability, then indeed they pressed her more intently.
   Three times had Phoebus removed the yokes from his horses when they had
                                                        plunged into the Spanish
stream, and on the fourth night the radiant stars   325
were twinkling, when the treacherous daughter of Aeetes put upon the raging
fire pure water and powerless herbs.
And now a death-like sleep, which her incantations
and the power of her magic tongue had given, relaxed
his body and possessed the king and, together with the king, his guards: 330
the daughters had, as ordered, entered his doorway with the Colchian
and had surrounded his bed: 'Why are you hesitating now, you sluggards?
Draw,' she said, 'your swords and drain out his old gore,
so that I may refill his empty veins with youthful blood.
Your father's life and age are in your hands;   335
if you have any piety and the hopes you exercise are not empty ones,
fulfil your duty to your father and drive out his old age
with your weapons, thrust your swords in and release his slime!' At these
encouragements, as each was pious, so she was the first to be impious
and, to avoid sin, committed sin; but there was not any who could   340
look upon her own thrusts. They averted their eyes,
and turning away gave blind wounds with savage hands.
He, flowing with blood, still lifted his body up onto his elbow
and, though half mangled, tried to rise up from his bed and in the midst

345 tot medius gladios pallentia bracchia tendens
'quid facitis, natae? quis uos in fata parentis
armat?' ait. cecidere illis animique manusque;
plura locuturo cum uerbis guttura Colchis
abstulit et calidis laniatum mersit in undis.
350   quod nisi pennatis serpentibus isset in auras,
non exempta foret poenae. fugit alta superque
Pelion umbrosum, Philyreia tecta, superque
Othryn et euentu ueteris loca nota Cerambi;
hic ope nympharum sublatus in aera pennis,
355 cum grauis infuso tellus foret obruta ponto,
Deucalioneas effugit inobrutus undas.
Aeoliam Pitanen a laeua parte relinquit
factaque de saxo longi simulacra draconis
Idaeumque nemus, quo nati furta iuuencum
360 occuluit Liber falsi sub imagine cerui,
quaque pater Corythi parua tumulatus harena est,
et quos Maera nouo latratu terruit agros,
Eurypylique urbem, qua Coae cornua matres
gesserunt tum cum discederet Herculis agmen,
365 Phoebeamque Rhodon et Ialysios Telchinas,
quorum oculos ipso uitiantes omnia uisu
Iuppiter exosus fraternis subdidit undis.
transit et antiquae Cartheia moenia Ceae,
qua pater Alcidamas placidam de corpore natae
370 miraturus erat nasci potuisse columbam.
inde lacus Hyries uidet et Cycneia tempe,
quae subitus celebrauit olor. (nam Phyllius illic
imperio pueri uolucresque ferumque leonem
tradiderat domitos; taurum quoque uincere iussus
375 uicerat, at spreto totiens iratus amore
praemia poscenti taurum suprema negabat.
ille indignatus 'cupies dare' dixit et alto
desiluit saxo. cuncti cecidisse putabant;
factus olor niueis pendebat in aere pennis.
380 at genetrix Hyrie, seruari nescia, flendo
deliquit stagnumque suo de nomine fecit.)
adiacet his Pleuron, in qua trepidantibus alis
Ophias effugit natorum uulnera Combe.
inde Calaureae Letoidos aspicit arua
385 in uolucrem uersi cum coniuge conscia regis.
dextra Cyllene est, in qua cum matre Menephron
concubiturus erat saeuarum more ferarum.
Cephison procul hinc deflentem fata nepotis
respicit in tumidam phocen ab Apolline uersi
390 Eumelique domum lugentis in aere natum.
tandem uipereis Ephyren Pirenida pennis
contigit; hic aeuo ueteres mortalia primo
corpora uulgarunt pluuialibus edita fungis.
sed postquam Colchis arsit noua nupta uenenis

BOOK VII [83

of so many swords stretched out his pallid arms 345
and said, 'Daughters, what are you doing? Who is arming you
for your father's doom?' Their courage and their hands fell;
he was about to say more but the Colchian took his throat out
together with his words and plunged his torn body into the hot water.
  But if she had not gone into the breezes with her winged snakes, 350
she would not have escaped punishment: she fled on high over
shady Pelion, the Philyreian dwelling, and over
Othrys and the places made famous by the tale of old Cerambus:
he, with the help of the nymphs, was lifted up into the air on wings
and when solid earth had been overwhelmed by the sea pouring in 355
he escaped Deucalion's waters unoverwhelmed.
She left Aeolian Pitane on the left-hand side,
and the figure of the long snake, made of stone,
and the copse of Ida, where Liber concealed the bullock
stolen by his son in the false guise of a stag, 360
and where Corythus' father lay beneath a little mound of sand,
and the fields that Maera terrified with her new bark,
and the city of Eurypylus where the Coan mothers wore
horns when Hercules' troop was departing,
and Phoebus' Rhodes and the Telchines of Ialysus 365
whose eyes blighted everything with their very gaze,
and Jupiter detested them and pushed them beneath his brother's waters.
She crossed the Cartheian walls of ancient Cea too,
where father Alcidamas was to be amazed that a gentle dove
could be born from his daughter's body. 370
From there she saw the lake of Hyrie and Cycneian tempe
which the sudden swan made famous. (For it was there that Phyllius
on the orders of a boy had tamed birds and a wild lion
and brought them to him; when he ordered him to break in a bull too,
he broke it in and, angry that his love had been scorned many times, 375
refused him the bull when he demanded it as the final gift;
he was resentful and saying, 'You'll want to give it,' leapt down
from a high rock. They all thought that he had fallen:
he had been made into a swan and was hanging in the air on snowy wings.
But his mother, Hyrie, not knowing he was safe, melted away 380
from weeping and made the pond which bears her name.)
Next to these lies Pleuron where on trembling wings
Ophius' daughter Combe escaped being wounded by her sons.
From there she saw the fields of Leto's Calaurea
which witnessed the turning of their king together with his wife into a bird. 385
On the right was Cyllene on which Menephron was
to lie with his mother in the manner of savage beasts.
Far from here she looked back at Cephisos bewailing the fate
of his grandson turned by Apollo into a fat seal,
and at the house of Eumelus grieving for his aerial son. 390
At last she touched down with her snaky wings at Pirenian
Ephyra: it was here, in the first age, so the men of old reported,
that mortal bodies sprang from mushrooms that grow in rain.
But after the new bride had been burnt by the Colchian poisons

```
395    flagrantemque domum regis mare uidit utrumque,
       sanguine natorum perfunditur impius ensis
       ultaque se male mater Iasonis effugit arma.
       hinc Titaniacis ablata draconibus intrat
       Palladias arces, quae te, iustissima Phene,
400    teque, senex Peripha, pariter uidere uolantes
       innixamque nouis neptem Polypemonis alis.
            excipit hanc Aegeus, facto damnandus in uno.
       nec satis hospitium est; thalami quoque foedere iungit.
       iamque aderat Theseus, proles ignara parenti,
405    qui uirtute sua bimarem pacauerat Isthmon;
       huius in exitium miscet Medea quod olim
       attulerat secum Scythicis aconiton ab oris.
       illud Echidnaeae memorant e dentibus ortum
       esse canis. specus est tenebroso caecus hiatu
410    et uia decliuis, per quam Tirynthius heros
       restantem contraque diem radiosque micantes
       obliquantem oculos nexis adamante catenis
       Cerberon abstraxit, rabida qui concitus ira
       impleuit pariter ternis latratibus auras
415    et sparsit uirides spumis albentibus agros.
       has concresse putant nactasque alimenta feracis
       fecundique soli uires cepisse nocendi;
       quae quia nascuntur dura uiuacia caute,
       agrestes aconita uocant. ea coniugis astu
420    ipse parens Aegeus nato porrexit ut hosti;
       sumpserat ignara Theseus data pocula dextra,
       cum pater in capulo gladii cognouit eburno
       signa sui generis facinusque excussit ab ore.
       effugit illa necem nebulis per carmina motis.
425         at genitor, quamquam laetatur sospite nato,
       attonitus tamen est ingens discrimine paruo
       committi potuisse nefas; fouet ignibus aras
       muneribusque deos implet feriuntque secures
       colla torosa boum uinctorum tempora uittis.
430    nullus Erecthidis fertur celebratior illo
       illuxisse dies; agitant conuiuia patres
       et medium uulgus, nec non et carmina uino
       ingenium faciente canunt: 'te, maxime Theseu,
       mirata est Marathon Cretaei sanguine tauri,
435    quodque suis securus arat Cromyona colonus,
       munus opusque tuum est; tellus Epidauria per te
       clauigeram uidit Vulcani occumbere prolem,
       uidit et immitem Cephisias ora Procrusten,
       Cercyonis letum uidit Cerealis Eleusin;
440    occidit ille Sinis magnis male uiribus usus,
       qui poterat curuare trabes et agebat ab alto
       ad terram late sparsuras corpora pinus;
       tutus ad Alcathoen, Lelegeia moenia, limes
       composito Scirone patet, sparsisque latronis
```

and the twin seas had seen the king's palace ablaze, 395
her impious sword was drenched with her children's blood
and the mother, having evilly avenged herself, escaped Jason's weapons.
Borne off from here by her Titanian snakes, she entered
Pallas' citadel, which saw you, most just
Phene, and you, old Periphas, flying together 400
and Polypemon's grand-daughter supported by her new wings.
    Aegeus took her in; for that one deed he was to be condemned;
and his hospitality was not enough: he also joined her in the marriage bond.
And now Theseus was there, an offspring unknown to his father,
and he had courageously subdued the isthmus of two seas: 405
on purpose to destroy him, Medea mixed the cliff-wort
she had brought with her long ago from the Scythian shores.
They say that it sprang from the teeth
of Echidna's dog; there is a blind cave with a shadowy opening,
there is a downward path by which the Tirynthian hero, 410
though he resisted and turned his eyes away against the daylight
and its flashing rays, dragged away in chains bound in adamant
Cerberus who, provoked by a raging anger,
filled the air equally with his triple barks
and sprinkled the green fields with white foam. 415
They think this hardened and, drawing nourishment from the fertile
and fruitful soil, took on the power to do harm,
and, because it was born to thrive on hard cliffs,
the country people call it 'cliff-wort'; because of his wife's cunning,
it was the father, Aegeus himself, who offered it to his son as if to an enemy. 420
Theseus had unwittingly taken hold with his right hand of the cup he had been given,
when his father, recognizing on the ivory hilt of his sword
the emblems of their family, struck the wicked thing from his mouth;
she escaped death by summoning clouds with her chants.
    But the father, though he rejoiced in the safety of his son, 425
was still stunned that a huge wrong could, but for a hair's
breadth, have been committed; he warmed the altars with fires,
he loaded the gods with gifts and his axes struck
the brawny necks of cattle bound with headbands round their temples.
No day, it is said, has dawned more festive 430
for the Erechthids than that one; the elders and the common folk
threw banquets and also, as the wine gave them
the talent, they sang songs: 'Marathon marvelled at you,
Theseus most great, for the shedding of the Cretan bull's blood,
and that the farmer ploughs Cremyon without fear of the pig 435
is your gift, your doing; it was through you that the land of Epidaurus
saw Vulcan's club-wielding offspring and the shore
of Cephisus saw pitiless Procrustes laid low;
and Ceres' Eleusis saw the death of Cercyon;
and Sinis died for misusing his great strength, 440
for he could bend tree trunks and used to draw
pines from on high to the ground so as to scatter bodies far and wide.
The path to Alcathoe and the Lelegeian walls lies safely
open with Sciron laid low, but the earth refused

```
445   terra negat sedem, sedem negat ossibus unda,
      quae iactata diu fertur durasse uetustas
      in scopulos; scopulis nomen Scironis inhaeret.
      si titulos annosque tuos numerare uelimus,
      facta premant annos. pro te, fortissime, uota
450   publica suscipimus, Bacchi tibi sumimus haustus.'
      consonat adsensu populi precibusque fauentum
      regia, nec tota tristis locus ullus in urbe est.
              nec tamen (usque adeo nulla est sincera uoluptas,
      sollicitumque aliquid laetis interuenit) Aegeus
455   gaudia percepit nato secura recepto;
      bella parat Minos, qui quamquam milite, quamquam
      classe ualet, patria tamen est firmissimus ira
      Androgeique necem iustis ulciscitur armis.
      ante tamen bello uires adquirit amicas,
460   quaque potens habitus, uolucri freta classe pererrat.
      hinc Anaphen sibi iungit et Astypaleia regna,
      promissis Anaphen, regna Astypaleia bello;
      hinc humilem Myconon cretosaque rura Cimoli
      florentemque thymo Syron planamque Seriphon
465   marmoreamque Paron, quamque impia prodidit Arne
      Siphnon et accepto, quod auara poposcerat, auro
      mutata est in auem quae nunc quoque diligit aurum,
      nigra pedes, nigris uelata monedula pennis.
      nec non Oliaros Didymeque et Tenos et Andros
470   et Gyaros nitidaeque ferax Peparethos oliuae
      Cnosiacas iuuere rates. latere inde sinistro
      Oenopiam Minos petit, Aeacideia regna.
      (Oenopiam ueteres appellauere, sed ipse
      Aeacus Aeginam genetricis nomine dixit.)
475           turba ruit tantaeque uirum cognoscere famae
      expetit; occurrunt illi Telamonque minorque
      quam Telamon Peleus et proles tertia Phocus;
      ipse quoque egreditur tardus grauitate senili
      Aeacus et quae sit ueniendi causa requirit.
480   admonitus patrii luctus suspirat et illi
      dicta refert rector populorum talia centum:
      'arma iuues oro pro nato sumpta piaeque
      pars sis militiae; tumulo solacia posco.'
      huic Asopiades 'petis inrita' dixit 'et urbi
485   non facienda meae; neque enim coniunctior ulla
      Cecropidis hac est tellus. ea foedera nobis.'
      tristis abit 'stabunt' que 'tibi tua foedera magno'
      dixit et utilius bellum putat esse minari
      quam gerere atque suas ibi praeconsumere uires.
490           classis ab Oenopiis etiamnum Lyctia muris
      spectari poterat, cum pleno concita uelo
      Attica puppis adest in portusque intrat amicos,
      quae Cephalum patriaeque simul mandata ferebat.
      Aeacidae longo iuuenes post tempore uisum
```

BOOK VII [87

a resting place, a resting place the waters refused for the brigand's scattered bones
which, it is said, a long age of tossing hardened 446
into rocks; rocks to which the name of Sciron clings.
If we wished to count your exploits and your years,
your deeds would dwarf your years. On your behalf, oh bravest of men,
we offer public prayers, for you we take draughts of Bacchus.' 450
The palace resounded to the applause of the people and the prayers
of his admirers, and there was no sad place in the whole city.
    And yet (truly there is no pure delight;
some trouble will break in upon the joyous) Aegeus
had realized that his pleasure in his son's return was not free from care: 455
Minos was preparing for war; and although in soldiery, although
in ships he was strong, yet was he most powerful in his paternal anger,
and he was avenging the death of Androgeus with a just use of arms.
But first he secured friendly forces for his war, 459
and traversed the seas with his swift fleet through which he was known as powerful.
And then he joined to himself Anaphe and the kingdom of Astypaleia,
Anaphe by promises, by war the kingdom of Astypaleia;
and then low-lying Myconos, Cimolus' chalky countryside,
Syros blooming with thyme, level Seriphos,
marble Paros and the Siphnos which impious Arne 465
betrayed: when she had received the gold which she had greedily demanded,
she was changed into a bird which even now adores gold,
the black-footed jackdaw wrapped in black wings.
And Oliaros, Didyme, Tenos, Andros,
Gyaros and Peparethos, prolific in the gleaming olive, 470
gave help to the Cnossan boats. From there Minos made for
Oenopia, the kingdom of the Aeacidae on his left hand side.
(The men of old called it Oenopia, but Aeacus
himself called it by his mother's name, Aegina.)
    A throng rushed out eager to get to know a man of such great 475
renown; Telamon ran out to meet him and, younger
than Telamon, Peleus and, the third offspring, Phocus;
there also emerged, slowed by the weight of old age,
Aeacus himself, and he asked what was the reason for his coming.
Reminded of his paternal grief, the ruler of a hundred 480
peoples sighed and replied to him in words like this:
'I am begging you to help the arms I have taken up for my son and to be
a part of my pious army: I am demanding solace for his burial mound.'
    'You ask in vain,' said Asopus' son to him, 'and for things
my city cannot do; for there is no other land 485
closer to the Cecropidae than this one: such is our bond.'
Sadly he went away saying, 'Your bond will cost you
dear,' but he thought it was more profitable to threaten war
than to wage it and use up his strength there prematurely.
    The Lyctian fleet could still be seen 490
from the Oenopian walls when, driven by full sail,
an Attic ship was there and was entering the friendly port
bringing Cephalus and also his country's requests.
Though it was a long time since they had seen him, the Aeacid young men

88] LIBER VII

495 agnouere tamen Cephalum dextrasque dedere
inque patris duxere domum. spectabilis heros
et ueteris retinens etiamnum pignora formae
ingreditur, ramumque tenens popularis oliuae,
a dextra laeuaque duos aetate minores
500 maior habet, Clyton et Buten, Pallante creatos.
      postquam congressus primi sua uerba tulerunt,
Cecropidum Cephalus peragit mandata rogatque
auxilium foedusque refert et iura parentum
imperiumque peti totius Achaidos addit.
505 sic ubi mandatam iuuit facundia causam,
Aeacus in capulo sceptri nitente sinistra
'ne petite auxilium, sed sumite,' dixit 'Athenae!
[nec dubie uires, quas haec habet insula, uestras
dicite, et omnia, quae rerum status iste mearum;]
510 robora non desunt; superat mihi miles et hoc est
(gratia dis!) felix et inexcusabile tempus.'
'immo ita sit;' Cephalus 'crescat tua ciuibus opto
urbs.' ait 'adueniens equidem modo gaudia cepi,
cum tam pulchra mihi, tam par aetate iuuentus
515 obuia processit; multos tamen inde requiro,
quos quondam uidi uestra prius urbe receptus.'
Aeacus ingemuit tristique ita uoce locutus:
'flebile principium melior fortuna secuta est;
hanc utinam possem uobis memorare sine illo!
520 ordine nunc repetam, neu longa ambage morer uos:
ossa cinisque iacent, memori quos mente requiris.
[et quota pars illi rerum periere mearum!]
      'dira lues ira populis Iunonis iniquae
incidit exosae dictas a paelice terras.
525 [dum uisum mortale malum tantaeque latebat
causa nocens cladis, pugnatum est arte medendi;
exitium superabat opem, quae uicta iacebat.]
principio caelum spissa caligine terras
pressit et ignauos inclusit nubibus aestus,
530 dumque quater iunctis expleuit cornibus orbem
luna, quater plenum tenuata retexuit orbem,
letiferis calidi spirarunt aestibus austri.
constat et in fontes uitium uenisse lacusque,
miliaque incultos serpentum multa per agros
535 errasse atque suis fluuios temerasse uenenis.
strage canum primo uolucrumque ouiumque boumque
inque feris subiti deprensa potentia morbi.
concidere infelix ualidos miratur arator
inter opus tauros medioque recumbere sulco;
540 lanigeris gregibus balatus dantibus aegros
sponte sua lanaeque cadunt et corpora tabent;
acer equus quondam magnaeque in puluere famae
degenerat palmas ueterumque oblitus honorum
ad praesepe gemit leto moriturus inerti;

BOOK VII [89

still recognized Cephalus and, giving him their right hands, 495
they led him into their father's palace. The hero, a fine sight,
still retaining reminders of his former beauty,
approached, and holding a branch of his people's olive
had, as the elder, two younger in age
on his right and left, Clytos and Butes, Pallas' sons. 500
　　After they had exchanged the words of first meeting,
Cephalus went through the requests of Cecrops' son and asked
for help; he recalled the bond and obligations of their fathers
and added that what was being sought was sovereignty over all of Achaea.
When his eloquence had thus helped the case he had been entrusted with, 505
Aeacus, his left hand leaning on the hilt of his sceptre,
said, 'do not ask for help, but take it, Athens,
[and do not hesitate to call the strength this island has
your own, and everything which the condition of my state affords;]
I do not lack strength; I have soldiery left and this is 510
(thanks to the gods!) a propitious time that offers no excuse.'
'At least, may it be so,' said Cephalus; 'I pray that your city
grow in citizens; for indeed, as I arrived just now I rejoiced
when such beautiful youths so matched in age came out
to meet me; and yet I miss from here many 515
whom once I saw when received by your city before.'
Aeacus groaned and spoke thus in a sad voice:
'A distressing start was followed by better fortune:
would that I could tell you of the one without the other!
I shall now recall it in order so as not to delay you with long ramblings: 520
they lie bone and ash, the ones you miss in your mindful memory.
[And how great a part of my realm has perished with them!]
　　A dreadful plague had befallen the peoples through the anger of Juno
unjustly hating the lands for being called after a wench.
[While it seemed to be a mortal ill, and the noxious cause 525
of such a great disaster was obscure, it was fought by the art of healing;
death was overcoming help which lay defeated.]
In the beginning, the sky pressed upon the lands with a dense
fog and trapped the sluggish heat in clouds,
and while the moon joined her horns to fill her orb 530
four times and shrank four times unravelling her full orb,
the warm south winds breathed with death-dealing heat.
It is known that the taint came even to our springs and lakes
and that many thousand snakes wandered through our untilled
fields and defiled our streams with their poisons. 535
At first it was from the destruction of dogs, birds, sheep and cattle
and among wild beasts that the power of the sudden disease was detected.
The unhappy ploughman was amazed at his powerful bulls
collapsing at their task and lying in the middle of their furrow;
as the wool-bearing flocks gave sickly bleats, 540
their wool dropped off of its own accord and their bodies decayed;
The once spirited horse, of great renown on the track,
could not live up to his prizes and, forgetful of his former glories,
stood groaning at his stall about to die a sluggard's death;

90] LIBER VII

545 non aper irasci meminit, non fidere cursu
cerua nec armentis incurrere fortibus ursi.
omnia languor habet. siluisque agrisque uiisque
corpora foeda iacent, uitiantur odoribus aurae.
mira loquar: non illa canes auidaeque uolucres,
550 non cani tetigere lupi; dilapsa liquescunt
adflatuque nocent et agunt contagia late.
       'peruenit ad miseros damno grauiore colonis
pestis et in magnae dominatur moenibus urbis.
uiscera torrentur primo flammaeque latentis
555 indicium rubor est et ductus anhelitus aegre;
aspera lingua tumet tepidisque arentia uentis
ora patent auraeque graues captantur hiatu;
non stratum, non ulla pati uelamina possunt,
nuda sed in terra ponunt praecordia, nec fit
560 corpus humo gelidum, sed humus de corpore feruet.
nec moderator adest inque ipsos saeua medentes
erumpit clades obsuntque auctoribus artes;
quo propior quisque est seruitque fidelius aegro,
in partem leti citius uenit. utque salutis
565 spes abiit finemque uident in funere morbi,
indulgent animis et nulla quid utile cura est.
(utile enim nihil est.) passim positoque pudore
fontibus et fluuiis puteisque capacibus haerent.
[nec sitis est extincta prius quam uita bibendo]
570 inde graues multi nequeunt consurgere et ipsis
immoriuntur aquis; aliquis tamen haurit et illas.
tantaque sunt miseris inuisi taedia lecti,
prosiliunt aut, si prohibent consistere uires,
corpora deuoluunt in humum fugiuntque penates
575 quisque suos, sua cuique domus funesta uidetur
[et, quia causa latet, locus est in crimine paruus].
semianimes errare uiis, dum stare ualebant,
aspiceres, flentes alios terraque iacentes
lassaque uersantes supremo lumina motu.
580 [membraque pendentis tendunt ad sidera caeli,
hic illic, ubi mors deprenderat, exhalantes.]
       'quid mihi tunc animi fuit aut quid debuit esse,
ni uitam odissem et cuperem pars esse meorum?
quo se cumque acies oculorum flexerat, illic
585 uulgus erat stratum, ueluti cum putria motis
poma cadunt ramis agitataque ilice glandes.
templa uides contra gradibus sublimia longis
(Iuppiter illa tenet); quis non altaribus illis
irrita tura dedit? quotiens pro coniuge coniunx,
590 pro nato genitor, dum uerba precantia dicit,
non exoratis animam finiuit in aris,
inque manu turis pars inconsumpta reperta est.
admoti quotiens templis, dum uota sacerdos
concipit et fundit purum inter cornua uinum,

BOOK VII [91

the boar did not remember to be angry nor the deer to trust   545
in flight nor bears to charge against the strong herds.
Lethargy held everything: in the woods and fields and roads
loathsome bodies lay and the air was blighted by the smell.
I shall tell you wonders: they were not touched by dogs or greedy
birds, nor by hoary wolves; they decayed and rotted,   550
polluting with their exhalation and bringing widespread contagion.
The pestilence came to the unhappy farmers with heavier
loss and became master within the walls of our great city.
The bowels burnt up first and, a symptom of the hidden
flame, there was a flush and difficulty in drawing breath; the tongue   555
was rough and swollen by the fire; dried by the warm winds,
their mouths opened up and the heavy air was snatched at by the gaping mouth.
They could bear no bed nor any covering
but laid their naked breasts upon the earth, and the body
was not cool from the ground, but the ground was heated from the body;   560
there was no one to control it, and the cruel disaster burst over
the healers themselves; their skills hurt those who used them.
The nearer each was to the sick and the more devotedly he served them,
the swifter he came into his share of death. And, as their hope of safety
went, and they saw only in their death an end to the disease,   565
they indulged their desires and had no care for what was helpful.
(For there was nothing helpful.) Everywhere, their modesty cast aside,
they clung to springs and rivers and capacious wells.
[And their thirst was not extinguished by their drinking till their life was.]
Many, weighed down, could not rise from there and died   570
in the very waters; yet there was someone to drink even those.
The unhappy people were so very weary of their hated beds
they leapt up or, if their strength prevented them from standing,
they rolled their bodies down onto the ground and each fled
his own penates, to each his own home seemed deadly   575
[and, because the cause was hidden, that small place was under suspicion].
You would see them wandering half-alive on the streets while they had the strength
to stand and others weeping and lying on the ground
and rolling weary eyes in their final movement.
[And they stretched their arms to the stars in the overhanging sky,   580
expiring here and there, where death had caught them.]
What was in my mind then, or what ought to have been,
if not that I was hating life and wanting to be part of my people?
Wherever the vision of my eyes turned to gaze, there
was a crowd prostrate, just as when rotten apples   585
fall from moving branches, or acorns from a shaken oak.
You see the lofty temple opposite with the long steps
(Jupiter inhabits it): who is there who has not given incense
in vain to those altars? How often, while a husband was speaking
words of prayer for his wife or a father for his son,   590
did he end his life on unresponsive altars,
and in his hands was found an unconsumed piece of incense!
How often, when they had been brought to the temple, while the priest was uttering
his prayers and pouring pure wine between their horns,

595 haud exspectato ceciderunt uulnere tauri.
ipse ego sacra Ioui pro me patriaque tribusque
cum facerem natis, mugitus uictima diros
edidit et subito conlapsa sine ictibus ullis
exiguo tinxit subiectos sanguine cultros.
600 exta quoque aegra notas ueri monitusque deorum
perdiderant; tristes penetrant ad uiscera morbi.
ante sacros uidi proiecta cadauera postes,
ante ipsas, quo mors foret inuidiosior, aras.
pars animam laqueo claudunt mortisque timorem
605 morte fugant ultroque uocant uenientia fata.
corpora missa neci nullis de more feruntur
funeribus (neque enim capiebant funera portae);
aut inhumata premunt terras aut dantur in altos
indotata rogos. et iam reuerentia nulla est
610 deque rogis pugnant alienisque ignibus ardent;
qui lacriment desunt indefletaeque uagantur
natorumque uirumque animae iuuenumque senumque;
nec locus in tumulos, nec sufficit arbor in ignes.
'attonitus tanto miserarum turbine rerum
615 "Iuppiter o!" dixi "si te non falsa loquuntur
dicta sub amplexus Aeginae Asopidos isse
nec te, magne pater, nostri pudet esse parentem,
aut mihi redde meos, aut me quoque conde sepulcro."
ille notam fulgore dedit tonitruque secundo.
620 "accipio sintque ista, precor, felicia mentis
signa tuae;" dixi "quod das mihi pigneror omen."
forte fuit iuxta patulis rarissima ramis
sacra Ioui quercus de semine Dodonaeo;
hic nos frugilegas aspeximus agmine longo
625 grande onus exiguo formicas ore gerentes
rugosoque suum seruantes cortice callem.
dum numerum miror, "totidem, pater optime," dixi
"tu mihi da ciues et inania moenia supple."
intremuit ramisque sonum sine flamine motis
630 alta dedit quercus. pauido mihi membra timore
horruerant stabantque comae; tamen oscula terrae
roboribusque dedi nec me sperare fatebar,
sperabam tamen atque animo mea uota fouebam.
nox subit et curis exercita corpora somnus
635 occupat; ante oculos eadem mihi quercus adesse
et ramos totidem totidemque animalia ramis
ferre suis uisa est pariterque tremescere motu
graniferumque agmen subiectis spargere in aruis,
crescere quod subito maius maiusque uidetur
640 ac se tollere humo rectoque adsistere trunco
et maciem numerumque pedum nigrumque colorem
ponere et humanam membris inducere formam.
   'somnus abit. damno uigilans mea uisa querorque
in superis opis esse nihil; at in aedibus ingens

BOOK VII [93

did the bulls fall without waiting for the wound!   595
When I myself was making sacrifice to Jove for myself, my country
and my three sons, the victim let forth a dreadful
lowing and, suddenly collapsing without any blows,
tinged the knives thrust into it with meagre blood.
The entrails too were sick and had lost their signs of truth and their warnings   600
from the gods: the grim disease penetrated to the bowels.
I saw corpses flung down before the sacred doors,
before the very altars, to make their death more odious.
Some closed off their breathing with a noose and were using death to put the fear
of death to flight and were, of their own accord, summoning their fate as it came. 605
The bodies of those sent to their death were carried in no proper
funerals (for indeed, the gates could not take the funerals);
either, unburied, they burdened the earth or they were given without a dowry
to high pyres; and there was now no respect:
they fought over the pyres and did their burning on strangers' fires.   610
There was no one to weep and, unbewailed, there wandered off
the souls of sons and husbands, of young and old,
and there was no room for burial mounds nor trees enough for fires.
     Thunderstruck by so great a whirlwind of unhappiness,
"Oh Jupiter," I said, "If they are not false words that say   615
you entered the embrace of Aegina, daughter of Asopus,
and if, great father, you are not ashamed to be my parent,
either return my people to me or bury me as well in a tomb."
He gave a sign with favourable lightning and thunder:
"I acknowledge it," I said, "and I pray those tokens of your   620
mind may be propitious; I claim the omen you give me."
There happened to be, nearby, a very special oak with spreading
branches, sacred to Jove and from the seed of Dodona:
here we saw in a long column, carrying a large
load in tiny mouths, corn-collecting ants   625
keeping to their track on the furrowed bark;
while I wondered at their number, "Give me," I said,
"oh best of fathers," as many citizens and fill up my empty walls."
The tall oak trembled and gave a sound, and its branches
moved without a breeze; my limbs had shuddered in fearful   630
fright and my hair was standing up; and yet I gave kisses
to the earth and to the tree and did not admit that I was hopeful,
and yet I was hopeful and cherishing my prayers in my heart.
Night came, and sleep overwhelmed bodies beset
with cares; the same oak seemed to be there before my eyes   635
and to have the same branches and to carry just as many insects
on its branches and to move and tremble as before
and to scatter the grain-bearing column on the fields below,
which suddenly seemed to grow bigger and bigger
and raise itself from the earth and stand with torso erect   640
and shed its thinness and the number of its feet and its black
colour and put human form on its limbs.
     Sleep left. Awake, I rejected what I had seen and complained
that there was no help in the gods; but in the house there was

645	murmur erat uocesque hominum exaudire uidebar
	iam mihi desuetas. dum suspicor has quoque somni
	esse, uenit Telamon properus foribusque reclusis
	"speque fideque, pater," dixit "maiora uidebis;
	egredere!" egredior, qualesque in imagine somni
650	uisus eram uidisse uiros, ex ordine tales
	aspicio noscoque; adeunt regemque salutant.
	uota Ioui soluo populisque recentibus urbem
	partior et uacuos priscis cultoribus agros,
	Myrmidonasque uoco nec origine nomina fraudo.
655	corpora uidisti; mores, quos ante gerebant,
	nunc quoque habent: parcum genus est patiensque laborum
	quaesitique tenax et quod quaesita reseruet.
	hi te ad bella pares annis animisque sequentur,
	cum primum, qui te feliciter attulit, Eurus'
660	(Eurus enim attulerat) 'fuerit mutatus in Austros.'
	talibus atque aliis longum sermonibus illi
	impleuere diem; lucis pars ultima mensae
	est data, nox somnis. iubar aureus extulerat Sol;
	flabat adhuc Eurus redituraque uela tenebat.
665	ad Cephalum Pallante sati, cui grandior aetas,
	ad regem Cephalus simul et Pallante creati
	conueniunt, sed adhuc regem sopor altus habebat.
	excipit Aeacides illos in limine Phocus;
	nam Telamon fraterque uiros ad bella legebant.
670	Phocus in interius spatium pulchrosque recessus
	Cecropidas ducit, cum quis simul ipse resedit.
	aspicit Aeoliden ignota ex arbore factum
	ferre manu iaculum, cuius fuit aurea cuspis;
	pauca prius mediis sermonibus ante locutus
675	'sum nemorum studiosus' ait 'caedisque ferinae,
	qua tamen e silua teneas hastile recisum
	iamdudum dubito. certe, si fraxinus esset,
	fulua colore foret; si cornus, nodus inesset.
	unde sit ignoro, sed non formosius isto
680	uiderunt oculi telum iaculabile nostri.'
	excipit Actaeis e fratribus alter et 'usum
	maiorem specie mirabere' dixit 'in isto.
	consequitur quodcumque petit fortunaque missum
	non regit et reuolat nullo referente cruentum.'
685	tum uero iuuenis Nereius omnia quaerit,
	cur sit et unde datum, quis tanti muneris auctor;
687	[quae petit ille refert et cetera nota pudori/e,
687a	quae patitur pudor, ille refert et cetera narrat;
687b	quae petit ille refert; ceterum narrare pudori
688	qua tulerit mercede, silet tactusque dolore]
688a	*ipse diu reticet Cephalus tactusque dolore*
	coniugis amissae lacrimis ita fatur obortis:
690	'hoc me, nate dea, (quis possit credere?) telum
	flere facit facietque diu, si uiuere nobis

BOOK VII [95

an enormous rumbling, and I seemed to hear men's voices 645
that I was by now unused to. While I was supposing that these too were
from a dream, Telamon came hurrying up, opened the doors
and said, "You, father, are about to see things beyond hope or faith.
Come out!" I came out, and just such men
as I had seemed to see in my dream, one by one 650
I looked at and knew: they approached and hailed me as their king.
I paid my vow to Jove and shared out the city, and the fields
emptied of their former cultivators, to my new people,
and I called them Myrmidons and did not divorce their name from their origin.
You have seen their bodies: and the character they showed before 655
they still have now; a thrifty race that endures toil
and clings to what it has acquired, and such as stores away its acquisitions.
These men, so matched in years and spirit, will follow you to war
as soon as Eurus which happily brought you'
(for Eurus had brought him) 'has been changed into Auster.' 660
   With this and other kinds of talk they filled
the long day: the last part of the day was given
to a banquet, the night to sleep; the golden sun had raised first light;
Eurus was still blowing and holding back the sails from returning;
Pallas' sons came to Cephalus, who was of greater age than them, 665
and Cephalus, together with the offspring of Pallas,
to the king, but deep sleep still held the king.
Phocus, son of Aeacus, received them on the threshold;
for Telamon and his brother were choosing men for war.
Phocus led the Cecropidae into an inner area, 670
to a handsome chamber, and himself sat down with them.
He noticed that Aeolus' grandson was holding in his hand a javelin
made from an unfamiliar tree and with a golden tip;
after speaking of a few things first in the midst of their talk,
'I'm an enthusiast for copses,' he said, 'and the killing of wild beasts; 675
but I've been wondering for a long time now from which grove was cut
that spearshaft you are holding; surely, if it were ash,
its colour would be yellow; if cornel, there'd be a knot in it.
I do not know from what it comes, but my eyes have not seen
a more beautiful casting spear than that.' 680
One of the Actaean brothers took hold of it and said,
'You will admire its effect more than its appearance.
It strikes whatever it is aiming at, chance does not
control its flight and, without anyone to return it, it flies back blood-stained.'
Then indeed the Nereid young man asked everything: 685
why and from where had it been given him; who was the source of so great a gift;
[what he asked the other answered, and other things, known for their shame, 687
which shame allowed he answered and told the other things; 687a
what he asked, the other answered; but to tell for shame 687b
the price for which he got it he was silent and touched by grief] 688
Cephalus himself was silent for a long time, and touched by grief 688a
for his lost wife, as the tears welled up spoke thus:
'This spear, goddess' son, (who could believe it?) makes 690
and will make me weep long, if the fates have given me

fata diu dederint; hoc me cum coniuge cara
perdidit; hoc utinam caruissem munere semper!
    'Procris erat, si forte magis peruenit ad aures
695 Orithyia tuas, raptae soror Orithyiae;
si faciem moresque uelis conferre duarum,
dignior ipsa rapi. pater hanc mihi iunxit Erectheus,
hanc mihi iunxit Amor; felix dicebar eramque.
(non ita dis uisum est, aut nunc quoque forsitan essem.)
700 alter agebatur post sacra iugalia mensis
cum me cornigeris tendentem retia ceruis
uertice de summo semper florentis Hymetti
lutea mane uidet pulsis Aurora tenebris
inuitumque rapit. liceat mihi uera referre
705 pace deae: quod sit roseo spectabilis ore,
quod teneat lucis, teneat confinia noctis,
nectareis quod alatur aquis - ego Procrin amabam,
pectore Procris erat, Procris mihi semper in ore.
sacra tori coitusque nouos thalamosque recentes
710 primaque deserti referebam foedera lecti;
mota dea est et 'siste tuas, ingrate, querellas;
Procrin habe!' dixit 'quod si mea prouida mens est,
non habuisse uoles' meque illi irata remisit.
dum redeo mecumque deae memorata retracto,
715 esse metus coepit ne iura iugalia coniunx
non bene seruasset. facies aetasque iubebat
credere adulterium, prohibebant credere mores;
sed tamen afueram, sed et haec erat, unde redibam,
criminis exemplum, sed cuncta timemus amantes.
720 quaerere quod doleam statuo donisque pudicam
sollicitare fidem; fauet huic Aurora timori
immutatque meam (uideor sensisse) figuram.
Palladias ineo non cognoscendus Athenas
ingrediorque domum; culpa domus ipsa carebat
725 castaque signa dabat dominoque erat anxia rapto.
uix aditus per mille dolos ad Erecthida factus:
et uidi, obstipui meditataque paene reliqui
temptamenta fide; male me quin uera faterer
continui, male quin, ut oportuit, oscula ferrem.
730 tristis erat (sed nulla tamen formosior illa
esse potest tristi) desiderioque dolebat
coniugis abrepti. tu collige qualis in illa,
Phoce, decor fuerit, quam sic dolor ipse decebat!
quid referam quotiens temptamina nostra pudici
735 reppulerint mores, quotiens "ego" dixerit "uni
seruor; ubicumque est, uni mea gaudia seruo."?
cui non ista fide satis experientia sano
magna foret? non sum contentus et in mea pugno
uulnera, dum census dare me pro nocte paciscor
740 muneraque augendo tandem dubitare coegi.
exclamo male uictor: "ego en, ego fictus adulter

long to live: it has destroyed me together with my dear
wife; would that I had done without this gift for ever!
    She was Procris; if perhaps it is Orithyia rather that has come
to your ears, she was the sister of the raped Orithyia; 695
if you wanted to compare the looks and character of the two of them,
she was more worthy to be raped. Her father, Erechtheus, joined her to me,
love joined her to me: I was said to be happy and I was;
but the gods did not approve, or perhaps I would be even now.
It was the second month after the wedding ceremonial 700
and I was stretching my nets for the antlered stags,
when from the very summit of ever-flowering Hymettus
saffron Dawn, as she drove off the shadows in the morning, saw me
and seized me against my will. May I be allowed to tell the truth
without offence to the goddess: she is a vision with her rosy face, 705
and she holds the boundaries of day and the boundaries of night
and she is nurtured on nectar water - Procris was the one I loved,
Procris was in my heart, Procris was always on my lips.
I was telling her of the rites of the wedding couch, of our new coupling and recent
marriage and of the first bonds of the bed I had left behind. 710
The goddess was moved to say, "Stop your complaints, ungrateful one;
have Procris! But if my mind is prophetic
you will wish not to have had her," and angrily she sent me back to her.
As I returned and was recalling what the goddess had said,
I began to have a fear that my wife had not kept 715
her marriage obligations well. Her looks and age commanded
me to believe in her adultery, her character forbade me to believe in it;
but still I had been away, still too there was her from whom I was returning,
an example of sin, but we lovers are afraid of everything. 719
I decided to seek out the sort of thing that was grieving me and to tempt her innocent
fidelity with gifts; Dawn helped this fear along
and altered my appearance (I seemed to feel it).
Unrecognizable I entered Pallas' Athens
and went into my house; the house itself was free of guilt
and gave off the signs of chastity and was worried for its seized lord. 725
Scarcely with a thousand tricks was an approach made to the daughter of Erechtheus:
seeing her I was dumbfounded and I almost abandoned the tests
of her fidelity I had devised; I could hardly contain myself from admitting
the truth, or from giving kisses to her as I ought to have.
She was sad (but yet there can be no woman more beautiful 730
than she was in her sadness), grieving with longing
for her husband snatched away. Imagine, will you, Phocus, what grace
there was in her when grief itself so graced her!
Why should I tell how often the innocence of her character
rebuffed my testings, how often, "I," she said, "keep myself 735
for only one; wherever he is, I keep my love only for him."?
To what sane man would that trial of fidelity not
have been great enough? I was not content and I fought to wound
myself, until I agreed to give her a fortune for a night
and by increasing the reward forced her to hesitate. 740
Basely victorious I cried out: "Look, it was me, me, a false adulterer

uerus eram coniunx; me, perfida, teste teneris."
illa nihil; tacito tantummodo uicta pudore
insidiosa malo cum coniuge limina fugit
745 offensaque mei genus omne perosa uirorum
montibus errabat, studiis operata Dianae.
tum mihi deserto uiolentior ignis ad ossa
peruenit; orabam ueniam et peccasse fatebar
et potuisse datis simili succumbere culpae
750 me quoque muneribus, si munera tanta darentur.
haec mihi confesso, laesum prius ulta pudorem,
redditur et dulces concorditer exigit annos.
dat mihi praeterea, tamquam se parua dedisset
dona, canem munus, quem cum sua traderet illi
755 Cynthia, "currendo superabit" dixerat "omnes."
dat simul et iaculum manibus quod (cernis) habemus.
muneris alterius quae sit fortuna requiris?
accipe; mirandi nouitate mouebere facti.
  'carmina Laiades non intellecta priorum
760 soluerat ingeniis, et praecipitata iacebat
immemor ambagum uates obscura suarum.
[scilicet alma Themis nec talia linquit inulta.]
protinus Aoniis immittitur altera Thebis
pestis et exitio multi pecorumque suoque
765 rurigenae pauere feram. uicina iuuentus
uenimus et latos indagine cinximus agros;
illa leui uelox superabat retia saltu
summaque transibat positarum lina plagarum.
copula detrahitur canibus, quos illa sequentes
770 effugit et coetum non segnior alite ludit.
poscor et ipse meum consensu Laelapa magno
(muneris hoc nomen); iamdudum uincula pugnat
exuere ipse sibi colloque morantia tendit.
uix bene missus erat nec iam poteramus ubi esset
775 scire; pedum calidus uestigia puluis habebat,
ipse oculis ereptus erat: non ocior illo
hasta nec excussae contorto uerbere glandes
nec Gortyniaco calamus leuis exit ab arcu.
collis apex medii subiectis imminet aruis:
780 tollor eo capioque noui spectacula cursus,
quo modo deprendi, modo se subducere ab ipso
uulnere uisa fera est; nec limite callida recto
in spatiumque fugit, sed decipit ora sequentis
et redit in gyrum, ne sit suus impetus hosti;
785 imminet hic sequiturque parem similisque tenenti
non tenet et uanos exercet in aera morsus.
ad iaculi uertebar opem; quod dextera librat
dum mea, dum digitos amentis addere tempto,
lumina deflexi. reuocataque rursus eodem
790 rettuleram: medio (mirum) duo marmora campo
aspicio; fugere hoc, illud latrare putares.

BOOK VII [99

but a true husband; you are caught, you cheat, and I am witness."
She said nothing; defeated by a silent shame she simply
fled from her base husband together with his treacherous house
and, in her resentment towards me hating the whole race of men, 745
she wandered on the mountains occupied in the pursuits of Diana.
Now that I was deserted a more violent fire came
into my bones; I began to beg forgiveness and admit that I had sinned
and that I too could have yielded to just such a guilty act
if given rewards, if such great rewards had been given. 750
With these admissions and after she had been avenged for her injured shame,
she was restored to me and spent sweet years harmoniously.
She gave to me besides, as if to have given herself were a small
gift, a dog as a present of whom her Cynthia had said
when she had given him to her, "He will outdo them all in running." 755
At the same time, she gave me the javelin too which (you see) I have in my hands.
Do you ask what was the fate of the other gift?
Listen; you will be moved by the strangeness of a wondrous deed.
    Laius' son had solved the incantations not understood
by the ingenuity of those before him, and the dark seer 760
lay fallen headlong unmindful of her ramblings.
[Of course bounteous Themis did not leave such things unavenged.]
At once a second scourge was sent to Aonian
Thebes and many countryfolk feared the wild beast would be
their own and their flocks' destruction. We, the young men of the neighbourhood, 765
came and surrounded the wide fields with a ring of nets.
With an easy leap it swiftly surmounted the meshes
and crossed the topmost lines of the toils we had placed.
The leash was taken off our dogs; but it escaped
their pursuit and, no slower than a bird, toyed with the pack. 770
With loud agreement, I myself was asked for Laelaps
(that was the name of her gift): he himself had already been fighting
to cast off the restraining lead from himself and from his neck.
Scarcely had he been released and we could not know where
he was; the warm dust kept his footprints, 775
but he himself had been snatched from our eyes: a spear is no swifter
than he was nor bullets shot from a whirling thong,
nor a light shaft leaving a Gortynian bow.
The summit of a hill between loomed over the fields that lay beneath:
I climbed up to it and caught sight of a strange race, 780
in which now the wild beast seemed to be caught, now to be extricating
itself from the very jaws; and skilfully it did not flee in a straight
line or into space, but dodged the mouth of its pursuer
and circled back so that its enemy could not keep its impetus;
he loomed behind her giving equal chase and as if holding on 785
did not hold on, but worked his empty jaws upon the air.
I turned to the javelin for help; while my right hand
balanced it, while I tried to put my fingers to the loop,
I averted my eyes. I had turned them back again
to the same point: in the middle of the plain I saw (a wonder) two marble 790
statues; you would think that one was fleeing and the other barking.

scilicet inuictos ambo certamine cursus
esse deus uoluit, si quis deus adfuit illis.'
  hactenus, et tacuit. 'iaculo quod crimen in ipso est?'
Phocus ait; iaculi sic crimina reddidit ille:
  'gaudia principium nostri sunt, Phoce, doloris;
illa prius referam. iuuat o meminisse beati
temporis, Aeacida, quo primos rite per annos
coniuge eram felix, felix erat illa marito!
mutua cura duos et amor socialis habebat,
nec Iouis illa meo thalamos praeferret amori,
nec me quae caperet, non si Venus ipsa ueniret,
ulla erat; aequales urebant pectora flammae.
sole fere radiis feriente cacumina primis
uenatum in siluas iuuenaliter ire solebam,
nec mecum famuli nec equi nec naribus acres
ire canes nec lina sequi nodosa solebant;
tutus eram iaculo. sed cum satiata ferinae
dextera caedis erat, repetebam frigus et umbras
et quae de gelidis exibat uallibus auram.
aura petebatur medio mihi lenis in aestu,
auram exspectabam, requies erat illa labori.
"aura," (recordor enim) "uenias" cantare solebam,
"meque iuues intresque sinus, gratissima, nostros,
utque facis, releuare uelis quibus urimur aestus."
forsitan addiderim (sic me mea fata trahebant)
blanditias plures et "tu mihi magna uoluptas,"
dicere sim solitus "tu me reficisque fouesque,
tu facis ut siluas, ut amem loca sola, meoque
spiritus iste tuus semper captatur ab ore."
uocibus ambiguis deceptam praebuit aurem
nescioquis nomenque aurae tam saepe uocatum
esse putat nymphae, nympham me credit amare.
criminis extemplo ficti temerarius index
Procrin adit linguaque refert audita susurra.
credula res amor est; subito conlapsa dolore
(ut mihi narratur) cecidit longoque refecta
tempore se miseram, se fati dixit iniqui
deque fide questa est et crimine concita uano
quod nihil est metuit, metuit sine corpore nomen
[et dolet infelix ueluti de paelice uera].
saepe tamen dubitat speratque miserrima falli
indicioque fidem negat et, nisi uiderit ipsa,
damnatura sui non est delicta mariti.
  'postera depulerant aurorae lumina noctem;
egredior siluasque peto uictorque per herbas
"aura, ueni," dixi "nostroque medere labori!"
et subito gemitus inter mea uerba uidebar
nescioquos audisse; "ueni," tamen "optima" dixi.
fronde leuem rursus strepitum faciente caduca
sum ratus esse feram telumque uolatile misi;

suppose a god wanted the running of both to be
inconquered in the contest, if any god was present in them.'
    He got so far, and fell silent. 'The javelin, what crime is there in that?'
said Phocus; and thus did he recount the javelin's crimes: 795
    'Joys were the start, Phocus, of my grief;
I shall tell of them first. Oh it is a delight to remember that blest
time, son of Aeacus, when I was, as was right, happy
with my wife in our first years and she was happy with her husband!
Mutual care and married love possessed the two of us,   800
neither would she prefer Jove's marriage bed to my love
nor was there any woman, not if Venus herself were to come,
who could win me; equal flames burnt our breasts.
When the sun was just striking the peaks with its first rays
I used to go, as a young man will, into the woods to hunt,   805
and neither attendants, nor horses, nor keen nosed dogs,
used to go with me nor follow the knotted lines.
I was safe with my javelin. But when my right arm had had its fill
of the killing of wild beasts, I would make for the cool again and the shade
and the breeze coming out from the chill valleys.   810
In the midst of the heat, it was the gentle breeze that I sought,
I waited for the breeze, it was the rest from my toil.
'Breeze," (for I remember it), "do come," I used to chant,
'and delight me and come, most welcome, to my breast,
and be willing, as you often do, to relieve the heat from which I burn.   815
Perhaps I added (so my fates were drawing me on)
more endearments and used to say, "You are my great
delight," or, "You restore and soothe me,
you make me love the woods and the lonely places, and that
breath of yours is always snatched at by my mouth."   820
Someone gave ear to these ambiguous words
and was deceived and thought that "breeze" which I had called out so often
was the name of a nymph, he believed I loved a nymph.
At once this rash informer of an imagined crime
went to Procris and in a whisper reported what he had heard.   825
A gullible thing is love; she collapsed and fell from sudden
grief (so it was told to me) and when, after a long time,
she was revived, she said that she was wretched, her fate unjust,
and she complained of my fidelity and, provoked by an empty charge,
she feared what was nothing, she feared a name without a body   830
[and grieved, unhappy one, as if over a real wench].
And yet she often doubted and hoped, most wretchedly, that she was deceived
and she refused to believe the informer and, unless she saw for herself,
would not convict her husband of misdeeds.
    The next dawn's lights had driven off the night;   835
I went out and sought the woods and, triumphant on the grass,
"Come, breeze," I said, "and assuage my toil!"
And suddenly I seemed to hear a kind of groaning
among my words; and still, "Come", I said, "best one."
As falling leaves again made a slight sound   840
I thought it was a wild beast and sent my weapon flying;

102] LIBER VII

```
        Procris erat medioque tenens in pectore uulnus
        "ei mihi!" conclamat. uox est ubi cognita fidae
        coniugis, ad uocem praeceps amensque cucurri;
845     semianimem et sparsas foedantem sanguine uestes
        et sua (me miserum!) de uulnere dona trahentem
        inuenio, corpusque meo mihi carius ulnis
        mollibus attollo scissaque a pectore ueste
        uulnera saeua ligo conorque inhibere cruorem,
850     neu me morte sua sceleratum deserat, oro.
        uiribus illa carens et iam moribunda coegit
        haec se pauca loqui: "per nostri foedera lecti
        perque deos supplex oro superosque meosque,
        per si quid merui de te bene perque manentem
855     nunc quoque cum pereo, causam mihi mortis, amorem:
        ne thalamis Auram patiare innubere nostris."
        dixit, et errorem tum denique nominis esse
        et sensi et docui. sed quid docuisse iuuabat?
        labitur, et paruae fugiunt cum sanguine uires.
860     dumque aliquid spectare potest, me spectat et in me
        infelicem animam nostroque exhalat in ore;
        sed uultu meliore mori secura uidetur.'
              flentibus haec lacrimans heros memorabat; et ecce
        Aeacus ingreditur duplici cum prole nouoque
865     milite, quem Cephalus consortibus accipit armis.
```

it was Procris and, holding the weapon in the middle of her breast,
"Ah me," she screamed. When I recognized it was the voice of my faithful
wife, I ran headlong and frantic to the voice;
I found her half-alive, her clothes spattered and stained   845
with blood and (wretch that I am) dragging her gift to me from
the wound, and with gentle arms I lifted up her body, dearer
to me than my own, tore her clothing from her breast,
bound up her cruel wounds and tried to stop the blood,
and begged her not to desert me shamed by her death.   850
She, in failing strength and already on the point of death, forced
herself to say these few words: "By the bonds of our bed
and by the gods above and by my own ones, by any service
I have done for you and by my love that remains even now
while I am dying and is the cause of my death, I beg, as a suppliant,   855
that you do not let Breeze marry into our bed."
She spoke, and then at last I realized her mistake
about the name and explained it to her. But how did it help to have explained it?
She was sinking, and her little strength was fleeing from her with her blood.
While she could still look at something, she looked at me   860
and breathed out her unhappy life onto me and in my mouth;
but she seemed to die relieved of care and with a better look upon her face.'
    The tearful hero was telling these things to them as they wept; and look,
Aeacus approached with his two offspring and fresh
soldiery, and Cephalus received them with shared arms.   865

LIBER VIII

Iam nitidum retegente diem noctisque fugante
tempora Lucifero cadit Eurus et umida surgunt
nubila; dant placidi cursum redeuntibus Austri
Aeacidis Cephaloque, quibus feliciter acti
ante exspectatum portus tenuere petitos.
    interea Minos Lelegeia litora uastat
praetemptatque sui uires Mauortis in urbe
Alcathoi, quam Nisus habet, cui splendidus ostro
inter honoratos medioque in uertice canos
crinis inhaerebat, magni fiducia regni.
sexta resurgebant orientis cornua lunae
et pendebat adhuc belli fortuna diuque
inter utrumque uolat dubiis Victoria pennis.
regia turris erat uocalibus addita muris,
in quibus auratam proles Letoia fertur
deposuisse lyram; saxo sonus eius inhaesit.
saepe illuc solita est ascendere filia Nisi
et petere exiguo resonantia saxa lapillo,
tum cum pax esset; bello quoque saepe solebat
spectare ex illa rigidi certamina Martis.
iamque mora belli procerum quoque nomina norat,
armaque equosque habitusque Cydoneasque pharetras.
nouerat ante alios faciem ducis Europaei,
plus etiam quam nosse sat est. hac iudice Minos,
seu caput abdiderat cristata casside pennis,
in galea formosus erat; seu sumpserat aere
fulgentem clipeum, clipeum sumpsisse decebat;
torserat adductis hastilia lenta lacertis,
laudabat uirgo iunctam cum uiribus artem;
imposito calamo patulos sinuauerat arcus,
sic Phoebum sumptis iurabat stare sagittis;
cum uero faciem dempto nudauerat aere
purpureusque albi stratis insignia pictis
terga premebat equi spumantiaque ora regebat,
uix sua, uix sanae uirgo Niseia compos
mentis erat: felix iaculum quod tangeret ille,
quaeque manu premeret felicia frena uocabat.
impetus est illi, liceat modo, ferre per agmen
uirgineos hostile gradus, est impetus illi
turribus e summis in Cnosia mittere corpus
castra uel aeratas hosti recludere portas,
uel si quid Minos aliud uelit. utque sedebat
candida Dictaei spectans tentoria regis,
'laeter' ait 'doleamne geri lacrimabile bellum
in dubio est; doleo quod Minos hostis amanti est
sed, nisi bella forent, numquam mihi cognitus esset.

BOOK 8

    Already Lucifer was revealing the gleaming day and making
the night-time flee, when the east wind fell and the moist clouds
rose; the gentle south winds gave good speed to the sons of
Aeacus and to Cephalus as they returned, and happily driven on by these
they arrived at the port they were seeking before they expected.   5
    Minos meanwhile was ravaging the Lelegeian shores
and trying out his martial strength on the city
of Alcathous which was ruled by Nisus, on the top of whose head
there clung among the honourable white hairs a lock
of bright purple, the guarantee of his great kingdom.   10
For the sixth time the horns of the rising moon were growing again,
and still the fate of the war was in the balance and for a long time
Victory flew between them both on undecided wings.
There was a royal tower, an addition to those speaking walls
on which Leto's offspring is said to have laid down   15
his gilded lyre; its sound clung to the stone.
Nisus' daughter often used to climb up there
and aim for the resounding walls with a little pebble
then, when there was peace; in war too she often used
to look from it at the contests of stern Mars.   20
And now, as the war dragged on, she knew even their nobles' names,
their weapons, horses, dress and Cydonean quivers.
She knew best of all the face of their leader, Europa's son,
more indeed than she needed to know him. Minos, in her judgement,
if he had hidden his head in a plume-crested helmet,   25
he was handsome in the head-piece; if he had taken up a gleaming
bronze shield, it suited him to have taken up the shield;
with arms drawn back he had hurled his pliant spears,
the maiden praised his skill and strength combined;
he had put a shaft to his broad bow and bent it back,   30
she swore that that was how Phoebus stood having taken up his arrows;
but when he had removed his bronze helmet and bared his face,
and in his purple was pressing down upon the back of his white horse,
glorious with its embroidered trappings, and was controlling its foaming mouth,
scarcely her own self, scarcely possessed of her right mind was   35
the Niseian maiden: she called his javelin lucky because it was touched by him,
and his reins lucky because they were pressed into his hand.
It was her impulse, if only it were allowed, to take her maiden's
steps through the enemy line, it was her impulse
to throw her body from the top of the towers into the Cnossian   40
camp, or to open the bronze gates to the enemy,
or anything else that Minos might wish. And as she sat down
and gazed upon the gleaming tents of the Dictaean king,
'I am in doubt,' she said, 'whether to rejoice or grieve that this lamentable
war is being waged; I grieve because Minos is an enemy to her who loves him,   45
but, if there had not been a war, he would never have been known to me.

LIBER VIII

  me tamen accepta poterat deponere bellum
  obside; me comitem, me pacis pignus haberet.
  si quae te peperit talis, pulcherrime regum,
50 qualis es ipse fuit, merito deus arsit in illa.
  o ego ter felix, si pennis lapsa per auras
  Cnosiaci possem castris insistere regis
  fassaque me flammasque meas qua dote rogarem
  uellet emi; tantum patrias ne posceret arces!
55 nam pereant potius sperata cubilia quam sim
  proditione potens—quamuis saepe utile uinci
  uictoris placidi fecit clementia uictis.
  iusta gerit certe pro nato bella perempto
  et causaque ualet causamque tenentibus armis
60 et, puto, uincemur. qui si manet exitus urbem,
  cur suus haec illi reseret mea moenia Mauors
  et non noster amor? melius sine caede moraque
  impensaque sui poterit superare cruoris;
  non metuam certe ne quis tua pectora, Minos,
65 uulneret imprudens. (quis enim tam durus ut in te
  derigere immitem non inscius audeat hastam?)
  coepta placent et stat sententia tradere mecum
  dotalem patriam finemque imponere bello;
  uerum uelle parum est. aditus custodia seruat
70 claustraque portarum genitor tenet; hunc ego solum
  infelix timeo, solus mea uota moratur.
  di facerent sine patre forem! sibi quisque profecto
  est deus; ignauis precibus Fortuna repugnat.
  altera iamdudum succensa cupidine tanto
75 perdere gauderet quodcumque obstaret amori.
  et cur ulla foret me fortior? ire per ignes
  et gladios ausim; nec in hoc tamen ignibus ullis
  aut gladiis opus est, opus est mihi crine paterno.
  ille mihi est auro pretiosior, illa beatam
80 purpura me uotique mei factura potentem.'
   talia dicenti curarum maxima nutrix
  nox interuenit tenebrisque audacia creuit.
  prima quies aderat, qua curis fessa diurnis
  pectora somnus habet; thalamos taciturna paternos
85 intrat et (heu facinus!) fatali nata parentem
  crine suum spoliat praedaque potita nefanda
  [fert secum spolium sceleris progressaque porta]
  per medios hostes (meriti fiducia tanta est)
  peruenit ad regem, quem sic adfata pauentem est:
90 'suasit amor facinus; proles ego regia Nisi
  Scylla tibi trado patriaeque meosque penates.
  praemia nulla peto nisi te; cape pignus amoris
  purpureum crinem nec me nunc tradere crinem,
  sed patrium tibi crede caput' scelerataque dextra
95 munera porrexit. Minos porrecta refugit
  turbatusque noui respondit imagine facti:

BOOK VIII [107

Still, he could lay aside the war if he took me
hostage; he would have me as his companion, me as a pledge of peace.
If she who bore you, most handsome of kings,
was such as you yourself are, the god was right to be on fire for her.   50
Oh three times happy would I be, if I could glide through the air
on wings and stand in the camp of the Cnossian king
and declare myself and the flames within me, and ask for what dowry
he would be willing to be bought; only let him not demand my father's citadel.
For rather let my hopes of the marriage bed perish than that I   55
achieve them by treachery—although often a mild conqueror's
clemency has made conquest profitable for the conquered.
He is surely waging a just war for the slaying of his son
and he is strong both in his cause and in the arms that uphold his cause,
and, I think, we shall be conquered. And if that is the outcome that awaits the city,   60
why is it to be his warfare that opens up our walls to him
and not my love? He will be able to overcome better without
slaughter and delay and the expenditure of his own blood;
I shall at least not be afraid that someone may unwittingly, Minos,
wound your breast. (For who is so harsh that he would,   65
unless unawares, dare to direct his pitiless spear at you?)
What I have begun is well, and my decision stands to hand over both myself
and my native land as a dowry, and to put an end to the war;
but to wish it is not enough. Guards protect the approaches
and my father holds the keys to the gates; he is the only one that I,   70
unhappy one, fear, he alone delays my hopes.
If only the gods would make me to be without a father! But, of course, each of us
is his own god; Fortune fights against slothful prayers.
Another girl, alight with so great a desire, would for a long time now
have been joyfully destroying whatever stood in the way of her love.   75
And why would any girl be braver than me? I would dare to go
through fire and the sword; but in this case there is no need
for any fires or swords, I need a lock of my father's hair.
That is more precious to me than gold; that purple
will make me blest through the achievement of my hopes.'   80
    So she spoke till night, the greatest nurse
of cares, broke in upon her, and boldness grew with the darkness.
The first rest had come, when sleep holds breasts
tired from the cares of day; silently she entered her father's
bed chamber and (what a crime!) the daughter despoiled her own   85
father of his lock and, having gained the abominable prize,
[she took the spoils of her crime with her and, having left the gate,]
she came through the middle of the enemy to the king (so great
was her confidence in her deserts), and spoke to the horrified man:
'Love urged me to the crime; I, the royal child of Nisus,   90
Scylla, hand over to you my native land's penates and my own.
I seek no reward but you; take as a pledge of my love
the purple lock, and do not think of me now as handing over
a lock to you but my father's head,' and the sinful girl proffered
her gift in her right hand. Minos shrank back from what was proffered   95
and, shocked by the sight of this novel act, replied,

'di te submoueant, o nostri infamia saecli,
orbe suo, tellusque tibi pontusque negetur.
certe ego non patiar Iouis incunabula, Creten,
qui meus est orbis, tantum contingere monstrum.'
dixit et, ut leges captis iustissimus auctor
hostibus imposuit, classis retinacula solui
iussit et aeratas impelli remige puppes.
    Scylla freto postquam deductas nare carinas
nec praestare ducem sceleris sibi praemia uidit,
consumptis precibus uiolentam transit in iram
intendensque manus passis furibunda capillis
'quo fugis' exclamat 'meritorum auctore relicta,
o patriae praelate meae, praelate parenti?
quo fugis immitis, cuius uictoria nostrum
et scelus et meritum est? nec te data munera nec te
noster amor mouit nec quod spes omnis in unum
te mea congesta est? nam quo deserta reuertar?
in patriam? superata iacet. sed finge manere:
proditione mea clausa est mihi. patris ad ora?
quem tibi donaui. ciues odere merentem,
finitimi exemplum metuunt. obstruximus orbem
terrarum, nobis ut Crete sola pateret.
hac quoque si prohibes et nos, ingrate, relinquis,
non genetrix Europa tibi est sed inhospita Syrtis,
Armeniae tigres austroque agitata Charybdis.
nec Ioue tu natus nec mater imagine tauri
ducta tua est (generis falsa est ea fabula); uerus
[et ferus et captus nullius amore iuuencae]
qui te progenuit taurus fuit. exige poenas,
Nise pater! gaudete malis modo prodita nostris
moenia! nam, fateor, merui et sum digna perire.
sed tamen ex illis aliquis quos impia laesi
me perimat. cur qui uicisti crimine nostro
insequeris crimen? scelus hoc patriaeque patrique est,
officium tibi sit. te uere coniuge digna est,
quae toruum ligno decepit adultera taurum
discordemque utero fetum tulit. ecquid ad aures
perueniunt mea dicta tuas, an inania uenti
uerba ferunt idemque tuas, ingrate, carinas?
iam iam Pasiphaen non est mirabile taurum
praeposuisse tibi; tu plus feritatis habebas.
me miseram! properare iubet diuulsaque remis
unda sonat mecumque simul mea terra recedit.
nil agis, o frustra meritorum oblite meorum;
insequar inuitum puppimque amplexa recuruam
per freta longa trahar.' uix dixerat, insilit undis
consequiturque rates faciente cupidine uires
Cnosiacaeque haeret comes inuidiosa carinae.
quam pater ut uidit (nam iam pendebat in aura
et modo factus erat fuluis haliaeetus alis),

'May the gods remove you,' oh scandal of our age,
from their world, and may both earth and sea be denied to you.
I certainly shall not allow Jove's cradle, Crete,
which is my world, to be touched by so great a monster. 100
He spoke, and, when with most just authority he had imposed laws
upon his captured enemy, he ordered the moorings of his fleet
to be untied and that his oarsmen drive his bronze-beaked boats away.
    After Scylla saw the ships launched and floating
on the sea and that their leader was not granting her the rewards of her crime, 105
and when she had used up her prayers she turned to violent anger
and, stretching out her hands in a frenzy, with her hair flowing loose,
'Where are you fleeing', she cried out, 'leaving the author of your success,
oh you who were preferred to my native land, preferred to my father?
Where are you fleeing, pitiless one, whose victory is both my sin 110
and my merit? Have neither the services I gave moved you,
nor my love, nor the fact that all my hope was
built on you alone? For, if I am abandoned, where am I to turn?
To my fatherland? It lies defeated. But suppose it did remain:
it is closed to me by my treachery. To face my father? 115
But I delivered him to you. The citizens hate me, deservedly;
the neighbouring peoples are afraid of my example. I blocked off
the world, for Crete alone to be open to me.
If you bar me from here too and, ungrateful one, leave me,
your mother was not Europa but inhospitable Syrtis, 120
Armenian tigresses, or Charybdis stirred up by the south wind.
Nor were you born to Jove nor was your mother seduced
by the guise of a bull (that story of your family is false); a true[,
wild, captivated by no heifer's love]
bull it was that fathered you. Exact your punishment, 125
Nisus, my father! Rejoice in my woes, oh walls I have just now
betrayed. For, I admit it, I have earned it, and I merit death.
But even so, let one of those that I have impiously harmed
destroy me. Why should you, who have conquered through my crime,
pursue the crime? Let what was a sin to my fatherland and father 130
be a service in your eyes. She truly deserved you for a husband,
the adulteress who tricked the grim bull with wood
and bore a discordant offspring in her womb. Do my words
reach your ears at all, or do the same winds
bear off my empty words, ungrateful one, and your ships? 135
Now, now it is not to be wondered at that Pasiphae preferred
the bull to you; you will have shown more savagery.
Unhappy me! He orders haste and the water cleft
by the oars resounds, and my land and I too are receding.
You are achieving nothing, vainly forgetful of my services; 140
I shall pursue you against your will and, by clinging to your curved stern,
I shall be dragged through the sea.' She had hardly spoken when she leapt
into the waves and, with desire bringing her strength, caught the ships up
and clung, a hated companion to the Cnossian boat.
And when her father saw her (for he was already hovering in the breeze 145
and had just been made into a sea-eagle with tawny wings),

LIBER VIII

        ibat ut haerentem rostro laceraret adunco.
        illa metu puppim dimisit et aura cadentem
        sustinuisse leuis, ne tangeret aequora, uisa est;
150   *pluma fuit; plumis* in auem mutata uocatur
        Ciris et a tonso est hoc nomen adepta capillo.
           uota Ioui Minos taurorum corpora centum
        soluit, ut egressus ratibus Curetida terram
        contigit, et spoliis decorata est regia fixis.
155   creuerat opprobrium generis foedumque patebat
        matris adulterium monstri nouitate biformis;
        destinat hunc Minos thalami remouere pudorem
        multiplicique domo caecisque includere tectis.
        Daedalus ingenio fabrae celeberrimus artis
160   ponit opus turbatque notas et lumina flexa
        ducit in errorem uariarum ambage uiarum,
        non secus ac liquidis Phrygius Maeandrus in undis
        ludit et ambiguo lapsu refluitque fluitque
        occurrensque sibi uenturas aspicit undas
165   et nunc ad fontes, nunc ad mare uersus apertum
        incertas exercet aquas: ita Daedalus implet
        innumeras errore uias uixque ipse reuerti
        ad limen potuit; tanta est fallacia tecti.
        quo postquam geminam tauri iuuenisque figuram
170   clausit et Actaeo bis pastum sanguine monstrum
        tertia sors annis domuit repetita nouenis,
        utque ope uirginea nullis iterata priorum
        ianua difficilis filo est inuenta relecto,
        protinus Aegides rapta Minoide Diam
175   uela dedit comitemque suam crudelis in illo
        litore destituit. desertae et multa querenti
        amplexus et opem Liber tulit, utque perenni
        sidere clara foret, sumptam de fronte coronam
        immisit caelo; tenues uolat illa per auras
180   dumque uolat gemmae nitidos uertuntur in ignes
        consistuntque loco, specie remanente coronae,
        qui medius Nixique genu est Anguemque tenentis.
           Daedalus interea Creten longumque perosus
        exilium tactusque soli natalis amore
185   clausus erat pelago. 'terras licet' inquit 'et undas
        obstruat, at caelum certe patet; ibimus illac!
        omnia possideat, non possidet aera Minos.'
        dixit et ignotas animum dimittit in artes
        naturamque nouat. nam ponit in ordine pennas,
190   [a minima coeptas, longam breuiore sequenti,]
        ut cliuo creuisse putes; sic rustica quondam
        fistula disparibus paulatim surgit auenis.
        tum lino medias et ceris alligat imas
        atque ita compositas paruo curuamine flectit
195   ut ueras imitetur aues. puer Icarus una

he went to tear at her with his curved beak as she clung there.
In her fear she let go of the stern, and a light breeze
seemed as she fell to hold her up so that she would not touch the sea;
there was plumage; when she was, *by her plumage*, changed into a bird, she was called
Ciris, and she acquired this name from the cutting of the hair. 151
    Minos paid his vows to Jove, a hundred head
of bulls, as he came off his ships and touched the Curetan
land, and he hung up his spoils to adorn his palace.
His family's dishonour had grown and the mother's disgusting 155
adultery was being exposed by the novelty of the two-formed monster;
Minos determined to remove this shame upon his marriage
and to shut it away in a house of many turns and blind rooms.
Daedalus, most famous for his talent in the craftsman's art,
set the building up, but confused its signs and led the eye 160
into error with the twisted ramblings of its many ways,
just as the Phrygian Meander plays in its clear
waters, flowing and flowing back in an uncertain course,
meeting up with itself and looking at its own approaching waves,
and driving its uncertain waters on, turned now towards its source, 165
now towards the open sea: so Daedalus filled
his countless ways with confusion and could himself scarcely
return to the entrance; so great was the deception of the structure.
And after he had shut into it the twin shape of bull
and young man, and the monster, twice fed on Actaean blood, 170
had been subdued by the third of the nine-yearly allotted groups,
and, by a maiden's help, the difficult gate, seen again
by none of those before, had been found by retracing a thread,
at once Aegeus' son took Minos' daughter and set sail
for Dia and cruelly abandoned his companion 175
on that shore. To the deserted and much complaining girl
Liber brought caresses and help, and, that she might be
famous with her own fixed star, he took the crown from her forehead
and set it up into the sky; it flies through the thin air
and as it flies its gems are turned into gleaming fires 180
and, keeping the appearance of a crown, they stay in their place
which is between the knee Flexer and the Snake holder.
    Daedalus meanwhile detested Crete and his long
exile and, though affected by a longing for his native soil,
had been shut off from it by the sea. 'He can block off', he said, 'the lands 185
and seas, but the sky at least is open. We shall go that way!
Though he may possess everything, Minos does not possess the air.'
He spoke and, directing his thoughts to skills unknown,
he changed nature. For he put feathers in a row
[beginning from the smallest, with the shorter following the long] 190
so that you would think they had grown on a slope; so does the rustic
pipe gradually expand with unequal stalks.
Then he bound them together in the middle and at the base with a thread and wax,
and when they had been arranged so, he bent them to a slight curve
to imitate real birds. His boy, Icarus, was with him 195

stabat et, ignarus sua se tractare pericla,
ore renidenti modo quas uaga mouerat aura
captabat plumas, flauam modo pollice ceram
mollibat lusuque suo mirabile patris
200 impediebat opus. postquam manus ultima coepto
imposita est, geminas opifex librauit in alas
ipse suum corpus motaque pependit in aura.
instruit et natum 'medio' que 'ut limite curras,
Icare,' ait 'moneo, ne, si demissior ibis,
205 unda grauet pennas, si celsior, ignis adurat.
inter utrumque uola, nec te spectare Booten
aut Helicen iubeo strictumque Orionis ensem;
me duce carpe uiam.' pariter praecepta uolandi
tradit et ignotas umeris accommodat alas.
210 inter opus monitusque genae maduere seniles
et patriae tremuere manus. dedit oscula nato
non iterum repetenda suo pennisque leuatus
ante uolat comitique timet, uelut ales ab alto
quae teneram prolem produxit in aera nido;
215 hortaturque sequi damnosasque erudit artes.
[et mouet ipse suas et nati respicit alas.]
hos aliquis tremula dum captat harundine pisces
aut pastor baculo stiuaue innixus arator
uidit et obstipuit, quique aethera carpere possent
220 credidit esse deos. et iam Iunonia laeua
parte Samos (fuerant Delosque Parosque relictae),
dextra Lebinthos erat fecundaque melle Caiymne,
cum puer audaci coepit gaudere uolatu
deseruitque ducem caelique cupidine tractus
225 altius egit iter. rapidi uicinia solis
mollit odoratas, pennarum uincula, ceras.
tabuerant cerae; nudos quatit ille lacertos
remigioque carens non ullas percipit auras,
oraque caerulea patrium clamantia nomen
230 excipiuntur aqua, quae nomen traxit ab illo.
at pater infelix nec iam pater 'Icare,' dixit
'Icare,' dixit 'ubi es? qua te regione requiram?'
'Icare' dicebat: pennas aspexit in undis
deuouitque suas artes corpusque sepulcro
235 condidit; est tellus a nomine dicta sepulti.
       hunc miseri tumulo ponentem corpora nati
garrula limoso prospexit ab elice perdix
et plausit pennis testataque gaudia cantu est,
unica tum uolucris nec uisa prioribus annis
240 factaque nuper auis, longum tibi, Daedale, crimen.
namque huic tradiderat fatorum ignara docendam
progeniem germana suam, natalibus actis
bis puerum senis, animi ad praecepta capacis.
ille etiam medio spinas in pisce notatas
245 traxit in exemplum ferroque incidit acuto

BOOK VIII [113

standing there and, unaware that he was handling his own danger,
was now with shining face trying to catch the feathers moved
by the wandering breeze, and now softening the yellow wax
with his thumb, and hindering his father's amazing work
with his play. After he had put the last touch   200
to what he had begun, the craftsman balanced his own body
on a pair of wings and hovered in the air they were moving.
And he fitted out his son and, 'I warn you, Icarus,' he said,
'to run on the middle path in case, if you go too low,
the water weighs down your wings, and, if too high, the sun's fire burns them. 205
Fly between each of them and do not, I tell you, look at
Boötes or Helice or Orion's drawn sword;
pick your way where I lead.' At the same time he gave him flying
instructions and fitted the unfamiliar wings to his shoulders.
In the midst of his work and warnings, the old man's cheeks grew wet   210
and the father's hands shook. He gave kisses to his son
that would never be repeated and, lifted on his wings,
he flew in front and feared for his companion, like a bird who has
led her tender offspring from a high nest into the air,
and he urged him to follow and trained him in ruinous skills.   215
[He both moved his own wings and looked back at his son's.]
And someone while trying to catch fish with a trembling rod,
or a shepherd leaning on his staff, or a ploughman on his shaft
saw them and was dumbfounded and, since they could press through the air,
believed that they were gods. And now Juno's Samos   220
was on the left side (Delos and Paros had been put behind them)
and Lebinthos was on the right as was honey-rich Calymne,
when the boy, beginning to enjoy his bold flight,
deserted his leader and, drawn by a desire for the heavens,
took too high a course. The nearness of the raging sun   225
softened the sweet-smelling wax that bound his wings.
The wings had melted; he shook his bare arms
but, lacking oarage, he did not grip the air at all,
but, with his mouth crying out his father's name, he was received
by the aquamarine water, which took its name from him.   230
But the unhappy father, not now a father, said, 'Icarus,'
'Icarus,' he said, 'where are you? In what region should I seek you?'
'Icarus,' he was saying; and caught sight of feathers in the waves
and cursed his skills and buried the body
in a tomb; the land was called after the name of the boy in the tomb. 235
    As he was placing the body of his unhappy son in the burial mound,
a chattering partridge looked out from a muddy ditch
and clapped with her wings and testified to her joy with a song.
She was then a unique bird, not seen in earlier years,
but recently made a bird and, Daedalus, a long standing reproach to you. 240
For, unaware of fate, his sister had handed
her offspring to him to be taught, a boy who had had
twice six birthdays with a mind receptive to instruction.
He even noticed the spine in the middle of a fish
and, taking it as his pattern, cut teeth all along   245

perpetuos dentes et serrae repperit usum;
primus et ex uno duo ferrea bracchia nodo
uinxit ut aequali spatio distantibus illis
altera pars staret, pars altera duceret orbem.
250 Daedalus inuidit sacraque ex arce Mineruae
praecipitem misit lapsum mentitus; at illum
quae fauet ingeniis excepit Pallas auemque
reddidit et medio uelauit in aere pennis.
sed uigor ingenii quondam uelocis in alas
255 inque pedes abiit; nomen, quod et ante, remansit.
non tamen haec alte uolucris sua corpora tollit
nec facit in ramis altoque cacumine nidos;
propter humum uolitat ponitque in saepibus oua
antiquique memor metuit sublimia casus.
260   iamque fatigatum tellus Aetnaea tenebat
Daedalon et sumptis pro supplice Cocalus armis
mitis habebatur, iam lamentabile Athenae
pendere desierant Thesea laude tributum.
templa coronantur bellatricemque Mineruam
265 cum Ioue disque uocant aliis, quos sanguine uoto
muneribusque datis et acerris turis honorant.
sparserat Argolicas nomen uaga fama per urbes
Theseos, et populi quos diues Achaïa cepit
huius opem magnis implorauere periclis;
270 huius opem Calydon, quamuis Meleagron haberet,
sollicita supplex petiit prece. causa petendi
sus erat, infestae famulus uindexque Dianae.
Oenea namque ferunt pleni successibus anni
primitias frugum Cereri, sua uina Lyaeo,
275 Palladios flauae latices libasse Mineruae.
coeptus ab agricolis superos peruenit ad omnes
ambitiosus honor; solas sine ture relictas
praeteritae cessasse ferunt Latoidos aras.
tangit et ira deos; 'at non impune feremus,
280 quaeque inhonoratae, non et dicemur inultae'
inquit et Olenios ultorem spreta per agros
misit aprum, quanto maiores herbida tauros
non habet Epiros, sed habent Sicula arua minores.
sanguine et igne micant oculi, riget horrida ceruix,
285 [et saetae similes rigidis hastilibus horrent.
stantque uelut uallum, uelut alta hastilia saetae.]
feruida cum rauco latos stridore per armos
spuma fluit, dentes aequantur dentibus Indis,
fulmen ab ore uenit, frondes adflatibus ardent.
290 is modo crescentes segetes proculcat in herba,
nunc matura metit fleturi uota coloni
et Cererem in spicis intercipit; area frustra
et frustra exspectant promissas horrea messes.
sternuntur grauidi longo cum palmite fetus
295 bacaque cum ramis semper frondentis oliuae.

a strip of sharp iron and invented the saw and its use;
he was the first also to bind two arms to one
hinge so that, when they stood apart at a fixed distance,
one side stood still and the other side drew a circle.
Daedalus was jealous and threw him head first from Minerva's 250
sacred citadel, and told a lie that he had slipped; but he
was caught by Pallas, who favours talent, and turned him
into a bird and, in mid-air, covered him in feathers.
But the vigour of his former quick talent went
to his wings and feet; his name remained even as before. 255
But this bird does not lift its body high
and does not make its nest in branches or high tree-tops;
it flies near the ground and lays its eggs in hedgerows
and, remembering its ancient fall, is afraid to be aloft.
    And now the land of Etna was keeping wearied 260
Daedalus, and Cocalus, by taking arms up for his suppliant,
was held to be lenient, now too Athens had stopped,
praise be to Theseus, paying their mournful tribute.
They garlanded the temples and called on the warrior 264
Minerva together with Jove and the other gods and honoured them with the blood
they had vowed and with the gift of offerings and caskets of incense.
Wandering rumour had spread the name of Theseus throughout the cities,
of the Argolid, and the peoples contained by rich Achaea
in their great perils begged for his help;
suppliant Calydon, though having Meleager, sought his help 270
in anxious prayer. The reason that they sought it
was a pig, the servant and avenger of outraged Diana.
They say that Oeneus had, for the successes of a plenteous year,
made offerings of the first-fruits of grain to Ceres, of his wines to Lyaeus,
and of Pallas' oil to fair haired Minerva. 275
The coveted honour came to all the gods
beginning with the farming ones; they say that only Leto's daughter
was passed over, her altars idle, left without incense.
Anger affects gods too; 'But we shall not let it go unpunished,
and, though dishonoured, we shall not also be called unavenged,' 280
she said, and to avenge being spurned she sent through the Olenian
fields a boar than which grassy Epirus has
bulls no bigger, but the Sicilian fields have smaller ones.
His eyes gleamed with blood and fire, his bristling neck was rigid[,
and his coarse hairs bristled like rigid spears. 285
And his coarse hairs stood like a palisade, like tall spears].
Boiling foam flowed over his broad shoulders
with a strident hiss, his tusks were the equal of Indian tusks,
lightning came from his mouth, the foliage caught fire from his breath.
First he trampled down the growing crops in the blade, 290
then he made the farmer weep by mowing down his ripe hopes
and cutting Ceres off in the ears; the threshing floor in vain,
in vain the barns waited for the promised harvest.
The swelling clusters with their long tendrils were flattened
and the berry of the ever-green olive together with its branches. 295

saeuit et in pecudes; non has pastorue canisue,
non armenta truces possunt defendere tauri.
diffugiunt populi nec se nisi moenibus urbis
esse putant tutos, donec Meleagros et una
300 lecta manus iuuenum coiere cupidine laudis:
Tyndaridae gemini, spectandus caestibus alter,
alter equo, primaeque ratis molitor Iason
et cum Pirithoo, felix concordia, Theseus
et duo Thestiadae prolesque Aphareia Lynceus
305 et uelox Idas et iam non femina Caeneus
Leucippusque ferox iaculoque insignis Acastus
Hippothousque Dryasque et cretus Amyntore Phoenix
Actoridaeque pares et missus ab Elide Phyleus.
nec Telamon aberat magnique creator Achillis
310 cumque Pheretiade et Hyanteo Iolao
impiger Eurytion et cursu inuictus Echion
Naryciusque Lelex Panopeusque Hyleusque feroxque
Hippasus et primis etiamnum Nestor in annis
et quos Hippocoon antiquis misit Amyclis
315 Penelopaeque socer cum Parrhasio Ancaeo
Ampycidesque sagax et adhuc a coniuge tutus
Oeclides nemorisque decus Tegeaea Lycaei.
rasilis huic summam mordebat fibula uestem,
crinis erat simplex, nodum collectus in unum,
320 ex umero pendens resonabat eburnea laeuo
telorum custos, arcum quoque laeua tenebat.
talis erat cultus; facies, quam dicere uere
uirgineam in puero, puerilem in uirgine possis.
hanc pariter uidit, pariter Calydonius heros
325 optauit renuente deo flammasque latentes
hausit et 'o felix, si quem dignabitur' inquit
'ista uirum!' nec plura sinit tempusque pudorque
dicere; maius opus magni certaminis urget.
      silua frequens trabibus, quam nulla ceciderat aetas,
330 incipit a plano deuexaque prospicit arua;
quo postquam uenere uiri, pars retia tendunt,
uincula pars adimunt canibus, pars pressa sequuntur
signa pedum cupiuntque suum reperire periclum.
concaua uallis erat, quo se demittere riui
335 adsuerant pluuialis aquae; tenet ima lacunae
lenta salix uluaeque leues iuncique palustres
uiminaque et longa paruae sub harundine cannae.
hinc aper excitus medios uiolentus in hostes
fertur ut excussis elisi nubibus ignes.
340 sternitur incursu nemus et propulsa fragorem
silua dat; exclamant iuuenes praetentaque forti
tela tenent dextra lato uibrantia ferro.
ille ruit spargitque canes, ut quisque furenti
obstat, et obliquo latrantes dissipat ictu.
345   cuspis Echionio primum contorta lacerto

BOOK VIII [117

He savaged the flocks too; neither shepherd nor dog could
protect them, nor the fierce bulls their herds.
The people fled away and did not think that they were safe
except within the city's walls, until Meleager with
a chosen band of young men came together in lust for renown: 300
Tyndareus' twin sons, one celebrated for the boxing gloves,
the other for his horse, the first ship's architect, Jason,
and, with Pirithous, together in happy harmony, Theseus,
Thestius' two sons, the offspring of Aphareus, Lynceus
and swift Idas, Caeneus, not now a woman, 305
fierce Leucippus, Acastus noted for his javelin,
Hippothous and Dryas, and Phoenix sprung from Amyntor,
Actor's pair of sons, and Phyleus sent from Elis.
Nor was Telamon absent, nor great Achilles' begetter,
and, with Pheres' son and Hyantean Iolaus, 310
there was tireless Eurytion, Echion unsurpassed in running,
Narycian Lelex, Panopeus, Hyleus, fierce
Hippasus, Nestor still in his first years,
those that Hippocoon sent from ancient Amyclae,
Penelope's father-in-law with Parrhasian Ancaeus, 315
Ampyx' shrewd son, Oecleus' son still safe
from his wife, and the Tegean girl, the glory of the Lycaean copse.
A burnished pin bit into the top of her cloak,
the style of her hair was simple, gathered in a single knot,
an ivory arrow case resounded as it hung 320
from her left shoulder, and her left hand held her bow too.
Such was her dress; her face was one that you could truly
say was maidenly in a boy, and boyish in a maid.
The moment that he saw her was the moment the Calydonian hero
desired her, though god disapproved, and, drinking down the hidden 325
flames, he said, 'Oh happy the man, if she will think any
worthy to be her husband!' Time and modesty allowed him to say
no more; the greater task of a great conflict drove him on.
A wood, crowded with tree trunks, which no generation had cut down,
starting level looked down over fields that sloped away from it; 330
and when the men came to it, some stretched their nets,
some slipped the leashes from their dogs, some followed deep
foot-prints and wanted to discover their own danger.
There was a hollow valley where streams of rain water
used to plunge down; the bottom of this depression was taken up 335
by pliant willow, light sedge, marsh rushes,
osiers and short reeds under tall bulrushes.
From here the savage boar was roused up into the midst of his enemies
and borne along, like fires struck from the clouds as they are shaken out.
The copse was flattened by his onset and the wood, thrust forward, 340
gave out a crash; the young men cried out and in strong right hands
held their weapons, flashing with broad iron, stretched out before them.
He charged and scattered the dogs as each stood in the way
of his frenzy, and, as they barked, he dispersed them with a sidelong blow.
    First a speartip was sent whirling by Echion's arm, 345

uana fuit truncoque dedit leue uulnus acerno.
proxima, si nimiis mittentis uiribus usa
non foret, in tergo uisa est haesura petito;
longius it. (auctor teli Pagasaeus Iason.)
350 'Phoebe,' ait Ampycides 'si te coluique coloque,
da mihi quod petitur, certo contingere telo.'
qua potuit, precibus deus adnuit: ictus ab illo est,
sed sine uulnere, aper; ferrum Diana uolanti
abstulerat iaculo, lignum sine acumine uenit.
355 ira feri mota est, nec fulmine lenius arsit;
emicat ex oculis, spirat quoque pectore flamma,
utque uolat moles adducto concita neruo
cum petit aut muros aut plenas milite turres,
in iuuenes certo sic impete uulnificus sus
360 fertur et Hippalmon Pelagonaque dextra tuentes
cornua prosternit; socii rapuere iacentes.
at non letiferos effugit Enaesimus ictus
Hippocoonte satus; trepidantem et terga parantem
uertere succiso liquerunt poplite nerui.
365 forsitan et Pylius citra Troiana perisset
tempora, sed sumpto posita conamine ab hasta
arboris insiluit, quae stabat proxima, ramis
despexitque loco tutus quem fugerat hostem.
dentibus ille ferox in querno stipite tritis
370 imminet exitio fidensque recentibus armis
Eurytidae magni rostro femur hausit adunco.
at gemini, nondum caelestia sidera, fratres,
ambo conspicui, niue candidioribus ambo
uectabantur equis, ambo uibrata per auras
375 hastarum tremulo quatiebant spicula motu.
uulnera fecissent, nisi saetiger inter opacas
nec iaculis isset nec equo loca peruia siluas.
persequitur Telamon studioque incautus eundi
pronus ab arborea cecidit radice retentus.
380 dum leuat hunc Peleus, celerem Tegeaea sagittam
imposuit neruo sinuatoque expulit arcu;
fixa sub aure feri summum destrinxit harundo
corpus et exiguo rubefecit sanguine saetas.
nec tamen illa sui successu laetior ictus
385 quam Meleagros erat; primus uidisse putatur
et primus sociis uisum ostendisse cruorem
et 'meritum' dixisse 'feres uirtutis honorem.'
erubuere uiri seque exhortantur et addunt
cum clamore animos iaciuntque sine ordine tela;
390 turba nocet iactis et quos petit impedit ictus.
ecce furens contra sua fata bipennifer Arcas
'discite femineis quid tela uirilia praestent,
o iuuenes, operique meo concedite;' dixit
'ipsa suis licet hunc Latonia protegat armis,
395 inuita tamen hunc perimet mea dextra Diana.'

BOOK VIII [119

it was in vain and gave only a light wound to the trunk of a maple tree.
The next one, if it had not used up too much of its thrower's
strength, seemed to be about to strike into the hide where he was aiming;
it went too far. (The thrower of the weapon was Pagasaean Jason.)
'Phoebus,' said Ampyx' son, 'if I have worshipped and do worship you,   350
grant me what I am aiming at, to hit him with my sure weapon.'
As far as he could, the god assented to his prayers: the boar was struck
by him but without injury; Diana had taken the iron
from the javelin in flight, and the shaft arrived without its point.
The wild beast's anger was aroused and burnt no more gently than lightning;   355
it flashed from his eyes, and flame breathed from his breast,
and, as a boulder flies when driven by the taut cord
when seeking either walls or towers full of soldiery,
with such a sure attack was the injury-making pig borne into
the young men, and he threw down Hippalmos and Pelagon who were protecting   360
the right flank; their companions snatched them as they lay there.
But Enaesimus did not escape the death-dealing blows,
he was Hippocoon's son; as he trembled and prepared to turn
his back, his sinews failed him when his knee tendon was severed.
Perhaps the Pylian too would have perished on that side of Trojan   365
times, but, taking the thrust from the placing of his spear,
he leapt into the branches of the tree which stood closest to him,
and from there he looked down in safety upon the enemy he had escaped.
Fiercely he scraped his tusks on the trunk of an oak,
bent on destruction, and, trusting in these refreshed weapons,   370
he gouged out the thigh of Eurytus' great son with his hooked snout.
But the twin brothers, not yet heavenly stars,
both resplendent, were both riding on horses
whiter than snow, were both shaking their spears with
quivering movement as the points flashed through the air.   375
They would have inflicted injuries if the bristle-bearer had not gone among
the dark woods, to places where neither javelin nor horse can penetrate.
Telamon followed after and, in his enthusiasm and careless of where he was going,
fell down flat, caught by the root of a tree.
While Peleus was raising him up, the Tegean girl put a swift   380
arrow to her bowstring and, bending the bow, shot it out;
the shaft lodged under the wild beast's ear, grazing the surface of his body, and
reddened his bristles with a little blood.
But she was no happier at the success of her shot
than Meleager was; he is thought to have seen it first   385
and to have been the first to show his companions the blood he had seen,
and to have said, 'Deservedly will you win honour for your manliness.'
The men flushed and urged one another on and added
spirit together with shouting and threw their weapons haphazardly;
their thronging hurt the shots they had made and impeded those they were attempting.
Look, the Arcadian of the double axe, raging beyond his fate,   391
said, 'Learn how much men's weapons surpass women's,
young men, and make way for me to act;
though Latonia herself protect him with her weapons,
my right hand will still destroy him against Diana's will.'   395

talia magniloquo tumidus memorauerat ore
ancipitemque manu tollens utraque securim
institerat digitis, primos suspensus in artus;
occupat audentem, quaque est uia proxima leto,
400 summa ferus geminos derexit ad inguina dentes.
concidit Ancaeus glomerataque sanguine multo
uiscera lapsa fluunt; madefacta est terra cruore.
ibat in aduersum proles Ixionis hostem
Pirithous, ualida quatiens uenabula dextra;
405 cui 'procul' Aegides 'o me mihi carior,' inquit
'pars animae consiste meae! licet eminus esse
fortibus; Ancaeo nocuit temeraria uirtus.'
dixit et aerata torsit graue cuspide cornum;
quo bene librato uotique potente futuro
410 obstitit aesculea frondosus ab arbore ramus.
misit et Aesonides iaculum, quod casus ab illo
uertit in immeriti fatum latrantis et inter
ilia coniectum tellure per ilia fixum est.
        at manus Oenidae uariat, missisque duabus
415 hasta prior terra, medio stetit altera tergo.
nec mora, dum saeuit, dum corpora uersat in orbem
stridentemque nouo spumam cum sanguine fundit,
uulneris auctor adest hostemque irritat ad iram
splendidaque aduersos uenabula condit in armos.
420 gaudia testantur socii clamore secundo
uictricemque petunt dextrae coniungere dextram,
immanemque ferum multa tellure iacentem
mirantes spectant neque adhuc contingere tutum
esse putant, sed tela tamen sua quisque cruentat.
425 ipse pede imposito caput exitiabile pressit
atque ita 'sume mei spolium, Nonacria, iuris'
dixit 'et in partem ueniat mea gloria tecum.'
protinus exuuias rigidis horrentia saetis
terga dat et magnis insignia dentibus ora.
430 illi laetitiae est cum munere muneris auctor;
inuidere alii totoque erat agmine murmur.
e quibus ingenti tendentes bracchia uoce
'pone age nec titulos intercipe, femina, nostros.'
Thestiadae clamant 'nec te fiducia formae
435 decipiat, ne sit longe tibi captus amore
auctor;' et huic adimunt munus, ius muneris illi.
non tulit et tumida frendens Mauortius ira
'discite, raptores alieni' dixit 'honoris,
facta minis quantum distent!' hausitque nefando
440 pectora Plexippi nil tale timentia ferro.
Toxea quid faciat dubium pariterque uolentem
ulcisci fratrem fraternaque fata timentem
haud patitur dubitare diu calidumque priori
caede recalfecit consorti sanguine telum.
445   dona deum templis nato uictore ferebat,

So had he spoken, puffed up by his eloquence,
and, lifting the two headed axe in both hands,
he had stood on tiptoe, raised up on the extremities of his legs;
he was forestalled in his daring by the wild beast who directed his twin
tusks to the top of his groin, which is the closest path to death. 400
Ancaeus fell and his guts, all rolled in with much
blood, slipped flowing out; the earth was drenched with gore.
There came against the advancing enemy Ixion's offspring,
Pirithous, shaking his mighty hunting spear in his right hand;
and to him, 'Away,' said Aegeus' son, 'oh dearer to me than my own self, 405
part of my soul, stay put! To stand at long range is allowed
to the brave; it was rash courage that hurt Ancaeus.'
He spoke and hurled his cornel spear heavy with its bronze tip;
but, though he aimed it well and it was about to fulfil his wish,
it was impeded by a leafy branch from an oak tree. 410
Aeson's son too threw a javelin which chance turned away
from the beast to be the undeserved fate of a barker; hurled
between its flanks, it stuck through its flanks into the ground.
     But the hand of Oeneus' son had varying luck; he threw two
spears, the first landed on the ground, the second in the middle of his hide. 415
And without delay, while he raged, while he turned his body in a circle
and gushed out hissing foam and fresh blood,
the author of the wound was there provoking his enemy to anger
and planting his shining hunting spear into the advancing shoulders.
His companions testified to their joy with a supportive shout 420
and sought to join right hand to right hand with the victor,
and, as the vast beast lay on so much ground,
they gazed at it in wonder and still did not think it safe
to touch it, but each still bloodied his own weapon.
He himself, placing his foot on its destructive head, pressed down on it 425
and spoke thus, 'Take up the spoil, Nonacria, rightly mine,
and let my glory be shared with you.'
At once he gave her trophies, the hide bristling
with stiff coarse hairs and the mouth remarkable for its great tusks.
She was delighted by the gift and by the gift's author; 430
others were jealous and there was murmuring in the whole company.
And from among them, Thestius' sons, stretching out their arms, cried out
with a huge shout, 'Come, put them down, and do not, woman, purloin
our glory. And don't let yourself be deceived by trust in your
beauty, in case the author of your gift, though held by your love, is 435
far away from you.' From her they took the gift and the rights over the gift from him.
The son of Mars did not endure it, and gnashing in seething anger,
'Learn,' he said, 'you plunderers of others' honour,
how far deeds are from threats!' And he gouged out with his accursed
sword the breast of Plexippus who was fearing no such thing. 440
Toxeus was hesitating what to do, wanting to avenge
his brother and, equally, fearing his brother's fate;
but he did not let him hesitate for long, but rewarmed in the brother's
blood his weapon still warm from the earlier slaughter.
     She was bearing gifts for her son's victory to the temple of the gods, 445

```
            cum uidet extinctos fratres Althaea referri,
            quae plangore dato maestis clamoribus urbem
            implet et auratis mutauit uestibus atras;
            at simul est auctor necis editus, excidit omnis
450         luctus et a lacrimis in poenae uersus amorem est.
            stipes erat quem, cum partus enixa iaceret
            Thestias, in flammam triplices posuere sorores
            staminaque impresso fatalia pollice nentes
            'tempora' dixerunt 'eadem lignoque tibique,
455         o modo nate, damus.' quo postquam carmine dicto
            excessere deae, flagrantem mater ab igne
            eripuit ramum sparsitque liquentibus undis.
            ille diu fuerat penetralibus abditus imis
            seruatusque tuos, iuuenis, seruauerat annos.
460         protulit hunc genetrix taedasque et fragmina poni
            imperat et positis inimicos admouet ignes.
            tum conata quater flammis imponere ramum
            coepta quater tenuit; pugnant materque sororque
            et diuersa trahunt unum duo nomina pectus.
465         saepe metu sceleris pallebant ora futuri,
            saepe suum feruens oculis dabat ira ruborem,
            et modo nescioquid similis crudele minanti
            uultus erat, modo quem misereri credere posses;
            cumque ferus lacrimas animi siccauerat ardor,
470         inueniebantur lacrimae tamen. utque carina
            quam uentus uentoque rapit contrarius aestus
            uim geminam sentit paretque incerta duobus,
            Thestias haud aliter dubiis adfectibus errat
            inque uices ponit positamque resuscitat iram.
475         incipit esse tamen melior germana parente
            et, consanguineas ut sanguine leniat umbras,
            impietate pia est. nam postquam pestifer ignis
            conualuit, 'rogus iste cremet mea uiscera' dixit
            utque manu dira lignum fatale tenebat,
480         ante sepulcrales infelix astitit aras
            'poenarum' que 'deae triplices, furialibus,' inquit
            'Eumenides, sacris uultus aduertite uestros.
            ulciscor facioque nefas; mors morte pianda est,
            in scelus addendum scelus est, in funera funus;
485         per coaceruatos pereat domus impia luctus.
            an felix Oeneus nato uictore fruetur,
            Thestius orbus erit? melius lugebitis ambo.
            uos modo, fraterni manes animaeque recentes,
            officium sentite meum magnoque paratas
490         accipite inferias, uteri mala pignora nostri.
            ei mihi, quo rapior? fratres, ignoscite matri!
            deficiunt ad coepta manus. meruisse fatemur
            illum, cur pereat; mortis mihi displicet auctor.
            ergo impune feret uiuusque et uictor et ipso
495         successu tumidus regnum Calydonis habebit,
```

BOOK VIII [123

when Althaea saw her brothers being brought back dead.
She gave out a wail filling the city with mournful
cries, and changed her golden clothes for black ones.
But when she was told the author of their death, all her grief
fell away and she was turned from tears to a passion for punishing.   450
There was a stick which, when Thestius' daughter lay in
childbirth, the threefold sisters placed in the flame
and, as they applied the thumb to spin the threads of fate,
'The same time,' they said, 'oh newly born, do we give to the wood
and to you.' After saying their solemn piece,   455
the goddesses withdrew and the mother snatched the blazing
branch from the fire and sprinkled it with pure water.
It had been hidden for a long time in the depths of the inner rooms
and its preservation had, young man, preserved your years.
The mother brought it out and ordered pinewood and shavings   460
to be set, and, when they were set, she applied harmful fire to them.
Then she tried four times to put the branch on the flames
and four times she stopped what she had begun; mother and sister fought
and two conflicting words tugged at one breast.
Often her face paled with fear at the crime that was to be,   465
often her burning anger gave its flush to her eyes,
and sometimes she had an expression like one threatening
something cruel, sometimes the sort you could have believed was pitying;
and when the wild fire in her mind had dried her tears
tears were still found, and, as a boat   470
driven by wind and wind-opposing tide
feels their twin violence and uncertainly obeys them both,
just do did Thestius' daughter waver between shifting emotions
and in turn checked her anger and, when it was checked, roused it up again.
And yet she began to be a better sister than parent   475
and, in order to appease the shades of her blood with blood,
she was impiously pious. For when the baleful fire
grew strong, 'Let that pyre burn my flesh,' she said
and, as she held the fateful wood in her grim hand,
she stood unhappy before the sepulchral altars   480
and, 'Three-fold goddesses of punishment ,' she said, 'turn,
Eumenides, your faces to the rites of fury.
I avenge and commit a sin; death must be by death expiated,
crime must be added to crime, a funeral to funerals;
Let the impious house perish from its heaped up griefs.   485
Is lucky Oeneus to enjoy his victorious son,
and is Thestius to be bereaved? Better will you both grieve.
Oh you, my brothers' shades and fresh ghosts, only
be aware of my service and receive my funeral offerings
prepared at such cost, the evil pledge of my womb.   490
Ah me, where am I rushing? Brothers, forgive a mother!
My hands have not the strength for what they have begun. I admit
that he has deserved to perish; but to be the author of his death dismays me.
So will he then get away unpunished, and will he, alive, victorious and puffed-up
with that very success, hold the kingdom of Calydon,   495

[124] LIBER VIII

uos cinis exiguus gelidaeque iacebitis umbrae?
haud equidem patiar; pereat sceleratus, et ille
spemque patris regnumque trahat patriaeque ruinam.
mens ubi materna est? ubi sunt pia iura parentum
500 et quos sustinui bis mensum quinque labores?
o utinam primis arsisses ignibus infans,
idque ego passa forem! uixisti munere nostro,
nunc merito moriere tuo. cape praemia facti
bisque datam, primum partu, mox stipite rapto
505 redde animam, uel me fraternis adde sepulcris.
et cupio et nequeo. quid agam? modo uulnera fratrum
ante oculos mihi sunt et tantae caedis imago,
nunc animum pietas maternaque nomina frangunt.
me miseram! male uincetis, sed uincite, fratres,
510 dummodo quae dedero uobis solacia uosque
ipsa sequar.' dixit dextraque auersa trementi
funereum torrem medios coniecit in ignes.
aut dedit aut uisus gemitus est ipse dedisse
stipes et inuitis correptus ab ignibus arsit.
515   inscius atque absens flamma Meleagros ab illa
uritur et caecis torreri uiscera sentit
ignibus ac magnos superat uirtute dolores.
quod tamen ignauo cadat et sine sanguine leto
maeret et Ancaei felicia uulnera dicit
520 grandaeuumque patrem fratresque piasque sorores
cum gemitu sociamque tori uocat ore supremo,
forsitan et matrem. crescunt ignisque dolorque
languescuntque iterum; simul est extinctus uterque,
inque leues abiit paulatim spiritus auras
525 paulatim cana prunam uelante fauilla.
      alta iacet Calydon: lugent iuuenesque senesque
uulgusque proceresque gemunt scissaeque capillos
planguntur matres Calydonides Eueninae.
puluere canitiem genitor uultusque seniles
530 foedat humi fusus spatiosumque increpat aeuum;
nam de matre manus diri sibi conscia facti
exegit poenas acto per uiscera ferro.
non, mihi si centum deus ora sonantia linguis
ingeniumque capax totumque Helicona dedisset,
535 tristia persequerer miserarum uota sororum.
immemores decoris liuentia pectora tundunt
dumque manet corpus, corpus refouentque fouentque.
oscula dant ipsi, posito dant oscula lecto;
post cinerem cineres haustos ad pectora pressant
540 adfusaeque iacent tumulo signataque saxo
nomina complexae lacrimas in nomina fundunt.
quas Parthaoniae tandem Latonia clade
exsatiata domus praeter Gorgenque nurumque
nobilis Alcmenae natis in corpore pennis
545 alleuat et longas per bracchia porrigit alas

and will you lie there, a tiny bit of ash and cold shades?
No, I shall not allow it; let the villain perish and let him
take with him his father's hope, his kingdom and the ruin of his fatherland.
Where is my maternal heart? Where are parents' pious obligations
and the pains I endured for twice five months? 500
Oh would that you had burnt as a baby in those first fires,
and would that I had allowed it! It was by my gift that you have lived,
now through your deserts you will die. Take the reward for your deed,
and the life twice given (first at birth, then when I snatched
the stick) give it back, or add me to my brothers' tombs. 505
I both want to act and cannot. What shall I do? At one point my brothers' wounds
are before my eyes and the image of such great slaughter,
now piety and the word mother break my resolve.
Unhappy me! Your victory will be evil, but be victorious, my brothers,
provided only that I myself may follow you and the solace 510
I shall give you.' She spoke and, as she turned away, with her trembling right hand
she threw the deadly brand into the middle of the fire.
The stick itself either gave or seemed to give
groans and, seized by the unwilling fires, it caught alight.
  Though unaware and absent, Meleager was burnt by that 515
flame and felt his flesh scorched by unseen
fires, but he overcame the great pains with his courage.
And yet that he was falling to an ignoble death without bloodshed
was grievous to him, and he called Ancaeus' wounds happy
and, with a groan, he summoned his aged father, his brothers, 520
his pious sisters and, with his last words, the companion of his marriage bed,
perhaps his mother too. The fire and pain grew
and subsided again; both were extinguished together,
and his spirit slowly went away into the light air
as a white ash slowly clothed the embers. 525
  High Calydon was brought down: young men and old men grieved,
the common people and the nobles groaned, the Calydonian mothers,
daughters of Euenus, tore their hair and beat their breasts.
His father, prostrate on the ground, defiled his grey head
and his old man's face with dust, and inveighed against his vast age; 530
for, from guilt at her dreadful deed, her hand had exacted
punishment from the mother by driving a sword through her bowels.
Not, if god had given me a hundred mouths with sounding
tongues and talent to match and all of Helicon,
would I catch the sad prayers of his unhappy sisters. 535
Unmindful of decorum, they beat their breasts to a livid hue
and, while the body remained, they caressed and recaressed the body.
Kisses they gave to him, and they gave kisses to the bier when it was in place;
when he was ash, they scooped the ashes up and pressed them to their breasts,
and lay prostrate on the burial mound and embraced his name 540
carved in the stone and poured their tears upon his name.
And Latonia, satisfied at last by the disaster
to the Parthaonian house, lifted them up on feathers that had sprung up
over their bodies, except for Gorge and the daughter-in-law of famous
Alcmena, and she stretched long wings over their arms 545

corneaque ora facit uersasque per aera mittit.
    interea Theseus sociati parte laboris
functus Erectheas Tritonidos ibat ad arces.
clausit iter fecitque moras Achelous eunti
imbre tumens. 'succede meis,' ait 'inclite, tectis, 550
Cecropide, nec te committe rapacibus undis.
ferre trabes solidas obliquaque uoluere magno
murmure saxa solent. uidi contermina ripae
cum gregibus stabula alta trahi, nec fortibus illic
profuit armentis nec equis uelocibus esse. 555
multa quoque hic torrens niuibus de monte solutis
corpora turbineo iuuenalia uertice mersit.
tutior est requies, solito dum flumina currant
limite, dum tenues capiat suus alueus undas.'
adnuit Aegides 'utor,' que 'Acheloe, domoque 560
consilioque tuo' respondit; et usus utroque est.
    pumice multicauo nec leuibus atria tophis
structa subit; molli tellus erat umida musco,
summa lacunabant alterno murice conchae.
iamque duas lucis partes Hyperione menso 565
discubuere toris Theseus comitesque laborum;
hac Ixionides, illa Troezenius heros
parte Lelex, raris iam sparsus tempora canis,
quosque alios parili fuerat dignatus honore
amnis Acarnanum, laetissimus hospite tanto. 570
protinus appositas nudae uestigia nymphae
instruxere epulis mensas dapibusque remotis
in gemma posuere merum. tum maximus heros
aequora prospiciens oculis subiecta 'quis' inquit
'ille locus?' (digitoque ostendit) 'et insula nomen 575
quod gerit illa, doce; quamquam non una uidetur.'
amnis ad haec 'non est' inquit 'quod cernitis unum;
quinque iacent terrae; spatium discrimina fallit.
quoque minus spretae factum mirere Dianae,
naides hae fuerant, quae cum bis quinque iuuencos 580
mactassent rurisque deos ad sacra uocassent,
immemores nostri festas duxere choreas.
intumui, quantusque feror cum plurimus umquam
tantus eram pariterque animis immanis et undis
a siluis siluas et ab aruis arua reuelli, 585
cumque loco nymphas memores tum denique nostri
in freta prouolui. fluctus nosterque marisque
continuam diduxit humum partesque resoluit
in totidem, mediis quot cernis Echinadas undis.
ut tamen ipse uides, procul en procul una recessit 590
insula, grata mihi; Perimelen nauita dicit.
huic ego uirgineum dilectae nomen ademi;
quod pater Hippodamas aegre tulit inque profundum
propulit e scopulo periturae corpora natae.
excepi nantemque ferens 'o proxima mundi 595

and made their mouths bony and sent them, changed, through the air.
    Theseus meanwhile now that he had performed his part of the
shared task was going to Tritonis' Erechthean citadel.
Achelous, swollen by a rainstorm, blocked his path and brought
delay to him as he went. 'Step into my house,' he said, 'famed 550
son of Cecrops and do not expose yourself to my rapacious waters.
They are wont to carry off whole tree-trunks and to roll rocks
sideways with great rumbling. I have seen high sheep pens
bordering the bank swept away flocks and all, nor there was it any help
to the herds to be strong nor to the horses to be swift. 555
When too the snows melt on the mountain, this torrent
has overwhelmed many young men's bodies in a swirling eddy.
It is safer to rest until the river runs within its usual
limits, till its proper channel holds its narrow waters.'
Aegaeus' son nodded in agreement and, 'I am using, Achelous, 560
your home and your advice,' he replied; and he used them both.
    The hall he entered was built of many-holed pumice
and rough tufa, the earth floor was damp with soft moss,
alternating conch and murex shells panelled the top.
And now, when Hyperion had measured two thirds of the day, 565
Theseus and his companions in toil reclined on the couches;
on this side was Ixion's son, on that the Troezenian
hero, Lelex, whose temples were already sprinkled here and there with white,
and the others deemed worthy of a like honour
by the Acarnanians' river, who was delighted to have so great a guest. 570
At once bare footed nymphs set up tables
and spread them for a feast and, when the banquet had been cleared away,
set down pure wine in jewelled cups. Then the great hero,
looking out over the sea stretched out beneath his eyes, said, 'What
is that place?' (and he pointed with his finger) 'Teach me 575
the name that island bears; although it does not seem to be just one.'
To this the river said, 'What you are looking at is not one;
there are five lands lying out there; the distance disguises the distinction.
And to make you wonder less at the act of the spurned Diana,
these were naiads, and when they had sacrificed twice five 580
bullocks and summoned the country gods to their rites,
they led the festal dances unmindful of me.
I swelled up with rage, and was as full as I ever am
borne along at my fullest and, with my anger and my waters equally out of hand,
I tore woods from woods and fields from fields, 585
and the nymphs, then at last mindful of me, I rolled,
together with the places where they were, out into the sea. My flood and the sea's
split their solid ground apart and loosened it into as many
parts as are the Echinades you are looking at in the middle of the waves.
But as you see yourself, one island, has withdrawn a distance, look, 590
a distance, it is my favourite; the sailor calls it Perimele.
I adored her and took the name of virgin from her;
but her father, Hippodamas, bore it ill and pushed
his daughter's body from a cliff into the deep, to die.
I caught her and bore her as she swam saying, 'Oh trident-bearer, 595

regna uagae' dixi 'sortite tridentifer undae,
[in quo desinimus, quot sacri currimus amnes,
huc ades atque audi placidus, Neptune, precantem.
huic ego, quam porto, nocui. si mitis et aequus,
600 si pater Hippodamas, aut si minus impius esset,
600a debuit illius misereri, ignoscere nobis.
600b cui quoniam tellus clausa est feritate paterna]
adfer opem mersaeque, precor, feritate paterna
da, Neptune, locum—uel sit locus ipsa licebit[—
hanc quoque complectar].' [mouit caput aequoreus rex
concussitque suis omnes adsensibus undas.
605 extimuit nymphe, nabat tamen; ipse natantis
pectora tangebam trepido salientia motu.
dumque ea contrecto, totum durescere sensi
corpus et inductis condi praecordia terris.]
dum loquor, amplexa est artus noua terra natantes
610 et grauis increuit mutatis insula membris.'
  amnis ab his tacuit. factum mirabile cunctos
mouerat; inridet credentes, utque deorum
spretor erat mentisque ferox, Ixione natus:
'ficta refers nimiumque putas, Acheloe, potentes
615 esse deos,' dixit 'si dant adimuntque figuras.'
obstipuere omnes nec talia dicta probarunt,
ante omnesque Lelex animo maturus et aeuo
sic ait: 'immensa est finemque potentia caeli
non habet et quidquid superi uoluere peractum est.
620 quoque minus dubites, tiliae contermina quercus
collibus est Phrygiis, modico circumdata muro.
(ipse locum uidi, nam me Pelopeia Pittheus
misit in arua suo quondam regnata parenti.)
haud procul hinc stagnum est, tellus habitabilis olim,
625 nunc celebres mergis fulicisque palustribus undae.
Iuppiter huc specie mortali cumque parente
uenit Atlantiades positis caducifer alis.
mille domos adiere locum requiemque petentes,
mille domos clausere serae. tamen una recepit,
630 parua quidem stipulis et canna tecta palustri,
sed pia; Baucis anus parilique aetate Philemon
illa sunt annis iuncti iuuenalibus, illa
consenuere casa paupertatemque fatendo
effecere leuem nec iniqua mente ferendo.
635 nec refert, dominos illic famulosne requiras:
tota domus duo sunt, idem parentque iubentque.
  'ergo ubi caelicolae paruos tetigere penates
submissoque humiles intrarunt uertice postes,
membra senex posito iussit releuare sedili,
640 cui superiniecit textum rude sedula Baucis.
inde foco tepidum cinerem dimouit et ignes
suscitat hesternos foliisque et cortice sicco
nutrit et ad flammas anima producit anili,

BOOK VIII [129

you who were allotted the kingdom next after the sky, that of the wandering wave,
[in whom we, all the sacred rivers that run, come to an end,
be present, Neptune, and graciously hear me as I pray.
I have hurt this girl that I am carrying. If he were gentle and fair,
if Hippodamas were fatherly, or if he were less impious, 600
he ought to have pitied her and forgiven us. 600a
But since her land is closed to her by a father's savagery,] 600b
bring her help and, I pray, since she was overwhelmed by a father's savagery,
grant her, Neptune, a place—or she may be herself a place[—
and also that I embrace her].' [The sea king moved his head
and shook all his waves with his agreement.
The nymph was terrified but still swam on; as she swam, I myself 605
was touching her breasts that quivered in a trembling motion.
And while I fondled them I felt her whole body
grow hard, and earth came over her abdomen and covered it.]
While I spoke, new earth embraced her limbs as they swam
and a heavy island grew from her body as it was changed. 610
    With this the river fell silent. The amazing event had moved
them all; Ixion's son mocked them for believing it,
being both a spurner of the gods and fierce in mind:
'You are telling falsehoods, and, Achelous, you think the gods
too powerful,' he said, 'if they give and take away forms.' 615
All were dumbfounded and did not approve such words,
and Lelex, who was mature in mind and age above them all,
spoke thus: 'Immeasurable is the power of heaven and it has
no limit, and whatever the gods want is brought about.
And, that you may be less in doubt, there is a linden tree close up against an oak 620
in the Phrygian hills, surrounded by a modest wall.
(I have seen the place myself for Pittheus sent me
to the fields of Pelops once reigned over by his father.)
Not far from there is a pond, once habitable land,
now water crowded with gulls and marsh coots. 625
Jupiter came here in mortal form as did, with his father,
the staff-bearer, grandson of Atlas, with his wings laid aside.
A thousand homes were approached by them in search of room and rest,
a thousand homes were shut and barred. But one took them in,
a small one, indeed, thatched with straw and marsh reed, 630
but pious; Baucis, an old woman, and Philemon, of like age,
had there in that hut been joined in the years of their youth, and there
had grown old together and, by admitting their poverty
and by bearing it with patient mind, had made it light.
And it did not matter there whether you looked for masters or slaves, 635
those two were the whole household, both alike obeyed and gave the orders.
    And so, when the heavenly-dwellers had reached the small penates
and dropped their heads to enter the low doorway,
the old man told them to rest their limbs on a seat he had placed for them
while Baucis bustled to throw a rough cloth over it. 640
And then she parted the warm ash in the hearth, roused
yesterday's fire, fed it with dry leaves and
bark, made it burst into flames with her old woman's breath,

	multifidasque faces ramaliaque arida tecto
645	detulit et minuit paruoque admouit aeno,
	quodque suus coniunx riguo collegerat horto
	truncat holus foliis; furca leuat ille bicorni
	sordida terga suis nigro pendentia tigno
	seruatoque diu resecat de tergore partem
650	exiguam sectamque domat feruentibus undis.
	interea medias fallunt sermonibus horas
	sentirique moram prohibent. erat alueus illic
	fagineus, dura clauo suspensus ab ansa;
	is tepidis impletur aquis artusque fouendos
655a	accipit. in medio torus est de mollibus uluis
656a	impositus lecto sponda pedibusque salignis;
655	[concutiuntque torum de molli fluminis ulua
656	impositum lecto sponda pedibusque salignis;]
	uestibus hunc uelant quas non nisi tempore festo
	sternere consuerant, sed et haec uilisque uetusque
	uestis erat, lecto non indignanda saligno.
660	accubuere dei. mensam succincta tremensque
	ponit anus, mensae sed erat pes tertius impar;
	testa parem fecit, quae postquam subdita cliuum
	sustulit, aequatam mentae tersere uirentes.
	ponitur hic bicolor sincerae baca Mineruae
665	conditaque in liquida corna autumnalia faece
	intibaque et radix et lactis massa coacti
	ouaque non acri leuiter uersata fauilla,
	omnia fictilibus; post haec caelatus eodem
	sistitur argento crater fabricataque fago
670	pocula, qua caua sunt, flauentibus inlita ceris.
	parua mora est, epulasque foci misere calentes;
	nec longae rursus referuntur uina senectae
	dantque locum mensis paulum seducta secundis.
	hic nux, hic mixta est rugosis carica palmis
675	prunaque et in patulis redolentia mala canistris
	et de purpureis collectae uitibus uuae;
	candidus in medio fauus est. super omnia uultus
	accessere boni nec iners pauperque uoluntas.
	'interea totiens haustum cratera repleri
680	sponte sua per seque uident succrescere uina;
	attoniti mouitate pauent manibusque supinis
	concipiunt Baucisque preces timidusque Philemon
	et ueniam dapibus nullisque paratibus orant.
	unicus anser erat, minimae custodia uillae,
685	quem dis hospitibus domini mactare parabant;
	ille celer penna tardos aetate fatigat
	eluditque diu tandemque est uisus ad ipsos
	confugisse deos. superi uetuere necari
	"di" que "sumus, meritasque luet uicinia poenas
690	impia;" dixerunt "uobis immunibus huius
	esse mali dabitur. modo uestra relinquite tecta

BOOK VIII [131

brought much-split kindling and dry twigs down
from the roof, chopped them up and put them under a small bronze pot, 645
and stripped the leaves from a cabbage which her husband
had pulled from his well-watered garden; with a two-pronged fork, he lifted down
a sooty side of bacon hanging from a blackened beam,
and cut from the long preserved chine a very small
piece and cut it up and softened what he had cut in the boiling water. 650
Meanwhile, they beguiled the intervening hours with conversations
and stopped the delay from being noticed. There was a tub there
of beechwood, hung by a nail from a stout handle;
it was filled with warm water and received their limbs
to soothe them. A bolster of soft sedge was placed 655a
in the middle of a couch with frame and feet of willow; 655b
and they shook the bolster of soft river sedge 655
[after placing it on the couch with frame and feet of willow;]
they covered it with draperies which were not usually spread
except at festal time, but even this was mean and old
drapery, not to be thought unworthy of the willow bed.
The gods reclined. The old woman, girt up and trembling, 660
placed a table there, but the table's third foot was uneven;
a potsherd made it equal, and when it had been put beneath to correct
the slope, green mint wiped the levelled surface.
On it she placed berries of pure Minerva, half-ripe,
autumn cornels preserved in clear wine-lees, 665
endives, radish, a lump of cheese,
and eggs lightly turned in ash no longer sharply hot,
all in earthenware; after this she set up a mixing-bowl
in the same engraved silver and cups fashioned
out of beech and smeared in the hollow part with yellow wax. 670
There was a slight delay, and then the hearth produced the hot feast;
and again wine of no great age was brought out
and taken away for a little to give room for a second course.
Here were nuts, here figs mixed with wrinkled dates,
plums and fragrant apples in flat baskets, 675
and grapes picked from purple vines;
in the middle was a white honeycomb. Above them all there was in addition
a look of goodness in their faces and a willingness neither sluggish nor mean.
　　　Meanwhile, they saw, as often as it was drained, the mixing-bowl
refilled of its own accord, and the wine replenished by itself; 680
stunned and fearful at the strangeness of it, Baucis and timid
Philemon uttered prayers with hands upturned
and begged pardon for their feast and lack of preparation.
There was a single goose, the guardian of the tiny house,
and its owners were preparing to sacrifice it to their divine guests; 685
but it was quick on the wing and wore them out, slowed as they were by
age, and it eluded them for a long time until at last it seemed to have taken refuge
with the gods themselves: the heavenly ones forbade that it be killed,
and, "We are gods," they said, "and your impious neighbourhood will pay
the penalties it deserves; to you it will be granted to be 690
exempt from this evil. Just leave your house

LIBER VIII

	ac nostros comitate gradus et in ardua montis
	ite simul." parent ambo baculisque leuati
693a	[ite simul." parent et dis praeeuntibus ambo
693b	membra leuant baculis tardique senilibus annis]
	nituntur longo uestigia ponere cliuo.
695	tantum aberant summo, quantum semel ire sagitta
	missa potest; flexere oculos et mersa palude
	cetera prospiciunt, tantum sua tecta manere.
	dumque ea mirantur, dum deflent fata suorum,
	illa uetus dominis etiam casa parua duobus
700	uertitur in templum; furcas subiere columnae,
	stramina flauescunt aurataque tecta uidentur
	caelataeque fores adopertaque marmore tellus.
	talia tum placido Saturnius edidit ore:
	"dicite, iuste senex et femina coniuge iusto
705	digna, quid optetis." cum Baucide pauca locutus
	iudicium superis aperit commune Philemon:
	"esse sacerdotes delubraque uestra tueri
	poscimus, et quoniam concordes egimus annos,
	auferat hora duos eadem, nec coniugis umquam
710	busta meae uideam neu sim tumulandus ab illa."
	uota fides sequitur; templi tutela fuere,
	donec uita data est. annis aeuoque soluti
	ante gradus sacros cum starent forte locique
	narrarent casus, frondere Philomena Baucis,
715	Baucida conspexit senior frondere Philemon.
	iamque super geminos crescente cacumine uultus
	mutua, dum licuit, reddebant dicta "uale" que
	"o coniunx" dixere simul, simul abdita texit
	ora frutex. ostendit adhuc Thyneius illic
720	incola de gemino uicinos corpore truncos.
	haec mihi non uani (neque erat cur fallere uellent)
	narrauere senes; equidem pendentia uidi
	serta super ramos ponensque recentia dixi:
	"cura deum di sint, et qui coluere colantur."'
725	desierat, cunctosque et res et mouerat auctor,
	Thesea praecipue; quem facta audire uolentem
	mira deum innixus cubito Calydonius amnis
	talibus adloquitur: 'sunt, o fortissime, quorum
	forma semel mota est et in hoc renouamine mansit;
730	sunt quibus in plures ius est transire figuras,
	ut tibi, complexi terram maris incole, Proteu.
	nam modo te iuuenem, modo te uidere leonem;
	nunc uiolentus aper, nunc quem tetigisse timerent
	anguis eras; modo te faciebant cornua taurum;
735	saepe lapis poteras, arbor quoque saepe uideri,
	interdum faciem liquidarum imitatus aquarum
	flumen eras, interdum undis contrarius ignis.
	'nec minus Autolyci coniunx, Erysicthone nata,

and accompany our steps and come to the mountain
heights with us." They both obeyed and, supported by their staffs,
[heights with us." They obeyed and, with the gods preceding, both   693a
supported their limbs on staffs and, slowed by their aged years,]   693b
struggled to put their footsteps on the long slope.
They were as far from the top as a single arrow shot   695
can go; they turned their eyes and saw all the rest
overwhelmed by water, only their house remained.
And while they wondered at that, while they bewailed the fate of their people,
that old hut, small even for its two owners,
was turned into a temple; columns took the place of forked poles,   700
the straw turned yellow and the house seemed gilded,
the doors engraved and the ground paved with marble.
Then the Saturnian, in gracious tones, spoke thus:
"Tell us, just old man, and you, wife worthy of your just husband,
what you desire." After a few words with Baucis,   705
Philemon revealed to the gods their joint decision:
"We ask to be your priests and to protect your
shrine and, since we have spent our years in harmony together,
let the same hour take us both and may I never see
my wife's tomb nor let her need to make a burial mound for me."   710
Their prayers were fulfilled; they were the temple's guardians
as long as they were granted life. Weakened by years and age,
they chanced to be standing before the sacred steps telling
the story of the place, when Baucis noticed foliage growing
on Philemon, and elder Philemon foliage growing on Baucis.   715
And now, as the tree-top grew over their two faces,
they were exchanging, while they could, answering words and, "Farewell,
my own dear one," they said together, and together their mouths were hidden
by a bushy covering. The Thyneian dweller still shows there
the neighbouring trees from their two bodies.   720
I was told this by reliable old men (and there was no reason why
they should want to deceive); I have myself seen garlands
hanging on the branches and as I laid fresh ones I said:
'Let those who care for the gods be gods, and those who have worshipped be
                                                                            worshipped.'"
    He had stopped, and both the story and its teller had moved them all,   725
Theseus especially; and since he wanted to hear the gods'
wondrous deeds, the Calydonian river leaning on his elbow
spoke thus to him: 'There are, oh bravest of men, those
whose form was changed once and stayed in that new state;
there are those who have the right to change into many shapes,   730
as you do, Proteus, dweller in the land-embracing sea.
For they have seen you now as a young man, now as a lion;
now you were a savage boar, now a snake they would fear
to have touched; now horns made you into a bull;
often you could seem to be a stone, often too a tree,   735
sometimes you mimicked the appearance of flowing waters
and you were a river, sometimes the opposite of water, fire.
    And you, Autolycus' wife and Erysichthon's daughter, have

```
         iuris habet; pater huius erat, qui numina diuum
740      sperneret et nullos aris adoleret odores.
         ille etiam Cereale nemus uiolasse securi
         dicitur et lucos ferro temerasse uetustos.
         stabat in his ingens annoso robore quercus,
         una nemus; uittae mediam memoresque tabellae
745      sertaque cingebant, uoti argumenta potentum.
         saepe sub hac dryades festas duxere choreas,
         saepe etiam manibus nexis ex ordine trunci
         circuiere modum mensuraque roboris ulnas
         quinque ter implebat, nec non et cetera tantum
750      silua sub hac, silua quantum fuit herba sub omni.
         non tamen idcirco ferrum Triopeius illa
         abstinuit famulosque iubet succidere sacrum
         robur et, ut iussos cunctari uidit, ab uno
         edidit haec rapta sceleratus uerba securi:
755      "non dilecta deae solum, sed et ipsa licebit
         sit dea, iam tanget frondente cacumine terram."
         dixit et, obliquos dum telum librat in ictus,
         contremuit gemitumque dedit Deoia quercus,
         et pariter frondes, pariter pallescere glandes
760      coepere ac longi pallorem ducere rami.
         cuius ut in trunco fecit manus impia uulnus,
         haud aliter fluxit discusso cortice sanguis
         quam solet, ante aras ingens ubi uictima taurus
         concidit, abrupta cruor e ceruice profundi.
765      obstipuere omnes aliquisque ex omnibus audet
         deterrere nefas saeuamque inhibere bipennem.
         aspicit hunc "mentis" que "piae cape praemia!" dixit
         Thessalus inque uirum conuertit ab arbore ferrum
         detruncatque caput repetitaque robora caedit,
770      redditus e medio sonus est cum robore talis:
         "nympha sub hoc ego sum Cereri gratissima ligno,
         quae tibi factorum poenas instare tuorum
         uaticinor moriens, nostri solacia leti."
         persequitur scelus ille suum, labefactaque tandem
775      ictibus innumeris adductaque funibus arbor
         corruit et multam prostrauit pondere siluam.
                  'attonitae dryades damno nemorumque suoque,
         omnes germanae, Cererem cum uestibus atris
         maerentes adeunt poenamque Erysicthonis orant.
780      adnuit his capitisque sui pulcherrima motu
         concussit grauidis oneratos messibus agros
         moliturque genus poenae miserabile (si non
         ille suis esset nulli miserabilis actis)
         pestifera lacerare fame. quae quatenus ipsi
785      non adeunda deae est (neque enim Cereremque Famemque
         fata coire sinunt), montani numinis unam
         talibus agrestem compellat oreada dictis:
         "est locus extremis Scythiae glacialis in oris,
```

BOOK VIII [135

this right no less; her father was a man to spurn the power
of the gods and to burn no incense on their altars.   740
It is said that he had even violated Ceres' copse
with an axe and defiled her ancient groves with iron.
There stood in them a huge oak with the sturdiness of many years,
a copse in itself; fillets, votive tablets and garlands
girt the middle of it, proofs of those who had been granted their prayers.   745
Often the dryads led festal dances under it,
often too with hands linked they went around the tree's
extent in order, and the measure of the oak was fully
three times five ells, and also the rest of the wood
was as far below it as the grass was below the whole wood.   750
Yet, even so, Triopas' son did not keep his iron
away from it but ordered his attendants to cut down the sacred
oak and, when he saw that, though ordered, they delayed, the villain
seized an axe from one of them and uttered these words:
"Though it turns out to be not only beloved of the goddess but   755
a goddess itself, it will now touch the ground with its top."
He spoke, and, while he aimed the tool for blows from the side,
the Deoian oak trembled and gave a groan,
and at once its foliage at once its acorns began
to turn pale and its long branches took on a pallor.   760
And as the impious hand made a wound in its trunk,
blood flowed from the shattered bark just as
happens when a huge bull, a victim before the altars,
falls and gore streams out from the severed neck.
All were dumbfounded and one man out of all of them dared   765
to deter the sin and restrain the cruel double axe.
The Thessalian looked at him and, "Take," he said, "the reward for your pious
mind," and turned the iron from the tree to the man,
lopped off his head and went back to the oak and hacked at it,
when a sound was returned from the middle of the oak like this: 770
"I, the nymph inside this tree, am very dear to Ceres,
and, as I die, I prophesy that punishments are looming
for your deeds, a solace for my fate."
He persisted in his crime, and at last, weakened
by countless blows and tugged at by ropes, the tree   775
collapsed and brought down much of the wood with its weight.
          The dryads were stunned at the copses' loss and at their own,
all of them sisters, and, grieving and dressed in black,
they approached Ceres and begged for punishment for Erysichthon.
She nodded her assent and most beautiful as she moved her head   780
she shook the fields laden with the swelling harvest
and set in motion a pitiable sort of punishment (were he not
pitiable to no-one because of his actions)
to tear at him with baleful hunger. But inasmuch as the goddess
could not herself approach her (for the fates do not allow   785
Ceres and Hunger to come together), she appealed to one of the mountain
divinities, a rustic oread, with such words as these:
"There is a place in the furthest reaches of icy Scythia,

triste solum, sterilis, sine fruge, sine arbore tellus.
790 Frigus iners illic habitant Pallorque Tremorque
et ieiuna Fames; ea se in praecordia condat
sacrilegi scelerata iube, nec copia rerum
uincat eam superetque meas certamine uires.
neue uiae spatium te terreat, accipe currus,
795 accipe quos frenis alte moderere dracones."
et dedit. illa dato subuecta per aera curru
deuenit in Scythiam rigidique cacumine montis
(Caucason appellant) serpentum colla leuauit,
quaesitamque Famem lapidoso uidit in agro
800 unguibus et raras uellentem dentibus herbas.
hirtus erat crinis, caua lumina, pallor in ore,
labra incana situ, scabrae rubigine fauces,
dura cutis, per quam spectari uiscera possent;
ossa sub incuruis exstabant arida lumbis,
805 uentris erat pro uentre locus; pendere putares
pectus et a spinae tantummodo crate teneri;
auxerat articulos macies genuumque tumebat
orbis et immodico prodibant tubere tali.
hanc procul ut uidit (neque enim est accedere iuxta
810 ausa), refert mandata deae paulumque morata,
quamquam aberat longe, quamquam modo uenerat illuc,
uisa tamen sensisse famem est retroque dracones
egit in Haemoniam uersis sublimis habenis.
   'dicta Fames Cereris, quamuis contraria semper
815 illius est operi, peragit perque aera uento
ad iussam delata domum est et protinus intrat
sacrilegi thalamos altoque sopore solutum
(noctis enim tempus) geminis amplectitur ulnis
seque uiro inspirat faucesque et pectus et ora
820 adflat et in uacuis spargit ieiunia uenis;
functaque mandato fecundum deserit orbem
inque domos inopes adsueta reuertitur arua.
lenis adhuc Somnus placidis Erysicthona pennis
mulcebat; petit ille dapes sub imagine somni
825 oraque uana mouet dentemque in dente fatigat
exercetque cibo delusum guttur inani
proque epulis tenues nequiquam deuorat auras.
ut uero est expulsa quies, furit ardor edendi
perque auidas fauces incensaque uiscera regnat.
830 nec mora, quod pontus, quod terra, quod educat aer
poscit et appositis queritur ieiunia mensis
inque epulis epulas quaerit; quodque urbibus esse
quodque satis poterat populo non sufficit uni,
plusque cupit, quo plura suam demittit in aluum.
835 utque fretum recipit de tota flumina terra
nec satiatur aquis peregrinosque ebibit amnes,
utque rapax ignis non umquam alimenta recusat
innumerasque trabes cremat et, quo copia maior

the soil is harsh, the land barren without crops, without a tree.
Sluggish Cold lives there with Pallor and Tremor, 790
and starving Hunger too; tell her to plant herself
in his villainous, sacrilegious breast, let no plentifulness
defeat her and let her overcome my strength in the contest.
And so that the extent of the journey will not terrify you, take my chariot,
take my dragons and the bridle to control them on high." 795
And she gave them to her. She was conveyed through the air in the chariot given her
and came down in Scythia and, on the summit of the stark mountain
(they call it Caucasus), she released the serpents' necks;
searching for Hunger, she saw her in a stony field
tearing at the sparse vegetation with her fingernails and teeth. 800
Her hair was shaggy, she had hollow eyes, a pallid face,
lips white from disuse, throat raw and blighted,
and hard skin through which her bowels could be seen;
shrivelled bones stood out under her hollow loins,
her belly was a space for a belly; you would think her breasts 805
were hanging off and only just held up by the rib cage on her spine;
her thinness had enlarged her joints, her knee joints
were bulging and her ankles stood out immensely swollen.
When she saw her from afar (for she did not dare to approach
close up), she reported the goddess' commands and, as she delayed a little, 810
although she was far from her, although she had just come there,
even so she seemed to feel hunger and, using the reins to turn around,
she drove the snakes on high back to Haemonia.
    Hunger, although she is always opposed to Ceres'
work, carried out what she had said and was brought through the air 815
on the wind to the house as bidden and at once entered
the chamber of the sacrilegious man and, while he relaxed in deep sleep
(for it was night time), she embraced him in both her arms
and breathed herself into him, blew upon his throat, breast
and mouth, and spread starvation in his empty veins. 820
With her commands performed, she abandoned the fertile world
and returned to her impoverished home, the fields she was used to.
Gentle Sleep was still soothing Erysichthon with his quiet
wings; but he sought banquets in the visions of his sleep
and moved his empty mouth, wore tooth on tooth, 825
worked his deluded gullet on unreal food,
and vainly devoured thin air instead of feasts.
But when sleep was driven from him, he raged with a burning desire to eat
which ruled his greedy throat and his inflamed guts.
And without delay, he demanded the produce of the sea, of the land 830
and of the air, complained of famine when the tables were set before him,
and in the midst of feasting he looked for feasts; and what could
have been enough for cities, enough for a nation, did not suffice for one,
and the more he sent down to his belly, the more he wanted.
And as the sea receives rivers from the whole earth 835
but is never sated by the waters and drinks dry the distant streams,
and as rapacious fire does not ever refuse nourishment
but burns up countless logs, and the greater the supply

est data, plura petit turbaque uoracior ipsa est,
sic epulas omnes Erysicthonis ora profani
accipiunt poscuntque simul. cibus omnis in illo
causa cibi est, semperque locus fit inanis edendo.
    'iamque fame patrias altique uoragine uentris
attenuarat opes, sed inattenuata manebat
tum quoque dira fames implacataeque uigebat
flamma gulae. tandem, demisso in uiscera censu,
filia restabat, non illo digna parente.
hanc quoque uendit inops. dominum generosa recusat
et uicina suas tendens super aequora palmas
"eripe me domino, qui raptae praemia nobis
uirginitatis habes" ait (haec Neptunus habebat).
qui prece non spreta, quamuis modo uisa sequenti
esset ero, formamque nouat uultumque uirilem
induit et cultus piscem capientibus aptos.
hanc dominus spectans "o qui pendentia paruo
aera cibo celas, moderator harundinis," inquit
"sic mare compositum, sic sit tibi piscis in unda
credulus et nullos, nisi fixus, sentiat hamos:
quae modo cum uili turbatis ueste capillis
litore in hoc steterat (nam stantem in litore uidi)
dic ubi sit; neque enim uestigia longius exstant."
illa dei munus bene cedere sensit et a se
se quaeri gaudens his est resecuta rogantem:
"quisquis es, ignoscas; in nullam lumina partem
gurgite ab hoc flexi studioque operatus inhaesi.
quoque minus dubites, sic has deus aequoris artes
adiuuet, ut nemo iandudum litore in isto,
me tamen excepto, nec femina constitit ulla."
credidit et uerso dominus pede pressit harenam
elususque abiit; illi sua reddita forma est.
ast ubi habere suam transformia corpora sensit,
saepe pater dominis Triopeida tradit, at illa
nunc equa, nunc ales, modo bos, modo ceruus abibat
praebebatque auido non iusta alimenta parenti.
uis tamen illa mali postquam consumpserat omnem
materiam deerantque graui noua pabula morbo,
ipse suos artus lacero diuellere morsu
coepit et infelix minuendo corpus alebat.
    'quid moror externis? etiam mihi nempe nouandi est
corporis, o iuuenis, numero finita potestas.
nam modo qui nunc sum uideor, modo flector in anguem,
armenti modo dux uires in cornua sumo—
cornua, dum potui. nunc pars caret altera telo
frontis, ut ipse uides.' gemitus sunt uerba secuti.

given the more it seeks and it is more voracious from its very abundance,
so did blaspheming Erysichthon's mouth take in every   840
feast and, at the same time, demand more. All food was
in him a reason for more food, and his eating always made an empty place.
    And now, through his hunger and the deep chasm of his belly, he had exhausted
his ancestral wealth, but even then his dreadful hunger
remained unexhausted and the flame of his appetite   845
thrived insatiably. At last, when he had sent his fortune down into his guts,
his daughter was left; she did not deserve him for a father.
Impoverished, he sold her too. The high-born girl refused to have a master
and, stretching her hands out over the sea nearby,
"Snatch me from my master, oh you who have the prize   850
of my snatched virginity," she said (Neptune it was who had it),
and he did not spurn her prayer and, although she had only just been seen
by her pursuing lord, he changed her form and put a man's face
on her and the dress appropriate to those catching fish.
Her master looked at her and said, "Oh you who hide   855
your dangling bronze in a little food, you, wielder of the rod,
so may the sea be calm for you and may the fish in the water
be gullible and let them see no hook unless they're caught:
the girl with dishevelled hair and mean dress who stood
just now on this shore (for I saw her standing on the shore)   860
tell me where she is; for her footprints stretch no further."
She realized that the god's gift had turned out well and, delighted
that she was being asked about herself, replied to her questioner so:
"Whoever you are, forgive me; I have not turned my eyes in any
direction from this part of the sea but have stayed here absorbed in this pursuit.   865
And that you may be less in doubt, may the god of the sea so help
these skills as truly as no man has stood on this shore
for a long time now, except, that is, for me, and no woman at all."
Her master believed her and, pressing his feet into the sand as he turned,
he went away duped; she had her form restored to her.   870
But when he realized that his daughter's body was transformable,
her father often sold Triopas' granddaughter to masters, but she
came back, now a mare, now a bird, sometimes a cow, sometimes a deer,
and provided nourishment for her greedy father unfairly.
But when the violence of his illness had consumed all   875
his substance and his grave disease lacked fresh sustenance,
he himself began to rend his own limbs apart with a tearing
bite and the unhappy man fed his body by diminishing it.
    Why do I delay you with outsiders? I too, of course, young man, have
a strictly limited power to change my body.   880
For sometimes I am as I now seem, sometimes I am turned into a snake,
sometimes as leader of the herd I put my strength into horns—
horns while I could, now one half of my forehead's weaponry
is missing, as you see yourself.' Groans followed his words.

COMMENTARY

1-235   *Perseus and Phineus*
A continuation of the chain of Perseus stories that began at 4.604. Otis (1970) 346-9 sees the stories as 'deliberate pathos, a true parody of epic'. At the end of the last book, Perseus rescued and subsequently married Andromeda; book 4 ends with Perseus telling the guests at the wedding feast of some of his exploits. Book 5 opens with the story of Phineus. Ovid's source is obscure since the story is hardly touched on in the extant literature and even Apollodorus (2.4.3) gives only the barest outline. What little else we know is in Bömer. Ovid's account of the battle and its antecedents is sympathetically analysed by Otis (1970) 346-9, though, in spite of a number of verbal echoes, I am not fully persuaded that Perseus/Andromeda/Cepheus/Phineus recall Virgil's Aeneas/ Lavinia/ Latinus/Turnus. Ovid's fondness for this sort of scene is revealed again in his treatment of the Lapiths and Centaurs (12.210ff.).

1   **And:** *-que*; a reminder that the book divisions are very artificial in this *carmen perpetuum*. The book divisions in the *Iliad* and *Odyssey* are, of course, only the work of Hellenistic scholars and are truly artificial. Many of the books of the *Aeneid* start with a direct connexion with what precedes, none more so than book 6 where Austin has an interesting note on scholars' reactions from the earliest days.
   Danaeian hero: Perseus. The genealogy will be useful:

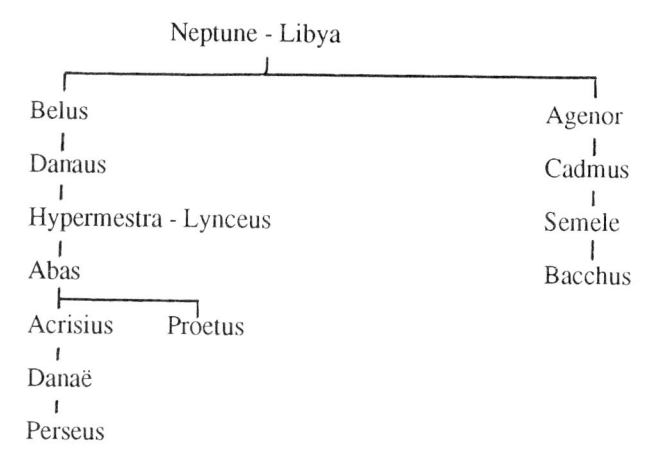

```
              Neptune - Libya
         _____|_____
        |                       |
      Belus                   Agenor
        |                       |
      Danaus                  Cadmus
        |                       |
   Hypermestra - Lynceus      Semele
        |                       |
       Abas                   Bacchus
      __|_____
     |         |
  Acrisius  Proetus
     |
   Danaë
     |
   Perseus
```

2   **Cephenes:** for a discussion of this tribe, see How and Wells on Herod. 7.61.6.

6   **you could compare:** as Hollis (on 8.323) points out, it is 'un-epic' to involve the reader in this way. It is all the more striking that the simile chosen is of such an epic type. The idea germinates at *Iliad* 2.144ff. though this is clearly not specifically an imitation of that simile.

142] NOTES: Book V

9 **ash-wood spear;** a characteristic weapon of Homeric heroes on both sides of the conflict (e.g. *Il.* 6.449, 19.388ff.) immediately gives this passage the flavour of high epic.

10 **the snatching of my bride:** *praereptae coniugis.* Andromeda had been betrothed to Phineus, her uncle. In a similar situation, Turnus uses the same two words of Lavinia, his betrothed, when Aeneas is about to marry her (Virg. *Aen.* 9.138).

11 **false gold:** Perseus had been born to Danaë after Zeus had visited her in a shower of gold (see 4.610-1 and the note on 6.113). Blasphemy in the mouth of a character, especially one just introduced, is a very common signal of impending disaster in the *Metamorphoses.* The same blasphemy at 4.611 precedes Acrisius' fate. See also Pentheus (3.513ff.), Arachne (6.1ff.), Niobe (6.170ff.), Erisychthon (8.738ff.) etc. There is, perhaps, a pun on 'false', *falsum,* 'he gold is false both because it deceives Danaë and because the whole story is, to Phineus, a lie.

17 **the grim deity of the Nereids:** Poseidon (Neptune); the story is in Apollodorus 2.4.3 (Frazer's translation):

> *For Cassiepea, the wife of Cepheus, vied with the Nereids in beauty and vowed to be better than them all; hence the Nereids were angry, and Poseidon, sharing their wrath, sent a flood and a monster to invade the land. But Ammon having predicted deliverance for the calamity if Cassiepea's daughter Andromeda were exposed as a prey to the monster, Cepheus was compelled by the Ethiopians to do it, and he bound his daughter to a rock.*

Ammon: sometimes Hammon, the Jupiter of North Africa where, of course, this story is set. Cf. 4.670, Fordyce on Catullus 7.5, Virg. *Aen.* 4.198ff.

19 **bowels of my own one:** *uisceribus...meis,* literally 'my bowels, (the word includes all or any of the inner organs), but Cepheus clearly means 'the bowels of my child', cf. English: 'my flesh and blood'; see also on 5.515, also 6.651, a particularly striking example.

19-25 **was snatched...snatch:** *rapta...eripies*; note how Cepheus plays with Phineus' words at lines 10-12: 'snatching...will snatch away': (*praereptae...eripiet*).

26 **it was fixed:** *adfixa,* the same word was used at 4.553 when we first met Andromeda on the rock. Here, he alludes to her as a 'reward', perhaps to suggest what he thinks of Phineus' attitude to her.

28 **secured:** *pactus,* a formal word used in making agreements. It picks up *paciscor* (4.703) where Perseus offered to rescue the girl in return for her hand.

30 **He...him:** i.e. Phineus...Cepheus. Latin's richer store of pronouns means that the obscurity in the English is absent in the Latin.

35 **coverlets:** i.e the coverings strewn on the couch on which he was reclining (Roman fashion, see on 5.155) to dine.

NOTES: Book V [143

38 **Rhoetus:** *'Phantasiename'* Bömer. The name recurs at 12.271ff. of a Centaur in the battle of the Lapiths and Centaurs; there are several other borrowing of names from this fight to that one (see on 5.60, 74, 103, 123, 130, 141, 144). This name may ultimately be borrowed from Virg. *Aen.* 9.344 (see also on 5.86). Many occurences of the name (though not this one) are discussed by Nisbet-Hubbard on Horace *Odes* 2.19.23.

40 **set:** i.e. for the wedding feast.

46 **Warrior Pallas:** *bellica Pallas*, i.e. Minerva (Pallas Athene). Cf. 2.752. Ovid is the first to use this epithet of Minerva but the idea behind it is as old as Homer who puts into the mouth of Zeus these words addressed to his other daughter, Aphrodite (*Il.* 5.733-42 Lattimore's translation):
> *No, my child, not for you are the works of warfare. Rather concern yourself only with the lovely secrets of marriage, while all this shall be left to Athene and sudden Ares.*

her brother: they were both children of Zeus (Jupiter).

aegis: Homer *Il.* 5.733-42 (Lattimore's translation):
> *Now in turn Athene, daughter of Zeus of the aegis, beside the threshold of her father slipped off her elaborate, dress which she herself had wrought with her hands' patience, and now assuming the war tunic of Zeus who gathers the clouds, she armed in her gear for the dismal fighting. And across her shoulders she threw the betasselled, terrible aegis, all about which Terror hangs like a garland, and Hatred is there, and Battle Strength, and heart-freezing Onslaught and thereon is set the head of the grim gigantic Gorgon, a thing of fear and horror, portent of Zeus of the aegis.*

See also 4.799-803. The word has entered English shorn of its mythological associations to mean merely 'protection', 'defence'.

47 The beautiful homosexual Athis comes from about as far east as was then known. Both in antiquity and to this day effeminacy is frequently associated with those who live to the east of the speaker's starting point.

49 **it is believed:** Ovid enjoys distancing himself in this way from the incredible; cf. 3.106, 4.45-6, 57; 5.187,541; 6.337, 561, 714; 7.408, and many other instances listed in Bömer.

51 **Tyrian:** i.e. 'purple' from the die associated with the Phoenicians.

52 **gold...golden:** *aureus...aurata*; this device where two forms of a word are put near to one another is known as polyptoton. It is common throughout Latin literature and is a special favourite of Ovid's. I list many examples from book 1-4 in my note on 1.33. Here should be added: 5.108-9, 123-6, 150-1, 161-2, 166, 185, 196-8, 248-9, 296-7; 300, 511, 622-4, 673; 6.13, 142, 242, 298-9, 303-8, 348, 447-8, 450-1; 598, 656, 667-8, 690-1; 7.16, 68-9, 200-1, 447, 476-7, 657, 691, 785-6, 823; 8.56-7, 471, 476-7, 477, 483-4.

144] NOTES: Book V

53 **myrrh-drenched locks:** the whole line is reminiscent of 3.555 spoken by Pentheus of Bacchus. Similar language is used of Aeneas in Virgil's *Aeneid* by his two great enemies (and rivals for Dido and Lavinia respectively) Iarbas (4.215-7) and Turnus (12.99-100). In all three cases, the intention is to suggest effeminacy. Here we have an archer; for the traditional attitude to archers, consider Diomedes' words to Paris at Hom. *Iliad* 11.385-7 (Lattimore's translation):
> 'You archer, foul fighter, lovely in your locks, eyer of young girls.
> If you were to make trial of me in strong combat with weapons
> your bow would do you no good at all, nor your close-showered arrows.'

55-6: **bow...bow:** *arcus... cornua*; the repetition in the English is unavoidable; there are not two distinct English words for bow as natural as *arcus* and *cornu*. Cf. 1.71-3, 157-8; 5.103-4, 232-3, 263-4, 319-20, 356-9, 532-4; 6.178-9, 349-57; 8.239-40.

59 **admired:** Ovid does not let us forget his effeminate appearance even for a moment.

60 **Lycabas:** like Rhoetus (see on 5.38) a name given to a Centaur (12.302). The name also occurs in a different context at 3.624.

61 **no concealer:** while homosexuality was far more acceptable in antiquity than it has generally been in the modern world, prejudice was not unknown.

64 **he:** i.e. Athis; see on 5.30.

68 **he...his:** i.e. Perseus...Perseus'; see on 5.30.

69 **Acrisius' son:** i.e.Perseus, actually his grandson; see on 5.1.
harpe: the Greek name for Perseus' curved sword already encountered at 4.666. It was also associated with Mercury (Hermes) (1.717); indeed, according to Apollodorus (2.4.2), Hermes gave it to Perseus, an idea that probably lies behind 'his Cyllenian harpe' at 5.176.

70 **Medusa:** Perseus had already related the story of his killing of Medusa at 4.772ff. There, however, he wrenched her head off, here he seems to have cut it off with the *harpe*, which is more in keeping with Hesiod *Theog.* 280-1 (Evelyn-White's translation):
> And when Perseus cut off her head there sprang forth great Chrysaor
> and the horse Pegasus.

74 **Phorbas:** once again, the name recurs in the battle of Lapiths and Centaurs (12.322), this time as one of the Lapiths. See the note on 5.38.
Syene: a town half-way up the Nile.

75 **Amphimedon:** a name from another famous domestic brawl, Odysseus' slaughter of the suitors (Hom. *Od.* 22.284).

76 **slipped...in the blood:** *sanguine... lapsi*; Virgil (*Aen.* 2.551) and his many imitators (see Austin) prefer the frequentative *lapso* ('slithering' Austin).

79   **Erytus, son of Actor:** see on 8.308.

80   **hook-shaped sword:** the harpe, see on 5.69.

81   **outstanding:** *exstantem*; the word can be either metaphorical (as translated) or literal: 'with high reliefs standing out'; either or both may be intended here.

85   **Semiramis:** a figure both of mythology (4.44-8) and history (Diod. Sic. 2.7.2-10.6) presumably founded on the 9th to 8th century Queen Sammu-ramat of Assyria.

86   **Abaris:** another name possibly borrowed from Virgil *Aen.* 9.344; see on 5.38.

89   Note the suggestion of cowardice; see further on 5.234.

91   **vainly kept out of the war:** for the sentiment, but not the language, see Horace *Odes* 2.14.13 and Nisbet-Hubbard who provide interesting parallels.

98   **Prothoenor:** a name from the catalogue of ships (Hom. *Il.* 2.495).

99   **Lynceus' son:** i.e. Perseus, actually his great-great-grandson; see on 5.1; also on 5.185.

99-106   This whole scene is inevitably reminiscent of Pyrrhus' slaughter of aged Priam at the altar (Virg. *Aen.* 2.526-58).

100   **Emathion:** The name occurs in a list of slayers and slain at Virg. *Aen.* 9.571.

103   **Chromis:** a name from Homer (*Il.* 2.858 etc.); the name also recurs in the battle of Lapiths and Centaurs (12.333); see on 5.38.

103-4   **altar...altar:** *altaria...arae*; see on 5.55-6.

105-6   There is a fascination in the literature with this sort of detail, as exemplified by the next but one incident (5.117-8); very similar are: Homer's picture of Dolon (*Il.* 10.454-7), Virgil's picture of Orpheus (*G.* 4.523-6) and Ovid's (11.50-3), also his picture of Philomela (6.555-61); not dissimilar are: Lucretius 3.640-7 and Virgil *Aen.* 10.395-6.

107   **Broteas and Ammon:** these brothers are not otherwise known; the name Broteas recurs for a Lapith at 12.262 etc.; see on 5.38.

108-9   **unconquerable...boxing gloves, if boxing gloves...conquer:** *caestibus... .inuicti uinci...caestibus*; Ovid juxtaposes *inuicti uinci* for which I have substituted the (near) juxtaposition of 'boxing gloves, if boxing gloves'. For the polyptoton, see on 5.52; for the chiasmus, see on 6.299-300.

111ff.   This and other examples of apostrophe are discussed by Fränkel (214). It was a favourite Hellenistic device used here to heighten the pathos. For other examples, see 5.242-7, 8.128. Austin has good discussions in his notes on Virgil *Aen.* 2.429 and 4.27.

NOTES: Book V

113-4 **you. . .your. . .he:** the change from second person to third for the same character is smoother in the Latin because of the use of a participle.

115-6 **Sing the rest to the Stygian shades:** editors compare Soph. *Ajax* 865: *I shall tell the rest to those below in Hades*. See also 12.321-2.

117-8 See on 105-6.

122 **like a bullock sacrificed:** the simile reminds us that we are indeed witnessing a slaughter at an altar.

123 **Cinyphian:** from the river Cinyps in Libya.
Pelates: recurs as the name of a Lapith (12.255); see on 5.38.

123-6 **tried. . .he tried. . .pinned. . .pinned there:** *temptabat...temptanti...cohaesit; haerenti*; for the polyptotons, see on 5.52.

125 **Marmarica:** a region of north Africa between Egypt and Cyrenaica.

126 **Abas:** a frequently encountered name; this one is not otherwise known and has, of course, no connexion with Perseus' great-grandfather.

128 **standards:** *castra*; literally 'camp'; but the essential point is that once again Ovid is using a Roman term out of context; see on 5.155.

129 **Nasamonian:** the Nasamones lived in Libya to the west of Marmarica.

129-30 **land. . .land:** *agri. . .agri*; English is more sensitive than Latin to this sort of repetition.

130 **Dorylas:** recurs as the name of a Centaur (12.380); see on 5.38.

138 **Abas'. . .son:** *Abantiades*; Perseus again; he was actually the great-grandson; see on 5.1.

141 **Clanis:** recurs as the name of one of the Centaurs (12.379); see on 5.38.
wounded differently: *diuerso uulnere*; *uulnus* normally means 'a wound' but it can refer to the weapon that inflicts the wound as at 9.126. Here, both the weapons and the wounds are different. The essential point is, of course, the contrast between the similarity of their birth and the difference between their deaths.

143 **his:** Perseus'; see on 5.30.

144 **Celadon:** recurs as the name of one of the Lapiths (12.250); see on 5.38.
Mendes: a town on the Nile delta.
Astreus: a name not otherwise known; as the scansion reveals, it is disyllabic.

149 **than had been accomplished:** *exhausto*; many translators take 'this to mean 'for him exhausted', but there is no suggestion of fatigue until 5.177.

150-1 **fight for. . .fought against:** *pugnant. . .pro. . .impugnante*; see on 5.52 and 129-30. Here, however, the Latin is clearly making a point, though it works out less well in English; cf. 5.160.

150-7 **him alone. . .Alone he:** *unum. . .unum*; Perseus' isolation is brought out by Cepheus' inactivity ('vainly loyal' 152) and his close association with the women, and reinforced by 'Alone he was surrounded by Phineus and by a thousand. . .' (157).

155 **penates:** Ovid, like Virgil before him, is very fond of introducing Roman terms and concepts into alien contexts. Perhaps the most familiar Virgilian examples are in *Aeneid* 4 (where Dido's foundation of her city is constantly described in Roman terms) and at *Aeneid* 8.337-69 (where Evander's tour of his primitive settlement is clearly intended to evoke the Rome that it is to become). In both cases, there is a serious point behind Virgil's choice of language; Ovid's practice is more self-indulgent. See also 1.170-6 (quoted in the note on 6.73), 4.122; 5.128, 207-8, 210, 372, 496, 640, 650; 6.10, 73, 283, 428ff.; 7.101, 701 (and the note), 739 (and the note); 8.91, 154 (and the note), 331, 562, 564, 566, 632, 637, 660, 846. Henderson's note on 3.111-4 is very instructive:

> *Ovid has chosen an anachronistic comparison, a favourite trick of his, and one of the ways in which he prevents the reader from practising for long that willing suspension of disbelief which most epic poets are careful to foster.*

161-2 **turned on. . .turned against. . .pressed on; pressing:** *aduersaque. . .uersus. . .instantes; instabant*; see on 5.52 and 150-51.

163 **Molpeus:** not otherwise known; he is from Chaonia in Epirus and so is much further from home than most of the others.
Echemmon: the name is taken from Hom. *Il.* 5.160 where it belongs to one of Priam's sons. This Echemmon, however, is from Nabataea in Arabia.

165 *armentorum:* normally (see Introduction 5). the fifth foot of the dactylic hexameter is a dactyl (- ∪ ∪ 'munching a turnip'): this spondaic fifth foot (- - 'munching turnips') is very suggestive of lumbering cattle. See also on 5.265.

166 **which. . .both:** *utro. . .utroque*; the Latin word-play is impossible to reproduce in English. It is, perhaps, a form of polyptoton; see on 5.52.

175-6 **stretched his weak arms out:** the standard gesture of supplication often, though not here, exploited by Ovid for pathetic, humorous or grotesque effect. For a full discussion, see my note on 2.487.

176 **Cyllenian harpe:** Hermes (Mercury) was born on Mt Cyllene; see *Homeric Hymns* 4.304, Virg. *Aen.* 4.252. For Mercury's association with the harpe, see on 5.69.

179 **my enemy:** Medusa's head which petrified all who saw her. That Perseus killed her was known to Hesiod (*Theog.* 280), but that her head would petrify all who saw it seems to appear first among literary writers in Ovid, though it also occurs in Apollodorus' version of this story (2.4.3). See also 4.614-9, 699, 741-3.

148] NOTES: Book V

184-5   **seeking...sought:** *petit, inque petendo*; see on 5.52.

185   **Lynceus'...descendant:** *Lyncidae*, rendered 'Lynceus' son at 5.99 (though he was actually his great-great-grandson; see on 5.1). The variation in my translation arises largely from considerations of euphony.

187   **lying claim:** see on 5.49. Virgil (*Aen.* 2.540) puts similar language into Priam's mouth to express contempt for Pyrrhus and to suggest his unworthiness to be Achilles' son. Here, however, as at 5.49, the motive seems more like authorial detachment.

188   **seven-branched Nile:** the reference is to the delta; seven was the traditional number of its streams; cf. 1.422, Herod. 2.17, Catullus 11.78, Virg. *Aen.* 6.800.

189   **partly...partly:** *partim...partim*; my literal translation may obscure an idiomatic sense 'some...others'; cf. 1.40-1 where I offer 'sometimes...sometimes'; consider also 1.436-7; 5.646-7; 7.226-7; 15.526.

191-2   **great is the consolation...so great a man:** the same sentiment recurs at 12.80-81. Cf. also Virgil *Aen.* 10.829-30 (West's translation):
> In your misfortune you will have one consolation for your cruel death,
> that you fell by the hand of the great Aeneas.

and 11.688-9:
> But it is no mean name you will be taking to your fathers when you
> tell them you fell by the spear of Camilla.

195   **and:** *que*; no attempt has been made in the translation to represent the idiosyncratic Ovidian trick of joining *inquit* ('he said') to *increpat* ('he reproached') by attaching the suffix *que* to the first word of the direct speech; cf. 5.327, 514, and for a much more daring extension of the use with *nec*, 5.414.

196-8   **charge...about to charge:** *incurrite...incursurus*; for the polyptoton, see on 5.52.

207   **It would take much time to tell:** *longa mora est*; Ovid enjoys this ploy for shortening lists; cf. 1.214, 3.224, 5.463 (see also my note on 3.206-33).

207-8   **of all the common soldiers:** *de plebe uirorum*; *plebe* is another example of the intrusion of deliberately inappropiate Roman terms (see on 5.155 and cf. 6.10); this one, however, has not been reflected in the translation.

208-9   Note how the parallelism of the two lines brings out the idea that those who survived the fight succumbed to Medusa.
       twice a hundred: simply a large indeterminate number.

210   **unjust war:** *iniusti...belli;* it is characteristic of Ovid to deploy elevated and Roman (see on 5.155) terminology in such an inappropriate context. Some feeling for the term can be gained from Cicero (*Att.* 7.14.3): 'Even an unjust (*iniusta*) peace is better than the most just (*iustissimum*) civil war'. Philosophical debate about the 'Just War' is, of course, still with us. That Phineus was in fact in the wrong has been stressed throughout; cf. 5.36-7, 89, 151, 200.

NOTES: Book V [149

214-5   turned away. . .to the side: a good example of Ovid's fondness for using the act of supplication to achieve a special effect; other striking examples include 1.635-6; 2.487 (where see my note); 3.241, 723-4; 4.683-4. Here, Phineus realises the power of Medusa's head and tries vainly to shield himself from it by turning away while supplicating. The idea of using supplication for humour may have come originally from Homer's picture of the naked Odysseus (*Od.* 6.141-7) pondering how to supplicate the maiden Nausicaa without frightening her.

224-6   most timid man. . .unmanly. . .fear: see on 5.89.

227   a monument: *monimenta*; the word can be used, like the English 'monument', either literally or metaphorically. Horace (*Odes* 3.30.1) exploits both uses by describing his poetry as a *monimentum* more lasting than bronze and higher than the pyramids. Ovid uses the word elsewhere at a story's climax. The dark fruit of the mulberry was described as *monimenta* (4.161) of Pyramus and Thisbe, while Juno threatened to turn the companions of Ino into '*monimenta* of her cruelty' (4.550) before petrifying them; see also 1.159. In all three of those cases I render the word 'memorial', but here the literal sense seems too strong for that.

232-3   eyes. . .eyes: *lumina. . .oculorum*; see on 5.55-6.

230   Phorcus' daughter: Medusa, cf. Hesiod *Theog.* 270-6.

234   timid. . .supplicating: the two jokes, on his cowardice (see on 5.89) and on his supplication (see on 5.214-5) are sustained to the end.

236-249 Perseus punishes Proetus and Polydectes.
The story of Proetus is otherwise known only from Apollodorus (2.2.1 and 2.4.1) and (in a rather different form from this) Pausanias (2.16.2 and 2.25.7). The twin sons of Abas, Acrisius and Proetus (see genealogy in the note on 5.1) quarrelled either in the womb (Apollod. 2.2.1) or over Acrisius' daughter, Danaë (Apollod. 2.4.1). Ovid may be the first to associate Perseus with the punishment of his great uncle. The story of Polydectes is found in Pindar (*Pyth.* 12.9-16) and Apollodorus (2.4.3). Ovid suppresses the reason for the ill-will between Perseus and Polydectes but, according to Apollodorus, Acrisius had banished his daughter Danaë and her son Perseus because he disbelieved her story that she had become pregnant by Zeus. He had cast them adrift in a chest which washed up on the island of Seriphos. They were rescued by the island's ruler, Dictys; his brother, however, Polydectes, became enamoured of Danaë only to be repulsed by Perseus, now grown up. To get rid of Perseus, Polydectes had him sent to get the gorgon's head. On his successful return, he found his mother at the altar seeking sanctuary from Polydectes' violence; so he petrified him with Medusa's head.

236   Abas'. . .descendant: *Abantiades*: Perseus; see on 5.138 and 185.
    his fathers' walls: his ancestral walls, Argos.

**242-7   For the apostrophe of Polydectes, see on 5.111ff.

242   small Seriphos: Seriphos is to the west of the Cyclades but it is still about 100 miles from Argos, a long way in a chest. By calling it 'small', Ovid reminds us that it

150] NOTES: Book V

was frequently the butt of jokes such as the one told by Plato (*Rep.* 1.329e-330a, Shorey's translation):

> But the retort of Themistocles comes in pat here, who, when a man from the little island of Seriphos grew abusive and told him that he owed his fame not to himself but to the city from which he came, replied that neither he himself would ever have made a name if he had been born in Seriphos nor the other if he had been born an Athenian.

248 **watch out for:** *parcite*: the Latin plural imperative makes it plain, as English cannot, that it is the bystanders, not Polydectes, that are being warned.

248-9 **face...face:** *oraque...ore*; see on 5.52.

250-678 *A panel devoted to the Muses*
Otis (128ff.) offers an analysis of the arrangement of these episodes. He sees the tales told by the Muses (341-661) framed by accounts about the Muses themselves (250-340 and 662-678), with the whole section balancing 4.1-415, itself similarly divided into a central panel of tales told by the Minyades (4.43-388) and a frame (4.1-42 and 389-415) about the Minyades themselves. The Perseus story (divided at the book division between the Ariadne story and the Phineus story) is seen as the pivot between these two great sections. However, as Otis' scheme frankly illustrates, the stories of Cadmus and Harmonia (4.563-603) seem to obtrude into this otherwise neat scheme.

250-72 *Hippocrene*
That there was a spring on Mt Helicon known as Hippocrene ('Horse spring') emerges as early as Hesiod (*Theog.* 6); the story that it was made by Pegasus occurs most notably before Ovid in Aratus (216-24). Antoninus Liberalis (9) offers a slightly different version.

250 **the Tritonian:** Minerva (Athene), the goddess of lake Tritonis; the title is as early as Homer (*Il.* 4.515); cf. Virg. *Aen.* 2.171, where Austin's note is instructive. The ostensible link between this story and the last is the very weak one of Minerva's leaving her brother on Seriphos to visit Helicon. Note, however, that Pegasus, born from Medusa's blood and the cause of Hippocrene, provides a less explicit but a more substantial link.

  golden-born: *aurigenae*; the word is a typical Ovidian whimsical invention. Danaë had conceived Perseus when visited by Zeus (Jupiter) in a shower of gold. See 4.610-1 and the note there.

  brother: both Minerva and Perseus were children of Jupiter.

252 **to the right:** Cynthos and Gyaros are islands to the north of Seriphos. Minerva, travelling north-west to Boeotia would indeed leave them on her right.

254 **Helicon of the Virgins:** according to Homer (*Il.* 2.484; see also on 5.313-4) and Hesiod (*Theog.* 36-43, 1021-2 etc.), the Muses lived on Olympus where they were born (Hesiod *Theog.* 60-62), but the Boeotian Hesiod associates them also and more prominently with Helicon and was generally followed (*Theog.* 1-2, 22-3, Evelyn-White's translation):

> *From the Heliconian Muses let us begin to sing, who hold the great and holy mount of Helicon...And one day they taught Hesiod glorious song while he was shepherding his lambs under holy Helicon...*

255 **learned:** *doctas*; the Latin word is indelibly associated with poetry, especially poetry in the Callimachean tradition. According to Nisbet-Hubbard, in a note (on *Odes* 1.1.29) well worth consulting, it is
> *a hard word to translate; 'learned' is too heavy, and 'cultured' too pretentious.*

257 **Medusa's flyer:** Pegasus. The story was alluded to at 4.786. Cf. Hesiod *Theog.* 280-4 (Evelyn-White's translation):
> *And when Perseus cut off her* [Medusa's] *head, there sprang forth great Chrysaor and the horse Pegasus who is so called because he was born near the springs* (pegae) *of Ocean... Now Pegasus flew away and left the earth...*

The clear indication of the last sentence is that the horse had wings.

260 **Urania:** Hesiod (*Theog.* 77-79) lists all nine Muses by name. Even by Ovid's time, the association of one Muse with one function had not developed.

262-3 **Pegasus is the source of this spring:** Hinds (4ff.) gives a full discussion of the implications of these words and their relationship to the Hesiodic etymology (see on 5.257).

263-4 **waters...water:** *latices... undas*; see on 5.55-6.

264-6 Note the idyllic picture: a poet's view of the home of poetry.

265 *antiquarum*: another spondaic fifth foot (see on 5.165); here it produces a Greek feel (Greek hexameters had spondaic fifth feet much more often), while the four word line was much favoured by Hellenistic taste.

267 **daughters of Memory:** see Hesiod *Theog.* 53-62, 915-7.

273-93 Pyreneus
The story occurs here only.

276-7 **Daulis and the Phocean countryside:** Phocis was a territory to the north-west of Boeotia, and Daulis was an ancient town just inside Phocis near the Boeotian border.

278 **We were seeking the temple of Parnassus:** Apollo's temple at Delphi; for the story of its founding, see *Hom. Hymns* 3.254-93. It is deep in Phocis, so that Pyreneus was in their way.

280-2 **(for he knew us)...(there was a rainstorm):** Ovid is very fond of these asides; cf. 1.591 (particularly like this passage), 597; 2.703; 6.262-3, 359, 421, 438, 472-3; 7.219, 453-4, 567, 660; 9.17, 344, 356-7, 782, 12.88. For a discussion, see Wilkinson, *Ovidiana* 235.

152] NOTES: Book V

285   **Aquilo:** the north wind, notorious as a violent wind; Dido rebukes Aeneas for contemplating sailing when the Aquilo is blowing (Virg. *Aen.* 4.310) but, in spite of Austin's comment ('The *Aquilo* was notoriously the wind of rain and storm') it was not especially a bringer of rain to Greeks and Romans for whom it had, after all, come from over land. (Dido, of course, lived to the south of the Mediterranean, which would make it a wet wind for her.)

   Auster: the south wind, so that the opposite considerations apply; cf. 1.66; Ennius (*Ann.* 444) offers *spiritus Austri imbricitor* ('the rain-producing spirit of Auster'). According to Ovid, when Jupiter decided to flood the whole world (1.262-7):
> At once he confined Aquilo in the Aeolian caves
> together with all the blasts that put the assembled clouds to flight,
> and he sent Notus [the south wind] out: Notus flew out with dripping wings,
> his terrible countenance covered with pitch-black fog;
> his beard was heavy with storm-clouds, streams flowed from his hoary locks;
> mists sat on his brow, his wings and his clothes' folds were wet with dew.

286   **swept clean again:** *repurgato*, a striking word to apply to the sky; it has a sense of cleansing; 'swept clean again' is an attempt to represent a rather striking image.

294-678 Pierus' daughters and the Muses
From Antoninus Liberalis (9), we may infer that Nicander told a story of the nine daughters of Pierus, king of Emathia (see on 5.313-4), competing unsuccessfully with the Muses and being transformed into nine different sorts of bird. The origin of this story is obscure and made stranger by the fact that as early as Hesiod (*Theog.* 1, 53 etc.) the Muses were said to be from Pieria (near Olympus; see on 5.254); subsequently, they were frequently referred to as *Pierides* either from Pieria or because they were thought of as the daughters of Pierus. For the confusion, cf. Cicero *de N.D.* 3.21.53 (Rackham's translation):
> Again the first set of Muses are four. . .the second set are the off-spring. . .of Jupiter and Menemosyne, nine in number; the third set are the daughters of Pierus and Antiope, and are usually called by the poets the Pierides or Pierian Maidens; they are the same in number and have the same names as the next preceding set.

296   **Jove's daughter:** Minerva.

296-7   **spoke. . .spoken:** *loquentes. . .locutum*; see on 5.52.

300   **Goddess. . .goddess:** *deae. . .dea*; the polyptoton (see on 5.52) is heightened in the Latin by the juxtaposition, impossible to achieve in English as is the change of form.

302   **Pella:** the Macedonian capital.

303   **Paeonian:** the Paeones were a people of northern Macedonia; see on 5.313.
   Euippe: not otherwise known. Her name ('Delighting in horses') is, however, very suitable for a Macedonian whose horsemanship was legendary.

304   **Lucina:** the goddess of childbirth.

NOTES: Book V [153

305   puff themselves up: *intumuit*; Hinds (131) sees a possible connexion with the use of the word *tumidus* by the new writers as a term of disparagement for what they saw as the overblown style of their rivals; see *OLD* s.v. 'tumidus' 6. This view must be reinforced by unlearned mob (*indoctum uulgus*, 308) with its echo of Horace *Odes* 3.1 where the Alexandrian attitude to 'the mob' (*uulgus*) is most memorably stated. See also on 5.255.

306   Haemonian: Thessalian; Thessaly is to the south of Macedonia.
     Achaean: often used, as in Homer (e.g. *Il.* 2.235), to mean Greek in general (cf. 4.606); here, however, much more likely to mean Achaea proper, the ancient region of Greece immediately south of Thessaly (not to be confused with the north-west region of the Peloponnese, also called Achaea, see on 5.577) so that we have a journey from Macedonia through Thessaly and Achaea to Boeotia.

310   Thespiae: a town to the east of mt Helicon.

312   Medusa's spring: Hippocrene, the spring made by Medusa's offspring, Pegasus; see on 5.250-72 and 257.
     Hyantean: according to Pliny (*Nat.* 4.26), *Hyantes* was an ancient name for the Boeotians.
     Aganippe: another spring on mt Helicon; cf. Cat. 61.30, Virg. *Ecl.* 10.12. Latin poets, unlike Greek ones, had, since before Ovid's time, normally avoided ending the hexameter with a quadrisyllabic word. It does, accordingly, give an extra Greek feel to lines such as this one, full of Greek proper names; cf. 5.409; 8.310 and Hollis.

313   Emathian: Emathia was a region of Macedonia; cf. Homer *Il.* 14.225-6 (Lattimore's translation):
     while Hera in a flash of speed left the horn of Olympus
     and crossed over Pieria and Emathia the lovely...

315-6   It was shameful...more shameful: *turpe...turpius*; the successive line starts are more effective in the Latin.

316   swore: i.e. to give a fair judgement.

317   living rock: *uiuo...saxo*; where nature left it, not where man put it; cf. 14.713 *durior...et saxo, quod adhuc uiuum radice tenetur* ('harder than the living rock still held by its root'); see also Virg. *Aen.* 1.167 and Austin's note.

318-331 Pierus' daughter sings of Typhoeus.
It is instructive to compare this competition with Arachne's challenge to Minerva's weaving. Arachne (6.103ff.) weaves a collection of divine crimes (*caelestia crimina*, 6.131) and is punished partly because of Minerva's jealousy of her skill (130) and partly because of her impiety; that at least seems to be implicit at 131. Similarly, the tale told here mocks the gods. Ovid has already told the story of the battle between the Giants and the Gods (1.151-62; see the note there). The Giants were defeated, but Pierus' daughter apparently corrupts the story to suggest a different outcome (319-20); and then goes on to the Typhoeus sequel, a story which first emerged in Hesiod (*Theog.* 820ff.) where Typhoeus challenges the gods and is overcome by Zeus; cf. 3.302-4:
     And yet, as far as he could, he tried to reduce his strength,

154]   NOTES: Book V

>*and did not equip himself with the fire which had hurled down
>Typhoeus of the hundred hands: there was too much ferocity in that one.*

Later, this different version emerged; cf. Anton. Lib. 28 (from Nicander) and Apollod. 1.6.3 where Frazer's note is relevant:

>*The story of the transformation of the gods into beasts in Egypt was probably invented by the Greeks to explain the Egyptian worship of animals, as Lucian shrewdly perceived (*De sacrificiis, *14).*

324   seven mouths: balanced by seven gods (5.327-31); see also on 1.188.

327   and: it is impossible in English to do full justice to this Ovidian trick described in the note on 5.195, but the strange placing of 'and' is an attempt. See also on 1.456.

328   Ammon: see on 5.17. Herodotus (2.42) confirms that he had ram's horns but offers a different explanation.

329   the Delian: *Delius*; Apollo, who was born on Delos. For his association with the raven, see 2.544-5 and the note. He was identified with the Egyptian Horus (Hdt. 2.149 and 156), the falcon god, and it is into a falcon that Apollo turns according to Antoninus Liberalis.
      Semele's offspring: Bacchus, see on 3.253-315. According to Herodotus (2.24), he was identified with Osiris. The goat, however, reflects the ancient view that the word 'tragedy', which originated in the festival of Dionysus (Bacchus), was derived from the Greek word *tragos*, ('a goat') and meant 'goat-song'; cf. Virg. *G.* 2.381ff. and Frazer's note 4 on Apollodorus 3.4.3 (vol. 1, p.320 of the Loeb edition).

329-31 Note the artistry with which Ovid varies the arrangement of god (A) and animal (B): ABAB, BAAB, BAAB, which I have preserved in the translation.

330   as a cat Phoebus' sister: Diana (Artemis) was identified with the Egyptian goddess Bubastis (Hdt. 2.156) to whose temples dead cats were taken (Hdt. 2.67).
      Saturnia as a cow: Juno (Hera) was called *boöpis* ('ox-eyed') by Homer (*Il.* 1.151 etc.), presumably a very ancient cult title.

331   as a fish Venus: possibly a reference to a story of the eastern goddess of sex, Dercetis, alluded to at 4.44 and told more fully by Diodorus Siculus (2.4.2-6); she is supposed to have been transformed into a fish.
      Cyllenius as a winged ibis: Mercury (Hermes), born on mt Cyllene; ibises were buried in Hermopolis ('Hermes' city', Hdt. 2.67), a centre of the ibis god, Thoth, who was identified with Hermes.

332-40   Introduction to the Muse's song
Note the rather perfunctory way Pierus' daughter's song has been reported and contrast that with the really full treatment accorded to Calliope's; it lasts almost to the end of the book. Note also how Ovid reminds us that we are in the middle of a conversation between Minerva and the Muses. Hinds (*passim*) has full discussions of the relationship between the Muses' songs and that of their rivals.

333   Aonides: the Muses; Aonia is another name for Boeotia.

341-661 Proserpina

The earliest extant account is *Hom. Hymns* 2. Among other treatments, Cicero's (*Ver.* 2.4.48.106-7) is important enough to warrant extensive quotation (Greenwood's translation):

> *It is an ancient belief, gentlemen, established by the oldest Greek books and inscriptions, that the island of Sicily as a whole is sacred to Ceres and Libera. . .They hold that these goddesses were born in Sicily: that corn was first brought to light in Sicilian soil; and that Libera, whom they also call Proserpina, was carried off from a wood near Henna, a place which, lying in the midst of the island, is known as the navel of Sicily. Ceres, the tale goes, in her eager search for traces of her lost daughter, lighted her torches at the fires that burst forth from the peak of Aetna, and roamed over all the earth carrying these in her hands. Henna, the traditional scene of the event I speak of, is built on a lofty eminence, the top of which is a table-land, watered by perennial springs, and bounded in every direction by precipitous cliffs, round which are numerous lakes and groves, and flowers in profusion at all seasons: one feels that the place itself confirms the story, familiar to us from childhood, of how the maiden was carried off.*

There is also Milton (*Paradise Lost*, 4.268-71):
> *Not that fair field*
> *Of Enna, where Proserpin gathering flowers*
> *Herself a fairer flower by gloomy Dis*
> *Was gathered.*

Ovid gives a parallel account at *Fasti* 4.417-620. For a general discussion, with particular reference to the relationship between Ovid's two treatments, see Otis 50ff. and Hinds. Otis's broad conclusion (built on foundations laid by Heinze) is that in the *Fasti* the style is elegiac and here epic, though a particular brand of epic more self-conscious and arch (my word) than Virgil's. Hinds's book is a full length study of Ovid's two treatments of the Persephone myth and its implications for our understanding of Ovid's method in general. It is impossible to do it justice in the scope of these notes, but I shall draw attention to some of its points as they arise.

341-408 Ceres, Proserpina and Dis

341-5   This praise of Ceres (Demeter) is modelled on Lucretius 5.14-15 and Virgil *G.* 1.147-9 which also starts *prima Ceres* ('Ceres was the first'). These hymnic lines immediately set a tone in contrast to her rival's song.

346-7   Note how Calliope specifically corrects her rival's account of the Giants' war (5.319-20).

347   **Trinacris:** literally 'triangular'; a very ancient name for the triangular island of Sicily.

350-2   **Pelorus. . .Pachynos. . .Lilybaeon:** the three promontaries at, respectively, the north-east, south-east and south-west corners of Sicily, giving it its triangular shape. Pelorus is Ausonian (Italian) because it is the nearest to Italy. The right hand under Pelorus, the left under Pachynos and the legs under Lilybaeon will indeed put Typhoeus

156] NOTES: Book V

on his back with his head under Etna, the volcano near the east coast between Pelorus and Pachynos. For Typhoeus under Etna, see Pindar *Pyth.* 1.15ff. and *Ol.* 4.8-9 (Lattimore's translation):
> *O son of Kronos, lord of Aitna,*
> *blast-furnace to hundred-headed Typhon's bulk.*

See also Virg. *Aen.* 3.578f. and Williams's note.

353 lay Typhoeus: an attempt to reproduce Ovid's effective delaying of the name to the end of the line.

356 king of the silent ones: Dis (Hades); see on 5.368.

356-9 king. . .king: *rex. . .tyrannus*; see on 5.55-6.

361-2 went round. . .inspection: *ambibat. . .exploratum*; cf. 2.401ff. where very similar words (*circuit. . .explorat*, 'went round. . .inspected') are used of a very similar situation, the inspection of the world after the flood by Jupiter (Dis' brother) during which he sees and ravishes Callisto.

363 Erycina: one of Venus' cult titles, from her temple on mt Eryx on the west coast of Sicily, and therefore especially appropriate here. Cf. Cat. 64.72, Hor. *Od.* 1.2.33 with Nisbet-Hubbard's note.

365 arms: *arma*; i.e. 'weapons'; note that 'arms', 'hands' and 'power' are all being addressed and identified with Cupid; cf. Virg. *Aen.* 1.664 (West's translation, adapted):
> *My son, source of my power, my great strength.*

Hinds (133f.) analyses this echo in some detail in a discussion of the 'epic flavour' of this section.

368 last lot: cf. 2.291 and Homer's report of the words of Poseidon (Neptune) (*Il.* 15.187-92, Lattimore's translation):
> *Since we are three brothers born by Rheia to Kronos,*
> *Zeus, and I, and the third is Hades, lord of the dead men.*
> *All was divided among us three ways, each given his domain.*
> *I when the lots were shaken drew the grey sea to live in*
> *forever; Hades drew the lot of the mists and the darkness,*
> *and Zeus was allotted the wide sky, in the cloud and the bright air.*

372 jurisdiction: *imperium*; the Roman technical term for magisterial authority. Ovid loves to introduce these anachronistic touches; see on 5.155. Hinds (109), however, sees it rather as a contribution to 'epic flavour'.

379 uncle: see on 5.368; cf. Hesiod *Theog.* 453-7 (Evelyn-White's translation):
> *But Rhea was subject in love to Cronus and bare splendid children,*
> *Hestia, Demeter* [Ceres], *and gold-shod Hera* [Juno] *and strong*
> *Hades* [Dis]. *. .and the loud crashing Earth-Shaker* [Poseidon (Neptune)] *and wise Zeus* [Jupiter], *father of gods and men.*

385-91 A typical ekphrasis, where the poet breaks off to set a scene. It is a device as old as Homer and more usually starts 'There is a place ('city'/'cave' etc.). . .', cf. 1.168,

5.409, and see Austin on Virg. *Aen.* 4.480ff. who compares Hom. *Il.* 6.152, *Od.* 13.32; see also *Od.* 7.112-31, the origin of the idealized garden. This passage has been widely seen as establishing a peaceful setting in contrast to the violence that is to follow. Hinds (*passim*) has a very elaborate analysis which is not always convincing. He also discusses Cicero's famous ekphrasis (*Ver.* 2.4.48.106-7, quoted in the note on 5.341-661). He sugests that *lacus est* ('there is a lake', 385) plays on the traditional *est locus* ('there is a place') and is picked up by *quo... luco* ('in this grove' 391) and that this playfulness is not unconnected with Cicero's *quam circa lacus lucique sunt plurimi... locus ut ipse...* ('round which are numerous lakes and groves...so that the place itself...'). It is, however, perhaps worth noting here that Virgil too offers *lucus in urbe fuit media... quo... loco...* ('There was a grove in the middle of the city...and in that place...', *Aen.* 1.441-3) and *est... lucus* ('There is a grove...', *Aen.* 8.597).

385 **Henna:** a city in the very middle of Sicily; Cicero's 'navel', (see on 5.341-661) the expression also occurs at Diod. Sic. 5.3.3.

386 **Cayster:** the swans on the Cayster (in Caria) became a commonplace based on Hom. *Il.* 2.461-3; see also 2.252-3. Hinds (44ff.) argues that this reminds us of the Nysean plain (also in Caria) where *Hom. Hymns* 2 set this whole story, so that this line amounts to a boast that Ovid's account is as good as the ancient poet's.

389 **like an awning:** *ut uelo*; I cannot follow Hinds (33ff.) in believing that this simile conjures up the amphitheatre (which did indeed have awnings; Hinds draws attention also to 'ringing them on every side', 388) and the violence associated with it.
Phoebus': i.e. Sol's (Sun's). Hinds (30ff.) argues unconvincingly for an additional association with the archer Apollo.

391 **perpetual spring:** cf. 1.107 and *Fasti* 5.207 in the context of Zephyr's rape of Flora.

395-6 For the speed, cf Jupiter's rape of Io (1.600-1); here it is all the more stark after the lingering description of nature. Otis (53f.) draws attention to the ways Ovid undercuts the epic pretensions of this passage. See also Leo Curran, 'Rape and Rape victims in the *Metamorphoses*', *Arethusa* 11 (1978) 213-41.

406 **Palici:** stress the middle syllable; these were ancient Sicilian deities, cf. Virg. *Aen.* 9.585.

407 **Bacchiadae:** the founders of Corinth (Hdt. 5.92), the city 'of two seas' since it is in the isthmus between the Adriatic and the Aegean. The Corinthian Archias was the traditional founder of Syracuse (Thuc. 6.3.2).

408 **unequal harbours:** Syracuse was famous for its two harbours, the Great Harbour and a smaller one (Thuc. 7.25.5).

409-37 Cyane and Anapis
The story is not in the *Homeric Hymn* but the creation of Lake Cyane does appear in Diodorus Siculus (5.4.1-2) in connexion with the rape of Persephone (Oldfather's translation):

158] NOTES: Book V

. . .*Corê* [Persephone], *we are told, received as her portion the meadows around Enna; but a great fountain was made sacred to her in the territory of Syracuse and given the name Cyanê or "Azure Fount." For the myth relates that it was near Syracuse that Pluton* [Dis] *effected the rape of Corê and took her away in his chariot, and that after cleaving the earth asunder he himself descended into Hades, taking along with him the bride whom he had seized, and that he caused the fountain named Cyanê to gush forth, near which the Syracusans each year hold a notable festive gathering.*
Cicero (*Ver.* 2.4.48.107) tells the same story but without naming the fountain. Note how Ovid here fleshes the story out and uses it to point a moral; in the *Fasti* (4.469), Cyane and Anapus (*sic*) are only waters past which Ceres goes when searching for her daughter; for an interesting discussion on these two treatments, see Hinds 82ff.

409ff. Another ekphrasis; see on 5.385-91.

409 Pisaean: Pisa was a district in Elis from which, legend has it, Alpheus chased Arethusa; cf. 5.494ff. where her story is told; see also the note on 5.487-508.
Arethusa: for the Greek feel achieved by Greek names and a quadrisyllabic ending, see on 5.312.

413 The same picture, perhaps, as at Cat. 64.18.

414 and, '. . .no. . .': *nec*, a much more daring extension of the use of *que* discussed at 5.195. Here, the connective part of *nec* ('and') joins *agnouit* ('recognized') to *inquit* ('said'), while the negative part belongs in the reported speech; the effect cannot survive translation; editors compare 10.569.

417 to compare great things with small: Bömer collects a host of examples of this saying, starting with Hdt. 2.10.1.

418 wooed, not terrified: no attempt has been made to catch the striking sound of the Latin *exorata. . .nec. . .exterrita*. For the sentiment, contrast 6.684-701.

420 the Saturnian: Dis; more usually of his brother, Jupiter, e.g. 1.163, 8.703. Both, together with Neptune (Poseidon), were sons of Saturn (Kronos in Greek), see on 5.368.

420-423 blocked his way. . .plunged it in: *obstitit. . .condidit*; the translation attempts to preserve the enjambments, a favourite device of poets to put great weight on a word by making it both the last word of its sentence and the first of its line.

424 crater: *crater*, the Greek word for a mixing bowl (e.g. 5.82) and then, metaphorically, of what we would call a 'crater'; Lucretius (6.701-2) points out that it is the word used by the Greek speaking natives for the top of Etna as opposed to the Latin *fauces* or *ora*. Similarly, Cicero (*Att.* 2.8.8) uses it of the Bay of Naples, another Greek speaking area. Bömer thinks that it has now become a natural Latin term (as it clearly was not for Lucretius), but is Ovid, in fact, maintaining a Greek colour here too?

426 inconsolable: *inconsolabile*, probably an Ovidian coinage.

NOTES: Book V [159

438-61 Ceres and Stellio (Ascalabus)
This story is not in the *Homeric Hymns*, though some of its details are, as will be shown (see also Hinds 83ff.). It was, however, in Nicander (*Ther.* 485, *Het.* fr. 56) and Antoninus Liberalis (24). There, the boy is identified as Ascalabus (the Greek for the spotted lizard) and his mother as Misme. Ovid offers no name for the mother; for Stellio, his name for the boy, see 460-1 and the note.

438-9 **Meanwhile...deep:** cf. *Hom. Hymns* 2.43-4 (Evelyn-White's translation):
and [she] sped, like a wild-bird, over the firm land and yielding sea, seeking her child.

441 **Hesperus:** *Hesperus*, the Greek for the Evening star (Latin *Vesper*); though both forms are quite common in the Latin poets, this may be a further contribution to Greek colour, see on 5.312 and 424.

441-3 **She lit...frosty dark:** cf. *Hom. Hymns* 2.47-8 (Evelyn-White's translation):
Then for nine days queenly Deo [Ceres] wandered over the earth with flaming torches in her hands...

445 **from the setting of the sun to its rising:** primarily a way of saying 'from west to east'; however, the arresting order must also serve as a reminder that the search goes on day and night.

446-7 **Tired out...mouth:** cf. *Hom. Hymns* 2.49-50 (Evelyn-White's translation):
...so grieved that she never tasted ambrosia and the sweet draughts of nectar, nor sprinkled her body with water.

449 **old woman:** Misme (Anton. Lib. 24).

450 This is ultimately the holy barley water drunk at the Eleusinian Mysteries; cf. *Hom. Hymns* 2.206-9 (Evelyn-White's translation [with slight corrections]):
Then Metaneira filled a cup with sweet wine and offered it to her [Demeter (Ceres)]; but she refused it, for she said it was not lawful for her to drink red wine, but bade them mix barley and water with soft mint and give her it to drink.

455 **was stained:** *combibit*, a word with both a literal meaning 'drink down' and a metaphorical one 'absorb', 'be stained by'; clearly, the metaphorical sense predominates here and is reflected in the translation; I have not, however, been able to catch the latent literal sense.

459 **monster:** *monstrum*, the standard term for a miraculous sign; since freaks of nature were often taken to be signs or portents, the word developed its modern meaning as well long before Ovid's time (*OLD* s.v. 3); see also Nisbet-Hubbard on Horace *Od.* 1.37.21.

460 **a name:** Stel(l)io; the most obvious explanation is a pun on *stellatus* ('starred', 461), an allusion to its spots. However, the force of the language *aptumque pudori nomen* ('a name to fit the disgrace') leads some commentators to point rather to Pliny

160] NOTES: Book V

N.H. 30.89 where we learn that the habits of the lizard have made it into a term of abuse, as indeed it is used by Petronius (50.5) and Apuleius (*Met.* 5.30); see Mynors on Virg. *G.* 4.243.

461   **disgrace:** *pudori*, which I have normally rendered 'shame'; however, the jingle 'name...shame' seemed intolerable.

462-86 Ceres punishes Sicily with famine.
This episode owes something to *Hom. Hymns* 2.305-9 (Evelyn-White's translation):
> Then she caused a most dreadful and cruel year for mankind over the all-nourishing earth: the ground would not make the seed sprout, for rich-crowned Demeter kept it hid. In the fields the oxen drew many a curved plough in vain, and much white barley was cast upon the land without avail.

463   **would take much time:** *longa mora est*; see on 5.207.

464   **Sicania:** an old name for Sicily (Hom. *Od.* 24.307); cf. Virg. *Aen.* 1.557.

465   **if she had not been changed:** see 5.427-37.

471   **she...she...she:** Ceres...Ceres...Proserpina; see on 5.30.

472   **dishevelled:** *inornatos*, the word can also mean 'unadorned' and Hinds (85ff.) would so take it, seeing it, ingeniously if implausibly, as a reference to the earlier loss of her veil at *Hom. Hymns* 2.39-41.

480   **default on their deposits:** *fallere depositum*, a technical banking term used commonly as a measure of bad conduct (it corresponds to *reddere depositum*, 'give back a deposit' for good conduct), cf. 9.120, *A.A.* 1.641, Pliny *Epp.* 10.96.34-5.

481-2   **well known throughout the wide world:** see, for example, Cic. *Ver.* 2.2.2.5 (Greenwood's translation):
> When has she [Sicily] failed to pay us punctually her tribute of grain?... Cato Sapiens called her in consequence "the nation's storehouse, the nurse at whose breast the Roman people is fed."

486   **darnel and caltrop:** *lolium tribolique*; cf. Mynors on Virg. *G.* 1.154 and 153.

487-508 Ceres and Arethusa
In the *Homeric Hymn* (2.52ff.), the truth is revealed to Demeter (Ceres) not by Arethusa but by Hecate and Helios (the Sun). In the *Fasti* (4.583-4), it is just the Sun; Arethusa's only rôle was to distract the matrons of Sicily with the result that Persephone was unattended when Dis approached. Arethusa had been pursued from Pisa in Elis (see on 5.409) to Sicily where their waters were finally united in Ortygia (but see on 5.499). Here, we get only a brief outline; for the full story, we must wait for 'a fitting hour...when you are relieved of care' (5.499-500) which occurs at 5.577ff. See also Virg. *Aen.* 3.692-6 (West's translation):
> At the entrance to the bay of Syracuse... there stands an island which men of old called Ortygia. The story goes that the river-god Alpheus

> *of Elis forced his way here by hidden passages under the sea and now mingles with Sicilian waters at the mouth of Arethusa's fountain.*

Williams's note gives a full account of other treatments from Pindar (*Nem.* 1.1-2) to Keats (*Endymion* 936-1017).

487 **Alpheias:** i.e. Arethusa, Alpheus' beloved, apparently an Ovidian coinage.

496 **penates:** see on 5.155.

499 **Ortygia:** 'quail island', an island between the two harbours of Syracuse (see on 5.408) where, in the standard versions (see on 5.487-508) Alpheus and Arethusa were united; here, however, makes no mention of Alpheus following her to Sicily.

507-8 **but still…still…still indeed:** *sed… tamen… sed… sed tamen*; 'still' in the sense of 'nevertheless'.

509-32 Ceres and Jupiter
In the *Homeric Hymn* (2.310ff.), it is Zeus (Jupiter) who, through Iris and Hermes, pleads with Demeter (Ceres).

510 **thunderstruck:** *attonitae*, 'thunderstruck' is the literal meaning, see on 7.614; Hinds (74ff.), however, would prefer to stress its undoubted associations with frenzy so as to relate the passage to *Hom. Hymns* 2.384-6.

510-1 **great frenzy…great grief:** *dolore… graui grauis… amentia*; an attempt at both the alliteration and the polyptoton (see on 5.52) of Ovid's Latin.

512 **clouded:** *nubila*; Ovid seems to have originated this extension of the word to people.

513 **resentfully:** *inuidiosa*, normally passive (e.g. 8.144) but probably active at 15.234 and certainly so at Prop. 2.28.10; see Bömer for more detail.

514 **and:** for this use of *que*, see on 5.195.

515 **blood:** *sanguine*, i.e. 'child'; for this quite common idiom, see Virg. *Aen.* 6.835 and Austin's note; cf. English 'my flesh and blood'; see also on 5.19.

520 **merely:** for Latin's idiomatic omission of this (for us) necessary detail, cf. 3.401, 4.115, 7.565, 8.346 and see Mayer on Lucan 8.51-2.

524 **pledge:** *pignus*, literally a 'pledge' or 'guarantee', the word is regularly used of children, the 'guarantees' of a marriage.

526-9 The author of the *Homeric Hymn* puts these sentiments into the mouth of Hades (Dis) addressing Persephone (Proserpina) (2.363-4, Evelyn-White's translation):
> *for I shall be no unfitting husband for you among the deathless gods, that am own brother to father Zeus.*

529 **his portion:** see on 5.360.

162] NOTES: Book V

530 **separate:** *discidium*, like 'separation', is used as a technical term for the break up of a relationship, but both words can also have a more informal sense.

531-2 This condition was revealed to us by Demeter (Ceres) herself at *Hom. Hymns* 2.393-402. For a full discussion, see Frazer on Apollod. 1.5.3.

532-4 **Fates...fates:** *Parcae...fata*; see on 5.55-6.

533-50 Proserpina eats and Ascalaphus tells.
In the *Homeric Hymn* (2.371-4), it is Hades' (Dis') trickery that persuades the girl to eat the fatal seeds. Ovid changes that, and has the girl eat spontaneously; Hinds (88ff.) believes that Ovid wishes us to refer this incident back to her original encounter with Dis. According to Apollodorus (1.5.3), Ascalaphus' punishment was to be turned into a stone (but see also on 5.550), the fate of another tale-bearer, Battus (2.676-707). Other tale-bearers punished in the work include Cornix and Corvus (2.531-632) and Clytie (4.190-273); see also Otis (120).

539 **not the least known:** Orphne (her name means 'dark', 'obscure') is in fact otherwise quite unknown.

541 **it is said:** see on 5.49.
Acheron: one of the rivers of the Underworld (Hom. *Od.* 10.513 etc.) was also the father according to Apollod. 1.5.3.

543 **Erebus:** the Underworld (cf. Hom. *Od.* 10.528); its queen is, of course, Proserpina, cf. 5.507.

544 **Phlegethon:** another Underworld river (Hom. *Od.* 10.513), a river of fire. Cicero (*de N.D.* 3.17.43) keeps the Greek form *Pyriphlegethon*; Ovid follows Virgil's shortening (*Aen.* 6.265).

546-8 A fine picture of the characteristic pose of the tawny owl, all head and claws.

549 **a messenger of grief:** note how the punishment fits the crime.

550 **owl:** the bird was regarded as of extremely ill omen, cf. 6.431-2; 7.269; 10.453; 15.791; see also Pease (who collects numerous parallels from ancient and modern literature) and Austin on Virg. *Aen.* 4.462, Thompson, 56, 66-7, 476-80. Apollodorus, long after his different main report (see on 5.533-50), has an isolated reference to a transformation of Ascalaphus into an owl (2.5.12). [His manuscripts suggest 'ass' and we owe 'owl' to his 16th century editor, Aegius.]

551-63 Sirens
Best known from Homer (*Od.* 12.39-54, 165-200). Hyginus (141) tells a variant on Ovid's story that their wings were a punishment for not saving Proserpina from Dis.

551 **Acheloides:** (i.e. daughters of Achelous) the Sirens; for their parentage, cf. Apollod. 1.3.4, *Epit.* 7.18, Hyg. 141.

555 **learned:** see on 5.255; ever since the Homeric story, it was their singing for which they were chiefly noted, as reinforced in the next few lines.

563 Ovid's haunting alliteration, *u̲irginei u̲ultus et u̲ox*, has not survived translation.

564-71 Jupiter's adjudication
An adaptation of the arrangement at *Homeric Hymns* 2.441-7 (459-65) (Evelyn-White's translation):
> Zeus [Jupiter]. . .agreed that her daughter should go down for the third part of the circling year to darkness and gloom, but for the two parts should live with her mother and the other deathless gods.

See also Frazer on Apollod. 1.5.3.

564   **sister:** see on 5.379.

572-641 Arethusa
For earlier treatments, see on 5.487-508.

572   This is the 'fitting hour. . .when you are relieved of care' (5.499-500) that Arethusa was waiting for to tell her story in full.

576   **old loves:** *ueteres amores*; 'long-standing', not 'old' in the sense of 'old flame'.

578   **Achais:** a variant on *Achaea* (according to Bömer, a form found only here and at 7.504), see on 5.306. Here, it is the one in the north-east Peloponnese.

583   **will delight in:** *gaudere solent*; see on 6.47-8.

585   **Stymphalian wood:** she has wandered eastwards and is now returning home.

587-90   **waters. . .waters:** *aquas. . .unda*; see on 5.55-6 and 636-8.

605-6   **will flee. . .will chase:** *fugere. . .solet. . .urgere*; see on 6.47-8. cf. also 1.506:
> *doves with trembling wing flee thus from an eagle.*

Ultimately this comes from the climax of the *Iliad*, Achilles' killing of Hector (22.139-42, Lattimore's translation):
> *As when a hawk in the mountains who moves lightest of things flying makes his effortless swoop for a trembling dove, but she slips away from beneath and flies and he shrill screaming close after her plunges for her again and again, heart furious to take her.*

Consider also, from Camilla's slaughter of Aunus' son, (Virg. *Aen.* 11.721-4, West's translation):
> *. . .as easily as the sacred falcon flies from his crag to pursue a dove high in the clouds, catches it, holds it and rips out its entrails with hooked claws while blood and torn feathers float down from the sky.*

It is indeed a commonplace as demonstrated by Nisbet-Hubbard on Hor. *Odes* 1.37.17ff., but it is characteristic of Ovid's playfulness that he takes a simile from two of the most famous episodes of epic violence and applies it in an erotic context; see also 1.533; 4.362-4; 8.19, 423-4, 533-5 and the notes. This is the first of a number of similes etc. appearing both here and in the Daphne story; see on 5.617, 618, 626-7, 628-9.

607   **Orchomenos:** Arcadian Orchomenos, to the south-west of Stymphalia.

Psophis: to the north-west of Orchomenos.
Cyllene: on the west coast of Elis.

608 Note that the places in this line fill in the journey described in the last line; thus the natural order would have been: Stymphalia-Orchomenos-Maenalos-Psophis-Erymanthus-Cyllene-Elis.
Maenalos: a mountain in Arcadia south of Orchomenos.
Erymanthus: a mountain betwen Psophis and Cyllene at the point where Achaea, Arcadia and Elis join.
Elis: a city and territory further east.

617 breathed...hair: also (see on 5.605-6) from the Daphne story (1.541-2):
and leant over the fugitive's
back and breathed on her hair as it flowed from her neck.
It is ultimately from Homer's foot-race (*Il.* 23.765, Lattimore's translation):
Great Odysseus was breathing on the back of the head of Aias.

618 Tired out from the effort of my flight: *fessa labore fugae*; also (see on 5.605-6) from the Daphne story (1.544): *uicta labore fugae* ('overcome by the effort of her flight').

622-4 Covered...had concealed: *tectum...texerat*; the translation has not reproduced the polyptoton (see on 5.52).

625 oh...oh: *io...io*; the Latin exclamation can have hunting associations; see 3.728 and my note.

626-7 Were they not a lamb's...high pens: also (see on 5.605-6) from the Daphne story (1.505): *Thus does a lamb flee from a wolf.*

628-9 or a hare's...body: also (see on 5.605-6) from the Daphne story (1.533-4):
As when a Gallic hound has seen in an empty field
a hare.

636 The same metamorphosis as that suffered by Cyane (5.427ff.).

636-8 water...waters...waters: *latices...aquas...undas*; see on 5.55-6, 587-90 and 3.171-3.

640 Ortygia: see on 5.499.
surname: Golding's solution for *cognomine*, the ordinary term for the Roman's last name. For this sort of intrusion, see on 5.155, although it should be noted that Virgil (*Aen.* 12.845) uses *cognomen* for the Furies' name, *Dirae*. For the fact, see Diod. Sic. 5.3.5 (Oldfather's translation):
And Artemis [Diana] *received from the gods the island at Syracuse*
which was named after her, by both the oracles and men, Ortygia.
The name was originally applied to her birthplace, Delos (Callimachus *Hymns* 2.58-9); see also Pindar *Nem.* 1.1-2, Apollod. 1.4.1 (quoted in the note on 6.107).

642-61 Triptolemus and Lyncus
Triptolemus had a small rôle in the Persephone story from early times (*Hom. Hymns* 2.473-9), but the Lyncus story is not otherwise extant till after Ovid (Hyg. 259, Serv. *ad Verg. Aen.* 1.323).

643   **dragons:** see Apollod. 1.5.2 and Frazer's note.

645   **city of Tritonis:** i.e. Athens, see on 5.250.

646-7 **some. . .some:** *partimque. . .partim*; see on 5.189.

650   **penates:** see on 5.155.

654   **ether:** *aether*, in Homer the word refers to heaven, but in Classical Greek it came to mean the upper air, as here. I have tranlated it as 'ether' throughout, but all thoughts of laughing gas or radio waves must be cleared from the mind.

660   **lynx:** *lynca* (Greek accusative); the metamorphosis clearly relates to his name.
       Mopsopian: (Athenian); it appears to be an ancient name revived by Hellenistic *doctrina*; cf. Callimachus fr. 351, Tib. 1.7.54.

662-678 Pierus' daughters and the Muses (again)
See on 5.294-678.

662   **learned:** *doctos*; see on 5.255.

665   **I said:** the speaker is 'one of the sisters' (5.268); she speaks in the first person also at 5.275.

669   **Emathides:** daughters of Macedon, see on 5.313.

673   **each. . .the other's:** *alteraque alterius*; the polyptoton (see on 5.52) is impossible to catch in English.

676   cf. 5.299.

NOTES: BOOK VI

Further elucidation and alternative views will often be found in Anderson's edition of books 6-10.

1-145 Arachne
The only earlier extant allusion to the story (Virg. *G.* 4.246-7: 'the spider hated by Minerva, hangs her traps loosely in the entrance') makes it plain that the story was known to the Augustan age. It may be no more than coincidence that the *stellio*, treated so recently in the *Metamorphoses*, (5.438-61), occurs three lines earlier in the *Georgics*. As has been widely observed, the Arachne story develops the theme of the story of Pierus' daughters (5.294-678), presumptuous human challenge to divine skill (see also on 5.11). Here, however, both the medium and the outcome are different. Otis (*passim*) and Anderson discuss the contrast more fully. See also on 5.318-31.

1-5 **Tritonia...Aonides...Maeonian:** note how easily Ovid transports us from Minerva (see on 5.250) and the Muses (see on 5.333) across the Aegean to Lydia; Maeonia was an eastern region of Lydia.

5 **Arachne:** the Greek word for 'spider'; both the name and the geography suggest a Greek origin for the story. Note how, in the next few lines, Ovid shows off his geographical learning.

8 **Colophonian:** Colophon was a town in Ionia to the west of Lydia.

9 **Phocaean:** Phocaea was an Ionian coastal town, north of Colophon.
  murex: a shell-fish from which purple dye was derived; see Austin on Virg. *Aen.* 4.262.

10-11 **she...she:** i.e. the mother...Arachne; see on 5.30.

10 **plebs:** for this deliberately inappropriate Roman intrusion, see on 5.155.

13 **small...small:** *parua paruis*; see on 5.52.
  Hypaepa: a small town in western Lydia, north-east of Colophon and south-east of Phocaea.

15 **Timolus:** usually 'Tmolus' (cf. 2.217, 11.151 etc., but the extra vowel is sometimes found in Greek too), a Lydian mountain range north-east of Hypaepa.

16 **Pactolid:** the Pactolus (stress the middle syllable) is a small Lydian river that flows north from mount Tmolus into the Hermus which then flows west to empty into the Aegean just south of Phocaea.

23 **taught:** *doctam*; while the word has its basic meaning here, there are clearly overtones of its specialized sense (see on 5.255), especially in this context of artistic competition.

NOTES: Book VI [167

5   **defeated:** our natural expectation that this will be the outcome, though it is reinforced as the story develops, is, in fact, frustrated or, at best, fulfilled in an unexpected way.

6-7   For this disguise, cf. Juno's appearance to Semele (3.275ff.); there, however, the victim received disastrous advice and acted on it; here, the advice is sound but ignored. Similar disguises occur at 11.310ff., 14.653ff. Cf also Virg. *Aen.* 5.620 (and Williams's note), 7.415ff.

8-9   Commentators compare Euripides (*Phoen.* 528ff.): 'not everything which comes with age is bad, but experience has something wiser to say than do the young'.

34   **she:** Ariachne; see on 5.30.
    grimly: *toruis*; the translation obscures the rather striking omission of *oculis*: 'with grim eyes'.

37   **enfeebled with...old age:** no attempt has been made to catch the Latin jingle *confecta senecta*. Is Ovid gently mocking his own clichés in this section?

42   **Why does she not come herself?:** Ovid delights in this sort of dramatic irony. Cf. 2.428ff. (an exchange between Callisto, Diana's devotee, and Jupiter disguised as Diana):
        'Welcome, oh divinity, greater, if I am
  the judge, than Jupiter, though he himself hears me.' He laughed as he
                                        heard her
    and rejoiced that he was preferred to himself...',
see also 2.704-5 and Fränkel 215.

45   **Mygdonian:** an alternative word for 'Phrygian'; Phrygia was immediately to the east of Lydia; see Nisbet-Hubbard on Hor. *Od.* 2.12.22.

46   **blushed...blush:** *erubuit...rubor*; see on 5.52.

46-7   **a...blush appeared on her...cheeks:** *notauit ora rubor*; the same phrase appears in Ovid's description of Hermaphroditus' reaction to Salmacis (4.329).
    will become: an attempt to catch implicitly the frequency which is explicit in *solet...fieri*.

47   **as the sky:** the simile is very 'epic' in tone; cf. 6.63ff.; see also on 5.605-6.

53   **both...twin:** not two looms each, of course.

61   **Tyrian:** the Phoenician cities of Tyre and Sidon were especially associated with the production of purple die. See on 5.51; 6.9.

63ff.   **just as:** another 'epic simile'; see on 6.47.

64   **will paint:** *solet...inficere*; see on 6.47-8.

NOTES: Book VI

69   **spun out:** *deducitur*; among the many senses of the Latin verb was the technical sense of 'spinning out'; from this, the Roman followers of Callimachus had developed a technical sense 'spinning out' the sort of poetry of which they approved. Its occurence at 1.4 is clealy significant. Here, despite its perfectly natural sense in a true spinning context, there is also a hint at its literary sense. For a discussion of the word and a bibliography, see Hinds 18ff., though he overlooks this passage.

     story: *argumentum*; another spondaic ending (see on 5.165) which further enhances the Hellenistic associations (see on 5.265) of this line.

70-82   The story is best known from Herodotus (8.55, de Sélincourt's translation):
> ...on the Acropolis there is a spot which is sacred to Erechtheus - the 'earth-born', and within it is an olive-tree and a spring of salt water [literally 'sea']. According to the local legend they were put there by Poseidon [Neptune] and Athene [Minerva], when they contended for possession of the land, as tokens of their claims to it.

See also Apollod. 3.14.1 and Frazer. Anderson offers a list of similar poetic descriptions of works of art starting with Achilles' shield (Hom. *Il.* 18.483ff.) and Aeneas' shield (Virg. *Aen.* 8.626ff.).

70   **Mars' rock:** *scopulum Mauortis*, a translation of the Greek Areiopagus (Ares' Hill), a hill immediately to the west of the Acropolis itself where the miracle was traditionally supposed to have occured.

70-1   **Cecropian citadel:** i.e. Athenian citadel (Cecrops was an ancient king of Athens, cf. 2.552ff.); presumably Ovid has the Acropolis in mind here though his apparent confusion with the Areiopagus seems strange in someone whose geography is usually so reliable.

72   **twice six heavenly ones:** the Latin for twelve, *duodecim*, cannot be accommodated in a hexameter; for the detail, see Apollodorus 3.14.1:
> 'Zeus...appointed arbiters, not, as some have affirmed, Cecrops and Cranaus, nor yet Erysichthon, but the twelve gods.'

73   **august:** *augusta*; the trick of introducing deliberately incongruous Roman ideas (see on 5.155) is here spiced with an obviously incautious allusion to the Emperor's title. There is a much more obvious example at 1.170-6 (a description of heaven):
> *This is the gods' route to the great Thunderer's dwelling,*
> *the royal home; to the right and to the left, the halls*
> *of the noble gods have open doorways and are thronged*
> *(the common gods live in separate areas); in this part, the powerful*
> *and famous heavenly ones have their penates.*
> *This is the place where, if I may speak boldly,*
> *I would not fear to speak of as great heaven's Palatine.*

The Palatine was, of course, where Augustus lived, hence English 'palace'. See also 1.204 and my note on 1.200-6.

77   **salt spring:** *fretum*; one of the many words for the sea, chosen, of course, to underline the miracle that it was not just a spring, but a salt water spring (see on 6.70-82) as befitted the god of the sea.

79   **aegis:** see on 5.46.

82   **Victory:** if Minerva can defeat Neptune our expectation of her victory over Arachne is raised higher still, a point reinforced by the four corners where she embroidered the fate of those who presumed against the gods.

87   **Thracian Rhodope and Haemus:** presumably the same Rhodope who, according to the *Homeric Hymn* (2.422), was one of Persephone's companions. However, this is the first extant reference to the story of the young couple who were so besotted that they addressed one another as Jupiter and Juno and were transformed into the two well known mountain ranges that lie side by side (running east to west) in Thrace. See Forbes Irving 290.

91   **the Pygmaean mother:** the basic story is as old as Homer (*Il.* 3.3-6, Lattimore's translation):

> *as when the clamour of cranes goes high to the heavens,*
> *when the cranes escape the winter time and the rains unceasing*
> *and clamorously wing their way to the streaming Ocean,*
> *bringing to the Pygmaian men bloodshed and destruction.*

From Antoninus Liberalis (16), we learn of a version of the story in which a Pygmaean woman was turned into a crane for challenging Hera (Juno); this, however, is our only extant reference to a contest. Herodotus (2.32) tells a story of a tribe of small men in Africa. See also Pliny *N.H.* 10.30.58.

93   **Antigone:** this is the earliest extant reference to the story known otherwise only from scholiasts; see Forbes Irving 225.

96   **Laomedon:** king of Troy and father of Priam.

97   **applauding herself:** it is very common for the metamorphosis to preserve, or even enhance, the most salient characteristic of the victim, cf. 6.145. The whole matter is treated at greater length by Hollis (xx) and in my note on 1.234.

98   **Cinyras:** the story is not otherwise known.

101   **olive leaves of peace:** olive bearing was a Greek practice according to Livy (29.16.6, de Sélincourt's translation):

> *The ten Locrian envoys made their appearance before the consuls in the Comitium in true Greek suppliant fashion, dressed in filthy rags, fillets on their brows, and branches of olive in their hands.*

Cf. Soph. *O.T.* 1-3. However, Livy also reports the practice as recognized in a quite different context (30.36.4, de Sélincourt's translation):

> *He [Scipio] was nearly there when he was met by a Carthaginian ship, hung with wollen fillets and olive branches of supplication, which was carrying ten envoys, leading citizens of Carthage, sent by Hannibal's order to sue for peace.*

For other examples, see Virg. *Aen.* 7.154; 8.116 with Eden's note.

102   **her own tree:** the olive; see on 6.70-82.

103 **The Maeonian woman:** Arachne, see on 6.5. As we return to her, so we return to the epithet with which she was introduced. Note that just as Minerva's tapestry was all about mortals who presumed to challenge gods, so Arachne (like the daughters of Pierus) depicts only misconduct by the gods.

104 **Europa:** her tale was told at 2.833-75 (see the note there).

107 **Asterie:** Hesiod (*Theog.* 409-10) mentions her as a daughter of Coeus and wife of Perses; Callimachus (*Hymns* 4.40) alludes to her name as having been borne once by Delos. Arachne's story is presumably the one related by Apollodorus (1.4.1, Frazer's translation):
> *Of the daughters of Coeus, Asteria in the likeness of a quail ['ortygia'] flung herself into the sea in order to escape the amorous advances of Zeus, and a city was formerly called after her Asteria, but afterwards it was named Delos.*

Hyginus (53) tells essentially the same story.

108 **eagle:** the bird of Jupiter (see Virg. *Aen.* 1.394 and Austin's note) and so here to represent Jupiter himself.

109 **Leda:** Apollod. 3.10. 7 (Frazer's translation):
> *But Zeus in the form of a swan consorted with Leda, and on the same night Tyndareus cohabited with her; and she bore Pollux and Helen to Zeus, and Castor and Clytaemnestra to Tyndareus.*

Frazer's note discusses other treatments.

lie back: *recubare*, like 'lie back', can have sexual associations, cf. Lucr. 1.38 where it is used of a very sensuous Mars leaning back on Venus; see also Livy 39.43.4.

110 **satyr:** Bömer discusses the evidence for supposing that this detail was in Euripides' *Antiope*.

111 **Nycteis:** i.e. Nycteus' daughter, Antiope; cf. Apollod. 3.5.5 (Frazer's translation):
> *Antiope was a daughter of Nycteus, and Zeus had intercourse with her. When she was with child, and her father threatened her, she ran away to Epopeus at Sicyon and was married to him. In a fit of despondency Nycteus killed himself, after charging Lycus to punish Epopeus and Antiope. Lycus marched against Sicyon, subdued it, slew Epopeus, and led Antiope away captive. On the way, she gave birth to two sons...Zethus and Amphion.*

See Frazer (p.337) on the Farnese Bull.

112 **Amphitryon:** this very famous story is told by Hesiod (*Shield* 27-56; cf. Hom. *Il.* 14.323-4.) though without the detail of Zeus' disguise as Amphitryon; but see Apollod. 2.4.8 (Frazer's translation):
> *But before Amphitryon reached Thebes, Zeus came by night and prolonging the one night threefold he assumed the likeness of Amphitryon and bedded with Alcmena...But when Amphitryon arrived and saw that he was not welcomed by his wife, he inquired the cause; and*

when she told him that he had come the night before and slept with her, he learned from Tiresias how Zeus had enjoyed her. And Alcmena bore two sons, to wit, Hercules, whom she had by Zeus and who was the elder by one night, and Iphicles, whom she had by Amphitryon.

See Frazer's note for other treatments.

Tyrinthian one: Alcmena; she was the daughter of Electryon of Tiryns (Eur. *Alc.* 838-9).

113 **Danaë:** see 4.610-1. Early references to Danaë as mother of Perseus by Zeus who came to her in a shower of gold include Pindar *Pyth.* 12.11-8 and Soph. *Ant.* 944ff. See also Hom. *Il.* 14.319-20.

Asopis: i.e. Asopus' daughter, Aegina; cf. Apollod. 3.12.6 (Frazer's translation):

The Asopus river was a son of Ocean and Tethys. . .Him Metope, herself a daughter of the river Ladon, married and bore two sons, Ismenus and Pelagon, and twenty daughters, of whom one, Aegina, was carried off by Zeus.

Jupiter's disguise as fire is not found elsewhere.

114 **Mnemosyne:** see on 5.267. The shepherd disguise is not found before Ovid.

Deois: i.e. daughter of Deo (another name for Ceres, (cf. *Hom. Hymns* 2.47), Proserpina. As Anderson observes, it is striking that Arachne should bring her list of Jupiter's misconduct to a climax with this allegation of incest with his own daughter, a point emphasised by Ovid's recent full treatment of the rest of her story (5.362ff.) and its stress on Jupiter's paternity (e.g. 5.514ff.) For this story, see Callimachus fr. 43.117; cf. also Diod. Sic. 3.64.1 and Cic. *de N.D.* 3.23.58 (Rackham's translation):

Likewise there are several Dianas. The first, daughter of Jupiter and Proserpine. . .

115 **she:** Arachne.

116 **Aeolian maiden:** Canace: Apollodorus 1.7.3-4 (Frazer's translation):
Aeolus reigned over the regions about Thessaly. . .He married Enarete. . .and begat seven sons. . .and five daughters, Canace, Alcyone etc. . .Canace had by Poseidon [Neptune] Hopleus and Nireus and Epopeus and Aloeus and Triops; Aloeus married Iphimedeia, daughter of Triops; but she fell in love with Poseidon. . . Poseidon met her and begat two sons, Otus and Ephialtes, who are called the Aloads [Aloidae].

116-7 **Enipeus. . .Aloidae:** here there seems to be a rare confusion between two different conquests by Neptune recounted in the *Odyssey* (11.235-54, Lattimore's translation):

There first I saw Tyro. . .
and she was in love with a river, godlike Enipeus. . .;
taking his likeness, the god who circles the earth and shakes it [Poseidon] lay with her. . .
       she conceived and bore Pelias and Neleus.

and 11.305-8:

172] NOTES: Book VI

> *After her I saw Iphimedeia, wife of Aloeus,*
> *but she told me how she had been joined in love with Poseidon*
> *and borne two sons to him, but these in the end had not lived*
> *long, Otos like a god, and the far-famed Ephialtes.*

As in Apollodorus quoted in the note on 6.116, Otus and Ephialtes were regularly referred to as the Aloidae from as early as Hom. *Il.* 5.385-6.

117 **Bisaltis:** known otherwise only from Hyginus 188; see Forbes Irving 222-3.

118 **fair-haired:** *flaua* can suggest the light yellow either of hair or of Ceres' crops; the absence of such a word in English makes the allusion impossible to render.

118-9 **mother of the grain crops:** Ceres; for the story, too long to quote here, see Paus. 8.25.4-10, 42.1-6.

119-20 **snake-haired mother. . .bird-horse:** Medusa and Pegasus; see 4.797, Hes. *Theog.* 278-81 (Evelyn-White's translation):
> *With her* [Medusa] *lay the Dark-haired One* [Poseidon] *in a soft meadow amid spring flowers. And when Perseus cut off her head there sprang forth great Chrysaor and the horse Pegasus.*

120 **Melantho:** this is the only extant pre-mediaeval reference to the story.

122 **countryman:** for Apollo's service as Admetus' herdsman, see Euripides *Alcestis* 1ff. Arachne is no doubt thinking of the more disreputable version of that story, see Call. *Hymns* 2.47-9 (Mair's translation):
> *Phoebus and Nomius* ['Pastoral'] *we call him* [Apollo] *ever since the time when by Amphrysus he tended the yoke-mares, fired with love of young Admetus.*

For further details, see Mynors on Virg. *G.* 3.1-2.

123-4 **hawk's feather. . .lion's skin:** these must refer to two more disreputable episodes in the story of Apollo, but they are no longer known.

124 **Isse:** we know the name otherwise only from an assertion by a grammarian that it occurs in Parthenius (fr. 15)

125 **Erigone:** this story is otherwise unknown. The more usual story (Hyg. 130 and alluded to at *Met.* 10.451) was that Dionysus had ordered Erigone and her father Icarius, to introduce the world to the joys of wine and that, when they came to Attica, the people became drunk and, thinking that Icarius was trying to murder them, killed him. Erigone hanged herself in grief for her father and was catasterised.

126 **two-formed:** *geminum*; cf. 2.630.
Chiron: Ap. Rhod. 2.1231-41 (Seaton's translation):
> *Cronos* [Saturn]. . .*lay beside Philyra, when he had deceived Rhea; and the goddess found them in the midst of their dalliance; and Cronos leapt up from the couch with a rush in the form of a steed with flowing mane, but Ocean's daughter, Philyra, in shame left the spot and those haunts, and came to the long Pelasgian ridges, where by*

NOTES: Book VI [173

*her union with the transfigured deity she brought forth huge Cheiron,
half like a horse, half like a god.*
See also Mynors on Virg. *G.* 3.92-4 whose note seems to overlook this passage.

128 ***intertextos:*** for the spondaic ending see on 5.165, 265.

129 **Spite:** *Liuor*; pace Bömer's doubts, the phrasing strongly suggests that Spite is personified here. For the history of personification, see my note on 2.760-82. Anderson sums up the situation well:

> *Much in the narrative has led us to believe that Arachne will be punished like the exemplary figures whom Minerva portrays in the four corners of her tapestry. Therefore, Ovid's comment, stated in measured spondees and emphasized by the repeated* non illud, [represented in the translation by the repeated 'not' with the proper names] *comes as a surprise. Arachne is not an inferior weaver; she is not defeated like the daughters of Pieros in the preceding tale, like Neptune in Minerva's earlier contest, like Niobe (somewhat differently) in the next...*

130 **manly-maid:** *uirago*, used by Ovid only here and at 2.765, both times for Minerva; the Latin word is a striking formation based on *uir*, 'man', but indelibly associated with *uirgo*, 'virgin'. Virgil uses the word of Juturna (*Aen.* 12.468). 'Manly-maid' is an attempt to capture the two elements that together give the word its peculiar flavour but it is too clumsy and contrived to do justice to *uirago*. The best alternative suggested to me is 'warrior-maid' but, to my mind, it loses the sexual prevarication implicit in *uirago*. In English, 'virago' has preserved the terrifying connotations of its Latin origin but has lost its awful purity and most of its sexual undertone.
her: i.e. Arachne's; see on 5.30.

131 **heavenly crimes:** the phrase well points up the issue that was offending Minerva.

132 **mount Cytorus:** behind the port of Cytorus in Paphlagonia lay hills famous for boxwood; cf. 4.311.

133 **three times or four:** *ter quater*; the ultimate origin of this phrase is Hom. *Od.* 5.306 where Odysseus, in the expectation of immediate drowning, claims that those Greeks who fell before Troy were '*three times and four* more happy' than he was; Virgil (*Aen.* 1.94) picks it up and puts it into Aeneas' mouth when he too thinks he is about to drown. These elevated associations clearly add to the humour here. For similar uses of the phrase, cf. Hor. *Od.* 1.31.13, Virg. *G.* 1.410.
Idmonian: cf. 6.8.
Arachnes: Greek genitive.

135 **raised her up:** *leuauit* can suggest 'raising up', the natural action taken to assist a victim of hanging. It also has a sense of 'making light' (cf. 8.798) which, in view of the metamorphosis, may also be suggested here.

139 **Hecataean:** Hecate was the archetypical witch. Cf. e.g. Eur. *Med.* 394ff., Cat. 34.15, Virg. *Aen.* 6.247.

142 **very small. . .small:** *minimum. . .parua*; if 'the best is the enemy of the good' is an example of polyptoton (see on 5.52), one might just think of this too as one, since *minimus* is the superlative of *paruus*, just as 'best' is the superlative of 'good'.

145 **as before:** once more, the continuity in metamorphosis is stressed; see on 6.97.

146-312: Niobe
One of the most familiar figures in antiquity. We meet her first in Homer where she is already well known since Achilles uses her story to persuade Priam to eat (*Il.* 24.601-17, Lattimore's translation):

> Now you and I must remember our supper.
> For even Niobe, she of the lovely tresses, remembered
> to eat, whose twelve children were destroyed in her palace,
> six daughters, and six sons in the pride of their youth, whom Apollo
> killed with arrows from his silver bow, being angered
> with Niobe, and shaft-showering Artemis killed the daughters;
> because Niobe likened herself to Leto of the fair colouring
> and said Leto had borne only two, she herself had borne many;
> but the two, though they were only two, destroyed all those others.
> Nine days long they lay in their blood, nor was there anyone
> to bury them, for the son of Kronos made stones out of
> the people; but on the tenth day the Uranian gods buried them.
> But she remembered to eat when she was worn out with weeping.
> And now somewhere among the rocks, in the lonely mountains,
> in Sipylos, where they say is the resting place of the goddesses
> who are nymphs, and dance beside the waters of Acheloios,
> there, stone still, she broods on the sorrows that the gods gave her.

Both Aeschylus and Sophocles wrote tragedies entitled *Niobe* but only fragments survive. For full accounts of Ovid's possible sources, see Otis (1966) 375-6, (1970) 404-5, Forbes Irving 294-6. The story clearly continues the theme of presumptuous humans. Otis (148-52), in a full and interesting discusion, suggests that Ovid's originality resides largely in seeing the eventual metamorphosis as a natural process rather than as a divine act. In view of 6.172ff. (and especially 176), I do not, however, understand why Otis (148) says:

> It is important to note that Ovid here ignores the tradition of Niobe's divine origin. Her claim to equality with Latona is represented solely as hybris of the worst sort (a mortal's claim to be a god). The ancestors of ll. 172f. prove nothing.

But the lines surely explain, though they do not excuse, Niobe's pretensions. For other points, see Forbes Irving 146-8.

149 **Sipylus:** a mountain on the border between Lydia and Ionia; for its association with Niobe, see Hom. *Il.* 24.615 quoted in the note on 6.146-312.

151 **give way:** *cedere*; the same word was used of Arachne at 6.6, 32.

152 **husband's:** she was married to Amphion of Thebes (6.221, Apollod. 3.5.6) and we know from the scholiast to *Iliad* 24.599ff. that Sophocles set the children's deaths in Thebes but had Niobe return home to Lydia.

skills: see on 6.178-9.

156 Anderson rightly compares 3.348 (Tiresias' comment on Narcissus): *'If he does not get to know himself'* and 3.517-8 (Tiresias' comment on Pentheus):
> *'How lucky you would be if you too were to be made*
> *bereft of this light, so that you could not see the Bacchic rights.'*

157 **Tiresias' daughter, Manto:** Tiresias was the long-lived blind seer most familiar to us from Sophocles' Theban plays, but important as early as Homer's *Odyssey* (11.90-151). For further details, see on 3.316-38. Manto was known to Apollodorus (3.7.4) as Tiresias' daughter but this is her first extant association with Niobe. In spite of Tiresias' longevity, it is striking that his daughter should be active at the time of Amphion when he himself was so important in the stories of Oedipus, the successor to Laius, who was himself the successor to Amphion (Apollod. 3.5.7).

159 **Ismenides:** daughters of the Ismenus, a river that flows near to Thebes; cf. 3.372.

160 **Latona and the two Latona-born:** Latona (Greek 'Leto') and her children Apollo and Diana (Artemis).

163 **Thebaides:** daughters of Thebes.

165 **all encompassed. . .companions:** the crowd is a measure of importance; see Austin on Virg. *Aen.* 2.40.

167 **and, as far as her anger allowed, beautiful:** note how neatly Ovid makes us recognize the sort of person Niobe was.

170-202 For the implications of this blasphemous speech, see on 5.11.

172 **Tantalus:** an unpropitious start to her claims; Tantalus had horribly abused his right to dine with the gods; see Pindar *Ol.* 1.36-58 (Lattimore's translation):
> *Son of Tantalos [Pelops], against older men I will say*
> *that when your father summoned the gods*
> *to that stateliest feast at beloved Sipylos,*
> *and gave them to eat and received in turn,*
> *then he of the shining trident caught you up,*
>
> *his heart to desire broken, and with his horses and car of gold*
> *carried you up to the house of Zeus and his wide honor,*
> *where Ganymede at a later time*
> *came for the same desire in Zeus.*
> *But when you were gone, and men from your mother looked,*
> *nor brought you back,*
> *some man, a neighbor, spoke quietly for spite,*
> *how they took you and with a knife*
> *minced your limbs into bubbling water*
> *and over the table divided and ate*
> *flesh of your body, even to the last morsel.*

176] NOTES: Book VI

> *I cannot understand how a god could gorge thus; I recoil.*
> *Many a time disaster has come to the speaker of evil.*
> *If they who watch on Olympos have honored*
> *any man, that man was Tantalos; but he was not*
> *able to swallow his great fortune, and for his high stomach*
> *drew a surpassing doom when our father*
> *hung the weight of the stone above him.*
> *He waits ever the stroke at his head and is divided from joy.*

For the next part of the story, see 6.401-11. He was horribly punished either as in Pindar or as in Homer (*Od.* 11.582-92, Lattimore's translation):

> *And I saw Tantalos also, suffering hard pains, standing*
> *in lake water that came up to his chin, and thirsty*
> *as he was, he tried to drink, but could capture nothing;*
> *for every time the old man, trying to drink, stooped over,*
> *the water would drain away and disappear, and the black earth*
> *showed at his feet, and the divinity dried it away. Over*
> *his head trees with lofty branches had fruit like a shower descending,*
> *pear trees and pomegranate trees and apple trees with fruit shining,*
> *and figs that were sweet and olives ripened well, but each time*
> *the old man would straighten up and reach with his hands for them,*
> *the wind would toss them away toward the clouds overhanging.*

This is the fate from which English 'tantalize' arises; see also 4.458.

174 **Pleiades:** cf. Apollod. 3.10.1 (Frazer's translation):
> *Atlas and Pleione, daughter of Ocean, had seven daughters called the Pleiades, born to them at Cyllene in Arcadia, to wit: Alcyone, Merope, Celaeno, Electra, Sterope, Taygete, and Maia.*

For their sister, Dione, Niobe's mother, see Hyginus 83: *Pelops the son of Tantalus and of Atlas' daughter, Dione...*

Atlas: readers have already encountered his metamorphosis to a mountain (4.657-62); here, Niobe's choice is not just unfortunate, it is also suggestive of her fate.

176 **grandfather...father-in-law:** Jupiter was father both of Niobe's father, Tantalus (Hyg. 82) and of her husband, Amphion (Apollod.3.5.5).

177 **Phrygian races:** the people of her birthplace (6.147).
Cadmus' palace: her home in Thebes after her marriage; Cadmus was the founder of Thebes (3.127-31).

177-9 **me...me...my...me:** *me...me...mei...meque*; a strikingly blasphemous parody of the standard hymnic form with its repeated *te* ('you'), cf. e.g. 1.559-60, 4.17-28, 7.433-50, Call. *Hymns* 1.6-9, Lucr. 1.6-8, Cat. 34.13-17, Virg. *Aen.* 8.293-9, Nisbet-Hubbard on Hor. *Od.* 1.10.9.

178-9 **assembled by my husband's lyre:** cf. Ap. Rhod. 1.736-41 (Seaton's translation):
> *Thebe [sic] still ungirt with towers was lying near, whose foundations they were just then laying in eager haste. Zethus on his shoulders was lifting the peak of a steep mountain...and Amphion after him, singing*

> *loud and clear on his golden lyre, moved on, and a rock twice as large followed his footsteps.*
>
> **husband's...husband:** *mariti... uiroque*; see on 5.55-6.

186-7 **the Titan daughter of...Coeus:** Uranus' (Heaven's) sons were called Titans (Hes. *Theog.* 207-8), and one of them, Coeus (Hes. *Theog.* 134), was father of Leto (Latona) (Hes. *Theog.* 405-6, Hom. *Hymns* 3.62).

some Coeus or other: *nescioquoque... Coeo*; vocabulary and sound combine to produce an effect of great contempt.

187 **refused a tiny lodging:** Latona's pregnancy by Jupiter had naturally angered Juno, and she saw to it that nowhere in the Greek world would she be allowed to rest and give birth, until eventually Delos did. Callimachus (*Hymns* 4.56ff.) tells the story in great detail.

192 **seventh part:** for a full discussion of how many children Niobe had according to the various authorities, see Frazer's exhaustive discussion on Apollod. 3.5.6. The essential point is, of course, that they far outnumber Latona's two.

193-200 The foolish confidence of these words prepare the reader for the inevitable outcome and even, in the repeated assertion that she can afford some loss (195-6 and 197-200), the manner of her undoing.

193 **lucky:** *felix*, picked up from 6.156; our cultural assumptions which still owe something to the doctrine of original sin make such words impossible to render precisely. *felix* suggests being favoured by fortune or the gods and *therefore* deserving favour. We are so suspicious of good fortune that our words, 'lucky', 'fortunate' or 'blessed' either have overtones of fortune beyond our deserts or are tinged with inappropriate piety. Of course, there was also in antiquity a more imprecise feeling that good fortune could not be relied on and that it was foolish to take it for granted; Niobe is a spectacular example of what happens to those who ignore that wisdom.

213 **her father's tongue:** the story is in Euripides (*Or.* 4-10, Way's translation):
> *He, the once blest,—I mock not at his doom—*
> *begotten of Zeus, as men say, Tantalus,*
> *dreading the crag which topples o'er his head,*
> *now hangs mid air; and pays the penalty,*
> *as the tale telleth, for that he, a man,*
> *honoured to sit god-like at meat with Gods,*
> *yet bridled not his tongue—O shameful madness!*

Niobe's fault was clearly hereditary.

215-6 **Phoebus...Phoebe:** Apollo and Diana.

217 **covered in cloud:** it is an epic convention as old as Homer (e.g. *Il.* 5.776) that gods cover themselves in cloud or mist when visiting the earth; cf. 2.790.

222-3 **backs...red from Tyrian juice:** shorthand for 'backs covered by a purple cloth'.

178] NOTES: Book VI

223   bridles heavy with gold: *habenae* strictly means 'reins' but 'reins heavy with gold' seems implausible. Bömer gives many parallels for the general picture starting with Hom. *Il.* 5.358. There it is certainly the head-stall that bears the gold. I believe we have a similar picture here; I have, accordingly, used 'bridle', a term for all the head gear and the reins.

224-66   Ovid's seven names for the seven sons coincide with those of Apollodorus (3.5.6) and Hyginus (11) except that instead of 'Alphenor' and 'Ilioneus', Apollodorus and Hyginus offer 'Eupinytus' and 'Agenor' ('Arche-' Hyginus). Bömer refers also to schol. Eur. *Phoen.* 159 etc.

224   Ismenus: the name of Thebes' river, a suitable name for a Theban boy.

226   steed: *quadripedis*, literally 'quadruped'; this sort of 'kenning' (the use of periphrasis instead of a more normal word) is an ancient device to produce poetic elevation. Hollis (on 8.376) has a very full discussion. The history of this particular example is traced by Harrison (on Virg. *Aen.* 10.892-3) as far back as Aristophanes (*Nub.* 659). It is not often effective for poetic elevation in English which prefers archaism; hence 'steed'.

229   forequarter: *armo*; Ovid uses the word only of animals and Centaurs. As 10.700 vividly reveals, the *umerus* of a man is the *armus* of an animal.

231   Sipylus: the name of a mountain in Niobe's home country (see on 6.149) another appropriate name.

233   any: *qua*, literally 'from anywhere'.

239   Phaedimus: a Greek name meaning 'shining' or 'famous'.

241   gleaming: *nitidae*; the word refers to the effect of the olive oil rubbed onto the wrestlers and dropping to the floor.

243   breast to breast: *pectora pectoribus*, see on 5.52.

247   *uersarunt. . .exhalarunt:* Anderson points out the unusual internal rhyme. The line also has a spondaic ending (see on 5.165), perhaps to represent the wrestlers' final gasp.

251   fateful iron tip: *fatifero. . .ferro*; no attempt has been made to reproduce the word-play and internal rhyme. *ferro* (literally 'iron') is frequently used alone of iron weapons' especially the sword, but here (as at 236) the arrow head. In English, however, 'iron' alone necessarily conjures up the humble domestic implement while '(arrow) tip' loses the telling contrast between the implicit softness of 'his inmost vitals' and the hardness of 'iron'.

254   non: with *simplex*.
     unshorn: *intonsum*, a sign of youth; Apollo (1.564) says of himself: *'as my head is youthful, my hair unshorn* [intonsis]'.

255 Damasichthon: 'Earth-subduer', an epithet of Poseidon (Neptune) at Bacchylides 15.19.

259-60 Ovid likes this picture of blood spurting through the air; cf. 4.121-4 of Pyramus' mortal wound (where, however, high spurting blood is essential to explain the staining of the mulberries):
> As he lay face up upon the earth, blood spurted high,
> just as when a pipe with faulty lead
> bursts and hissing through the hole there is a long thin
> jet of water which cleaves the air with its impact.

emico and *eiaculor* occur in both passages; neither is a very common word and *eiaculor* does not occur elsewhere in the *Metamorphoses*.

260 drilled: *terebrata*; the Latin verb is a technical term from carpentry and surgery. (The English 'trepan' is ultimately derived from the related Greek word for the tool.) The earliest literary appearance of the carpentry version is in the memorable scene in the *Odyssey* (9.384ff.) where the actions of Odysseus and his men in putting out Polyphemus' eye are likened to it. Virgil uses *terebro* for his description of the same incident (*Aen.* 3.63, see Williams's note for further details) and also for the sensible suggestion that the Trojans bore a hole in the Trojan horse to inspect what was within (*Aen.* 2.38). Once again, Ovid transfers a word from a most elevated moment in epic to a far less dignified context.

263 (unaware...ask): for the aside, see on 5.280-2.

265-6 Cool comfort indeed. The same idea occurs more memorably in Shakespeare (*Romeo and Juliet* 3.1.100, almost the last words of Mercutio):
> No, 'tis not so deep as a well, nor so wide as a church-door; but 'tis enough, 'twill serve.

271 Amphion: according to Apollodorus (3.5.6), he survived; according to Hyginus (9), he was shot by Apollo. By having him commit suicide, Ovid surely suggests a more natural reaction than Niobe's.

273 Niobe...Niobe: *Niobe Niobe*; notice how Latin can greatly increase the force of the repetition by juxtaposing the two mentions of the name. The two Latin forms are identical; even so, they are in different cases so that there is some sense of polyptoton (see on 5.52).

281-2 The double 'she said' (*ait* and *dixit*) has persuaded most editors that one or other of these lines is spurious. Many have deleted 281 on the grounds that *efferor* ('I am being carried out') requires the explanation afforded by *per funera septem* ('through seven funerals'), though, as Bömer shows, the argument is not decisive. On the other hand, the repeated *pascere* ('feed yourself') is effective and Ovidian whereas *corque... satia* ('Glut your wild heart') seems lame by comparison.

283 I am being carried out: *efferor*, a technical term for being carried out for burial. Niobe despairs for a moment but her stupidity quickly reasserts itself.

triumph: *triumpha*; another example of the deliberate introduction of intrusive and anachronistic Roman concepts (see on 5.155); Niobe momentarily sees herself and her sons being carried in a Roman triumph.

283-5 **victorious. . .victorious. . .victor:** *uictrixque. . .uictrix. . .uinco*; note Niobe's fixation on the idea of conquest. These words both confirm Niobe's folly and prepare us for the inevitable outcome.

288-301 Ovid devotes 43 lines to the death of the sons but only 14 to that of the daughters. This is achieved partly by omitting the daughters' names, though they are in Apollodorus (3.5.6) and Hyginus (11). Homer (see on 6.146-312) does not make it clear whether the sons or the daughters were killed first. According to Apollodorus the daughters died first, in the house, and the sons later while hunting on Cithaeron; Hyginus (9) agrees with Apollodorus on the settings but (*pace* Anderson) has Ovid's order.

294 A line almost universally condemned as, in Anderson's words, 'impossibly bad'.

297-301 With one child left, even Niobe finally realises, too late, the full horror of what she has brought upon herself. Both Apollodorus and Hyginus report one surviving daughter (for further details, see on 6.418), but Ovid's version is more effective dramatically and morally.

298-9 **all. . .all:** *toto. . .tota*; the polyptoton (see on 5.52) underlines the pathos.

299-300 one, the youngest. . .youngest. . .alone: *unam minimamque. . .minimam. . .et unam*; the chiasmus (a repetition in the form ABBA named after the Greek letter 'chi' (X)) is clearer in the Latin than the English because *unam* can mean both 'one' and 'alone'. Like many rhetorical devices, it has no effect in itself but it heightens the effect of the words it highlights. Here, the pathos of 'one' and 'youngest' (literally 'smallest') is vividly underlined. After despising Niobe for her stupidity, suddenly we cannot fail to feel sympathy.

301 **childless:** *orba*; the very word Niobe had used to taunt Latona (6.200).

303-8 **moved. . .unmoving. . .to be moved. . .movements:** *mouet. . .immota. . .moueri. . . motus*; here the polyptoton (see on 5.52) draws attention to movement or, rather, lack of movement in the petrified Niobe.

305 **sad sockets:** *maestis. . .genis*; the *genae* are the upper part of the cheek including the area around the eyes; sometimes, though clearly not here, the word is used to mean 'eyes'; here, we are presumably to think of red-rimmed eyes.

306 **even her tongue itself:** the cause of her undoing, cf. 6.213.
hardened: *duro*; the adjective is used proleptically (i.e. in anticipation), the palate hardened when it froze. The usage is less common in English, but consider, 'Dig a deep hole'.

310-11 Cf. Pausanias 1.21.3 (Frazer's translation):

> *This Niobe I myself saw when I ascended Mount Sipylus. Close at hand it is merely a rock with no resemblance to a woman, mourning or otherwise; but if you stand farther off, you will think you see a weeping woman bowed with grief.*

311 **snatched off to:** Ovid sides with those who see Niobe's end back in her native Phrygia (see on 6.152). The obvious problem of motivating her return is solved in this radical way. See Anderson for a fuller discussion.

fixed: *fixa*; in both languages the word can mean either 'fixed in place' or 'rendered motionless' (see *OLD* s.v. 'figo' 6,7); both senses seem to be hinted at here.

313-81 Lycian farmers
Antoninus Liberalis (35) attributes this story to Menecrates and Nicander. His version is more complex and includes an intervention by wolves (Greek 'lykoi') apparently introduced to explain the origin of 'Lycia'.

313 **the anger of the divinity:** such comments on public reaction to divine punishment are not uncommon in the *Metamorphoses*; cf. e.g. 3.732-3 and 4.416ff. (a very close parallel), both adduced by Anderson. At 3.253-5, after Actaeon's punishment, the format is superficially quite different, openly inviting speculation on Diana's fairness:
> *Opinion was divided: to some the goddess seemed*
> *more savage than was fair, others praised her and called her worthy*
> *of her strict virginity; both sides could find their reasons.*

That specific invitation to judge is made more subtly here; as Anderson suggests, the juxtaposition of the two stories, in one of which Latona promptly punishes foolish pride with great severity and in the other she punishes wanton cruelty relatively slowly and more leniently, must cause us to reflect on divine punishment, a theme which has dominated since the beginning of book 3 (see Otis 84) and which was hardly absent in books 1-2.

315 **twin-bearing:** *gemelliparae*; almost certainly an Ovidian coinage occuring only here and at *F.* 5.542, also of Latona.

316 **retold:** *renarrant*; the most familiar occurrence of this rare word is at Virg. *Aen.* 3.717 where it is used to sum up Aeneas' account of his adventures in books 2-3. There, as Williams points out, the verb does not mean 'tell again' but the *re-* has more the force associated with the prefix in English 'recite' or 'recount'; the same is true of the only other Ovidian use of the word (5.635). Here, however, 'tell again' seems more plausible. 'Retell' (like *renarro*) is an unusual formation and seems capable of bearing either sense.

321 **for my father:** this inconsequential introductory story is surely an Ovidian invention to create suspense and plausibility.

327-8 'Ovid cleverly constructs 327 and 328 with identical metrical arrangements . . . and repeated words disposed in identical positions, to enhance the effect of the imitative action of the young man, copying his guide's reverence.' Anderson.

332 **king's wife:** *regia coniunx*; here, of course, Juno, wife of the king of heaven. Both in Latin and English, the phrase would more naturally refer to a human queen as it

NOTES: Book VI

does at 13.483 and Virg. *Aen.* 7.56. Twice elsewhere (9.259, 14.592), Ovid uses the phrase of Juno but in both cases the context makes the meaning more immediately obvious; at 10.46 he uses the phrase of Proserpina.

333-4 For the story, see on 6.187.

335 **palm:** as early as Homer (*Od.* 6.163), we are told of a famous palm on Delos. Its rôle as a support for Latona as she gives birth emerges at *Hom. Hymns* 3.117; cf. Eur. *Hec.* 458-61 (where it is entwined with the laurel), Call. *Hymns* 4.210.

Pallas' tree: the olive (see on 6.70-82) at the birth of Apollo and Diana seems to be known only from here.

336 **stepmother:** *nouerca*; strictly, in both languages, the term is used of a father's new wife who replaces the mother. Here it is used of Juno, the legitimate wife in relation to the children of the husband's mistress (Latona). In most cultures, the stepmother is proverbially an evil figure (cf. 1.147, Hor. *Epod.* 5.9) and the term is used here to draw attention to Juno's hostility.

337 **they say:** see on 5.49.

339 **Chimera-bearing:** *Chimaeriferae*, probably another Ovidian coinage; the word occurs nowhere else. For the Chimera and its association with Lycia, see Hom. *Il.* 6.171-3, 179-82 (Lattimore's translation):

*Bellerophontes went to Lykia in the blameless convoy
of the gods; when he came to the running stream of Xanthos, and Lykia,
the lord of wide Lykia tendered him full-hearted honour.*

*... he sent him away with orders to kill the Chimaira
none might approach; a thing of immortal make, not human,
lion-fronted and snake behind, a goat in the middle,
and snorting out the breath of the terrible flame of bright fire.*

'Chimera' has, of course, entered English meaning 'a mere wild fancy'.

341 **starry:** *sidereo*; i.e. 'of the sun' as at 1.779, 4.169.

343 **of moderate size:** *mediocris aquae*; literally 'of moderate water'.

346 **Titania:** Latona, daughter of the Titan Coeus (see on 6.186-7). At 3.173, *Titania* is used for her daughter, Diana and at 1.395 for Pyrrha, daughter of the Titan Iapetus. Shakespeare uses the name for his Queen of the Fairies in *A Midsummer-Night's Dream*.

348 **forbade...forbade:** *uetat... uetantes*; see on 5.52.

349-57 **water...water...waters...water... water:** *aquis... aquarum... undas... aquae... unda*; see on 5.55-6.

359 For the aside, see on 5.280-2.

366 **Coeus' daughter:** see on 6.186-7.

369 Fränkel (215 n.42): 'In the story of the Lycian peasants, the thirsty Latona asks them to let her drink from the pond, and adds: "you will have given me life in the water" (6.357). The phrasing strikes us as strange. . .: when the peasants refused, Latona gave them life in the water (369)." As my translation shows, Ovid actually goes from *aqua* [water] to *stagno* [pond], but the point still seems valid.

376 **under water, under water:** *sub aqua. . .sub aqua*; the Latin must be an onomatopoeic attempt to produce the sound of frogs croaking.

382-400 Marsyas
Another story of foolish human rivalry with the gods to follow Pierus' daughters (see on 5.294-678), Arachne (see on 6.1-145) and Niobe (see on 6.146-312). This is by far the most savage, and the savagery is accentuated because the story itself is passed over - only the grim punishment is described in full. For the story see Apollod. 1.4.2 (Frazer's translation):
> *Apollo also slew Marsyas, the son of Olympus. For Marsyas, having found the pipes which Athena had thrown away because they disfigured her face, engaged in a musical contest with Apollo. They agreed that the victor should work his will on the vanquished, and when the trial took place Apollo turned his lyre upside down in the competition and bade Marsyas do the same. But Marsyas could not, so Apollo was judged the victor and despatched Marsyas by hanging him on a tall pine tree and stripping off his skin.*

384 **Latous:** i.e. Apollo, Latona's son; the epithet links this with the previous story. For the Doric form (instead of *Letous*), see Nisbet-Hubbard on Hor. *Od.* 1.31.18.
 Tritoniac: Athenian; Tritonia was a cult title of Minerva (Athene) as early as Homer (e.g. *Il.* 4.515); for a fuller discussion see Austin on Virg. *Aen.* 2.171.
 reed: the flute (*tibia*, 386) played by Minerva and taken over by Marsyas (see on 6.382-400). By 'reed' is meant here a plant stem to provide a wind instrument, not the small piece of reed used in the mouth-piece of the modern bassoon etc.

392-5: The lament for the lost poet is a common motif, cf. Virg. *Ecl.* 5.20-44. This lament, however, is much shorter and seems much less elevated; see in particular on 395.

393 **Olympus:** either Marsyas' father (see on 6.382-400) or his pupil (Hyg. 161, 273.11).

395 **grazed. . .herds:** the line is a close imitation of a line in Lucretius' list of animals useful to man (5.866): *lanigerasque simul pecudes* [= greges] *et bucera saecla* [= armenta]. The imitation surely undercuts the apparent solemnity. For the double 'kenning', see on 6.266, though here, the elevation of language may have a slightly mocking effect.

400 **the river:** See Herod. 7.26 (Bettenson's translation):
> *. . .and another river, too, of equal size, called (as its proper name) the Cataract. This latter stream rises in the actual market-square of Celaenae and joins the Maeander. Here too the skin of Marsyas the*

184] NOTES: Book VI

> *Silenus is exhibited; according to the Phrygian legend Apollo flayed Marsyas and hung the skin up here in the market-place.*

Also Livy 38.13.6 (de Sélincourt's translation):

> *This river [the Meander] has its source in springs at Celaenae, a city which was at one time capital of Phrygia; from there there was a migration to a spot not far from old Celaenae, and to the new city was given the name of Apamea. . .The river Marsyas also rises not far from the source of the Meander and empties itself into that river: and the story goes that it was at Celaenae that Marsyas had his pipe-playing contest with Apollo.*

401-11 Pelops

This is, of course, a continuation of the story of Tantalus' family (see on 6.172). The story is in Hyginus (83):

> *When Pelops, the son of Tantalus and Atlas' daughter, Dione, had been killed by Tantalus at the banquet of the gods, Ceres ate his shoulder, but he had his life restored by the gift of the gods; when the rest of his limbs had been brought together as they had been, Ceres fitted an ivory shoulder in place of his incomplete one.*

Euripides (*I.T.* 385-8) assumes that his audience is familiar with the story.

404-5   pulled his cloak from his breast: a standard gesture of grief; cf. 3.480.

412-674 Procne and Philomela

For a detailed discussion of possible sources, see Frazer on Apollod. 3.14.8, Otis (1966) 377-81, (1970) 406-10 and Forbes Irving 248-9. Ovid now turns from the relationship between gods and humans to that between one human and another. It is a powerful story told with all Ovid's skill. For speculation on a development in the narrative possibly introduced by Ovid, see on 6.506-7. For an analysis of the underlying meaning of the myth in its various forms, see Forbes Irving 99-107.

412-23   This transition from Niobe to Procne and Philomela is reminiscent of 1.577-87 where the rivers assemble to console Peneus on the loss of his daughter Daphne, but Inachus is absent because of his loss of Io. See also on 7.162.

414   Pelopian: Pelops was Niobe's brother and the father of Atreus and Thyestes and so grandfather of Agamemnon, Menelaus and Aegistheus. The connexion with Niobe clearly helps in the transition.

415   Calydon: for the story, see 8.260ff. Calydon is near the northern shore of the Corinthian Gulf towards the western end. Otherwise, all the towns in this list are in the Peloponnese.

416   Orchomenos: see on 5.607. In view of the preponderance of Peloponnesian towns, I am asuming that this is the Arcadian Orchomenos (Hom. *Il.* 2.603-5) and not the one in Boeotia (*Il.* 2.511).

417   fierce Messene: presumably a reference to the Messenian Wars of the eighth and seventh centuries.

low-lying: *humiles*; by far the best known Cleonae was just south-west of Corinth (for the others in Laconia, Phocis and Chalcidice, see Bömer). *humiles* is either literal 'low-lying' (it was situated in the Tretus valley) or metaphorical 'humble'. Neither is altogether satisfactory in view of Strabo 8.6.19 p.377 (Jones's translation):

> *Cleonae is a town situated by the road that leads from Argos to Corinth, on a hill which is surrounded by dwellings on all sides and is well fortified, so that in my opinion Homer's words "well-built Cleonae" [Il. 2.570] were appropriate.*

For further details, see Bömer.

418 **Nelean:** Neleus was king of Pylos and was succeeded by his only surviving son, Nestor (Hom. *Il.* 11.691-2). It is possible that here Ovid is also drawn by the alternative version of the Niobe legend according to which one daughter survived (see on 6.297-301); both Apollodorus (3.5.6) and Hyginus (9, 10) name her as Chloris and claim that she went on to marry Neleus. This too then would provide a link.

Pitthean: Pittheus was Pelops' son (another link with Tantalus' family) and king of Troezen; see Eur. *Med.* 683-4, *Hipp.* 11.

419-20 A view of Greece from the Peloponnesian point of view. 419 describes those cities within the Peloponnese thought of as 'confined' (*clauduntur*) by the Isthmus and 420 those to the north of the Isthmus and visible from (or by means of) it. See also on 5.407.

421 The intrusion of the poet's surprise and the address to Athens itself both suggest that something significant is afoot. These interventions are much commoner than usual in this section, see 6.438, 472-3. For the device itself, see on 5.280-2.

422-5 Notice both the speed of the action here and Ovid's choice (invention?) of a much more exciting war than the one found in Apollodorus (3.14.8, Frazer's translation):

> *Pandion married Zeuxippe, his mother's sister, and begat two daughters, Procne and Philomela. . .But war having broken out with Labdacus on a question of boundaries, he called in the help of Tereus, son of Ares [Mars], from Thrace, and having with his help brought the war to a successful close, he gave Tereus his own daughter Procne in marriage.*

427 **Gradivus:** (stress the middle syllable) a Roman title of Mars of uncertain origin, cf. Virg. *Aen.* 3.35 and Williams, 10.542 and Harrison. Only here, we are told, is the -a- short.

428 *pronuba*: an untranslatable term for the matron who conducted the bride to the marriage chamber; cf. Virg. *Aen.* 4.166 (and Austin) and the pseudo-marriage between Aeneas and Dido. Indeed, the two descriptions have much in common linguistically, and both also display anachronistic Roman terminology (see on 5.155), Virgil's presumably to relate Rome's past to its present, and Ovid's in his normal sense of playfulness. The outlook for this ceremony is even more bleak than for the Virgilian one as the language foreshadows. Anderson speculates that contemporaries would also think of numerous disastrous dynastic marriages of the late republic and early empire.

186] NOTES: Book VI

429 **Hymenaeus:** the marriage hymn; it is as early as Homer (*Il.* 18.493); for a full discussion see Fordyce on Cat. 61.

430-1 **Eumenides:** 'the Kindly Ones', the standard Greek euphemism for the Furies. Their participation, accentuated by the anaphora at the start of two consecutive lines, is a clear indication of the trouble to come. Virgil excludes them from the Dido story until they appear in a simile (*Aen.* 4.469) just as she is contemplating suicide.

430 **from a funeral:** lighted torches were a prominent feature of Roman weddings; the symbolism of their being carried by the Furies and snatched from funeral pyres is not hard to interpret.

432 **owl:** *bubo*; the onomatopoeia of the Latin word seems to bring out its sinister associations (see on 5.550). Like *Eumenides*, it is kept back by Virgil in the Dido story for the suicide scene (*Aen.* 4.462). Throughout its history, the owl has been associated with Athens (see D'Arcy Thompson s.v. 'glaux') so that it is just possible that Ovid expects the victims to misinterpet its presence here.

433-4 **under this bird of omen:** *hac aue*, literally 'with this bird' but, because, Romans used birds for augury, the phrase can regularly mean 'with this omen'; see Nisbet-Hubbard on Hor. *Od.* 1.15.5. For the anaphora, see on 6.430-1.

438 **So...us!:** once again, the authorial intervention brings us up short; see on 6.421. For the sentiment, cf. 7.453-4.
Titan: according to Hesiod (*Theog.* 371-2), the Titan, Hyperion, was the father of the Sun, the Moon and Dawn. Hence Cicero, in his translation of Aratus (589) [*de Nat. Deorum* 2.42] uses *Titan* for the sun, followed by Virgil (*Aen.* 4.119), Seneca and others. See also on 1.10.

447-8 **right hand...with right hand:** *dextera...dextrae*; see on 5.52.

448 **with that happy omen:** an ironical pointer to the future.

451-2 **rich...richer:** *diues...diuitior*; see on 5.52.

456-7 For the simile, cf. 1.492 (of Apollo catching light with love for Daphne): '*And as light stubble is fired after the ears are cut*'. There, the 'inappropriateness' of the humble rustic simile must contribute to the absurd image of Apollo. Here too, as Anderson suggests, there must be some element of undercutting especially in 457 where we pass from a normal agricultural practice (see Mynors on Virg. *G.* 1.84-93) to, presumably, an accidental conflagration.

459-60 For the general wildness of the Thracians, see Hor. *Od.* 1.27.2 and Nisbet-Hubbard; it is a commonplace that peoples thought of as inferior are also thought to be excessively devoted to the pleasures of Venus (for the metonymy see on 6.488); for Thracians in particular, see Nepos *Alcibiades* 11.4: '...*Thracians, drunkards and given to sex...*'.

465-6 **held...hold:** *captus... capiunt*; hardly a polyptoton (see on 5.52) for which one would expect some rhetorical point, but an example of Latin's much greater tolerance for this sort of repetition than there is to be found in English.

472-3 **Ye gods...breasts:** Another authorial intervention; see on 6.421.

473-4 A characteristic Ovidian paradox.

476-7 **by her life, and against it:** *perque suam contraque suam... salutem*; literally 'by her safety...'; it is impossible in English to do full justice to this daring and witty syllepsis. The wit reminds us not to take the story too seriously. Cf. 7.347-9; 8.561; see also on 2.312-3; 9.135. Ovid's use of this figure is discussed by Fränkel (197).

478 **prefondled:** *praecontrectat*; the prefix is found, with this verb, only here and must be an Ovidian coinage.

479 **his neck:** i.e. her father's neck as the context makes plain.

480 **spurs...torches...food:** the mixed metaphors are certainly striking and unusual.

482 **no less impious:** litotes; he means that if he were the father he would be much more impious than he in fact is, because he would be contemplating incest.

486 **Phoebus:** Sol, the sun, see on 5.389.

488 **Bacchus:** i.e. 'wine'; this sort of metonomy is widespread in Greek and Roman literature. Other examples in the *Metamorphoses* are to be found at e.g. 2.68; 3.123, 323, 437, 540; 4.258; 6.460; 7.104, 140, 450; 8.7, 292; 9.251.

490 **Odrysian:** the Odrysae lived near the Thracians (Herod. 4.92) and the adjective is used loosely to mean 'Thracian'.

490-3 Cf. Hom. *Il.* 2.1ff. where all the other gods are asleep but Zeus cannot sleep. This becomes an epic cliché; Dido's inability to sleep after Aeneas' recounting of his exploits has made her fall in love with him (Virg. *Aen.* 4.1ff.) is a famous example, and Virgil repeats the motif as she approaches the end (*Aen.* 4.522ff.; see Pease and Austin). Cf. also 7.185-7, 634-5; 8.83ff.

491-2 Again (see on 6.456-7), Ovid invokes his account of Apollo's passion for Daphne (1.500-2):

> he admired her fingers and her hands
> and her arms, bare almost to her shoulders;
> the parts that were covered he supposed were better still.

493 **care:** *cura*; both the Latin word and the English can mean either 'anxiety' or 'affection'; I believe that only 'anxiety' is appropriate here.

496 **I give her to you:** *hanc ego... do*; this echo of the formula for giving a daughter in marriage (cf. *OLD* s.v. 'do' 4a) must give the reader a certain *frisson*. See also on 6.506-7.

188] NOTES: Book VI

497-8 **(and you wanted it too, Tereus):** the parenthesis brings out just how deceived Pandion is; his remark is so much truer than he knows.

502 **piety:** see on 6.630.

506-7 Another even more explicit echo of the betrothal ceremony. Anderson thinks it may relate to another version of the myth according to which Tereus feigns the death of Procne so that he can go through a form of marriage with Philomela. This indeed is the version told by Apollodorus (3.14.8) and Hyginus (45). Whether the change is Ovid's is impossible to tell.

511 **painted:** a stock epithet of ships, cf. 3.639, Nisbet-Hubbard on Hor. *Od.* 1.14.14, Fordyce on Virg. *Aen.* 7.431.

513 **My prayers:** *uota*; the word can mean both 'prayers' and 'the thing prayed for'.

514 Many editors suspect this line because it seems to have been copied from 4.350.

515 **barbarian:** *barbarus*; Anderson's comment is to the point:
> He has avoided using this word to describe Tereus until it is justified by his moral behavior, but has prepared us for it by his remarks on the whole nation of Thracians in 459-60.

Once established, the word is repeated at 533 and 576. Forbes Irving (102), however, correctly observes that 6.460 has prepared us for Tereus' character.

516 **predatory:** the English word has strong animal associations absent from *praedator*; (do not infer from *OLD* that Statius *Theb.* 4.316 is a counter example); 'plundering' might have been a closer choice but there was a need to keep that root for *raptor* (518).

516-8 The epic simile, as so often from Homer on, anticipates and teasingly delays a climax in the story. See also on 6.527-30.

526 **but above all to the great gods:** the climax of the tricolon serves to draw attention to Philomela's piety and the uselessness of the gods.

527-30 Two more similes to add to the one at 516-8. It is characteristic of Homer to group similes at climactic points. In *Iliad* 22, for instance, at the final encounter between Achilles and Hector, there are similes at 93-5, 127-8, 135, 139-42, 162-4, 189-92, 199-200; less overwhelmingly, the brief account in *Odyssey* 9 of Odysseus and his men blinding the Cyclops is framed by two elaborate similes at 384-6 and 391-3. As Anderson and Forbes Irving (105 n.34) observe, the bird similes anticipate the transformation.

532 Perhaps a scribe's crude re-working of 4.138.

533 **barbarian:** see on 6.515.

537 Perhaps a crude anticipation of 6.606.

542-3 Cf. Virg. *Aen.* 1.603-4 (West's translation):

NOTES: Book VI

> ...*if there are any gods who have regard for goodness, if there is any justice in the world, if their minds have any sense of right.*

555-61   See on 5.105-6.

559   Another simile at a memorable moment; see on 6.527-30.
will jump: *salire solet*; see on 6.47-8.

561   **(I would scarcely dare to believe it) they say:** Note that at this peculiarly telling moment, Ovid uses two distancing (see on 5.49) devices.

567   **broad gold:** i.e. a broad gold stripe.

571   **The god:** Sol (Sun).
the twice six signs: the signs of the zodiac; see on 2.70-5.

574-5   **Great...grief:** Anderson reminds us of 'Necessity is the mother of invention'. At *Ars Amat.* 2.43, Ovid expresses much the same idea in similar language: 'Evils often bring out ingenuity' (*ingenium mala saepe mouent*).

576   **barbarian:** see on 6.515.

582   **warp:** *stamen*; the manuscripts read *carmen* ('poem'), but Philomela's work was weaving, not poetry; cf. 6.576.

586   **all engrossed in the idea of punishment:** *poenaeque in imagine tota est*; the phrase recurs at 13.546. I have offered the traditional translation but am slightly tempted to assume a personified *Poenae* and render 'totally took on the look of Punishment'. On balance, however, 13.456 tells against that interpretation.

587-600   The Bacchic scene takes us back to Virgil's Dido (*Aen.* 4.300-3, West's translation):

> *Driven to distraction and burning with passion, she raged and raved around the whole city like a Bacchant stirred by the shaking of the sacred emblems and roused to fury when she hears the name of Bacchus at the biennial orgy and the shouting on Mount Cithaeron calls to her in the night.*

See also on 6.430-1. In the *Aeneid*, it was only a simile; here, the notorious Bacchic orgies were the background and cover for Philomela's revenge.

587   **Sithonian:** strictly speaking, Sithonia was the middle of the three peninsulas of Chalcidice. However, it was often used, as here, to mean Thracian in general.

588   **trieteric:** *trieterica*, borrowed from Virg. *Aen.* 4.302. It means, literally, 'every third year' but, because we no longer employ ancient inclusive reckoning, we would call it 'every other year', hence West's 'biennial' (see on 6.587-600). Pease gives a full history of the word starting at *Hom. Hymns* 1.11-2.

588-90 Night. . .by night. . .by night: the anaphora brings out the point. The nocturnal aspect of Bacchic worship was regarded as one of its most disreputable features; cf. Eur. *Bacchae* 487-9 and Dodds's note.

592   vine wreath, deerskins: standard Bacchic accoutrements; cf. e.g. Eur. *Bacchae* 11-2, 249.

597   'euhoe': the Bacchic cry; cf. e.g. Eur. *Bacchae* 141.

598   seized. . .was seized: *rapit raptae*; see on 5.52.

599   ivy leaves: another standard feature of Bacchic worship; cf. e.g. Eur. *Bacchae* 106.

606   supplanter: *paelex*; a word I usually render 'wench', see on 7.524, where its full range of meaning is discussed.

611ff.   This section on Procne's plans for revenge and especially on her attitude towards the killing of her child should be compared to Euripides' classic exploration of the same theme in the case of Medea which Ovid is clearly imitating and developing (*Med.* 1021-80).

628   tears forced from her: *lacrimis. . .coactis*; Virgil uses the phrase at *Aen.* 2.196 to mean 'crocodile tears' and Austin cites other examples. He is wrong, however, to include our passage since, plainly, these tears are only too sincere.

630   piety: *pietate*, an untranslatable word because it conveys a range of qualities, such as dutiful devotion to the gods, family and country, that we do not see as parts of a single coherent virtue. I translate it 'piety' so that the reader can gain a sense of the range of this important word; here, of course, the predominant sense is 'devotion to family'. See also on 1.149.

635   piety. . .sin: Ovid enjoys this sort of striking oxymoron to bring out the moral dilemma. There is a very similar example at 7.339-40.

636   Ganges tigress: for the tigress as a symbol of cruelty, see on 7.33. It seems to be an Ovidian idea to trace the beast not, as Virgil does, to Hyrcania, but to the Ganges.

643-6   Cf. Ovid's description of Lycaon's conduct (1.226-9):
   And he was not content with that; with his sword-point he cut open
   the throat of a hostage sent from the Molossian tribe
   and boiled part of the half-dead limbs
   in bubbling water and roasted part over the fire.
Both these passages clearly descend from Virg. *Aen.* 1.212-3.

651   his own flesh: *sua uiscera*; i.e. Itys; see on 5.19.

652   night in his mind: exemplifying the more general point made at 6.472-3.

NOTES: Book VI   [191

655   **within:** *intus*; she means 'inside you'; he takes her to mean 'within the room', as at 10.457.

656   **asked. . .he asked:** *quaerit; quaerenti*; a peculiarly poignant example of polyptoton (see on 5.52).

662   **snaky sisters:** the Furies, cf. 4.490-9, Aesch. *Eum.* 128, Virg. *Aen.* 12.845-51. We now remember that the Furies were also present at the beginning of this marriage (6.430-1).

667   **Cecropides:** i.e. Procne and Philomela, descendants of Cecrops, an ancient king of Athens; cf. 2.552ff.

667-70   Note how allusively Ovid treats the metamorphosis. Apollodorus (3.14.8) and Hyginus (45) both report it as the result of merciful divine intervention but, as Anderson points out, this would not suit Ovid's bleaker outlook. According to Apollodorus (and the Greek sources in general), it was Procne who became a nightingale and Philomela a swallow; Hyginus reverses that which prompts Frazer to make this comment:
> *The later Roman mythographers somewhat absurdly inverted the transformation of the two sisters, making Procne the swallow and the tongueless Philomela the songstress nightingale.*

Ovid is not explicit but the bird that 'went up under the roof' must be the swallow because of its nesting habits (*hirundo* covers the house-marten as well as the swallow), while the one that 'sought the woods' must be the shyer nightingale. However, if there is any point to this way of identifying them it may be to suggest that each returns to the scene of her crime, Philomela to the woods where she was ravished, Procne to the house where she organized the slaughter of her son. At *Ars Amat.* 2.383-4, *Fasti* 2.853ff., *Trist.* 3.12.9-10 it is again Procne who becomes the swallow, but at *Trist.* 2.390 and 5.1.60 it seems to be the nightingale. For further details, see Bömer.

667-8   **hovering. . .hovering:** *pendere. . .pendebat*; see on 5.52.

670   **plumage marked with blood:** for the 'chestnut-coloured patch' on the swallow's throat, see Mynors on Virg. *G.* 4.15.

674   This crude line does not sit well with the allusiveness of the rest of the metamorphosis section.

675-721 *Orithyia and Boreas*

Cf. the list in Apollonius Rhodius of those embarking with Jason in search of the Golden Fleece (1.211-23, Seaton's translation):
> *Next came Zetes and Calais, sons of Boreas, whom once Oreithyia, daughter of Erechtheus, bare to Boreas on the verge of wintry Thrace; thither it was that Thracian Boreas snatched her away from Cecropia as she was whirling in the dance, hard by Ilissus' stream. And, carrying her far off, to the spot that men called the rock of Sarpedon, near the river Erginus, he wrapped her in dark clouds and forced her to his will. There they* [Zetes and Calais] *were making their dusky wings quiver upon their ankles on both sides as they rose, a great wonder to behold, wings that gleamed with golden scales: and*

round their backs from the top of the head and neck, hither and thither, their dark tresses were being shaken by the wind.
Plato (*Phaedrus* 229b-c) discusses whether the story is literally true or whether it would be more appropriate to see it as a garbled version of Orithyia's accidental fall into the sea from a blast of the north wind.

681-2   Cephalus...Procris: their story is told at 7.661-865. For the genealogy, see on 7.490-522.

682   had spoilt things for: the disgraceful conduct of Tereus meant that no other Thracian was a welcome suitor for an Athenian princess.

684   entreaties rather than strength: see on 5.418.

690-1   violence...with violence...with violence: *uis...uis...ui*; once again the anaphora (and the polyptoton, see on 5.52) draws attention to the essential issue.

690-9   Ovid enjoys this sort of confusion between the wind as a god and the wind as a natural phenomenon. Virgil plays similarly with Atlas (*Aen.* 4.246-51) and is directly imitated by Ovid (4.657-66, and see my note; there is another particularly amusing example at 11.156-9, 164). Here, as Anderson on 695-6 discusses in detail, the humour depends significantly on the introduction of allusions to Lucretius' rationalist accounts of wind causing thunder, lightning and earthquakes at 6.121-9, 173-7, and 557-60 (Bailey's translation):

> *In this way, too, all things seem often to tremble with heavy thunder, and the great walls of the containing world to be torn apart suddenly and leap asunder, when all at once a gathered storm of mighty wind has twisted its way into the clouds, and, shut up there with its whirling eddy, constrains the cloud more and more on all sides to hollow itself out with thickening all around; and then, when the force and fierce onslaught of the wind have weakened it, it splits and makes a rending crash with a frightful crashing sound.*

> *In this manner, too, the clouds colour places with leaping light, and the storm lightens with quivering dart. When wind has come within a cloud, and whirling there has, as I have shown before, made the hollow cloud grow thick, it grows hot with its own swift movement.*

> *Moreover, when the wind gathering throughout the cavernous places of the earth blows strong from one point, and with all its weight presses on the lofty caves with mighty strength, the earth leans over to where the swooping force of the wind presses it.*

710   Ciconian: the Cicones lived on the Southern coast of Thrace and were known as early as Hom. *Il.* 2.846.

711   Actaean: i.e. 'Athenian'. The adjective occurs in Callimachus (fr. 230) and was taken into Latin apparently by Virgil (*Ecl.* 2.24). Acte was an old name for Attica (Apollod. 3.14.1).

NOTES: Book VI [193

714 **they say:** see on 5.49.

720 **Minyans:** a tribe said to have originated in Thessaly but later migrated to Boeotia; the Argonauts were said to have descended from them; see 4.1, Herod. 1.146, 4.145.

721 **first ship:** Jason's Argo, traditionally the first ship; we must overlook Athens' enemies (6.423) and Tereus' voyages (6.444 ff., 511ff.).

NOTES: BOOK VII

1-424   Medea
Almost half the book is devoted to Medea and her various adventures. Her large part seems to break naturally into subdivisions.

1-158   Jason and Medea
Here Ovid takes a story that filled 1,618 lines from the beginning of Apolloniu Rhodius 3 and distils from it Medea's inner conflict between love and duty (Ap. Rhod 3.299-438, 4.744-801) and the story of her assistance to Jason both in his struggles wit the bulls as well as with the soldiers born from the viper's teeth, and in his gaining of th Golden Fleece (Ap. Rhod. 3.912-4.211). This is achieved by largely assuming th narrative and concentrating on several moments of high emotion. The story had als been told by Pindar (*Pyth.* 4); for his portrayal of Medea's character, Ovid is als dependent to some extent on Euripides' tragedy. Only two lines of Ovid's own traged on this theme survive, so that we can make no sensible judgement on the relationshi between that treatment and this one.

1   **Pagasaean:** Pagasae was a town on the borders of Magnesia and Thessaal where the Argo was built (Ap. Rhod. 1.238).

2   **Phineus:** a blind seer tormented by the Harpies until the Argonauts came an Zetes and Calais chased them away. For the details, see Apollod. 1.9.21 (and Frazer Ap. Rhod. 2.178-499. According to Apollodorus (1.9.21), Phineus lived at Salmydessu (on the Black Sea coast of Thrace); according to Apollonius Rhodius (2.176-8), he live just inside the Bosphorus on the Thracian side. Either way, as Anderson observes, th mention of Phineus establishes that the Argo has already crossed the Aegean and passe through the Hellespont, the Propontis and the Bosphorus to be well on the way t Colchis which is at the far end of the Black Sea.

3   **Aquilo:** an alternative Latin name for Boreas; cf. Cic. *Leg.* 1.3.

4   **virgin birds:** *uirgineas uolucres*; the Harpies; cf. Virgil's description (*Aer* 3.216, West's translation):
> These are the vilest of all monsters. No plague or visitation of the gods sent up from the waves of the river Styx has ever been worse than those. They are birds with the faces of girls [uirginei], with filth oozing from their bellies, with hooked claws for hands and faces pale with a hunger that is never satisfied.

Later, by the time Aeneas and his men met them they had, as Virgil explains, bee banned from Phineus' Thracian home to the Strophades, small islands off the west coas of the Peloponnese.

8   **a dreadful condition:** see Apollod. 1.9.23 (Frazer's translation):
> The other [Aeetes] *promised to give it* [the Golden Fleece] *if single-handed he* [Jason] *would yoke the brazen-footed bulls. These were two wild bulls that he had. . .they had brazen feet and puffed fire from*

their mouths. These creatures Aeetes ordered him to yoke and to sow dragon's teeth; for he had got from Athena half of the dragon's teeth which Cadmus sowed in Thebes.

See also Ap. Rhod. 3.407-16. For the origin of the Golden Fleece, see Apollod. 1.9.1; for why Jason was sent to fetch it, see Apollod. 1.9.16. (Frazer's translation):
Aeson. . .had a son Jason. . .Now Jason dwelt in Iolcus, of which Pelias was king. . .when Pelias consulted the oracle concerning the kingdom, the god warned him to beware of the man with a single sandal. . .when he was offering a sacrifice. . .he sent for Jason. . .to participate in it. . .Jason. . .hastened to the sacrifice, and in crossing the river Amarus he lost a sandal in the stream and landed with only one. When Pelias saw him, he bethought him of the oracle, and going up to Jason asked him what. . .he would do if he had received an oracle that he should be murdered by one of the citizens. Jason answered. . ."I would command him. . .to bring the Golden Fleece." No sooner did Pelias hear that than he bade him go in quest of the fleece. Now it was at Colchis in a grove of Ares, hanging on an oak and guarded by a sleepless dragon.

For Cadmus' dragon's teeth, see *Met.* 3.106-10.

9-99 Ovid's real interest here is not in the narrative that he has so savagely truncated but in Medea's inner torment. There are, of course, many previous ancient treatments of the struggle between duty and passion. Consider, for example, Ap. Rhod. 3.439-70, 744-801 (on this part of Medea's story) and Virg. *Aen.* 1-89 (on the equivalent situation in Dido's life). Particular borrowings will be noted as they arise, but the total effect in all its brilliance is very much Ovid's own.

9 **conceived:** *concipit*; the word is in fact the standard word for 'caught' in 'caught fire' (*OLD* s.v. 1b); however the word is repeated at 7.17 (in the same sense) and at 7.22 in the metaphorical sense of 'conceive', also a recognized sense of the word (*OLD* s.v. 3) and, of course, giving rise to the English derivative. I use 'conceive' in all three places to draw attention to the repetition.

mighty fire: for earlier examples of this very familiar image of passion, see Ap. Rhod. 3.285-98, Virg. *Aen.* 4.2 (with Pease's monumental note) and *passim*. In this scene, Ovid returns to the image more than once.

10-11 *postquam. . .poterat:* repeated at 14.701.

11 **passion with reason:** *ratione furorem*; the same contrast also occurs at 1.618-9 (and see my note). Here, Ovid has developed the idea into a neat verbal play from the more pedestrian approach of Apollonius Rhodius (3.797-801, Seaton's translation):
And what disgrace will not be mine? Alas for my infatuation! Far better would it be for me to forsake life this very night in my chamber by some mysterious fate, escaping all slanderous reproach, before I complete such nameless dishonour.
Virgil, however had prepared the ground (*Aen.* 4.23-7, West's translation):
But I would pray that the earth open to its depths and swallow me or that the All-powerful Father of the gods blast me with his thunderbolt and hurl me down to the pale shades of Erebus and its bottomless night before I go against my conscience [pudor] *and rescind its laws.*

19-20 desire...thought: *cupido...mens*; see on 7.11.

20-1 I see the better things...the worse: perhaps Ovid's most famous sentence; no doubt it has its origins in Eur. *Med.* 1078-80 (Warner's translation):
> I know indeed what evil I intend to do,
> but stronger than all my afterthoughts is my fury,
> Fury that brings upon mortals the greatest evils.

Page's note gives other examples of the sentiment. Once again, note how Ovid sharpens what he has inherited and changes its focus from contemplation of infanticide to contemplation of immoral love.

22 marriage: like Virgil's Dido, Medea deludes herself into believing that she can enjoy a secure marriage with her beloved; cf. 7.49, 91 and contrast 7.69-70.

30-1 the greedy snake: the snake that guarded the Golden Fleece; see on 7.8.

33 tigress...iron and stone: for this motif, see on 8.120-5. See also Eur. *Med.* 1279-80.

49 ceremonial torch: i.e. 'marriage'; see on 7.22.
     Pelasgian: an ancient term for 'Greek', originally restricted to Greeks from the north; see Eden on Virg. *Aen.* 8.600.

55 greatest god: here, Medea must mean Love (*Amor*).

**57-8 Cf. Eur. *Med.* 534-8 (Warner's translation):
> But on this question of saving me [Jason], I can prove
> you [Medea] have certainly got from me more than you gave.
> Firstly, instead of living among barbarians,
> you inhabit a Greek land and understand our ways,
> how to live by law instead of the sweet will of force.

Once again, Ovid changes the focus of the ideas he inherits. In Euripides, the words are used by Jason in retrospect as an obviously threadbare attempt at self-justification; here, they are used by Medea in prospect to illustrate her naive expectations.

62 mountains that rush together: the Symplegades, rocks that clashed together, one of the hazards Jason had encountered on his way to Colchis; see Eur. *Med.* 2 (and Page's extensive note), Ap. Rhod. 2.593-602.

63-5 Charybdis...Scylla: Charybdis was the whirlpool opposite the monstrous Scylla who snatched men from ships. For a full account, see Hom. *Od.* 12.66-110, 234-59. According to Homer, Scylla and Charybdis were near the Wandering Rocks through which the Argo had passed on its way home (*Od.* 12.64-90, cf. Ap.Rhod. 4.922-81). Since they were traditionally at the straits of Messina between Sicily and Italy, they were certainly far out of Jason's way; the confusion, if there was one, is as old as Homer; for a full discussion, see Page on Eur. *Med.* 2.

68-9 **husband...marriage:** *coniuge...coniugium*; Ovid's language brings out the train of thought; Golding was perhaps right to sacrifice literalness for the polyptoton (see on 5.52):
> Or if I chaunce to be afraide, my feare shall only tende
> But for my husband. Callste thou him thy husband? Doste pretende
> Gay titles to thy foule offence, Medea?

69-70 **Do you think...guilt?:** *coniugiumne...tuae?* There is a very close verbal echo of Virg. *Aen.* 4.172:
> coiniugium uocat, hoc praetexit nomine culpam

or in West's translation (slightly adapted):
> She called it marriage, using the word to cover her guilt.

Once again, the closeness of the imitation must not blind us to the contrast in the focus. In the *Aeneid*, the line is the narrator's and seems to represent Virgil's own judgement on Dido's self deception. In our passage, it is Medea herself who, if only for a moment, glimpses the moral truth of her situation.

72 **Piety:** see on 6.630
   Shame: *Pudor*; the sense of moral shame so specifically flouted by Dido (Virg. *Aen.* 4.27 and 55).

74 **Hecate, Perses' daughter:** cf. Hes. *Theog.* 409-12, Ap. Rhod. 3.478. According to Apollonius (3.475ff.), Argus persuaded Jason to invoke Hecate's assistance; Ovid simplifies by assuming that it was Medea who took the initiative to involve her. For Hecate, the archetypal witch, see on 6.139.

77-83 **flame...spark...caught fire:** see on 7.9.

91 **marriage-bed:** see on 7.22.

95 **three-formed goddess:** Hecate, Diana and Luna (the Moon) regarded as the infernal, terrestrial and heavenly aspects of one goddess; cf. Cat. 34, Hor. *Od.* 3.22.1-4. Dido too invoked this concept (Virg. *Aen.* 4.509-11, West's translation [adapted]):
> There were altars all around and the priestess with hair streaming
> called with a voice of thunder upon three hundred gods, Erebus,
> Chaos, and triple Hecate, virgin Diana of the three faces.

There, the ceremony was the prelude to Dido's suicide, here, by a change of focus and a dreadful irony, it is presented in an apparently optimistic context, though the reader, of course, knows better.

96 **all-seeing father of his future father-in-law:** see Hom. *Od.* 10.135-8 (Lattimore's translation):
> We came to Aiaia, which is an island. There lived Circe
> of the lovely hair, the dread goddess who talks with mortals,
> who is own sister to the malignant-minded Aietes;
> for they both are children of Helios [the Sun], who shines on mortals.

99 **shelter:** *tecta*; Ovid is unspecific about where this was; Anderson toys with 'tents'.

198] NOTES: Book VII

101   **Mars' sacred field:** *sacrum Mauortis in agrum*; editors point out that Apollonius too (3.411) set this conflict in a field of Ares (Mars); Anderson, however, may be wrong to dismiss the idea of an association with Rome's Campus Martius. Ovid chooses to keep only some of Apollonius' detail and his choice of this detail in particular may well be motivated by his taste for this sort of anachronistic Roman incongruity (see on 5.155), especially since the picture here of the people assembling will almost inevitably conjure up for a Roman the *Comitia* assembling in the Campus Martius.

104   **Vulcan:** i.e. 'fire'; see on 6.488.

105   **adamantine:** *adamanteis*; a Greek word used as early as Hesiod (*Theog*. 161) for a very hard mythical substance. Literally, the word means 'that cannot be overcome'. Virgil introduced the word into Latin, see *Aen*. 6.552 and Austin.

106-10   A blacksmith's simile and one based on a Roman lime kiln. Note how *sonant* ('sound') at the end of the simile picks up *resonare* ('resound') at the beginning. Anderson, who gives a full technical account of the kiln, regards it as a clear example of deliberate Roman incongruity and anachronism (see on 5.155; 7.101) and he also wonders whether the humble blacksmith simile implies that Ovid is 'slyly irreverent towards the myth'; it is at least equally plausible, however, that such a simile adds to the epic tone; consider Homer who illustrates the sound of Polyphemus' eye boiling on the red hot point of Odysseus' stake thus (*Od*. 9.391-4, Lattimore's translation):

> As when a man who works as a blacksmith plunges a screaming
> great ax blade or plane into cold water, treating it
> for temper, since this is the way steel is made strong, even
> so Cyclops' eye sizzled about the beam of the olive.

117   **dewlaps:** *palearia*; see on 2.854.

123   **pre-steeped:** *praetincta*; another Ovidian coinage; the teeth had, of course, come from the poisonous snake; see on 7.8.

128   **bowels:** *uisceribus*; both words can suggest either specifically the lower intestine or can be used of almost any internal organ; here, of course, (and see also 8.532) the poet is thinking of the womb; for the usage in English, cf. *Gen*. 25.23, *Psalm* 71.6 (A.V.):

> By thee have I been holden up from the womb: thou art he that took
> me out of my mother's bowels.

132   **Aesonian:** *Aesonii*; the manuscripts read *Haemonii*; Iolcus is close enough to Haemonia (i.e. Thessaly, see on 5.306) for that to be possible. However, Ovid does not use the adjective otherwise of Jason, though he does use it of the Argonauts' mothers (7.159) and of the whole expedition (*Ars Amat*. 1.6). On the other hand, *Aesonius* (a correction suggested by Heinsius) occurs of Jason at *Met*. 7.156, *Am*. 1.15.22, *Her*. 12.66, 134; 17.232, and he appears very frequently as *Aesonides* or *Aesone natus* ('Aeson's son').

138   **relieving:** *auxiliare*, a military technical term for military reinforcement or 'relief', which is the sense of 'relieving' intended here; cf. 6.424.

140 **war:** *Martem*; here the metonomy (see on 6.488) seems too harsh to reproduce in English: *'drove Mars from himself and turned it [him?] against them.'* See also on 7.141.

141 The same teeth (see on 7.8) produced the same situation at 3.122-3: *'as the sudden / brothers fell in their own war from mutual injuries'* (suoque / Marte *[see on 7.140]* cadunt subiti per mutua uulnera fratres).

142 **civil war:** as Anderson observes, no poet of this period could contemplate fraternal conflict without thinking of Rome's civil wars; cf 3.117, again of the products of the same teeth.

151 **golden tree:** i.e. the tree with the Golden Fleece upon it.

152 **Lethean:** i.e. 'sleep-inducing' from the supposed characteristics of Lethe ('Forgetfulness'), a place in the Underworld (Aristoph. *Frogs* 186) which much later, and only in Latin literaure, is thought of as a river (Virg. *Aen.* 6.705); Austin observes that Virgil never uses *Lethe* of the river (he uses various periphrases); indeed, Ovid *Met.* 11.603 seems to be the first extant example of its use for the river.

155 *ubi uenit:* the text is surely defective here; I have ignored *ubi* in the translation.

157-8 Note the astonishing compression of these lines, remarkable even for Ovid. Apollonius' account of these events takes all 1,781 lines of his fourth book; his epic then ends with no reference to the rest of the story.

159-293 Aeson
According to the ancient *Argument* to Euripides' *Medea*, the story of Aeson's rejuvenation by Medea was in the lost *Nostoi* (ancient epics on the return of the various warriors who went to Troy); the fragments are conveniently available in Evelyn-White's Loeb edition of Hesiod and the *Homerica* where this fragment appears on page 526:
> Forthwith Medea made Aeson a sweet young boy and stripped his old
> age from him by her cunning skill, when she made a brew of many
> herbs in her golden cauldrons.

According to Page (edition of *Medea*, page lv), the *Argument* probably originated in work done in the first century A.D.; Page also reports an argument by C. Robert (*Bild und Lied*, pp. 36ff.) that Ovid himself drew on the *Argument* for this section. Bömer lists other fragmentary references to the story in early Greek lyric poetry.

162 **was absent from the congratulations:** *abest gratantibus*; the same style of link has been used before when, after Daphne has been changed to a laurel to escape from Apollo, the local rivers gathered round her father not knowing whether to congratulate him (*gratentur*, 1.578) and only Inachus was absent (*abest*, 1.583) because he was mourning the fate of his daughter, Io, the subject of the next story. See also on 5.412-23.

169 **piety:** see on 6.630.

177 **three-formed goddess:** Hecate, see on 7.95.

182-3 Knots of all kinds are antipathetic to magic. Dido lets her hair down, removes one shoe and undoes her cincture before she begins the ritual that ends in her suicide (Virg. *Aen.* 4.511-8); cf. also 1.382.

183 **uncovered...uncovered:** *nuda...nudos*; unfortunately, the obviously neat equivalents to *nudus*, 'bare' or 'naked', are not applicable both to 'feet' and 'hair'.

185-7 See on 6.490-3.

188 **stretching her arms towards them:** the standard gesture of supplication; see on 2.487.

194 **three-fold Hecate:** see on 7.95.

199-200 Cf. 7.154.

200-1 **stay...shaken...shake...still:** an attempt at the polyptoton (see on 5.52) and (see on 6.299-300) of *concussaque sisto, stantia concutio*; note that *sisto* and *stantia* come from two distinct but closely cognate verbs. English 'stay' and 'still' are not cognate but their alliteration and similarity of sense make them into a common and natural pair.

203 **break the viper's throat:** cf. Virg. *Ecl.* 8.71 for a similar case. Bömer quotes other parallels.

204 **living rocks:** see on 5.317.

207 **draw down:** the trick, especially associated with Thessalian witches, of drawing the moon down from the sky. Editors sometimes confuse it with eclipse but see my article in *Rh. Mus.* 116 (1973) 221-38.
  Temesaean bronzes: Temese (or Tempse) was a town in southern Italy noted for its bronze (possibly the same town of that name refered to at Hom. *Od.* 1.184). For the apotropaic use of cymbals, see Tibullus 1.8.21-2:
  And her song tried to bring the Moon down from her chariot
  and would have done so, had not the clashing bronze sounded out.

208 **grandfather's:** i.e. 'Sun's'; see on 7.96.

210 **You:** *uos*; the plural makes it plain that Medea here reverts to her invocation of the gods in general (cf. 7.198) after concentrating for a few lines on the Moon (7.207-9).

212 **serpent-born:** *serpentigenis*; probably another Ovidian coinage.

214-5 Note that Medea's account of the transition from Colchis to Iolcus enjoys the same degree of compression as Ovid's at 7.157-8.

218 **chariot..snakes:** for the idea of flying snakes drawing Sun's chariot, see Page's edition of Euripides' *Medea*, p. xxvii. In that play (1321-2), Medea summons her grandfather similarly; the text has no allusion to snakes, but the scholiast has.

NOTES: Book VII [201

219   For the parenthesis, see on 5.280-2.

223   **Tempe:** the Thessalian valley through which the Peneus flows; it was noted for its beauty; see on 1.569.

224-30: Ovid cannot resist this list of Thessaly's mountains (see 1.154-5, 570; 2.221, see also on 7.352, 353) followed by a list of her rivers (see on 1.569-80).

229   **many too from Amphrysus:** the Latin makes it plain without repeating *ripis* ('banks') that here too 'banks' is meant.

231   **Boebe:** the lake was well known though usually called Boebeian after the unimportant town Boebe on its shore (Hom. *Il.* 2.711-2). Here, Ovid transfers the town's name to the lake.

232   **long-lived:** appropriately, in context; see also on 7.273.
         Anthedon: a town on the Boeotian coast (Hom. *Il.* 2.508) called Euboean by Ovid presumably because it faces the island of Euboea, as he points out himself at 13.905.

233   **not yet widely known:** *nondum.. .uulgatum*; cf. 1.164, where the same formula was used to prepare for the later telling of Lycaon's story.
         Glaucus' change of body: for the story, see 13.898-968.

236   **her snakes:** i.e. the ones drawing her chariot.
         the smell: i.e. 'of the herbs'.

239-40   Sexual abstinence was a common feature of ritual purity; cf. 10.434-5.

240   **altars out of turf:** see Nisbet-Hubbard on Hor. *Od.* 1.19.13.

241   **Youth:** *Iuuentae*; in Greek, she is called Hebe and, as here, represents all the joys associated with youth (cf. Hom. *Il.* 4.2). For some account of a more austere view in earlier Roman cult till, in the late republic, the Greek picture seemed to become more prominent, see Pease on Cic. *de Nat. Deorum* 1.40.112 and Nisbet-Hubbard on Hor. *Od.* 1.30.7.

243-5   This is the standard form of ritual for summoning up the denizens of the Underworld. Consider what Odysseus does when he wishes to summon up the dead (Hom. *Od.* 10.570-2; 11.23-8, 34-7, Lattimore's translation):

Circe
meanwhile had gone down herself to the side of the black ship,
and tethered aboard it a ram and one black female.

There Perimedes and Eurylochos held the victims
fast, and I, drawing from beside my thigh my sharp sword,
dug a pit, of about a cubit in each direction,
and poured it full of drink offerings for all the dead, first
honey mixed with milk, and the second pouring was sweet wine,

202] NOTES: Book VII

> *and the third, water, and over it all I sprinkled white barley.*
>
> *Now when with sacrifices and prayers, I had so entreated*
> *the hordes of the dead, I took the sheep and cut their throats*
> *over the pit, and the dark-clouding blood ran in, and the souls*
> *of the perished dead gathered to the place, up out of Erebos.*

Aeneas (Virg. *Aen.* 6.243-63), as Anderson observes, goes through a far more complex ritual before he can enter the Underworld. However, Odysseus and Medea, unlike Aeneas, are not hoping to travel down to the Underworld so that Ovid is not so much abbreviating Virgil as returning to (an admittedly abbreviated) Homer. It should be noted that Odysseus' brief presence in the Underworld (Hom. *Od.* 11.565-600) clearly originated in some other part of the tradition unconnected with this ritual.

246-7 The text is much confused in the manuscripts. In Homer's ritual, there was honey, milk, wine, water and barley. Unless several lines have fallen out it would appear that Ovid reduced this list to two; the manuscripts all offer *lactis* ('milk') but are divided as to whether the other substance should be *mellis* ('honey') or *uini* (or *Bacchi*) ('wine'). The manuscripts also divide as to which is the correct line for each of the two adjectives, *liquidi* ('clear' or 'flowing') and *tepidi* ('warm'). However, in a ritual context, warmth seems much more appropriate for 'milk' (suggesting, as it does, freshness); *liquidus* is not found elsewhere in Ovid of wine, and where it does occur (e.g. Hor. *Epist.* 1.14 34) it seems to mean 'strained so as to remove the impurities'); it is, however, used as a technical term with *mel* (e.g. Varro *R.R.* 3.16.26) to suggest the form of honey known to us as 'clear', the only form possible for this ritual.

249 **king...and his ravished wife:** Dis and Proserpina, see 5.341-661.

256 **profane:** *profanos*; the technical term for the unitiated who must be kept from the holiest parts of a ceremony; cf. Cat. 64.260, Hor. *Od.* 3.1.1, Virg. *Aen.* 6.258.

259 **much-split:** *multifidas*, probably another Ovidian coinage; the word is repeated (again with *faces*) at 8.644. Torches were produced by splitting resinous wood.

263 **put on:** *posito*; 'fire' is not mentioned as in 'Polly, put the kettle on'; the usage seems to be recorded neither in Latin nor in English dictionaries.

264-78 Ovid enjoys this wonderful list of exotic ingredients.

267 **ebbing:** the stones will be at their cleanest as the tide goes out.
Ocean: the name both of the all-encircling sea (Hom. *Il.* 18.489) and of one of the Titans (Apollod. 1.1.4). The ancients assumed the Atlantic to be part of Ocean, hence the reference to tides.

269 **ill-famed...owl:** see on 5.550.

270 **changeling wolf:** presumably a reference to Lycaon whose story was told at 1.218-39.

272 **Cinyphian:** see on 5.123.

NOTES: Book VII [203

water-snake: a rare word probably introduced into Latin by Virgil (*G.* 2.214 and 3.415 where Mynors gives further details including the observation that the snake was noted for its foul stench).

273 **liver. . .lived:** the 'pun' is, of course, an accident of translation and represents no Latin word-play.

long lived stag: *uiuacis. . .cerui*; the phrase occurs also at 3.194 and at Virg. *Ecl.* 7.30. Here, of course, it is particularly apt; cf.7.232.

274 **nine generations:** i.e. 'of men'; Plutarch quotes Hesiod (a fragment not otherwise known) to the same effect (*Mor.* 415c, Babbitt's translation):
 Nine generations long is the life of a crow and his cawing,
 Nine generations of vigorous men.
Aratus (1,022) also attributes nine generations to the crow but Aristophanes (*Birds* 609) allows only five.

277 **sweet:** *mitis*; OLD cites a number of places where the comparative of *mitis* is used to suggest 'cultivated' as opposed to 'wild'. Here, *oliuae* must refer to the plant rather than the fruit which suggests that here too 'cultivated' may be the sense intended, for which I have coined 'sweet'.

292 **swelled out:** his limbs were suddenly restored from the emaciation of old age.

294-6 *Bacchus' nurses.*
A very brief tale (the subject of Aeschylus' lost play, *The Nurses of Dionysus*, according to the ancient *Argument* to Euripides' *Medea*) to separate the Pelias story from that of Aeson.

296 **the Colchian:** Medea.

297-349 *Pelias*
For the history of this story, see Apollod. 1.9.27 and Frazer who, in particular, gives a brief account of its appearance on Greek vases. Oddly, both Plautus (*Pseud.* 869ff.) and Cicero (*de Sen.* 23.83 and see Powell) seem to know of a version of the story in which Pelias' rejuvenation is successful. For the origin of Jason's hatred for Pelias, see on 7.8.

297 **the Phasian:** Medea, cf. 7.6.

300-1 **took her in. . .had taken them in:** *excipiunt. . .cepit*; the word-play is only a little less striking in the Latin.

302 An echo of 7.168. As Anderson observes, this whole section echoes the rejuvenation of Aeson.

312 **wool-bearer:** *laniger*; for the 'kenning' see on 6.266.

315 **meagre blood:** it was long thought that the old had little blood, cf. 13.409 of Priam. Lady Macbeth (Shakespeare *Macbeth* 5.1.40-1) had clearly read such a passage and so was unprepared for the blood that flowed from old king Duncan:

204] NOTES: Book VII

Yet who would have thought the old man to have had so much blood in him.

316-7 **limbs. . .body:** *membra. . .corpus*; *membra*, literally 'limbs' is here used idiomatically to mean 'body'; but so to translate it would give a false impression of ugly repetition.

324-5 **Spanish stream:** the Atlantic (see on 7.267). Virgil (*Aen.* 11.913) has a similar expression.

328-9 Cf. 7.252-4 and see on 7.302.

333-8 **gore. . .blood. . .slime:** *cruorem. . .sanguine. . .saniem*; Medea seems to suggest that the old man's blood is inferior and must be replaced with good young blood. At 338, she goes further and calls his blood *saniem*, normally 'pus' as at 4.495. Golding renders it 'filthy matter', I have tried 'slime'.

339-40 Ovid enjoys these conceits; there is a very similar one at 6.635.

347-9 **Their courage and their hands. . .his throat together with his words:** the double syllepsis reinforces the impression that Ovid takes the story light-heartedly; see also on 6.476-7.

350-401 *The flight of Medea*
Ovid uses the journey to insinuate a host of obscure metamorphoses, almost all only hinted at. In any given case it is impossible to know whether the obscurity is real or whether it arises only from the accident of what we have lost. However, it seems unlikely that it is mere chance that so many so close together are of obscure origin.

350 **winged snakes:** for Medea's access to a flying chariot, see on 7.218.

352 **Philyreian:** Philyra was Chiron's mother (Hes. *Theog.* 1001-2); Chiron, the most famous of the Centaurs, dwelt on mount Pelion; cf. Hom. *Il.* 143-4, Lattimore's translation):
> *the Pelian ash spear which Cheiron had brought to his* [Achilles'] *father from high on Pelion to be death for fighters.*

Pelion: the mountain immediately to the north-east of Iolcus (cf. 7.158).

353 **Othrys:** another mountain, across the Pagasaean Bay and to the south-west.
Cerambus: this version of the story is apparently found only here. The details are obscure but the outline is clear enough: Cerambus (the Greek for 'beetle') escaped Deucalion's flood (1.253-312) by being transformed into a beetle. For further details, see Anderson and Forbes Irving (314).

356 **unoverwhelmed:** *inobrutus*; another Ovidian coinage.

357 **Pitane:** (stress the first syllable), across the Aegean on the Aeolian coast where Apollo petrified the snake that tried to eat Orpheus' severed head. The story is told in full at 11.50-60.

NOTES: Book VII [205

359   **Ida:** a mountain in the Troad further north up the Aeolian coast. This story is not otherwise known.

360   The line is largely a repeat of 3.250.

361   **Corythus' father:** Paris; for the relationship. see Parthenius 34. 'Ovid presumably refers to the humiliating end of the prince of Troy. . .'. Anderson.

362   **Maera:** another unknown story. It is reminiscent of Hecuba's transformation into a dog (13.565-9) but that occurred in Thrace and, in any event, Maera cannot be Hecuba.

363   **Eurypylus:** king of Cos (an island much further south down the coast of Asia Minor, cf. Hom. *Il.* 2.677); yet another story not otherwise known. It must, however, be related to a myth told by Apollodorus (2.7.1, Frazer's translation):
> *Hercules sailed to Cos, and the Coans, thinking he was leading a piratical squadron, endeavoured to prevent his approach by a shower of stones. But he forced his way in and took the city by night, and slew the king Eurypylus. . .*

365   **Phoebus' Rhodes:** i.e. Sol's (Sun's) Rhodes, an island, a little to the south-east of Cos, which was (and, in a more modern idiom, still is) a great centre of sun-worship. Pindar (*Ol.* 7.14) calls her 'bride of Helios'.
       Telchines: their story seems to be alluded to by Callimachus (*Aetia* fr. 75.644ff.). What little else we know is discussed by Forbes Irving (178).
       Ialysus: a town in the north of the island of Rhodes.

368   **Cartheian. . .Cea:** Cartheia was a town near the southern tip of Cea (according to *OLD* the normal Latin form of the Greek *Ceos*; it is intriguing that it is the Latin form that has survived into modern Greek, the Greek form that has come into English); the island was just off the eastern coast of the Peloponnese so that Medea has now recrossed the Aegean.

369   **Alcidamas:** according to Antoninus Liberalis (1), Nicander had told this story in which Hermochares had tricked Alcidamas' daughter, Ctesylla, into swearing to marry him; at first Alcidamas swore to allow the marriage but later he broke his oath by promising her to another. By this time Ctesylla had fallen in love with Hermochares and they fled to Athens to marry. However, she died in child-birth but, at her funeral, a dove flew out of her and her body vanished. For a full discussion, including an account of the possible connexion with the happier story of Acontius and Cydippe, see Forbes Irving (232-3).

371   **Hyrie:** north of the Corinthian Gulf, in Aetolia.
       Cycneian: the story of Cycnus (Greek for 'swan') and Phyl(l)ius is attributed to Nicander and Areus by Antoninus Liberalis (12); his details are, however, not the same as Ovid's: in his version, the labours are different, the mother is called Thyria and she is changed into a bird, not a lake. For a full discussion, see Forbes Irving (257).
       tempe: *tempe*; here, a common noun based on Tempe (see on 7.223) and used of any beautiful valley. For a discussion of this usage, which starts as early as Theocritus (1.67), see Mynors on Virg. *G.* 2.469.

NOTES: Book VII

373   **a boy:** Cycnus.

374   **him...he...him:** Cycnus...Cycnus...Phyllius; see on 5.30.

377   **he:** Cycnus; see on 5.30.

382   **these:** Hyrie and Cycneian tempe (7.371).
               Pleuron: a town just south of Hyrie.

383   **Ophius' daughter Combe:** not otherwise known. Forbes Irving (229) offers some very tentative speculation.

384   **she:** Medea
               Leto's Calaurea: see Strabo 8.6.14 (C373-4) (Jones's translation):
               Troezen is sacred to Poseidon...Off its harbour, Pogon by name, lies
               Calauria, an isle with a circuit of about one hundred and thirty
               stadia. Here was an asylum sacred to Poseidon; and they say that this
               god made an exchange with Leto, giving her Delos for Calauria.
Pausanias 2.33.2 and Frazer's note; the island is just off the east coast of the Argolid so that, from Hyrie, Medea has flown straight over Corinth, her eventual destination (391), all the way to the Peloponnesian coast.

385   Another story not otherwise known.

386   **Cyllene:** a mountain to the west of Corinth; once again Medea has overshot.
               Menephron: known otherwise only from Hyginus 253, a list of incestuous couples according to which he lay not only with his mother, Blias, but also with his daughter, Cyllene.

387   **in the manner of savage beasts:** Myrrha (10.324-31) tries to justify her own incest with her father on the grounds that it is natural among animals.

388   **Cephisos:** (stress the middle syllable), a river in Phocis, back north in Boeotia. Forbes Irving (313) offers some speculation on this otherwise unknown story.
               fat seal: the ancients thought of seals as ugly; cf. 1.300 and Mynors on Virg. G. 4.394-5.

390   **Eumelus:** the story is told by Antoninus Liberalis (18) who attributes it to Boios. Eumelus' son, Botres, began to eat his father's sacrificial lamb before the ceremony was complete. Eumelus struck him down but Apollo turned him into a bird.

391   **touched down...at:** *contigit*; regularly used of 'arriving at' but its literal meaning is 'touched' and the modern flying term seemed irresistible.

391-2   **Pirenian Ephyra:** Ephyra was an ancient name for Corinth (Hom. *Il.* 6.152); Pirene was a spring there (*Met.* 2.240).

393   The theory is not reported elsewhere.

394-7 An extremely rapid rehearsal of the plot of Euripides' *Medea*.

394 **the new bride:** Jason's new bride, Glauce or Creusa, who was to supplant Medea.

395 **twin seas:** see on 5.407.

398 **Titanian:** *Titaniacis*, a very rare form (perhaps only here). The snakes belonged to Sol (see on 7.218); the Titan Hyperion was Sol's father (see on 6.438).

400 **Phene...Periphas:** the story is in Antoninus Liberalis (6): Periphas, king in Athens, was so popular that he attracted divine honours. Zeus wanted to destroy him but Apollo interceded and he was changed into an eagle (Zeus' bird) and his unnamed wife into a vulture (*phene* in Greek).

401 **Polypemon:** an alternative name for Procrustes (Apollod. *Epit.* 1.4, and see Frazer). This story of his grand-daughter, Alcyone (Greek for 'kingfisher'), is otherwise known only from Probus on Virg. *G.* 1.399. This Alcyone is probably not the same as Ceyx' wife (11.266-345). See also Forbes Irving 240-1.

402-9.97Theseus
Though Theseus himself is never very prominent, he or his exploits provide the essential links and background throughout this long panel.

402-24 Theseus and Aegeus
Note that this section may be seen both as the final section of a Medea panel starting at 7.1 and as the first section of a Theseus panel. The story told here appears in Apollodorus (3.15.6-7, 16.1, *Epit.* 1.4-6, Frazer's translation):

> *As no child was born to him [Aegeus], he feared his brothers, and went to Pythia and consulted the oracle concerning the begetting of children. The god answered him:*
> *"The bulging mouth of the wineskin, O best of men,*
> *Loose not until thou hast reached the height of Athens."*
> *Not knowing what to make of the oracle, he set out on his return to Athens. And journeying by way of Troezen, he lodged with Pittheus, son of Pelops, who, understanding the oracle, made him drunk and caused him to lie with his daughter Aethra...Now Aegeus charged Aethra that, if she gave birth to a male child, she should rear it, without telling whose it was; and he left a sword and sandals under a certain rock, saying that when the boy could roll away the rock and take them up, she was then to send him away with them.*
>
> *Aethra bore to Aegeus a son Theseus, and when he grew up, he pushed away the rock and took up the sandals and sword, and hastened on foot to Athens.*
>
> *...Theseus came to Athens. But Medea being then wedded to Aegeus, plotted against him and persuaded Aegeus to beware of him as a traitor. And Aegeus, not knowing his own son, was afraid and sent him against the Marathonian Bull. And when Theseus had killed it,*

208] NOTES: Book VII

> Aegeus presented to him a poison which he had received.. .from Medea. But just as the draught was about to be administered to him, he gave his father the sword, and on recognizing it Aegeus dashed the cup from his hands.

402   **her:** Medea.

405   **the isthmus of two seas:** see on 5.407.

406   **cliff-wort:** see on 7.419.

408   **they say:** *memorant*; it is typical of Ovid to distance himself from some of his more fantastic stories; see on 5.49.

409   **Echidna's dog:** Cerberus, cf. Hes. *Theog.* 304-12.

410   **the Tirynthian hero:** Hercules who was made to perform twelve labours for Eurystheus of Tiryns (Apollod. 2.4.12). The last of these was to bring up Cerberus from Hades (Apollod. 2.5.12), a story known even to Homer (*Il.* 8.361-9).

411   **he:** Ceberus from 413; this arrangement preserves Ovid's dramatic delaying of the name.

412   **adamant:** *adamante*; a Greek word used as early as Hesiod (*Theog.* 161) for a very hard, mythical substance; literally, the word means 'that cannot be overcome'. Virgil introduced the idea into Latin (*Aen.* 6.552 and see Austin). Its adjectival use in English to mean 'stubbornly inflexible' is recent.

414   **triple:** Hesiod (*Theog.* 312) assigned fifty heads to Cerberus. The normal number was three, cf. 4.450, Austin on Virg. *Aen.* 6.417-25, and Nisbet-Hubbard on Hor. *Od.* 2.13.34.

419   **cliff-wort:** *aconita*, the Greek term, well established in Latin; a poisonous plant, known in English as 'wolf's bane'; Ovid's suggested derivation ties the Greek name of the plant to the Latin *cautes* ('cliff') through the Greek and Latin words for 'whetstone' (*acone* and *cos* respectively).

425-52 Theseus
Theseus' celebration of the saving of his son leads into a hymn to his praise.

433-50 you ... your ... through you ... your ... on your behalf ... for you: *te ... tuum ... per te.. .tuos.. .pro te.. .tibi*; for the hymnic repetition of 'you' and 'your' (*tu* and *tuus*), see on 6.177-9. It should, however, be noted that English idiom requires 'you' and 'your' more often than Latin requires *tu* and *tuus*, see especially, 449-50. The hymn should be compared to Bacchylides' hymn to Theseus (18.16-30, Fagles's translation); the numbers in square brackets give the corresponding line in Ovid's hymn:

> *Fresh from his heat*
> *on the Corinth road,*
> *a runner tells out*
> *unbelievable acts*

of a mighty man:
he's brought down Sinis [448]
the Bender of Pines,
a son of Looser Poseidon
who racks the earth;
he's killed the boar
that devoured men
in the woods of Cremmyon [435],
put an end to the reckless Sciron,
shut the wrestling ring
of Cercyon [439], *and snapped*
Polypemon's [see on 438] *club from the Butcher*
who with a better man met.

433-4 **Marathon. . .Cretan bull's blood:** for the exploit, see Apollod. *Epit.* 1.5 (quoted on 7.402-24); for the bull, see Apollod. 2.5.7 (Frazer's translation):

Acusilaus says that this was the bull that ferried across Europa for Zeus; but some say it was the bull that Poseidon sent up from the sea when Minos promised to sacrifice to Poseidon what should appear out of the sea. And they say that when he saw the beauty of the bull he sent it away to the herds and sacrificed another to Poseidon; at which the god was angry and made the bull savage. To attack the bull Hercules came to Crete, and when, in reply to his request for aid, Minos told him to fight and catch the bull for himself, he caught it and brought it to Eurystheus, and having shown it to him he let it afterwards go free. But the bull roamed to Sparta and all Arcadia, and traversing the Isthmus arrived at Marathon in Attica and harried the inhabitants.

Callimachus told the story of Theseus' defeat of the Marathonian Bull in his *Hecale*, but only scanty fragments survive.

437 **Vulcan's. . .offspring:** Periphetes; cf. Apollod. 3.16 1.

438 **Procrustes:** also known as Polypemon.

443-4 **Alcathoe. . .Lelegeian. . .Sciron:** Pausanias 1.39.6; 1.42.1 (Frazer's translation):

The Megarians say that Lelex came from Egypt and reigned in the eleventh generation after Car, the son of Phoroneus, and that the people were called Leleges in his reign; and that Cleson, son of Lelex, begat Pylas, and Pylas begat Sciron and Sciron. . .afterwards claimed the throne against Pandion's son Nisus. Aeacus, they say, arbitrated between them, awarding the kingdom to Nisus and his posterity, but to Sciron the command in war. . .but about the Cretan war and the capture of the city in the reign of Nisus they profess to know nothing.

The Megarians have yet another acropolis, which takes its name from Alcathous.

NOTES: Book VII

444-5 **refused a resting place, a resting place. . .refused:** *negat sedem, sedem negat*; this chiasmus (see on 6.299-300) works more neatly in Latin than in English.

447 **into rocks; rocks:** *in scopulos; scopulis*; for the polyptoton, see on 5.52.

450 **of Bacchus:** i.e. 'of wine'; for the metonomy, see on 6.488.

453-89 Minos
The basic story is to be found in Apollodorus (3.15.7, Frazer's translation):
> But he himself [Aegeus] *came to Athens and celebrated the games of the Panathenian festival, in which Androgeus, son of Minos, vanquished all comers. Him Aegeus sent against the bull of Marathon, by which he was destroyed. . .But when the tidings of his death were brought to Minos, as he was sacrificing to the Graces in Paros, he threw away the garland from his head and stopped the music of the flute, but nevertheless completed the sacrifice. . .But not long afterwards, being master of the sea, he attacked Athens. . .*

The involvement of Aeacus, however, is probably an Ovidian invention.

453-4 **(there. . .joyous):** for the sentiment, cf. 6.438; for the authorial intervention see on 5.280-2.

458 **just use of arms:** see on 5.210.

461-70 A geographical romp through the Cyclades (which lie between Crete and Attica) to list the islands which did (and did not) support Minos.

461 **Anaphe:** about eighty miles north of Cnossus.
Astypaleia: a few miles to the east of Anaphe.

462 **Anaphe by promises, by war the kingdom of Astypaleia:** *promissa Anaphen, regna Astypaleia bello*; for the chiasmus, see on 6.299-300.

463 **low-lying Myconos:** (stress the first syllable), an island just north of Delos among the more northerly Cyclades; cf. Virgil *Aen.* 3.75-6 (West's translation):
> *It* [Delos] *used to float from shore to shore until in gratitude the Archer God Apollo moored it to Gyaros and high Myconos. . .*

Commentators worry that Virgil calls the island 'high' (*celsa*), Ovid 'low-lying' (*humilem*); see Bömer.
Cimolus': (stress the midle syllable), about seventy-five miles south-west of Myconus.
chalky: *cretosa*; see Pliny *N.H.* 20.81.212 (Jones's translation):
> . . .*complaints of the breasts* [are relieved] *with honey or Cimolian chalk.*

464 **Syros:** about fifty miles north of Cimolus. However, the manuscript tradition here is deeply corrupt and both 'Syros' and 'thyme' (*thymo*) are emendations by Heinsius.
Seriphos: between Cimolus and Syros.

NOTES: Book VII [211

465   **marble Paros:** about 40 miles east of Seriphos; for its proverbial marble, see Nisbet-Hubbard on Hor. *Od.* 1.19.6.
   Siphnos: about thirty miles west of Paros.
   Arne: otherwise unknown.

466   The line is almost identical to 2.759.

468   **jackdaw:** for the habits of this bird, see Pliny *N.H.* 10.41.77 (Rackham's translation):
   *. . .jackdaws (a bird whose unique fondness for stealing especially
   silver and gold is remarkable).*
Thomas Ingoldsby's *The Jackdaw of Rheims* is a more modern literary reminder of the jackdaw's proclivities.

469   **Oliaros:** (stress the second syllable), between Paros and Siphnos.
   Didyme: (stress the first syllable), otherwise known only as a small island off the north coast of Sicily. Here, however, it must be one of the Cyclades.
   Tenos: an island about forty miles north of Oliaros.
   Andros: a somewhat larger island immediately north-west of Tenos.

470   **Gyaros:** (stress the first syllable), a few miles south of Andros; see also on 7.463.
   Peparethos: (stress the penult), an island over a hundred miles north-west of Andros just off the north of Euboea, well out of the Cyclades. It was noted for its wine, cf. Athen. 1. p.29a and e-f (Gulick's translation):
   In this play [the second edition of *Thesmophoriazousae*] *the master of
   comedy* [Aristophanes] *mentions Peparethian wine: "I'll not permit
   the drinking of Pramnian wine, or Chian, or Thasian, or Peparethian,
   or any other which will rouse your passion."*

   *Hermippus, I believe, makes Dionysus mention several varieties: ". . .
   .my enemies shall have Peparethan* [sic].
See also Bömer.

472   **Oenopia:** for the change of name, see Apollod. 3.12.6 (Frazer's translation):
   *And having conveyed Aegina to the island then named Oenone, but
   now called Aegina after her, Zeus cohabited with her and begot a son
   Aeacus on her.*
Pindar knew Aegina both as 'Oenone' (*Nem.* 4.46) and as 'Oenopia' (*Isthm.* 8.21).
   on his left hand side: from Peparethus, Minos would have to sail the whole length of Euboea, past Cape Sunium at the tip of Attica from where he would sail north-west till he was between Aegina on the left and Athens on his right.

476-7 **Telamon. . .Peleus. . .Phocus:** for their relationship and eventual fate see Apollod. 3.12.6 (Frazer's translation):
   *As Phocus excelled in athletic sports, his brothers Peleus and Tela-
   mon plotted against him, and the lot falling on Telamon, he killed his
   brother in a match by throwing a quoit at his head, and with the help
   of Peleus carried the body and hid it in a wood. But the murder being
   detected, the two were driven fugitives from Aegina by Aeacus.*

Pindar (*Nem.* 5.13-8) clearly knows the story but feigns too much embarrassment to tell it.

480-1   **ruler of a hundred peoples:** Minos. Crete was known as 'Crete of the hundred cities' by Homer (*Il.* 2.649).

483   **pious:** here, of course, the stress is on duty to family; see on 6.630.

484   **Asopus' son:** Aeacus was, in fact, his grandson through Aegina. See Pindar *Isthm.* 8.18-25.

486   **Cecropidae:** Athenians, see on 6.70-1. In fact, the hostility between Athens and Aegina was notorious and it lasted from before the Persian Wars till Hellenistic times and beyond.

487-9   Interestingly, Minos' threats come to nothing. Of course, the whole episode seems to be an Ovidian invention and he does not return to it; see on 7.453-89.

490-522 Aeacus and Cephalus
This meeting was probably contrived by Ovid chiefly to introduce the story of Cephalus and Procris, and perhaps to offer a contrast to Aeacus' story. A genealogical table may prove useful:

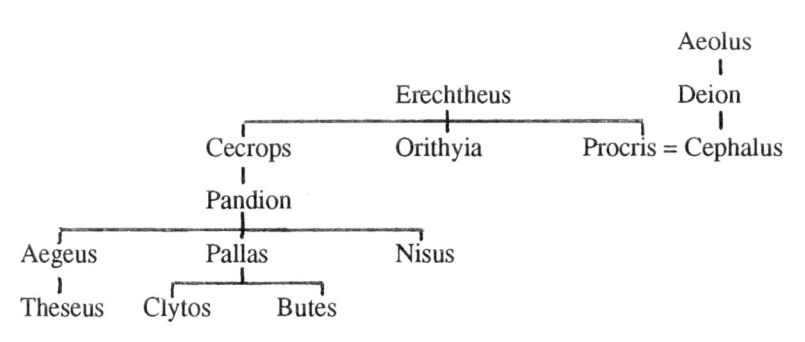

```
                                                              Aeolus
                                                                |
                                Erechtheus                    Deion
                                    |                           |
              Cecrops           Orithyia        Procris = Cephalus
                |
              Pandion
                |
        ┌───────┼───────┐
     Aegeus  Pallas   Nisus
       |       |
    Theseus ┌──┴──┐
          Clytos Butes
```

For an account, see Apollod. 1.7.3, 1.9.4, 3.15.1, 3.15.5-8 and Frazer.

490   **Lyctian:** Lyctos was a Cretan city (Hom. *Il.* 2.647); Virgil (*Ecl.* 5.72, *Aen.* 3.401) seems to have introduced the adjective, meaning 'Cretan', into Latin.

493   **Cephalus:** he was representing his father-in-law, Erechtheus, king of Athens, see table in note on 7.490-522; see also 6.677-82.

494   **a long time since he had seen him:** both the present meeting and its predecessors seem to be Ovidian inventions; see on 7.490-522..
    Aeacid young men: Peleus, Telamon and Phocus (7.476-7).

496   **the hero:** Cephalus.

498 **his people's olive:** the olive was sacred to Athene (see 6.102) and given to Athens by her (see on 6.70-82).

500 **Clytos and Butes, Pallas' sons:** Pallas was the son of Pandion, Clytos and Butes were probably both an Ovidian invention; see the table in the note on 7.490-522.

502 **Cecrops' son:** Aegeus, actually his grandson, see the table in the note on 7.490-522.

504 **what was being sought:** i.e. by Minos.

523-613 The Aeginetan Plague
While this particular plague seems to be Ovid's invention, it may have been suggested by an earlier mythological plague suffered by Athens and recorded by Apollodorus (3.15.8, Frazer's translation):
> When the war lingered on and he [Minos] could not take Athens, he
> prayed to Zeus that he might be avenged on the Athenians. And the
> city being visited with a famine and a pestilence...

The description of the plague owes almost everything to Thuc. 2.46-55, Lucr. 6.1138-286, and Virg. G. 3.478-566. Thucydides was describing a historical plague at Athens from which he had himself suffered; it was an important event during the Peloponnesian War, though he presented it with great skill to form a stark contrast with the confidence and idealism of Pericles' Funeral Speech which immediately precedes it in his narrative. Lucretius devoted the last book of his *de Rerum Natura* to accounts in Epicurean terms of all sorts of phenomena he had not touched on earlier. The last of these was plague and, after an explanation in general terms (6.1090-137), he launched into a passionate account of the Athenian Plague closely based on Thucydides' description. This makes for a strange and harrowing end to the work, but a very memorable one that has exercised scholars' ingenuity over the centuries in the search for a convincing explanation. Similarly, the third book of Virgil's *Georgics* ends with a description of a cattle plague at Noricum significantly based on Thucydides and Lucretius but necessarily adapted since its primary victims were animals. Once again, the question of the precise purpose of the piece has provoked much controversy, but its emotional power has never been doubted. By Ovid's time a tradition had clearly been established and he could not resist joining in any more than could so many of his successors, e.g. Seneca (*Oed.* 35ff.), Lucan (6.80-117), Silius Italicus (14.580-617). It would have been possible to point out parallels throughout the description, but I have preferred to invite the reader to compare the treatments as a whole. According to Anderson (on 7.520):
> Ovid combines the elements of the human and animal plagues, heightens the details, and thus transforms a plausible epidemic into a lues
> poetica ['a poetical plague'], a melodramatic episode which is spectacularly amusing and exercises no hold on the audience's emotions.'

The reader must decide how far this judgement is fair. Professor Tarrant believes that the section has attracted much interpolation. It is certainly plausible that such a passage would attract interpolators; I think the reader will agree that the excisions suggested here (many of which are Professor Tarrant's) improve both the quality and the continuity of the writing.

524 **wench:** this is the word I have generally used for *paelex*, whose basic meaning, to quote *OLD*, is: 'A mistress installed as a rival or in addition to a wife'. In Ovid, however, the word seems frequently to have a jocular connotation as, perhaps, here (certainly at 1.622), only sometimes a pejorative one, as at 4.235, 277. While 'wench' does not necessarily carry the connotation of 'mistress', it does cover the range from cheerful ribaldry to moral disapprobation. For a different solution, see on 6.606. For Aegina's story, see on 7.472.

565 **only:** see on 5.520

567 **(for there was nothing helpful):** see on 5.280-2.

599 **meagre blood:** not only old age but sickness too was thought to diminish the supply of blood; see on 7.315, cf. Virg. *G.* 3.492.

611 **unbewailed:** *indefleta*; another Ovidian coinage.

614-60 The repopulation of Aegina
The story of the birth of the Myrmidons from ants presumably arose (as Ovid suggests at 7.654) from a false derivation from *myrmex*, the Greek for 'ant'. The story is at least as old as Hesiod (fr. 205 M-W [*Scholiast on Pind. Nem. 3.21*], Evelyn-Whites's translation' p.185):
> Concerning the Myrmidons Hesiod speaks thus: 'And she conceived and bare Aeacus, delighting in horses. Now when he came to the full measure of desired youth, he chafed at being alone. And the father of men and gods made all the ants that were in the lovely isle into men and wide-girdled women.'

But the connexion with a plague seems to be an Ovidian invention.

614 **Thunderstruck...whirlwind:** *attonitus...turbine*; as we learn from Lucretius (6.395) and Virgil (*Aen.* 1.42-5; 6.592-4), the *turbo* ('whirlwind') was especially associated with Jupiter's thunderbolt; *attonitus*, therefore, probably maintains its association with thunder; of course, the whole phrase is metaphorical though it may be preparing us for the literal at 7.619.

620 **I acknowledge it:** *accipio*; a technical term for accepting an omen as favourable. Bömer compares Livy 1.7.11.

623 **Dodona:** the story of the famous oracle of Zeus at the oak of Dodona is to be found at Herod. 2.53.

634-5 **bodies beset with cares:** probably not a poetic plural referring to himself but another example of the epic cliché of the hero acting while most sleep, though here the difference between them is that the hero is dreaming constructively while the others are not. See on 6.490-3.

654 **divorce their name from their origin:** for the etymology, see on 7.614-60.

657 **and acquired...acquisitions:** *quaesitique...quaesita*; for the polyptoton see on 5.52. Suspicions have been expressed on the authenticity of this line.

659-60 Eurus. . .Auster: Anderson questions Ovid's choice of the Eurus, but Aegina is south-west of Athens so that if Eurus is thought of as the east (rather than as the south-east) wind it could, with a little skill, have brought Cephalus from Athens to Aegina. Similarly, Auster, the south wind, could be used for the return journey. For the aside, see on 5.280-2.

661-865 Cephalus and Procris
For a very full analysis of Ovid's probable sources and how he has treated them, see Otis 176-83, (1966) 381-4 (1970) 410-3. The issues are complex in detail, but it is clear that Ovid has transformed a rather crude story into a beautiful analysis of genuine love gone tragically wrong.

666 offspring of Pallas: Clytos and Butes, see on 7.500.

672 Aeolus' grandson: Cephalus, see the table in the note on 7.490-522.

677-8 ash. . .cornel: for ash spears, see on 5.9; for cornel spears, cf. Virg. *Aen.* 9.698.

685 the Nereid young man: Phocus, cf. Hesiod *Theog.* 1003-5 (Evelyn-White's translation):
> *But of the daughters of Nereus, the Old man of the Sea, Psamathe the fair goddess, was loved by Aeacus. . .and bare Phocus.*

687-8 As the most casual glance will reveal, there is major confusion in the manuscript report of these lines. I have followed Professor Tarrant's excisions and his suggested reconstruction identified as line 688a.

694 Orithyia: see on 6.675-721. For the genealogy, see the table in the note on 7.490-522

694-5 if perhaps. . .has come to your ears: *si forte. . .peruenit ad aures. . .tuas*; for the formula, cf. Virg. *Aen.* 1.375-6; 2.81 and Austin.

697 more worthy to be raped: i.e. 'more beautiful'. Anderson is surely right to suggest that this point reflects badly on Cephalus' character. It would be no more acceptable for an ancient than for a modern husband to compliment his wife's looks in such a way.

701 nets: it was a Roman practice to hunt by driving the quarry into nets (see on 3.148); this, then, is another example of a Roman practice anachronistically and inappropriately brought into a Greek story; see on 5.155.

702 ever-flowering Hymettus: a mountain in Attica noted for its honey, see Nisbet-Hubbard on Hor. *Od.* 2.6.14. See also on 7.804-62.

703 Dawn: for her love for Cephalus, see Hesiod *Theog.* 984-7 (Evelyn-White's translation):
> *And Eos [Dawn] bare. . .to Cephalus. . .a splendid son, strong Phaethon. . .*

Normally, of course, as at 2.1ff., Sol is the father of Phaethon.

NOTES: Book VII

705 **rosy:** that Dawn was rosy is one of the most famous of Homeric commonplaces; cf. e.g. *Il.* 6.175: 'rosy-fingered dawn'.

706 **boundaries. . .boundaries:** readers interested in repetition should note that Ovid repeats *teneat* ('holds') and not *confinia* ('boundaries'). In English, it seemed easier to repeat the noun rather than the verb.

709 **her:** Dawn.

739 **fortune:** *census*; the Latin word is a technical term for a property qualification from which it develops the sense 'fortune'. The translation conceals the hint at another Roman anachronism; see on 5.155.

741-2 There is considerable manuscript confusion here. However, there should be no doubt that the central point is the witty contrast between the novel meaning of 'false adulterer' (i.e. that you cannot truly commit adultery with your own wife) and the 'true husband'.

744 **her base husband together with his treacherous house:** I have reversed Ovid's Latin which would give 'the house together with the husband'. That is elegant enough in Latin but seems clumsy in English.

746 **Diana:** the goddess of chastity provides a natural refuge for a woman disappointed in love.

757-8 A transparent device to remind the reader that this is Cephalus' narration to Phocus. There is no danger that Phocus will deny interest.

759 **Laius' son:** Oedipus. His story is most familiar from Sophocles' tragedies.

760 **dark seer:** the Sphinx, known even to Hesiod (*Theog.* 326) as the destroyer of the Thebans.

763 **a second scourge:** the Teumessian vixen. For the story, see Apollod. 2.4.6-7 (Frazer's translation):

> *Amphitryon. . .undertook an expedition against the Teleboans, and invited Creon to assist him. Creon said he would join in the expedition if Amphitryon would first rid the Cadmea of the vixen; for a brute of a vixen was ravaging the Cadmea. But though Amphitryon undertook the task, it was fated that nobody should catch her. As the country suffered thereby, the Thebans every month exposed a son of one of the citizens to the brute, which would have carried off many if that were not done. So Amphitryon betook him to Cephalus. . .and persuaded him. . .to bring to the chase the dog which Procris had brought from Crete as a gift from Minos; for that dog was destined to catch whatever it pursued. So then, when the vixen was chased by the dog, Zeus turned both of them into stone.*

Frazer and Forbes Irving (299) collect other reports.

NOTES: Book VII [217

766 **nets:** see on 7.701.

771 **Laelaps:** a Greek word for a violent storm.

778 **Gortynian:** *Gortyniaco*; the adjective is found nowhere else. Gortyn was a Cretan city, and Crete was famous for its archers; cf. Hom. *Il.* 10.260, Nisbet-Hubbard on Hor. *Od.* 15.17.

782 **from the very jaws:** *ab ipso uulnere*; literally, 'from the very wound(ing)'.

785-6 This part of the narrative clearly owes much to Virgil's famous simile to illustrate the final chase by Aeneas of Turnus at the very climax of the *Aeneid* (12.753-5, West's translation):
 . . .*but the untiring Umbrian hound stays with him with jaws gaping;*
 now he has him; now he seems to have him [tenet similisque tenenti]
 and the jaws snap shut, but he is thwarted and bites the empty air.
Note that Ovid plays with his Virgilian model by substituting *non tenet* ('did not hold on') for *tenet* ('he has him'). See also 1.535-6. The point is also reinforced by the polyptoton, see on 5.52.

796 Contrast the start of Aeacus' story at 7.518.

804 Cf. 7.703 where first light also heralded disaster for Cephalus.

804-62 Ovid had already told this part of the story in his more youthful *Ars Amatoria* (3.687-746) starting off with a reference to 'flowering Hymettus' (see on 7.702).

823 **nymph. . .nymph:** *nymphae, nympham*; the point is underlined by the polyptoton (see on 5.52).

827 **(so it was told to me):** not authorial detachment (see on 5.49) but an explanation of how Cephalus knows something he could not have seen.

852 **by the bonds of our bed:** an echo of 7.710.

853 **my own ones:** i.e. 'my own gods', the gods of the underworld, since she is moribund. Ovid cannot resist undercutting this tragic moment with his verbal wit.

854 **by any service I have done for you:** a standard formula; cf. Virgil *Aen.* 4.317; Catullus 76 is almost a study on the idea.

861 **in my mouth:** another predominantly Roman custom (see on 5.155) very familiar from Virgil *Aen.* 4.684-5 (West's translation):
 . . .*and catch any last lingering breath with my lips.*
See also Pease and Austin.

NOTES: BOOK VIII

For book 8, readers may wish to consult not only Anderson's commentary but also Hollis's very full edition.

1-151   Scylla
The story was ancient even for Aeschylus (*Choeph.* 612-22, Lattimore's translation):
> And in the legends there is one more, a girl
> of blood, figure of hate
> who, for the enemy's
> sake killed one near in blood, seduced by the wrought
> golden necklace from Crete,
> wherewith Minos bribed her. She sundered
> from Nisus his immortal hair
> as he all unsuspecting
> breathed in tranquil sleep. Foul wretch,
> Hermes of death has got her now.

There is the motive is clearly greed, not love. However, lust, if not love, has supplanted greed by the time we reach Callimachus (*Hec.* fr. 288, Trypanis's translation):
> Scylla, a whore, having no untrue name [see on 8.151], cut the purple lock.

By Virgil's time, the double metamorphosis has appeared in the tradition (*G.* 1.404-9):
> Nisus appears high up in the clear air,
> and Scylla pays the penalty for the purple lock:
> wherever, in flight, she cuts the light ether with her wings,
> look, her fierce enemy Nisus follows after with a great screeching
> through the breezes; where Nisus goes through the breezes,
> she, in flight, cuts the light air eagerly with her wings.

Ovid himself (*Tr.* 2.393-4) refers to a tragedy on the topic in which the motive was love. The pseudo-Virgilian *Ciris* tells the whole story buts its date and relationship to Ovid have been hotly debated. The prevailing view is, however, that it was written later than our account. For a fuller discussion of this and other questions on the history of the myth, together with full bibliographies, see Otis 62-5, Hollis on 8.1-151, Anderson on 8.1-151, Mynors on Virg. *G.* 1.404-9, and Forbes Irving 226-8.

1   **Lucifer:** i.e. 'Light-bringing', the Morning Star, beautifully described by Homer (*Od.* 13.93-4). For more details, see on 2.114.

2   **for the East wind fell:** for the situation, see 7.659-69.

4   **returned:** strictly speaking, Cephalus is indeed returning to Athens but 'the sons of Aeacus' (i.e. the Aeginetan forces) are going for the first time.

6-8   **Lelegeian...Alcathous:** see on 7.443-4.

NOTES: Book VIII [219

7   **martial strength:** *uires Mauortis*; literally, 'strength of Mars' see on 6.488; but this sort of metonomy is much rarer in English than in Latin and 'martial' is derived from *Mars*.

8   **Nisus:** see on 7.443-4.

14-6   **speaking walls...Leto's offspring:** from Theognis (1.773-4), we learn of Apollo as the god who built Megara for Alcathous. For 'speaking walls', cf. Pausanias 1.42.2 (Frazer's translation):
When he [Alcathous] was building the wall, as the Megarians say, Apollo helped him in the work, and laid down his lyre on the stone; and if any one chance to hit the wall with a pebble, it sounds exactly like a lyre that is struck.

18   **and aim for the resounding walls:** cf. Pausanias' account quoted in the note on 8.14-16.

19   **then, when there was peace:** cf. Hom. *Il.* 22.152-6 (Lattimore's translation):
Beside these
in this place and close to them, are the washing hollows
of stone, and magnificent, where the wives of the Trojans and their lovely
daughters washed the clothes to shining, in the old days
when there was peace, before the coming of the sons of the Achaians.
Characteristically, Ovid takes one of the great moments of pathos in high literature and applies it in this very different context. See also on 5.605-6.

21-4   The woman's rehearsal of the names of the leaders of the besieging force as seen from the defending walls originates in Helen's survey (Hom. *Il.* 3.161-242) of the Achaean troops she sees from the walls of Troy.

23   **Europa's son:** *Europaei*; see Hom. *Il.* 14.313-6, 321-2. For the spondaic ending, see on 5.165, 265.

24-36   Hollis, in the course of a full account of this conceit, quotes [Tibullus] 3.8 (= 4.2) 7-12 (Postgate's translation):
Whatsoever she does, whithersoever she turns her steps, Grace follows her unseen to order all aright. Hath she loosed her hair? Then flowing locks become her. Hath she dressed it? With dressed hair she is divine. She fires the heart if she chooses to appear in gown of Tyrian hue; she fires it if she comes in the sheen of snowy robes.
Anderson compares Propertius' account (4.4) of Roman Tarpeia falling in love with Tatius, the besieging Sabine king.

24   **in her judgement:** perhaps an oblique reference to Minos' later rôle as judge in the Underworld; cf. Hom. *Od.* 11.568-71 (Lattimore's translation):
There I saw Minos, the glorious son of Zeus, seated,
holding a golden scepter and issuing judgments among
the dead, who all around the great lord argued their cases,
some sitting and some standing, by the wide-gated house of Hades.

51-2   **if I could glide through the air on wings:** an ambition she achieves, but not in the way she wanted.

56-7   **conqueror's...conquest...conquered:** *uinci uictoris...uictis*; the polyptoton (see on 5.52) underlines the importance of the argument.

220] NOTES: Book VIII

57 **clemency:** *clementia*; one of the most emotive words of Roman politics. Caesar's *clementia* was famous or notorious depending on whether it was seen as magnanimity in victory (see Austin on Virg. *Aen.* 6.853) or a device for demeaning traditional defenders of republican ideals.

58 **a just war:** see on 5.210.
son: Androgeus, cf. 7.458.

68 **native land:** *patriam*; as at 3.7-8, where too the word is found in a context in which 'father' is also prominent, it may seem at first sight tempting to render 'fatherland', the literal sense. However, quite apart from the slightly jarring sense 'fatherland' still has in English, it is notable that in neither place does Ovid put the word *pater* anywhere nearby. Two lines later, for instance, he uses *genitor* for 'father'. Cf. 8.109 and contrast 8.114-5, 130.

83ff. See on 6.490-3.

85 The Latin juxtaposition of *nata* ('daughter') and *parentem* ('father') reinforces the sense of guilt but cannot be reproduced in English.

91 **penates:** see on 5.155.

98 **earth and sea be denied to you:** she ended, of course, in the air. This curse does not seem to be in the extant literature but Bömer cites many inscriptions. Editors also refer to Lattimore (1962) 114 where some of them are translated and discussed.

99 **Jove's cradle, Crete:** for the story of Zeus' birth in Crete, see Hes. *Theog.* 468-80.

109 **native land...father:** *patriae...parenti*; see on 8.68.

111-2 **have neither the services I gave you nor my love:** *nec te data munera nec te / noster amor*; cf., from Dido's plea to Aeneas (Virg. *Aen.* 4.307), *nec te noster amor nec te data dextera* ['right hand'].

113-6 **For, if...to you:** the cry of the abandoned unfaithful daughter is a commonplace. From a long list in Bömer, I select some of the more well-known: Euripides *Medea* 502-3 (Rex Warner's translation):
> *Where am I to go? To my father's?*
> *Him I betrayed and his land when I came with you.*

Ap. Rhod. 4.378 (Seaton's translation):
> *How shall I come to my father's sight?*

Catullus 64.177,180-1 (Cornish's translation):
> *For whither shall I return, lost, ah, lost?...Shall I hope for the aid of*
> *my father? - whom I deserted of my own will, to follow a lover*
> *dabbled with my brother's blood?*

Virgil's Dido has a similar cry but she is thinking not of a father but of suitors unwisely spurned (*Aen.* 4.534-6, West's translation):
> *So then, what am I to do? Shall I go back to those who once wooed me*
> *and see if they will have me? I would be a laughing stock. Shall I beg*

NOTES: Book VIII [221

a husband from the Numidians after I have so often scorned their offers of marriage?

114-5   **fatherland...father:** *patriam...patris*; see on 8.68.

120   **your mother was not Europa...fathered you:** the origin of this commonplace is in Homer (*Il.* 16.33-5, Lattimore's translation):
> *Pitiless: the rider Peleus was never your father*
> *nor Thetis was your mother, but it was the grey sea that bore you*
> *and the towering rocks, so sheer the heart in you is turned from us.*

The version apparently clearest in Ovid's mind is Catullus 64.154-7 (Cornish's translation):
> *What lioness bore thee under a desert rock? what sea conceived thee and vomited thee forth from his foaming waves? what Syrtis, what ravening Scylla, what waste Charybdis bore thee, who for sweet life returnest such meed as this?*

Cf. also Virg. *Aen.* 4.365-7, (West's translation):
> *You are not the son of a goddess and Dardanus was not the first founder of your family. It was the Caucasus that fathered you on its hard rocks and Hyrcanian tigers offered you their udders.*

Pease gives an exhaustive history of the motif.

120   **Syrtis:** cf. Catullus 64.156 (quoted on 8.120-5); dangerous shallows of the North African coast.

121   **Armenian tigresses:** perhaps more often called Hyrcanian as at Virg. *Aen.* 4.367 (quoted on 8.120-5) and see Pease and Austin. Stand at the southern end of the Caspian Sea and Armenia will be to the west and north-west, Hyrcania to the east. Indeed Statius (*Theb.* 10.288-9) refers to a 'Caspian tigress'.

       Charybdis: see on 7.63-5; usually mentioned with Scylla, as at Catullus 64.156 (quoted on 8.120-5); however, as Hollis suggests, she is probably omitted here 'because of the coincidence of names.' Hollis goes on to give an account of where these two distinct figures (*pace* Otis 63 n.1) are sometimes confused.

123   **the guise of a bull:** see 2.833ff.

130   **my fatherland and father:** *patriaeque patrique*; see on 8.68.

131   **She:** Pasiphaë, Minos' wife. For the story, see Apollod. 3.1.3-4 (Frazer's translation):
> *And in sacrificing to Poseidon he [Minos] prayed that a bull might appear from the depths, promising to sacrifice it when it appeared. Poseidon did send him up a fine bull, and Minos obtained the kingdom, but he sent the bull to the herds and sacrificed another...angry at him for not sacrificing the bull, Poseidon...contrived that Pasiphae should conceive a passion for it. In her love for the bull she found an accomplice in Daedalus, an architect, who had been banished from Athens for murder. He constructed a wooden cow on wheels, took it, hollowed it out in the inside, sewed it up in the hide of a cow which he had skinned, and set it in the meadow in which the*

222] NOTES: Book VIII

> *bull used to graze. Then he introduced Pasiphae into it; and the bull came and coupled with it, as if it were a real cow. And she gave birth to Asterius, who was called the Minotaur. He had the face of a bull, but the rest of him was human...*

134-5 This commonplace is said to go back to Homer (*Od.* 8.408-10, Lattimore's translation):

> *Farewell, father and stranger, and if any word was let slip that was improper, may the stormwinds catch it away and carry it off...*

There, however, the thrust is quite different; far more similar is Catullus 64.139-42 (Cornish's translation):

> *Not such were the promises thou gavest me once with winning voice, not this didst thou bid me hope, ah me! no, but a joyful wedlock, but a desired espousal; all which at once the winds of heaven blow abroad in vain.*

This is itself an echo of 64.59; see also Quinn on Catullus 30.10.

141 In the general tradition, Minos seems to have punished Scylla by tying her to his ship (see e.g. Apollod. 3.15.8), whereas Ovid paints a more romantic picture. For more details, see the discussions referred to in the note on 8.1-151.

150 *pace* Hollis, the lame repetition *pluma...plumis*, hardly a neat polyptoton, must call the text into question.

151 **she acquired the name from the cutting of the hair:** from 'keiro', the Greek for 'I cut'. No convincing suggestion has ever been made for the identity of what is probably a mythological bird; see Hollis on 8.145-6.

152-82 *Minos, Daedalus and Ariadne*

The first part of the story is found in Apollodorus (3.1.4, Frazer's translation, starting where our quotation broke off in the note on 8.131):

> *and Minos, in compliance with certain oracles, shut him* [the Minotaur] *up and guarded him in the Labyrinth. Now the Labyrinth which Daedalus constructed was a chamber "that with its tangled windings perplexed the outward way."*

These last poetic words are usually taken to be a quotation, perhaps from Sophocles' *Daedalus*. We then pick up the story where we left it at 7.489 with Minos seeking help from Aeacus to attack Athens in vengeance for the loss of his son Androgeus there (see on 7.453-89). First, he had attacked Nisus of Megara (8.1-151), then, according to Apollodorus (3.15.8, Frazer's translation):

> *When the war lingered on and he* [Minos] *could not take Athens, he prayed to Zeus that he might be avenged on the Athenians. And the city being visited with a famine and a pestilence, the Athenians, at first...slaughtered the daughters of Hyacinth...But when this was of no avail, they inquired of the oracle how they could be delivered; and the god answered them that they should give Minos whatever satisfaction he might choose. So...Minos ordered them to send seven youths and the same number of damsels without weapons to be fodder for the Minotaur.*

NOTES: Book VIII [223

The story continues in the *Epitome* (1.7-9, Frazer's translation [adapted]):
> And he [Theseus] *was numbered among those who were to be sent as the third tribute to the Minotaur. . . .And when he came to Crete, Ariadne, daughter of Minos, being amorously disposed to him, offered to help him if he would agree to carry her away to Athens and have her to wife. Theseus having agreed on oath to do so, she besought Daedalus to disclose the way out of the Labyrinth. And at his suggestion she gave Theseus a thread when he went in; Theseus fastened it to the door, and, drawing it after him, entered in. And having found the Minotaur. . .he killed him. . .and drawing the thread after him made his way out again. And by night he arrived with Ariadne. . . at Naxos. There Dionysus fell in love with Ariadne and carried her off.*

Further details will be discussed in their place.

153 **Curetan:** here to mean Cretan from the Curetes who protected the infant Zeus on Crete; see on 4.282.

154 **hung up his spoils:** another anachronistic Roman touch (see on 5.155); editors compare *Aen.* 2.504-5 but there Virgil's attribution of the practice to the Trojans arises naturally from his wish to suggest that Roman customs are of ancient origin.

161-2 Editors put a full stop at the end of 161, taking the simile with what follows. The more expected construction with *non secus ac* (cf. 9.40; 15.180), as opposed to *non secus*, is for it to introduce a following not preceding simile or, as at Virg. *Aen.* 3.236, to introduce a one word comparison.

162 **Meander:** the winding Phrygian river whose name, even in antiquity, had become a word for 'sinuous'. Editors observe that Seneca (*Ep.* 104.15) regarded it as a poetic *cliché* though, as Hollis observes, he used it himself at *H.F.* 683ff. See also on 2.246.

174 **Aegeus' son:** editors explain the history of the Theseus and Ariadne story in detail. Ovid himself, however, seems interested only in the opportunity it affords for the metamorphosis of catasterism. As editors observe, the romantic story of Ariadne abandoned by Theseus is perhaps too close in spirit to the Scylla story for inclusion here. Furthermore, Catullus (64) had treated Ariadne in a way that Ovid may have felt he could not surpass. It cannot, however, be accidental that Ovid quotes Catullus 64 so very often during the Scylla story as the notes above reveal.

Dia: according to Callimachus (fr. 601), an alternative name for Naxos. Frazer, however, (on Apollod. *Epit.* 1.9 and quoting Merry on Hom. *Od.* 11.322) takes a different view:
> *Later writers. . .identified Dia with Naxos, but it is rather the little island, now Standia, just off Heracleion, on the north coast of Crete. Theseus would pass the island in sailing for Athens.*

178-82 crown. . .knee Flexer. . .Snake holder: cf. Aratus 63-6, 71-6 (Mair's translation):

> *Right there in its orbit wheels a Phantom form, like to a man that strives at a task. That sign no man knows how to read clearly, nor on what task he is bent, but men simply call him On His Knees.*
>
> *Here too that Crown, which glorious Dionysus set to be memorial of the dead Ariadne, wheels beneath the back of the toil-spent Phantom.*
> *To the Phantom's back the Crown is near, but by his head mark near at hand the head of Ophiuchus...*

Cicero, in his translation of Aratus (*de Nat. Deorum* 2.42) specifically tells us that the Latin term for *Ophiuchus* (i.e. 'Snake-holding') was *Anguitenens*. Ovid seems to go out of his way to avoid the compound technical term either in its Greek or its Latin form.

183-259 Daedalus and Icarus

The story is not in the extant literature before Ovid, if we ignore Virgil's allusion to it (*Aen.* 6.30-3), but that must be purely by chance, especially since there is sixth and fifth century vase reference to Icarus' fall. For the details, see Hollis on 8.183-259. Ovid himself treated the story before at *Ars Amat.* 2.21-96.

188 **directing his thoughts to skills unknown:** *ignotas... artes*; as Anderson points out, Joyce places this on the fly-leaf of *Portrait of the Artist as a Young Man*. The 'Young Man' was, of course, Joyce himself but he wears the mask of the pseudonym, Stephen Dedalus.

189 **he changed nature:** such a suggestion is a clear challenge to the natural order and should bring a *frisson* to the alert reader. At *Ars Amat.* 2.42, Daedalus goes so far as to say: '*I must change the laws of nature*'. See also on 5.11.

191 **the rustic pipe:** the syrinx or Pan-pipe; see on 1.677.

204-5 The advice is reminiscent of that given by Sol to his son, Phaethon, in similar circumstances (2.134-7):
> *So that heaven and earth endure the heat fairly,*
> *don't push your course down and do not drive it through the highest ether.*
> *You will burn heaven's houses if you go up too high;*
> *too low, and it will be the earth; you will go safest in the middle.*

207 **Boötes or Helice or Orion's drawn sword:** Boötes and Helice (Greek for 'winding', an alternative name for Ursa Minor [The Little Bear] from the fact that she 'winds round' the pole) are permanently up near the top of the sky (from the point of view of an observer in the northern hemisphere); Orion appears only just above the horizon and not all year round. So this is an instruction to fly neither too high nor too low.

211 **and the father's hands shook:** *et patriae tremuere manus*; a clear echo of Virgil *Aen.* 6.33, *bis patriae cecidere manus* ('twice the father's hands slipped'), a description of Daedalus trying to carve a picture of his son's death but defeated by emotion.

216 This line, identical to *Ars Amat.* 2.73, seems out of place here.

217   This line is repeated from *Ars Amat.* 2.77 but here the idea is developed much further. Hollis and Bömer offer further parallels.

220-2   The list of islands at *Ars Amat.* 2.79-82 is much the same, but longer. They journey north from Crete through the Sporades so that Icarus can drown in what is to be called the Icarian sea. Daedalus then turns west towards home.

220   **Juno's Samos:** cf. Virg. *Aen.* 1.15-16 (West's translation):
> *Juno is said to have loved it* [Carthage] *more than any other place, more even than Samos.*

See also Austin on Virg. *Aen.* 1.16.

222   **honey-rich Calymnae:** known to extant poetry only here and at *Ars Amat.* 2.81 where its shady woods are noted rather than its honey. Strabo, however (10.5.19) stresses its honey.

227   Taken verbatim from *Ars Amat.* 2.89.

229-31   **crying out. . .said:** *clamantia. . .dixit*; the first of Icarus, the second of Daedalus. This is a subtle improvement on the earlier version in the *Ars Amatoria* where Icarus 'says' (*inquit*, 2.91) "Father, o father" while Daedalus 'cries out' (*clamat. . . clamat. . .clamabat*, 2.93, 94, 95) "Icarus. . .Icarus. . .where are you?"

229   **his father's name:** *patrium. . .nomen*; as Hollis points out, this must mean not 'Daedalus' but 'father'. I cannot, however, see a neat way to make that clear in English.

230   **took its name:** the Icarian Sea.

231-2   Ovid clearly enjoyed this section and its humour; it is repeated almost verbatim from *Ars Amat.* 2.93-5.

235   **land:** the island of Icaria is to the west of Samos. A slightly different version was known to Apollodorus (2.6.3, Frazer's translation):
> *And having put in at the island of Doliche, he* [Hercules] *saw the body of Icarus washed ashore and buried it, and he called the island Icaria instead of Doliche. In return Daedalus made a portrait statue of Hercules at Pisa, which Hercules mistook at night for living and threw a stone and hit it.*

236-59 Perdix
The outline of the story is told by Apollodorus to explain why Daedalus had fled from Athens to Crete in the first place (3.15.8, Frazer's translation):
> *He had fled from Athens, because he had thrown down from the Acropolis Talos, the son of his sister Perdix; for Talos was his pupil, and Daedalus feared that with his talents he might surpass himself, seeing that he had sawed a thin stick with a jawbone of a snake which he had found. Daedalus was tried in the Areopagus, and having been condemned fled to Minos.*

NOTES: Book VIII

For detailed discussion of the history of the story (traceable at least as far back as Sophocles fr. 323), see Frazer, Hollis, Forbes Irving 256-7. In giving the name 'Perdix' to the boy rather than to the mother, Ovid seems to be reverting to the Sophoclean tradition.

239-40   bird...bird: *uolucris...auis*; see on 5.55-6.

237   **a muddy ditch:** *limoso...elice*; the manuscripts read *ramosa...ilice* ('a well-branched oak') but this seems to fit ill with the climax of the story at 8.256-9. For that reason, many editors have followed Auctor de Dubiis Nominibus (*GLK* 5.587), an early grammarian, interested in the gender of *ilex*, who quotes the line as printed here. For a full discussion coming to the opposite conclusion, see Hollis.

244-9   Note the delicate care Ovid lavishes on these fine descriptions of a saw and of a pair of compasses.

255   **his name:** Perdix, from 8.237. Note that the metamorphosis involves a change of sex as well as of species.

260-546 The Calydonian Boar Hunt
Hollis offers a very full history of the legend, while Anderson points out various examples of Ovid's undercutting of his predecessors. Suffice it to say here that its presence in the *Iliad* (9.529-99), in a fascinatingly different form, reveals its great antiquity, while its constant recurrence in literature and art demonstrates its popularity.

260-3   In this transition, Ovid returns to Theseus, whom we left at 8.175, by bringing to a final conclusion Minos' feud against the Athenians. Theseus then leads on naturally to the Calydonian Boar Hunt. For Minos' death in Sicily, cf. Apollod. *Epit.* 1.13-5 (Frazer's translation):

> And Minos pursued Daedalus, and in every country that he searched he carried a spiral shell and promised to give a great reward to him who should pass a thread through the shell, believing that by that means he should discover Daedalus. And having come to Camicus in Sicily, to the court of Cocalus, with whom Daedalus was concealed, he showed the spiral shell. Cocalus took it, and promised to thread it, and gave it to Daedalus; and Daedalus fastened a thread to an ant, and, having bored a hole in the spiral shell, allowed the ant to pass through it. But when Minos found the thread passed through the shell, he perceived that Daedalus was with Cocalus, and at once demanded his surrender. Cocalus promised to surrender him, and made an entertainment for Minos; but after his bath Minos was undone by the daughters of Cocalus; some say, however, that he died by being drenched with boiling water.

This story too is early; cf. Herod. 7.169 (de Sélincourt's translation):

> The story goes that Minos went to Sicania (or Sicily, as it is now called) in search of Daedalus, and there met a violent death.

272   **pig:** *sus*; Ovid's choice of the undignified general term instead of *aper* 'boar' is presumably a deliberate undercutting of this traditional tale. For a full discussion, see on 8.359.

274 **Lyaeus:** a Greek cult-title of Bacchus meaning 'Loosener'; see on 3.520.

281 **Olenian:** Olenos was a town in southern Aetolia; here the adjective probably means no more than 'Aetolian'.

282-3 Commentators note the awkwardness of the Latin construction which the translation attempts to mirror.
Epirus...Sicilian: according to Pliny (*N.H.* 8.176), Pyrrhus, the fourth century king of Epirus, had established an excellent breeding programme for bulls; the claims of Sicily seem to be less well documented; for the details, see Bömer.

285-6 The first of these lines has long been suspected because of the feeble repetition of *riget...rigidis* (exaggerated in the translation where 'was rigid...rigid' partly conceals the shift from verb to adjective); the second line is absent from most manuscripts; both lines, in spite of the parallels adduced by Hollis, seem to over-stress the bristles.

288 **Indian tusks:** i.e. elephant tusks.

289 **lightning:** *fulmen*; a word frequently used by Ovid of the boar; cf. 1.305 (regrettably concealed in my translation), 8.339, 356; 10.550; 11 368 (of a wolf).

292 **Ceres:** i.e. 'wheat'; see on 6.488.

298-328 *Catalogue of Hunters*
Lists of names were a feature of epic from Homer onwards. At 3.206-33, Ovid listed Actaeon's hunting dogs with a degree of self-mockery. This list is more straightforward and, with thirty-six heroes, is more elaborate than either Apollodorus' version (1.8.2) with twenty or Hyginus' (173) which we have only in a mutilated version.

301-2 **Tyndareus' twin sons:** Castor and Pollux; cf Hom. *Il.* 3.237 (Lattimore's translation):
    Kastor, breaker of horses, and the strong boxer, Polydeuces.

302 **Jason:** see 6.719-7.8.

303 **Pirithous...Theseus:** like Orestes and Pylades, these two were a famous type of friendship, cf. 8.405. They appear together at Hom. *Od.* 11.631; for a discussion, see Frazer on Apollod. 2.5.12.

304 **Thestius' two sons:** named later (8.432-42) as Toxeus and Plexippus, brothers of Althaea, and so uncles of Meleager. Bömer gives a full account of the history of the names of Meleager's uncles. See also Apollod. 1.7.10-8.1 where Plexippus is an uncle of Meleager but Toxeus is a brother killed long before by their father, Oeneus.

304-5 **offspring of Aphareus, Lynceus and...Idas:** see Apoll. Rhod. 1.151-5 (Seaton's translation):
    *The sons of Aphareus, Lynceus and proud Idas, came from Arne both
    exulting in their great strength; and Lynceus too excelled in keenest*

228] NOTES: Book VIII

sight, if the report is true that that hero could easily direct his sight even beneath the earth.

305   **Caeneus:** for the story of Caeneus' sex change, see 12.459-531; see also Frazer on Apollod. *Epit.* 1.22, Austin on Virg. *Aen.* 6.448.

306   **Leucippus:** according to Apollodorus (3.10.3), a brother of Aphareus (8.304).
        Acastus: one of the Argonauts, see Apoll. Rhod. 1.224 etc.

307   **Hippothous:** son of the notorious Cercyon (see on 7.433-50); see Paus. 8.5.3, Hyg. 173.
        Dryas: a son of Ares, cf. Apollod. 1.8.2.
        Phoenix sprung from Amyntor: he was, of course, to be Achilles' tutor, cf. Hom. *Il.* 9.448.

308   **Actor's pair of sons:** Eurytus and Cteatus (Hom. *Il.* 2.621); see also Frazer on Apollod. 2.7.2. Eurytus is presumably not the same as the 'Erytus, son of Actor' killed by Perseus (5.79-84) and perhaps confused with Hermes' son, Erytus, one of the Argonauts (Apoll. Rhod. 1.52). See also on 8.312.
        Phyleus: a man of this name appears at Hom. *Il.* 2.628-9 as the father of Meges who led the men of Elis. At *Il.* 2.624, Homer mentions another leader from Elis called Augeas; according to Apollodorus (2.5.5), he was Phyleus' father and the owner of the stables that were the scene for Hercules' fifth labour.

309   **Telamon:** see on 7.476-7.
        Achilles' begetter: Peleus, see on 7.476-7; see also Hom. *Il.* 1.1.

310   **Pheres' son:** Admetus (Apollod. 1.8.2); for his story, see on 6.122.
        Hyantean: see on 5.312.
        Iolaus: Hercules' charioteer (Apollod. 2.5.2) and son of his twin brother, Iphicles (Apollod. 2.4.11).
        For the quadrisyllabic ending, see on 5.312.

311   **Eurytion, Echion:** according to Apollodorus (1.8.2), Eurytion was a son of Actor (see on 8.308); clearly there may be some confusion between him and Eurytus (8.308). Apollonius Rhodius (1.52) presents Erytus and Echion together as sons of Hermes and lists Eurytion separately (1.71).

312   **Narycian Lelex:** this Lelex is known only from this episode (see also 8.567-8, 617). Naryx was a settlement of the Opuntian Locrians on the mainland opposite Euboea.
        Panopeus: as Bömer observes, there is nothing in Ovid's account of the Teumessian Vixen (see on 7.763) to connect it with Panopeus. However, according to Apollodorus (2.4.7), Amphitryon went with Panopeus from hunting down the Teumessian Vixen to ravaging the Taphians.
        Hyleus: known otherwise only from a modern reconstruction of the text at Apollod. 1.8.2.

NOTES: Book VIII [229

313 **Hippasus:** according to Apollodorus (1.9.16), he was the father of Actor the Argonaut (see on 8.311), and, according to Hyginus (173), the son of Eurytus. If so, Hippasus is the Eurytiades of 8.371.
Nestor still in his first years: no reader of Homer could imagine a youthful Nestor, for he was the type of the garrulous old man both in the *Iliad* (e.g. 1.245-84; 24.624-30) and the *Odyssey* (e.g. 3. *passim*).

314 **Hippocoon...Amyclae:** Hippocoon was king of Sparta (for the poetic use of *Amyclae* for 'Sparta', see *OLD*); Apollodorus (3.10.5) attributes twelve sons to him though Enaesimus, mentioned by Ovid at 8.362-3, is not one of them. Hyginus (173) however, lists Enaesimus, Alcon and Leucippus as sons of Hippocoon who went to the Calydonian Boar Hunt. Of these, only Alcon appears in Apollodorus' list.

315 **Penelope's father-in-law:** this is, of course, Odysseus' father, Laertes.
Parrhasian: as early as Homer (*Il.* 2.608), Parrhasian is used as a poetic equivalent for 'Arcadian'; cf. 2.460 and see Fordyce on Virg. *Aen.* 8.344.

316 **Ampyx' shrewd son:** the seer, Mopsus. Not in Apollodorus' list but in Hyginus'.

316-7 **Oecleus' son...wife:** for the story of how later Amphiaraus was tricked into joining Polynices' fatal war against his brother, Eteocles, through the treachery of his wife, Eriphyle, see Apollod. 3.6.2.

317 **the Tegean girl:** Atalanta; because of her importance in the story, Ovid gives her a very full description. He never, however, names her, preferring various epic periphrases. See also on 8.738.

322-3 **you could truly say:** see on 5.6.

329-444 The Hunt
The account, as Hollis observes, is very epic in style. Whether he is right to judge that after a 'splendid and visually brilliant' setting of the scene Ovid's account loses 'impetus' must be left for the reader to judge.

329-30 For this description of virgin territory so favoured by devotees of Diana, goddess of chastity and hunting, cf. e.g. Eur. *Hipp.* 72-82. For the ekphrasis, see on 5.385-91; note that the normal introduction with the verb 'to be' is delayed till 8.344.

331 **nets:** see on 7.701, 5.155.

339 **fires struck from the clouds:** i.e. lightning, cf. Lucr. 6.96-422; see on 8.289.

346 **only:** see on 5.528.

355 **lightning:** see on 8.289.

357 **cord:** *neruo*; a technical term for the 'cord in a ballistic engine' (*OLD* s.v. 3a).

230] NOTES: Book VIII

359 **injury making pig:** *uulnificus sus*; the comic effect of the common word for 'pig' has already been exploited at 8.272, but here it is greatly enhanced by the monosyllabic line ending. Horace (*Ars Poetica* 139) exploits that effect in his famous line 'The mountains will be in travail and there will be born a ridiculous mouse', a line that ends *ridiculus mus*, exactly the same rhythmic pattern as is found here. Hollis and Anderson both argue that the rhythm imparts something of antique epic grandeur or is intended to indicate violent action; but this is to ignore the effect that the word *sus* itself must arouse. Furthermore, there are two lines that Ovid is very likely to have had in mind: Lucretius 5.25, which also ends with the same rhythmic pattern: *Arcadius sus* ('Arcadian pig'), a clear attempt to belittle Hercules' killing of the Erymanthian Boar, and Virg. *G.* 3.255, again the same rhythmic ending: *dentesque Sabellicus exacuit sus* ('and the Samnite pig sharpens his tusks'), attracting this from Mynors:

> The terminal monosyllable sus, *following a four-syllable word, sharpens the effect, adding here. . .a touch of astonishment, that so unheroic a beast should behave in such a warlike manner; in Lucr. 5.25 it adds contempt. . .For* sus = aper *we have no evidence earlier than Ovid; for in Lucr. 5.25 the famous Calydonian* [he means Erymanthian] *boar is to the true philosopher only a 'bristly Arcadian pig'.*

For a detailed discussion of monosyllabic endings, see Fordyce on Virg. *Aen.* 7.592.

362-3 **Enaesimus. . .Hippocoon's son:** see on 8.314.

365 **the Pylian:** Nestor, see on 8.313. He came from 'sandy Pylos' (Hom. *Il.* 1.247-8); commentators rightly remark on the comic absurdity of the self-opinionated Nestor escaping danger by pole-vaulting into a tree.

371 **Eurytus'. . .son:** see on 8.313.

376 **bristle-bearer:** *saetiger*; for the 'kenning' see the very full discussion by Hollis and the note on 6.226.

387-8 **manliness. . .men:** *uirtutis. . .uiri*; the word-play brings out the issue. Was 8.323 a preparation for this?

390 **thronging:** *turba*; Bömer is surely right that the throng is of hunters, not weapons. No attempt has been made to catch the word-play of *petit* ('attempting') *impedit* ('impeded').

391 **the Arcadian:** Ancaeus, cf. 8.401, see on 8.315.

394 **Latonia:** Diana, daughter of Leto, cf 1.696.

403-4 **Ixion's offspring, Pirithous:** see Apollod. 1.8.2

405 **dearer to me than my own self:** see on 8.303.

411 **Aeson's son:** *Aesonides*; Jason, see on 7.132.

412 **barker:** for the 'kenning', see on 6.226.

423-4 An incongruous reminder of the Achaeans' attitude to Hector's body (Hom. *Il.* 22.371-2, Lattimore's translation):
> And the other sons of the Achaians came running about him,
> and gazed upon the stature and on the imposing beauty
> of Hector; and none stood beside him who did not stab him.

See on 5.605-6.

425 **He himself:** i.e. Meleager.

426 **Nonacria:** Nonacris was a mountain and city in Arcadia so the adjective comes to mean 'Arcadian' and here refers to Atalanta. See on 8.317.

437 **the son of Mars:** Meleager; cf. Apollod. 1.8.2 (Frazer's translation):
> *Althaea had also a son Meleager, by Oeneus, though they say that he was begotten by Ares [Mars].*

As Hollis observes, here it is his divine parentage that is the more relevant.

440-1 **Plexippus...Toxeus:** see on 8. 304.

443 **rewarmed:** *recalfecit*; another Ovidian neologism.

445-525 Althaea and Meleager

The conflict between love for brother and love for husband or son occurs more than once in classical literature. A striking example comes from Herodotus (3.118) where the wife of Intaphernes the conspirator surprised Darius by choosing her brother rather than her husband or a son when she was offered mercy for any one (de Sélincourt's translation):
> 'My lord', she replied, 'God willing, I may get another husband, and other children when these are gone. But as my father and mother are both dead, I can never possibly have another brother...'

Readers will also remember Antigone. In all cases, it should be noted that the bystanders are no less surprised than we are. If these stories do reflect a primitive social attitude, it is certainly very ancient.

According to Hollis, 'this seems...the least satisfactory part of the book'; according to Anderson, 'the delineation of Althaea's dilemma, by narrative and soliloquy, is one of his masterpieces.' Suffice it to say that Ovid welcomes the story as an opportunity to explore an inner conflict. For the basic story, see Apollod. 1.8.2-3 (Frazer's translation):
> *It is said that when he [Meleager] was seven days old, the Fates came and declared that Meleager should die when the brand burning in the hearth was burnt out. On hearing that, Althaea snatched up the brand and deposited it in a chest.*

There then follows an account of the Calydonian Boar Hunt including Meleager's killing of his uncles. Apollodorus continues:
> *However, from grief at the slaughter of her brothers Althaea kindled the brand, and Meleager immediately expired.*

451 **Thestius' daughter:** Althaea, see on 8.304.

452 **the threefold sisters:** the Fates; cf. Hes. *Theog.* 901-6 (Evelyn-White's translation):

> *Next he [Zeus] married bright Themis who bare. . .the Moerae [Fates]*
> *to whom wise Zeus gave the greatest honour, Clotho, and Lachesis,*
> *and Atropos who give mortal men evil and good to have.*

471 **wind and wind-opposing:** *uentus uentoque. . .contrarius*; for the polyptoton, see on 5.52.

476-7 **in order to appease the shades of her blood with blood:** an attempt to get the polyptoton (see on 5.52) of *consanguineas. . .umbras* ('blood-related shades') sandwiching *ut sanguine leniat* ('in order to appease with blood').

477 **impiety pious:** *impietate pia*; for the sense of these words, see on 6.630; for the polyptoton, see on 5.52.

483-4 **death. . .by death. . .crime. . .to crime. . .a funeral to funerals:** *mors morte. . .scelus. . .in scelus. . .funera funus*; see on 5.52.

500 **twice five months:** then, as now, a human pregnancy lasted approximately ten lunar (or nine calendar) months.

509 **victory. . .victorious:** as Anderson observes, the language picks up 'mother and sister fought' (8.463); the terms frame the conflict.

520 **father:** Oeneus; see on 8.437.

520-1 **his brothers, his pious sisters:** Ovid is uninterested in their names; the tradition is complex (see Bömer).

521 **the companion of his marriage bed:** according to Homer his wife was called Cleopatra (*Il.* 9.556) with Alcyone (*Il.* 9.562) as a by-name.

526-46 The Meleagrides
Their story is clearly reminiscent of the Heliades (2.340-66). *meleagris* is a transliteration of the Greek for guinea-fowl (see D'Arcy Thompson s.v. 'Meleagris' (198-200). We are told that Nicander called Meleager's sisters *Meleagrides* which would normally mean 'daughters' not 'sisters' of Meleager. Similarly, Virgil called the Heliades (Phaethon's sisters) *Phaethontiades* (*Ecl.* 6.62). For a full history of the story which may be traceable to Hesiod, see Forbes Irving (245-6).

528 **daughters of Euenus:** the Euenus was Calydon's local river, so this is an allusive way of referring to the Calydonian women.

532 **bowels:** see on 7.128.

533-5 This grandiose introduction comes ultimately from *Il.* 2.488-93 where Homer uses it as a prelude to the catalogue of ships (Lattimore's translation):
> *I could not tell over the multitude of them nor name them,*
> *not if I had ten tongues and ten mouths, not if I had*
> *a voice never to be broken and a heart of bronze within me,*
> *not unless the Muses of Olympia, daughters*

NOTES: Book VIII   [233

of Zeus of the aegis, remembered all those who came beneath Ilion.
Virgil puts a similar cry into the mouth of the Sibyl as a climax to her account of the damned in the underworld (*Aen.* 6.625-7, West's translation):
> *If I had a hundred tongues, a hundred mouths and a voice of iron, I could not encompass all their different crimes or speak the names of all their different punishments.*

Austin gives a full history of this 'rhetorical flourish', but the point to make here is that, once again (see on 5.605-6), Ovid takes a famous passage and undercuts it by placing it in a relatively trivial context.

535   **catch:** *persequerer*; the word means 'pursue', 'catch up with' and is here used metaphorically exactly as in the English 'to catch a good likeness of'.

543   **Parthaonian:** Portheus (elsewhere 'Porthaon' or 'Parthaon') was Oeneus' father and so Meleager's grandfather; see Hom. *Il.* 14.115-7 (Lattimore's translation):
> *For there were three blameless sons who were born to Portheus, and their home was in Pleuron and headlong Kalydon. Agrios was first, then Melas, and the third was Oineus the horseman.*

544-5   **Gorge and the daughter-in-law of famous Alcmena:** their preservation is also recorded by Antoninus Liberalis (2.7) 'through the good will of Dionysus', which is perhaps partly explained by Apollod. 1.8.1 (Frazer's translation):
> *Oeneus. . .married Althaea. . .and begat. . .a daughter Gorge, whom Andraemon married, and another daughter Deianira, who is said to have been begotten on Althaea by Dionysus.*

For Alcmena as Hercules' mother, see on 6.112, and for the story of Deianira's marriage to Hercules, see 9.1-238.

547-610 Achelous and the Echinades
Ovid is our only extant source for this story. For some thoughts on its possible history, see Forbes Irving 308.

549   **Achelous:** the river is not, in fact, on the way from Calydon to Athens, but in precisely the opposite direction.

550   **famed:** *inclite*; a word of archaic grandeur, see Austin on Virg. *Aen.* 6.479.

556   **When too the snows melt:** it is striking to find this rational explanation in the midst of such a mythological passage; here reason is undercutting myth.

561   **your home and your advice:** for Ovid's love of syllepsis, see on 6.476-7.

562   **hall:** *atria*; Anderson has a good discussion of this 'palace' built into a cave in the volcanic rock. The use of the Roman term *atria* is another example of Ovid's taste for using inappropriate Roman terms (cf 8.564, 566 and see on 5.155), but this is especially striking since the centre of the *atrium* was open to the sky, very unlike a cave. The whole passage should be compared with Diana's cave at 3.157-60 where there is less artifice in the construction and decoration.

NOTES: Book VIII

564 **panelled:** *lacunabat*; an Ovidian coinage but formed from the Roman technical term *lacunar*; see on 8.562, 5.155.

565 **Hyperion:** normally the name of the father of Sun, as at *Hom. Hymn* 31.4-7. However, Homer uses both *Hyperionides* ('son of Hyperion') to mean Sun (*Od.* 12.176) and *Hyperion* (*Od.* 1.24). Later, poets clearly felt licensed by this and Ovid calls Sun both 'son of Hyperion' (4.192) and 'Hyperion' (15.406-7). For further details, see *LSJ* and *OLD*.

566 **reclined on the couches:** more Roman anachronism, see on 8.562, 660; 5.155.

567 **Ixion's son:** Pirithous, see 8.403-4.

568 **the Troezenian. . .Lelex:** at 8.312, he was Narycian, from his birthplace. Later, however, he was adopted by Pittheus of Troezen (8.622-3, see also on 7.402-24).

573 **jewelled cups:** *gemma*; the word can refer to jewels but, according to *OLD* (s.v. 3) quoting this passage, it may also refer to the material ('perhaps glass') of which the cup is made. See also Mynors on Virg. *G.* 2.506.

579 **the spurned Diana:** see 8.271ff.

587-9 Herodotus (2.10) offers a more rational explanation for the formation of these particular islands.

596 **allotted:** see on 5.368.

598-608 The lines within square brackets are in only some manuscripts. Some scholars think they are Ovid's second thoughts, others that they have been interpolated. For fuller discussions see Anderson who rejects the lines in square brackets and Hollis who would admit all the lines except 601 and 609-10.

609-10 **limbs. . .body:** *artus. . .membris*; both words, literally, mean 'limbs'; for a similar problem see on 7.316-7.

611-724 Baucis and Philemon
This story is not extant before Ovid and there has been much speculation as to whether it has a Greco-Roman origin or whether, as Ovid's Phrygian setting would suggest, it comes from the East. Hollis and Bömer write at great length but can provide little evidence to point decisively either way. On the other hand, they offer much fascinating evidence on flood myths, especially from the Near East. Ovid tells a strikingly similar story at *Fasti* 5.493ff. while many readers will be put in mind of Abraham, Lot, Sodom and Gomorrah (*Genesis* 18-19).

612 **Ixion's son:** Pirithous, see 8.403-4; it is wholly appropriate that the son of so notorious a sinner (see on 4.461, 465) should blaspheme. Normally in the *Metamorphoses*, blasphemy precedes disaster (see on 5.1), but no punishment is recorded for Pirithous by Ovid. Perhaps we are expected to remember that he was left in Hades after Hercules had rescued Theseus, his partner in crime; see Apollod. 2.5.12 and Frazer.

NOTES: Book VIII [235

614-5 Pirithous would not have approved of the *Metamorphoses*.

622 **his father:** Pelops, see on 7.402-24.

626-7 Commentators compare *Acts* 14.11-12:
And when the people saw what Paul had done, they lifted up their voices, saying in the speech of Lycaonia, The gods are come down to us in the likeness of men.
And they called Barnabas, Jupiter; and Paul, Mercurius, because he was the chief speaker.

627 **Atlas' granson:** Mercury, see on 2.697-704.

632 **hut:** *casa*, a very evocative term for Romans since it was always used of Romulus' hut, preserved on the Palatine in Ovid's day. See Livy 5.53.8, Ovid *Fasti* 1.199, Prop. 2.16.19-20. See also on 5.155.

637 **penates:** see on 5.155.

644 **much-split:** see on 7.259.

652-6 652-4 are omitted by some manuscripts while the tradition offers two versions of 655-6. The solution adopted here is argued for, on slightly different grounds, by Hollis and Anderson.

660 **reclined:** see on 8.566; 5.155.

661 **third foot:** the advantage of a three-legged over a four-legged table is that it cannot be unstable, even on an uneven surface; a short leg can, however, give it a surface that is not level, the fault Baucis is here correcting.

664 **berries of pure Minerva:** olives, see on 6.70-82.
half ripe: *bicolor*; literally 'of two colours', i.e. green and black, leaving the green stage but not yet fully black. It is, perhaps, just possible that a choice between green and black olives is being offered.

668 **engraved:** *caelatus*, the technical term for metal engraving. Anderson is surely right to see wit here; in more luxurious places you might expect to see engraved silver bowls; Ovid wryly reminds us that this bowl is not of metal by describing it as 'in the same engraved silver' i.e. 'the same as the other earthenware', i.e. 'neither engraved nor of silver'. Contrast 8.701-2 which, otherwise, loses something of its point.

670 **smeared with yellow wax:** 'to make them impermeable' (Hollis) or 'they have been mended with wax' (Anderson) or, just possibly, to imitate gold; see on 8.668.

676 **grapes. . .from purple vines:** the transferred epithet, moving the adjective from its noun to another noun, is common in ancient poetry. It is especially common in Latin hexameters where there was an almost overwhelming preference for sharing the adjectives in a line evenly among the nouns, regardless of strict logic.

684 The plot moves on with something very like an ekphrasis (see on 5.385-91).
goose, the guardian of the tiny house: no Roman could escape the association with the story of how the Sacred Geese saved Rome (Livy 5.47); see on 2.538-9.

693-3b Here the choice is between accepting only 693 (the reading of three good manuscripts) or the two line version of it (693a-b), the reading of most others. Hollis argues for omitting 693, Anderson for omitting 693a-b; the arguments offered rely entirely on subjective preference, probably the only criterion available in this case.

699 **hut:** *casa*, see on 8.632.

703 **the Saturnian:** Jupiter, see on 5.420. The word has rather an archaic ring.

718 **my own dear one:** *coniunx*, literally 'spouse' except that, as here, the word can have a much warmer sense than 'spouse' can convey.

718-9 Kenney believes the sound here to be especially important:
the sibilants of the Latin suggest the rustling of the miraculously burgeoning leaves: 'o coniunX diXere Simul, Simul abdita teXit/ora fruteX.'

719 **Thyneian:** *Thyneius*; for the use of this adjective to include Phrygia, see Hollis.

721 **I:** Lelex, see 8.617.

724 **those who care for the gods:** *cura deum*; of itself, the Latin can mean either 'those who care for the gods' or 'those for whom the gods care'. For the former, Hollis cites *Her.* 1.104 (where Eumaeus is referred to as *cura fidelis harae*) and for the latter Virg. *Aen.* 3.476 (where Anchises is called *cura deum*); there are many more parallels in Bömer. Hollis and Anderson both prefer the latter interpretation on the grounds that it responds better to 8.619. But the former makes for a far more balanced line here (as Hollis concedes) and the reader is not asked to provide a very difficult step in the argument in order to marry 8.619 to 8.724. Some readers will recall a similar controversy at *Luke* 2.14.

725-878 Erysichthon and Mestra
Once again, Hollis and Bömer give very full accounts of what we know of the origins of this story; it is at least as old as Pseudo-Hesiod *Catalogue of Women*; the earliest version to which Ovid was certainly indebted is Callimachus *Hymns* 6.31-117. See also K.J. McKay, *Erysichthon, a Callimachean Comedy*, *Mnemosyne* (Supplementum Septimum), Leiden, 1962.

727 **Calydonian river:** Achelous (cf. 9.2); see 8.549, 561.

731 **Proteus:** the supreme answer to Pirithous' disbelief in metamorphosis (8.614-5). For his abilities, cf. Hom. *Od.* 4.456-8 (Lattimore's translation):
*First he turned into a great bearded lion,
and then to a serpent, then to a leopard, then to a great boar,
and he turned into fluid water, to a tree with towering branches.*

NOTES: Book VIII [237

See also on 2.9 and Forbes Irving 174-9.

738 **Autolycus' wife and Erysichthon's daughter:** Mestra; Ovid never names her, relying entirely on this sort of periphrasis; see also on 8.317. This is our only extant reference to her subsequent (presumably) marriage to Autolycus, a notorious character (11.313-4). He is most remembered as Odysseus' maternal grandfather (Hom. *Od.* 19.392-466).

739-40 **a man to spurn the power of the gods:** for blasphemy as a prelude to disaster, see on 5.11.

749 **ells:** *ulnas*; the *ulna* was a measure largely used in poetic contexts and is the origin of English 'ell'; it means 'forearm' but, as a measure, meant 'apparently the span of the outstretched arms' (*OLD* s.v. b), which, assuming six feet, would make the oak 90 feet tall. The 'ell' varied in length but was never more than 45 inches.

751 **Triopas' son:** *Triopeius*; in spite of its poor manuscript support, modern editors (apart from Hollis) have, on the whole, accepted it. For Triopas as father of Erysichthon, see Call. *Hymns* 6.96-100. Essentially the same manuscript problem recurs at 8.872.

758 **Deoian:** *Deoia*; i.e. 'belonging to Ceres, daughter of Deo'; see on 6.114.

767 **the Thessalian:** Erysichthon.

772 **-orum...-orum:** a jingle usually avoided in Augustan poetry. I have allowed a faint echo, 'as I die, I prophesy'.

785-6 **(for the fates...together):** there is a similar parenthesis to explain why Minerva keeps her distance from Envy at 2.766-7. See also 8.814.

788-808 This ekphrasis (see on 5.385-91) on Hunger and her abode is to be compared with Ovid's similar *tour de force* on Envy at 2.760-82 where I give a brief history of this sort of personification; it begins as early as Homer (*Il.* 4.439-43, 9.505-12). See also Hollis. In recent times, television has brought many grim reminders of what starvation looks like.

795 **dragons:** see on 5.643.

820 **spread:** *spargit*; the word is also used of Envy's ministrations at 2.801. Here it may be especially piquant because it is also a standard term for 'sowing seeds', the great antidote to hunger.

828-9 **burning...inflamed:** *ardor...incensaque*; the image of fire is picked up again at 8.845.

836 **drinks dry:** *ebibit*; cf. 6.342.

845 **unexhausted:** *inattenuata*; this negative form is another Ovidian coinage.
 flame: *flamma*; see on 8.828-9.

846 **fortune:** *censu*; it is impossible to catch the nuance of this Roman technical term (see on 5.155) for a citizen's property qualification. Hollis is surely correct to see humour here.

853 **he changed her:** for Mestra's metamorphosis, see Forbes Irving 173.

856 **bronze:** *aera* i.e. 'bronze fishing hooks'.

861 **footprints stretched no further:** for a similar situation, cf. 5.631-2.

871 **transformable:** *transformia*; another Ovidian coinage.

872 **Triopas' granddaughter:** Mestra, see on 8.751.

879-884 Transition to Achelous' story.
This passage returns us to the conversation at 8.725-37: now, Achelous suddenly remembers that he too (as well as Proteus and Mestra) has the power of metamorphosis. It also serves to draw us into the next book where the full story will be told. For the story and its history, see Apollod. 2.7.5 (and Frazer), Forbes Irving 172-3.

884 **Groans followed his words:** a powerful inducement to read on into book 9.

BIBLIOGRAPHY

To save space in the notes, authors frequently cited are cited only by name and page number together with, where more than work is involved, date of publication or other suitable indication. The references are fully expanded here.

Anderson

Ovid's Metamorphoses book 6-10 Edited, with Introduction and Commentary, by William S. Anderson, Norman, Oklahoma, 1972.

Austin

P. Vergili Maronis Aeneidos Liber Primus with a commentary by R.G. Austin, Oxford, 1971.
P. Vergili Maronis Aeneidos Liber Secundus with a commentary by R.G. Austin, Oxford, 1964.
P. Vergili Maronis Aeneidos Liber Quartus edited with a commentary by R.G. Austin, Oxford, 1955.
P. Vergili Maronis Aeneidos Liber Sextus with a commentary by R.G. Austin, Oxford, 1977.

Babbit

Plutarch's Moralia with an English translation by Frank Cole Babbitt (Loeb Classical Library), London and Cambridge, Mass., 1936.

Bailey

Titi Lucreti Cari de Rerum Natura Libri Sex edited etc. by Cyril Bailey, Oxford, 1947.

Bettenson

Livy Rome and the Mediterranean Books XXXI-XLV of the History of Rome from its Foundation Translated by Henry Bettenson (Penguin Classics), Harmondsworth, 1976.

Bömer

P.Ouidius Naso Metamorphoses Kommentar von Franz Bömer, Heidelberg, 1969-86.

Cornish

Catullus Translated by Francis Warre Cornish (Loeb Classical Library), London and Cambridge, Mass., 1913 [*Second Edition, revised by G.P. Goold*, 1988].

BIBLIOGRAPHY

D'Arcy Thompson

See Thompson

de Sélincourt

Herodotus the Histories translated and with an introduction by Aubrey de Sélincourt, (Penguin Classics), Harmondsworth, 1954.
Livy the War with Hannibal: books xxi-xxx of The History of Rome from its foundation, translated by Aubrey de Sélincourt, (Penguin Classics), Harmondsworth, 1954.

Dodds

Euripides Bacchae edited with introduction and commentary by E.R. Dodds, Oxford, 1944 (1st edition), 1960 (2nd edition).

Eden

A commentary on Virgil: Aeneid VIII by P.T. Eden, Leiden, 1975.

Evelyn-White

Hesiod The Homeric Hymns and Homerica with an English translation by Hugh G. Evelyn-White (Loeb Classical Library), London and Cambridge, Mass., 1914.

Fagles

Bacchylides complete poems Translated by Robert Fagles, New Haven, Conn., 1961.

Forbes Irving

Metamorphosis in Greek Myths P.M.C. Forbes Irving, Oxford, 1990.

Fordyce

Catullus a Commentary by C.J. Fordyce, Oxford, 1961.
P. Vergili Maronis Aeneidos Libri VII-VIII with a commentary by C.J. Fordyce, Oxford, 1977.

Fränkel

Ovid, a Poet between two Worlds, Hermann Fränkel, Berkeley and Los Angeles, 1945.

BIBLIOGRAPHY [241

Frazer

Apollodorus The Library with an English Translation by James George Frazer (Loeb Classical Library), London and Cambridge, Mass., 1921.
Pausanias's description of Greece translated with a commentary by J.G. Frazer, London, 1898.

Golding

The xv Bookes of P. Ouidius Naso, entytuled Metamorphosis, translated oute of Latin into English meeter, by Arthur Golding Gentleman, A worke very pleasaunt and delectable, London, 1567. See also *Ovid's Metamorphoses The Arthur Golding Translation 1567 edited, with an introduction and notes, by John Frederick Nims*, New York, 1965.

Greenwood

Cicero the Verrine Orations with an English Translation by L.H.G. Greenwood (Loeb Classical Library), London and Cambridge, Mass., 1935.

Gulick

Athenaeus the Deipnosophists with an English translation by Charles Burton Gulick (Loeb Classical Library), London and Cambridge, Mass., 1927.

Harrison

Vergil Aeneid 10 with introduction, translation and commentary by S.J. Harrison, Oxford, 1991.

Heinze

Ovids elegische Erzählung (Berichte. . .Sächsischen Akad. der Wiss., Phil. Hist Klasse 71 (1919) 7 [reprinted in R. Heinze, *Vom Geist des Römertums*, 1960.]

Henderson

Ovid Metamorphoses III with Introduction, Notes and Vocabulary by A.A.R. Henderson, Bristol, 1979.

Hinds

The Metamorphosis of Persephone, Stephen Hinds, Cambridge, 1987.

Hollis

Ovid Metamorphoses Book VIII edited with an introduction and commentary by A.S. Hollis, Oxford, 1970.

BIBLIOGRAPHY

How and Wells

A commentary on Herodotus with introduction and appendices by W.W. How and J. Wells, Oxford, 1912.

Jones

The Geography of Strabo with an English translation by Horace Leonard Jones (Loeb Classical Library), London and Cambridge, Mass., 1927.

Jones

Pliny Natural History with an English translation by W.H.S. Jones (Loeb Classical Library), London and Cambridge, Mass., 1951.

Kenney

See Melville

Lattimore

The Iliad of Homer Translated with an introduction by Richmond Lattimore, Chicago, 1951.
Themes in Greek and Latin Epitaphs by Richmond Lattimore, Urbana, Ill. 1962.
The Odyssey of Homer Translated with an introduction by Richmond Lattimore, New York, Evanston and London, 1965.
The Odes of Pindar translated by Richmond Lattimore, Chicago and London, 1947.

Mair

Callimachus with an English Translation by A.W. Mair, Aratus with an English Translation by G.R. Mair (Loeb Classical Library), London and Cambridge, Mass., 1921.

Mayer

Lucan Civil War VIII Edited with a Commentary by R. Mayer, Warminster, 1981.

Melville

Ovid Metamorphoses translated by A.D. Melville with an introduction and Notes by E.J. Kenney (The World's Classics), Oxford, 1986.

Mynors

Virgil Georgics Edited with a Commentary by R.A.B. Mynors, Oxford, 1990.

Nisbet-Hubbard

A Commentary on Horace: Odes Book I, by R.G.M. Nisbet and Margaret Hubbard, Oxford, 1970.
A Commentary on Horace: Odes Book II, by R.G.M. Nisbet and Margaret Hubbard, Oxford, 1978.

Oldfather

Diodorus of Sicily with an English Translation by C.H. Oldfather (Loeb Classical Library), Cambridge, Mass. and London, 1923.

Otis

Brooks Otis, *Ovid as an Epic Poet*, Cambridge, 1966 (1st edition), 1970 (2nd edition).

Page

Euripides Medea the text edited with introduction and commentary by Denys L. Page, Oxford, 1938.

Pease

Publi Vergili Maronis Aeneidos Liber Quartus edited by Arthur Stanley Pease, Cambridge, Mass., 1935.
M. Tulli Ciceronis de Natura Deorum edited by Arthur Stanley Pease, Cambridge, Mass., 1955.

Postgate

Tibullus translated by J.P. Postgate (Loeb Classical Library), London and Cambridge, Mass., 1913 [*Second Edition, revised by G.P. Goold*, 1988].

Powell

M. Tullius Cicero Cato Maior de Senectute edited with introduction and commentary by J.G.F. Powell, Cambridge, 1988.

Rackham

Cicero de Natura Deorum with an English translation by H. Rackham, (Loeb Classical Library), London and Cambridge, Mass., 1933.
Pliny Natural History with an English translation by H. Rackham (Loeb Classical Library), London and Cambridge, Mass., 1940.

Rand

Ovid and his Influence, **Edward Kennard Rand**, London, 1925, New York, 1963.

244] BIBLIOGRAPHY

Seaton

Apollonius Rhodius The Argonautica with an English Translation by R.C. Seaton (Loeb Classical Library), London and New York, 1912.

Shorey

Plato the Republic with an English translation by Paul Shorey (Loeb Classical Library), London and New York, 1930.

Thompson

A Glossary of Greek Birds, a new edition by D'Arcy Wentworth Thompson, London, 1936.

Warner

Euripides Medea translated by Rex Warner, London, 1944; see also *The Complet Greek Tragedies edited by David Grene and Richmond Lattimore*, Chicago, 1955.

Way

Euripides with an English translation by Arthur S. Way, in four volumes, (Loeb Classical Library), London, 1912.

West

Virgil The Aeneid a new prose translation by David West, (Penguin Classics) Harmondsworth, 1990.

Wilkinson

Ovid Recalled by L.P. Wilkinson, Cambridge, 1955.
'The World of the Metamorphoses' in *Ovidiana, recherches sur Ovide Publiées l'occasion du bimillénaire de la naissance du poète par N.I. Herescu*, Paris, 1958.

Williams

P. Vergili Maronis Aeneidos Liber Tertius edited with a commentary by R.D. Williams, Oxford, 1962.
P. Vergili Maronis Aeneidos Liber Quintus edited with a commentary by R.D. Williams, Oxford, 1960.

INDEX

This index is to head words in the explanatory notes. The references refer to the line numbers of the translation and are rarely, if ever, more than one line from the Latin reference.

Abas 5.126
Abas (Perseus' grandfather) 5.1, 138, 236
Abaris 5.86
Acastus 8.306
Achaean 5.306
Achais 5.577
Acheloides 5.551
Achelous 8.547-610, 549, 879-884
Acheron 5.541
Achilles 8.309
Acrisius 5.1, 69
Actor (father of Erytus) 5.79
Actor (father of Eurytus and Cteatus) 8.308
Aeacid 7.494
Aeacus 7.490-4522
Aegeus 7.402-24, 490-522; 8.174
Aegina 7.614-60
Aeginetan 7.523-613
Aeolian 6.116
Aeolus 7.490-522, 672
Aeson 7.159-293; 8.411
Aesonian 7.132
Aganippe 5.312
Agenor 5.1
Alcathoe 7.443-4
Alcathous 8.6-8
Alcidamas 7.369
Alcmena 8.544-5
Aloidae 6.116-7
Alpheias 5.487
Althaea 8.445-525
Ammon (Broteas' brother) 5.107
Ammon (god) 5.17, 328
Amphimedon 5.75
Amphion 6.271
Amphitryon 6.112
Amphrysus 7.229
Ampyx 8.316
Amyclae 8.314
Amyntor 8.307
Anaphe 7.461, 462
Anapis 5.409-37
Andros 7.469
Anthedon 7.232
Antigone 6.93
Aonides 5.333; 6.1-5
Aphareus 8.304-5
Aquilo 5.285; 7.3
Arachne 6.1-145, 1-5
Arcadian 8.391
Arethusa 5.409, 487-508, 572-641
Ariadne 8.152-82
Armenian 8.121
Arne 7.465

Ascalabus 5.438-61
Ascalaphus 5.533-50
Asopis 6.113;
Asopus 7.484
Asterie 6.107
Astreus 5.144
Astypaleia 7.461, 462
Atlas 6.174; 8.627
Auster 5.285; 7.659-60
Autolycus 8.738

Bacchiadae 5.407
Bacchus 5.1; 6.488; 7.294-6, 450
Baucis 8.611-724
Belus 5.1, 69
Bisaltis 6.117
Boebe 7.231
Boötes 8.207
Boreas 6.675-721
Broteas 5.107
Butes 7.490-522, 500

Cadmus 5.1; 6.177
Caeneus 8.305
Calaurea 7.384
Calydon 6.415
Calydonian 8.727
Calydonian Boar Hunt 8.260-546
Calymnae 8.222
Cartheian 7.368
Cayster 5.386
Cea 7.368
Cecropian 6.70-1
Cecropidae 7.486
Cecropides 6.667
Cecrops 7.490-522, 502
Celadon 5.144
Cephalus 6.681-2; 7.490-522, 493, 661-865
Cephenes 5.2
Cephisos 7.389
Cerambus 7.353
Cercyon 7.433-50
Ceres 5.341-408, 438-61, 487-508, 509-32; 8.292
Charybdis 7.63-5; 8.121
Chimera 6.339
Chiron 6.126
Chromis 5.103
Ciconian 6.710
Cimolus 7.463
Cinyphian 5.123; 7.272
Cinyras 6.98
Clanis 5.141
Clytos 7.490-522, 500
Coeus 6.186-7

INDEX

Colchian 7.296
Colophonian 6.8
Combe 7.383
Corinth 6.416
Corythus 7.361
Cremmyon 7.433-50
Cretan 7.433-4
Crete 8.99
Curetan 8.153
Cyane 5.409-37
Cycneian 7.371
Cyllene 5.607; 7.386
Cyllenian 5.176
Cyllenius 5.331
Cytorus 6.132

Daedalus 8.152-82, 183-259
Damasichthon 6.255
Danaë 5.1; 6.113
Danaeian 5.1
Danaus 5.1
Daulis 5.276-7
Dawn 7.703
Deion 7.490-522
Delian 5.329
Deoian 8.758
Deois 6.114
Dia 8.174
Diana 7.746; 8.579
Didyme 7.469
Dis 5.341-5
Dodona 7.623
Dorylas 5.130
Dryas 8.307

Echemmon 5.163
Echidna 7.409
Echinades 8.547-610
Echion 8.311
Elis 5.608
Emathian 5.313
Emathides 5.669
Emathion 5.100
Enaesimus 8.362-3
Enipeus 6.116-7
Ephyra 7.391-2
Epirus 8.282-3
Erebus 5.543
Erechtheus 7.490-522
Erigone 6.125
Erycina 5.363
Erymanthus 5.608
Erysichthon 8.725-878, 738
Erytus 5.79
Euenus 8.528
Euippe 5.303
Eumelus 7.390
Eumenides 6.430-1
Europa 8.23, 120
Eurus 7.659-60
Eurypylus 7.363
Eurytion 8.311
Eurytus 8.371

Flexer 8.178-2

Ganges 6.636
Glaucus 7.233
Gorge 8.544-5
Gortynian 7.778
Gradivus 6.427
Gyaros 7.470

Haemonian 5.306
Haemus 6.87
Hecataean 6.139
Hecate 7.74, 194
Helice 8.207
Helicon 5.254
Henna 5.385
Hesperus 5.441
Hippasus 8.313
Hippocoon 8.314, 362-3
Hippocrene 5.250-72
Hippothous 8.307
Hyantean 5.312; 8.310
Hyleus 8.312
Hymenaeus 6.429
Hymettus 7.702
Hypaepa 6.13
Hyperion 8.565
Hypermestra 5.1
Hyrie 7.371

Ialysus 7.365
Icarus 8.183-259
Ida 7.359
Idas 8.304-5
Idmonian 6.133
Indian 8.288
Iolaus 8.310
Ismenides 6.159
Ismenus 6.224
Isse 6.124
Ixion 8.403-4, 567, 612

Jason 7.1-158; 8.302
Jove 5.296; 8.99
Juno 8.220
Jupiter 5.509-32, 564-71

knee Flexer see Flexer

Laelaps 7.771
Laius 7.759
Laomedon 6.96
Latona 6.160
Latonia 8.394
Latous 6.384
Leda 6.109
Lelegeian 7.433-4; 8.6-8
Lelex 8.312, 568
Lethean 7.152
Leto 7.384; 8.14-6
Leucippus 8.306
Libya 5.1

INDEX [247

Lilybaeon 5.350-2
Lucifer 8.1
Lucina 5.304
Lyaeus 8.274
Lycabas 5.60
Lycian 6.313-81
Lyctian 7.490
Lynceus (Theseus' ancestor). 5.1, 99, 185
Lynceus (an Argonaut) 8.304-5
Lyncus 5.642-61

Maenalos 5.608
Maeonian 6.1-5, 103
Maera 7.362
Manto 6.157
Marathon 7.433-4
Marmaria 5.125
Mars 7.101; 8.437
Mars' Rock 6.70
Marsyas 6.382-400
Meander 8.162
Medea 7.1-424, 350-401
Medusa 5.70, 257, 312
Melantho 6.120
Meleager 8.445-525
Meleagrides 8.526-46
Memory 5.267
Mendes 5.144
Menephron 7.386
Messene 6.417
Mestra 8.725-878
Minerva 8.664
Minos 7.453-89; 8.152-82
Minyans 6.720
Mnemosyne 6.114
Molpeus 5.163
Mopsopian 5.660
Muses 5.250-678, 294-678, 642-678
Myconos 7.463
Mygdonian 6.45

Narycian 8.312
Nasamonian 5.129
Nelean 6.418
Neptune 5.1
Nereids 5.17; 7.685
Nestor 8.313
Nile 5.188
Niobe 6.146-312, 6.273
Nisus 7.490-522; 8.8
Nonacria 8.426
Nycteis 6.111

Ocean 7.267
Odrysian 6.490
Oecleus 8.316-7
Oenopia 7.472
Olenian 8.281
Oliaros 7.469
Olympus 6.393
Ophias 7.383
Orchomenos 5.607; 6.416
Orion 8.207

Orithyia 6.675-721; 7.490-522, 694
Othrys 7.353
Ortygia 5.499, 640

Pachynos 5.350-2
Pactolid 6.16
Paeones 5.314
Paeonian 5.303
Pagasaean 7.1
Palici 5.406
Pallas 5.46; 6.335; 7.490-522, 500, 666
Pandion 7.490-522
Panopeus 8.312
Parnassus 5.278
Paros 7.465
Parrhasian 8.315
Parthaonian 8.543
Pegasus 5.262-3
Pelasgian 7.49
Pelates 5.123
Peleus 7.476-7
Pelias 7.297-349
Pelion 7.352
Pella 5.302
Pelopian 6.414
Pelops 6.401-11
Pelorus 5.350-2
Penelope 8.315
Peparethos 7.470
Periphas 7.400
Perdix 8.236-59
Perses 7.74
Perseus 5 1-235, 236-249
Phaedimus 6.239
Phasian 7.297
Phene 7.400
Pheres 8.310
Philemon 8.611-724
Philomela 6.412-674
Philyreian 7.352
Phineus 5.1-235; 7.2
Phlegethon 5.544
Phocaean 6.9
Phocean 5.276-7
Phocus 7.476-7
Phoebe 6.215-6
Phoebus (Apollo) 5.330; 6.215-6
Phoebus (Sol [Sun]) 5.389; 6.486; 7.365
Phoenix 8.307
Phorbas 5.74
Phorcas 5.230
Phrygian 6.177
Phyleus 8.308
Pierus 5.294-678, 318-31, 642-678
Piety 7.72
Pirenian 7.391-2
Pirithous 8.303, 403-4
Pitane 7.357
Pitthian 6.418
Pleiades 6.174
Pleuron 7.382
Plexippus 8.440-1
Polydectes 5.236-249

INDEX

Polypemon 7.401, 433-50
Procne 6.412-674
Procris 6.681-2; 7.490-522, 661-865
Procrustes 7.438
Proetus 5.1, 236-249
Proserpina 5.341-661, 341-5, 533-50
Proteus 8.731
Prothoenor 5.98
Psophis 5.607
Pygmaean 6.91
Pylian 8.365
Pyreneus 5.273-93

Rhodes 7.365
Rhodope 6.87
Rhoetus 5.38

Samos 8.220
Saturnia 5.330
Saturnian 5.420; 8.703
Sciron 7.433-4
Scylla 7.63-5; 8.1-151
Semele 5.1, 329
Semiramis 5.85
Seriphos 5.242; 7.464
Shame 7.72
Sicania 5.464
Sicilian 8.282-3
Sicily 5.462-86
Sinis 7.433-50
Siphnos 7.465
Sipylus 6.149, 231
Sirens 5.551-63
Sithonian 6.587
Snake holder 8.178-82
Spanish 7.324-5
Spite 6.129
Stellio 5.438-61
Stygian 5.115-6
Stymphalian 5.585
Syene 5.74
Syros 7.464
Syrtis 8.120

Tantalus 6.172
Tegean 8.317
Telamon 7.476-7; 8.309
Telchines 7.365
Temesaean 7.207
Tempe 7.223
Tenos 7.469
Tereus 6.497-8
Thebaides 6.163
Theseus 7.402-9.97, 402-24, 425-52, 490-522; 8.303
Thespiae 5.310
Thessalian 8.767
Thestius 8.304, 451
Thyneian 8.719
Timolus 6.15
Tiresias 6.157
Tirynthian 7.410
Titan 6.186-7, 438
Titania 6.346

Titanian 7.398
Toxeus 8.440-1
Trinacria 5.347
Triopas 8.751, 872
Triptolemus 5.642-61
Tritonia 6.1-5
Tritoniac 6.384
Tritonian 5.250
Tritonis 5.645
Troezenian 8.568
Tyndareus 8.301-2
Typhoeus 5.318-31, 353
Tyrian 6.61

Urania 5.260

Victory 6.82
Vulcan 7.104, 437

Youth 7.241